Clarke County Virginia

Personal Property Tax Lists, 1836–1870

Volume 2
1854–1870

Marty Hiatt, CG

HERITAGE BOOKS
2015

HERITAGE BOOKS
AN IMPRINT OF HERITAGE BOOKS, INC.

Books, CDs, and more—Worldwide

For our listing of thousands of titles see our website at
www.HeritageBooks.com

Published 2015 by
HERITAGE BOOKS, INC.
Publishing Division
5810 Ruatan Street
Berwyn Heights, Md. 20740

Copyright © 2015 Marty Hiatt, CG

All rights reserved. No part of this book may be reproduced or transmitted in any form or by any means, electronic or mechanical, including photocopying, recording or by any information storage and retrieval system without written permission from the author, except for the inclusion of brief quotations in a review.

International Standard Book Numbers
Paperbound: 978-0-7884-5673-2
Clothbound: 978-0-7884-6239-9

Clarke County, Virginia Personal Property Tax Lists 1854-1870

Table of Contents

Introduction	vii
1854	1
1855	15
1856	28
1857	41
1858	54
1859	69
1860	82
1861	95
1862	109
1865	121
1866	121
1867	143
1868	165
1869	187
1870	211
Index	230

Clarke County, Virginia Personal Property Tax Lists 1836-1853

Heritage Books by Marty Hiatt:

Clarke County, Virginia Register of Births, 1853–1896
Clarke County, Virginia Personal Property Tax Lists, 1836–1870: Volume 1, 1836–1853
Clarke County, Virginia, Personal Property Tax Lists, 1836-1870: Volume 2, 1854-1870
Early Church Records of Loudoun County, Virginia, 1745–1800

Loudoun County, Virginia Death Register, 1853–1896
Elizabeth R. Frain and Marty Hiatt

New Jerusalem Lutheran Church Cemetery
Marty Hiatt and Craig R. Scott

Northern Virginia Genealogy: Volume 1, Numbers 1, 1996
Northern Virginia Genealogy: Volume 1, Number 2, April 1996
Northern Virginia Genealogy: Volume 1, Number 3, July 1996
Northern Virginia Genealogy: Volume 1, Number 4, October 1996
Northern Virginia Genealogy: Volume 2, Number 1, January 1997
Northern Virginia Genealogy: Volume 2, Number 2, April 1997
Northern Virginia Genealogy: Volume 2, Number 3, July 1997
Northern Virginia Genealogy: Volume 2, Number 4, October 1997
Northern Virginia Genealogy: Volume 3, Number 1, January 1998
Northern Virginia Genealogy: Volume 3, Number 2, April 1998
Northern Virginia Genealogy: Volume 3, Number 3, July 1998
Northern Virginia Genealogy: Volume 3, Number 4, October 1998
Northern Virginia Genealogy: Volume 4, Number 1, Winter 1999
Northern Virginia Genealogy: Volume 4, Number 2, Spring 1999
Northern Virginia Genealogy: Volume 4, Number 3, Summer 1999
Northern Virginia Genealogy: Volume 4, Number 4, Fall 1999
Northern Virginia Genealogy: Volume 5, 2000
Northern Virginia Genealogy: Volume 6, 2001
Northern Virginia Genealogy: Volume 7, 2002
Northern Virginia Genealogy: Volume 8, 2003
Northern Virginia Genealogy: Volume 9, 2004

*Those at Rest: Lovettsville Union Cemetery,
Loudoun County, Virginia, 1879–1999*

Clarke County, Virginia Personal Property Tax Lists 1854-1870

Dedication

To Mary Thomason Morris, archivist at the Clarke County Historical Association, Berryville, Virginia. Transcribing the Clarke County Personal property tax lists would have been a one volume effort if not for Mrs. Morris' encouragement, and her desire to know "what happened after the War." She urged me to continue abstracting past 1860, so this 5 year project is finally coming to an end.

Appreciation

To my friend Betty Frain. Without her skills and generously giving her time to format the text, this information would still be a manuscript.

Clarke County, Virginia Personal Property Tax Lists 1854-1870

Clarke County, Virginia Personal Property Tax Lists 1854-1870

Introduction

Personal property taxes have been assessed and collected in Virginia almost annually since 1782. Names of free adult men and single women who owned taxable items were collected by a commissioner of revenue or his deputies. The poll tax (on heads of adult males) was used to support county needs. Taxes on slaves, horses, carriages, clocks and other items were sent to the state. The taxable age for white males varied from sixteen to twenty-one years, depending on the time period.

An explanation of the columns on the first page for each year tells the age at which men were *supposed* to be taxed. This isn't to say that every 16-20 year-old young man was named or even indicated by a number in the lists. People didn't enjoy paying taxes any more in the 19th century than they do today. When a name appears on a Clarke County tax list, you can be fairly certain that person was head of a household.

This book does not have all of the information that is available on the complete tax lists. The heads of households, slaves, and horses are indicated. The dates that the individual lists of names and taxable property were received are on the original lists for most years. Space did not allow for their inclusion here.

Additional information about families can be determined by reading the complete tax lists. They are available at the Library of Virginia, or can be ordered through inter-library loan.

        Auditor of Public Accounts, Clarke County
        microfilm reel No. 469 (1851-1860)
        microfilm reel No. 470 (1861-1870)

Clarke County, Virginia Personal Property Tax Lists 1854-1870

Because of the war, no taxes were assessed in 1863 and 1864.

When reading the tax lists in this book:

- Always check the first page of each year to determine the column headings.
- Brackets were used to enclose comments by the compiler. When a name was misspelled [sic] meaning "as written" was inserted after the name. If the name is not clear, and could be interpreted more than one way a question mark [?] was added.
- A few abbreviations are found, mainly Est. for estate; Rev. or Revd. for reverend; Dr. or Doct. for doctor, and various military ranks.
- Periods were not used after abbreviated given names on the original lists or in this book.
- Blank lines mean nothing was written in that space on the original lists.
- When there are no numbers after a woman's name, it means she was not married, and paid taxes on property that was not extracted for this book.
- Occasionally you will see "back of book." That refers to the original tax booklet, not this book. Look at the end of that year's list for additional information.
- For the last two years in this book, the names are presented last name first. That is the way they were written on the original lists.
- A line space was inserted in the text before and after names that are not listed within their appropriate letter group.

Clarke County, Virginia Personal Property Tax Lists 1854-1870

1854

1) Free male persons above 16 years of age, 2) slaves who have attained the age of 16 years, 3) White male inhabitants who have attained the age of 21 years, except those exempted from taxation on account of bodily infirmity, 4) Male free negroes between the ages of 21 and 55 years, 5) Slaves who have attained the age of 12 years, 6) Horses, mules, asses & jennets

Buckner Ashby	0-10-2-0-0-11	Thos. H. Alexander	1-1-1-0-0-6
James M. Allen	0-3-1-0-2-11	Nimrod Ashby	0-0-1-0-0-0
Mason Anderson	1-4-1-0-1-6	John Ashby	0-0-1-0-0-1
John H. Anderson	0-2-1-1-0-1	Wm Asbury	0-0-1-0-0-0
David H. Allen	0-12-2-0-5-18	Jos E. Anderson	0-0-1-0-0-1
Jesse Allen	0-0-1-0-0-1	Jno & Nimrod Anderson	0-2-2-0-0-8
John Alexander	0-23-1-0-0-23	John Amick	0-0-1-0-0-0
John Anderson	0-0-1-0-0-0	Evan P. Anderson	0-0-1-0-0-2
James Athey	0-0-1-0-0-0	Joseph Anderson	0-0-1-0-0-1
Levi Athey	0-0-1-0-0-1	John W. Anderson of Joe	0-0-0-0-0-0
Robt Ashby Junr.	0-0-1-0-0-0	Nimrod F. Anderson	0-0-0-0-0-0
Robt Ashby Senr.	0-0-1-0-0-0	John W. Anderson	0-0-1-0-0-0
Geo W. Allen	0-4-1-0-0-9	D. T. Armstrong	0-0-1-0-0-0
Augustine C. Ashby	0-0-1-0-0-1	Saml J. Austin	0-0-1-0-0-0
A. S. Allen	0-0-1-0-0-1	Thomas Ashby	1-0-2-0-0-1
Jeremiah Ashby	0-0-1-0-0-0	Nathl Burwell	0-9-1-0-2-20
James Allison	0-0-1-0-0-0	Bowen & Everheart	3-2-2-0-0-7
Wm T. Allen	0-5-1-0-3-12	Wm C. Benson	0-0-1-0-0-0
Geo W. Ashby	0-1-1-0-0-1	John Burchell	0-7-2-0-0-13
Capt. Geo B. Ashby	0-0-1-0-0-0	Andrew J. Berlin	0-0-1-0-0-0
John Allison	0-0-1-0-0-0	Archibald Bowen	2-4-1-0-1-10
James Ash	0-0-1-0-0-0	Hiram O. Bell	0-3-1-0-2-4
Washington Anderson	0-0-1-0-0-2		
Richard Adams	0-0-1-0-0-1		
Augt Athey	0-0-1-0-0-3		
Joel Alexander	0-0-1-0-0-0		

Clarke County, Virginia Personal Property Tax Lists 1854-1870
1854

Francis O. Byrd	0-12-1-0-0-11	Cornelius Bussey Junr.	0-0-1-0-0-0
Philip Berlin	0-6-2-0-0-6	Strother H. Bell	2-0-3-1-0-0
Geo C. Blakemore	0-7-1-0-0-11	Richd S. Bryarly	0-8-1-0-1-14
D⁰ as guardian for L. Enders		Christian Bowser	0-0-1-0-0-0
Neille Barnett	0-5-2-0-1-9	N. B. Balthrope	3-1-1-0-0-4
Thos Briggs Est.	0-2-0-0-2-5	John Blue	10-1-2-0-0-8
Danl S. Bonham	1-2-1-1-1-9	Capt. A. Beevers	0-0-1-0-0-3
Strother H. Bell	0-0-0-0-0-0	Peter Bennett	0-0-1-0-0-0
Robt Burchell	0-6-1-0-2-8	Adam Barr	0-0-1-0-0-0
H. W. Brabham	0-0-1-0-0-0	Saml Bonham	1-11-1-0-4-19
Arthur Briggs	0-0-0-0-0-2	A. J. Billmire	0-0-1-0-0-0
Squire Bell	0-0-1-0-0-0	Jesse Butler	0-0-1-0-0-1
John W. Byrd	0-11-1-0-3-9	Juliet Boyston	0-1-0-0-0-0
Thos Briggs	0-6-4-0-2-12	T. T. Byrd's Est	0-1-0-0-1-1
John S. Briggs	0-0-1-0-0-0	Richd E. Byrd	0-1-0-0-0-1
John Brumly	0-0-2-0-0-16	John R. Bell	0-1-1-0-0-5
Susan R. Burwell	0-9-0-0-2-2	James Brown	0-0-1-0-0-0
John C. Bonham	2-1-1-0-0-5	Richard Billmire	0-0-1-0-0-0
Lewis Berlin	0-3-1-0-0-1	Jesse Bowen	0-2-1-0-1-6
Wm Brentten	0-0-1-0-0-0	James J. Board	1-0-1-0-1-1
Strother H. Bowen	0-2-1-0-0-0	Jonas Berkheimer	0-0-1-0-0-1
		Wm Berlin	0-3-2-0-1-0
Ann C. Benn	0-0-0-0-0-2	Benjn F. Boley	0-2-1-0-0-1
Charles T. Benn	0-0-1-0-0-0	Geo H. Bell	0-0-1-0-0-0
John H. Barr	0-0-1-0-0-0	Geo W. Berlin	0-0-1-1-0-0
Wm Berry	0-7-2-0-3-11	Geo W. Bradfield	1-2-1-0-0-1
Hector Bell	0-0-1-0-0-0	Henry M. Bowen	0-2-1-0-1-10
Miss Nancy Boyston	0-1-0-0-0-0	Conrad Bowman	0-0-1-0-0-0
		George Board	0-0-1-0-0-0
John Bussey	0-0-1-0-0-0	James Berlin	0-0-1-0-1-1
Geo H. Burwell	0-50-1-0-6-39	Miss Emily Bell	0-0-0-0-0-1
James Bell	0-0-1-0-0-1	Robt Bull	0-1-1-0-0-0
Rosannah Berlin	0-1-0-0-0-0	Jos C. Bartlett	2-3-1-0-1-10
George Bolen	0-0-1-0-0-0	Columbus Brown	0-0-1-0-0-0
Cornelius Bussey Senr.	0-0-1-0-0-0	Middleton Bowen	0-0-1-0-0-0
		Geo W. Board	0-0-1-0-0-1
H. T. Barton	0-0-1-0-0-1	Robt & James Briggs	0-5-2-0-0-6

Clarke County, Virginia Personal Property Tax Lists 1854-1870
1854

David Brandt	0-0-1-0-0-0	Elizabeth N. Carter	0-0-0-0-0-1
James W. Board	0-0-1-0-0-1	Henry Canniford	0-0-1-0-0-0
Thomas Brown	0-0-1-0-0-0	James Carter	0-0-2-0-0-3
Geo W. Brumly	0-1-1-0-0-4	Thos Cornwell	1-0-1-0-0-1
John Beattey	0-0-1-0-0-0	Aaron Chamblin	0-0-1-0-0-3
Dr. Wm A. Bradford	0-5-1-0-1-11	Isaac Cornwell	0-0-1-0-0-0
James J. Brown	0-0-1-0-0-0	Michael Copenhaver	0-0-1-0-0-1
Charles Bales	0-0-1-0-0-0	Mrs. Ury Castleman	0-3-0-0-2-1
Alfred Castleman	1-9-1-0-1-12	John Carroll Junr.	0-0-1-0-0-0
Osborn D. Castleman	0-0-1-0-0-0	Stephen D. Castleman	1-4-2-0-0-2
Fredk Clopton	0-5-1-0-3-6	John N. Collier	0-0-1-0-0-2
Nathl & Wm Castleman	0-0-2-0-0-2	Charles D. Castleman	0-5-1-0-0-8
Geo F. Calmes	1-6-2-0-2-8	Henry C. Carr	0-0-1-0-0-0
Wm Carper	0-0-1-0-0-3	Stephen B. Cook	0-2-2-0-0-6
Robt A. Colston	0-4-1-0-1-9	John B. Carter & Bro	0-5-2-0-1-6
Elizabeth K. Carter	0-2-3-0-1-6	Peter Cain	0-1-3-0-0-7
John Copenhaver	1-4-2-0-1-10	Wm K. Carter	0-1-1-0-1-4
Geo D. Cooper	0-0-1-0-0-0	John P. Chamberlain	0-0-1-0-0-2
Miss M. Catlett	0-4-1-0-1-9	Franklin Canniford	0-0-1-0-0-0
James N. Clarke	1-4-1-0-0-1	Daniel Carroll	0-0-1-0-0-0
Thos H. Crow	3-5-1-0-1-9	Samuel Camel	0-0-1-0-0--0
Dr. R. T. Colston	0-6-0-0-1-12	Eloesa M. Castleman	0-0-0-0-0-0
Geo W. Cooper	0-0-1-0-0-0	Edward Cauthorn	0-0-1-0-0-0
Wm A. Castleman	0-4-1-0-1-13	Wm G. Carter	0-0-1-0-1-2
John Cooper	0-0-1-0-0-3	McLean Clingen	0-0-1-0-0-1
Parkison Corder	0-0-1-0-0-1	Henry W. Castleman	0-4-1-0-0-10
James Castleman	0-15-2-0-0-25	John A. Carter	0-2-1-0-0-5
Wm A. Cooper	0-0-1-0-0-0	David Carper	0-5-1-0-0-5
Thomas Carter	1-10-1-0-2-13	H. J. Chamblin	0-0-1-0-0-0
John Carroll Senr.	1-0-1-0-0-0		
Dabney Cauthun	0-0-1-0-0-0		
Peter Cooley	0-1-1-0-0-0		

Clarke County, Virginia Personal Property Tax Lists 1854-1870
1854

Name	Values	Name	Values
Anne B. Cooke	0-18-0-0-2-15	John D. Davis	0-0-1-0-0-0
Elisha Carver	0-1-0-0-1-5	James Davis	0-0-1-0-0-0
Jacob Clink	0-2-1-0-0-6	Aaron Dubal	0-2-2-0-0-1
Jeremiah Cain	0-0-1-0-0-0	Joseph Detter	0-0-1-0-1-1
Creager & Wharton	0-1-3-0-1-3	Jefferson Dove	0-0-1-0-0-0
Geo W. Castleman	0-0-1-0-0-0	Robt N. Duke	0-5-1-0-1-7
John Carper Senr.	0-5-1-0-1-10	Saml Deardorff	0-0-1-0-0-0
Andrew Cornwell	0-0-1-0-0-0	Edward Dorsey	0-1-1-0-0-0
John P. Caragan	0-0-1-0-0-0	Lewis Dick	0-0-1-0-1-0
Wm Chapman	0-0-1-0-0-0	John L. Detter	0-0-1-0-0-1
John B. Carper	0-0-1-0-0-1	Hugh Davis [at the bottom]	0-0-1-0-0-0
John R. Crockwell	0-0-1-0-0-0	Henry Edwards	1-0-1-0-0-2
John H. Crebs	1-3-1-0-2-7	Wm G. Everhart	2-1-2-0-0-7
Fielding H. Calmes	0-1-0-0-0-1	John Elleyett	0-0-1-0-0-2
Wm L. Chipley	0-0-1-0-0-0	Henson Elliott	1-2-3-0-0-6
Philemon Cromwell	0-0-1-0-0-0	Elliott & Parker	0-0-0-0-0-0
		Alexander M. Earle	0-5-1-0-1-11
		Hiram P. Evans	0-3-2-0-0-1
		Jacob Enders	0-7-1-0-0-11
Peter Dearmont	0-1-1-0-0-1	John Eberhart	0-2-1-0-0-0
Moses T. Davis	0-0-1-0-0-0	Jacob W. Everhart	0-0-1-0-0-1
Wm Deahle	2-1-1-0-0-1	Edward Eno	0-4-1-0-0-2
James W. Doran	0-0-1-0-0-0	Wm H. Edwards	0-0-1-1-0-1
Saml Davis	1-0-1-0-0-0	Henry Evans	0-1-1-0-0-1
John Drish	0-0-1-0-0-1	Christopher Elliott	0-0-1-0-0-0
Michael Dearmont	1-8-1-0-1-13	John R. Evans	0-0-1-0-0-0
Washington Dearmont	0-0-1-0-0-3	Albert Elsey	0-1-1-0-0-0
Baalis Davis	0-1-1-0-1-2	Isaac N. Elsey	0-0-1-0-0-0
John Donovan	0-0-1-0-0-0	Robt Eddy	0-0-1-0-1-4
James Doran	1-0-1-0-0-2	Edward Franks	0-0-1-0-0-0
Samuel Dobbins	0-0-1-0-0-3	Ephraim Furr	0-0-1-0-0-0
John Dow	0-2-1-0-0-5	Dr. J. F. Fauntleroy	0-4-1-0-2-4
Jefferson H. Davis	0-0-1-0-0-0	O. R. Funsten	0-12-1-0-2-15

Clarke County, Virginia Personal Property Tax Lists 1854-1870
1854

Name	Values	Name	Values
Henry G. Flagg	0-0-1-0-0-0	James F. Green	0-0-1-0-0-2
James A. Foster	0-2-1-0-0-5	Thos E. Gold	0-5-2-0-2-16
Moses Furr	0-1-1-0-0-1	Do as guardian	
Israel Fiddler	0-0-1-0-0-0	or B. Crampton	
Granville Farnsworth	1-0-1-0-0-2	Geo F. Gordon	0-0-1-0-0-0
		Mrs. Mary Green	0-6-0-0-1-6
Elizabeth Fleming	0-2-0-0-0-4	Stephen J. Gant	0-4-1-0-0-3
James Furr	0-0-1-0-0-1	John S. Gordon	0-2-1-0-0-7
Jos Fleming Senr.	0-0-1-0-0-0	Geo W. Gordon	0-0-1-0-0-2
Wm Fowler Senr.	0-0-1-0-0-4	Henry N. Grigsby	0-6-1-0-0-14
Washington Ferguson	0-1-1-0-0-3	Wm Gourley	0-0-1-0-0-0
		Saml Grubs	0-0-1-0-0-0
Enoch Furr	0-0-1-0-0-0	Geo W. Green	0-7-1-0-0-8
Martin Feltner	2-0-1-0-0-2	Richard N. Green	0-5-1-0-0-6
Jos Fleming Junr.	1-0-1-0-0-5	John L. Grant	0-0-1-0-0-4
Thomas Fowler	0-0-1-0-0-1	Lewis F. Glass	0-6-1-0-1-9
Marcus R. Feehrer	0-2-1-0-2-4	Martin Gant	0-5-1-0-1-8
		Mrs. Isabella Glass	0-0-0-0-0-0
John Frasier	0-2-0-0-0-0	Thornbury Grubb	0-0-1-0-0-0
Josiah Ferguson	0-2-1-0-2-5	Wm Grubbs Junr.	0-0-1-0-0-0
Johnson Furr	1-1-1-0-1-6	John J. Gordon	0-2-2-0-0-10
Christopher Fonda	0-0-1-0-0-0	John Gruber	0-2-2-0-0-5
Ebin Frost	0-0-1-0-0-0	John Green	0-2-1-0-0-8
Joshua Fellows	0-0-1-0-0-0	Geo W. Grubbs	0-0-1-0-0-0
Wm M. Fergerson	0-0-1-0-0-1	Geo Gardiner	0-0-1-0-0-0
		Elias M. Green	0-0-1-0-0-0
Everett Fowler	0-0-1-0-0-0	Jefferson Grubb	0-0-1-0-0-0
Henry Franks	2-0-1-0-0-0	Nathan Grubbs	0-0-1-0-0-0
Thomas J. Flagg	0-0-1-0-0-0	Adam Greenwald	0-0-1-0-0-0
John A. Finnell	0-1-1-0-0-0	Zebedee Gray	1-1-1-0-0-0
Dennis Fenton	0-0-1-0-0-0	Robt Gill	0-0-1-0-0-0
		Geo W. Grayson	1-2-1-0-0-1
Emanuel Garmong	2-0-1-0-0-2	Whiting Hamilton	1-0-1-0-0-2
James W. Galloway	0-0-1-0-0-0	A. J. Harford	0-0-1-0-0-0
		John T. Hilliard	0-0-1-0-0-0
Edward Gormon	0-0-1-0-0-1	James Hamilton	0-0-1-0-0-0
Jos Gormon	0-0-1-0-0-0	Carter J. Harris	0-0-1-0-0-1

Clarke County, Virginia Personal Property Tax Lists 1854-1870
1854

Henry D. Hooe	2-1-1-0-0-3	Rev. Jno F. Hoff	0-5-1-0-0-0
Abram Huyett	0-0-1-0-0-2	Adrian D. Hardesty	0-2-1-0-0-10
John Huyett	0-0-1-0-0-0	John Hodge	0-0-1-0-0-0
Saml Huyett	0-3-1-0-0-9	Wm Heskitt	0-0-1-0-0-0
Henry A. Hibbard	0-0-1-0-0-0	Harrison Hoof	0-0-1-0-0-0
James A. Haynes	0-4-1-0-0-5	James M. Howard	0-0-1-0-0-0
James M. Hite	0-1-1-0-0-3	E. C. Hutchison	collateral tax
Wm Hanvey	1-0-1-0-0-0	John Hooff	0-0-1-0-0-0
Wm Hummer	0-0-1-0-0-1	Nelson E. Hall	0-0-1-0-0-0
Mason Hummer	0-0-1-0-0-1	Willoughby Hanvey	1-0-1-0-0-0
Charles F. Hennis	0-0-1-0-0-1	Thos L. Humphrey	0-1-1-0-1-2
Wm Heflin	1-0-1-0-0-0	Edward E. Hall	0-6-1-0-1-8
Jos H. Hooe	0-0-1-0-0-0	John E. Hilbert	0-0-1-0-0-0
Charles W. Hardesty	0-2-1-0-0-0	Nimrod Henry	0-0-1-0-0-0
Wm G. Hardesty	0-2-1-0-1-14	Saml Heflebower	0-6-1-0-2-10
Jacob Heflebower	0-6-1-0-1-10	Wm Holland	0-0-1-0-0-1
Wm Holtsclaw Senr.	0-0-1-0-0-0	James M. Hardesty	0-1-1-0-2-5
Wm Holtsclaw Junr.	0-0-1-0-0-1	James E. Hesser	0-0-1-0-1-2
Blackwell Holtsclaw	0-0-1-0-0-0	Abram Hess	0-0-1-0-0-0
Mary Howard	0-4-0-0-0-0	John Henry	0-0-1-0-0-0
Cornelius Hoff	0-0-1-0-0-0	Eliza G. Hay	0-0-7-0-0-2
Philip Hansucker	1-0-1-0-1-0	William Hay	0-0-1-0-0-1
Geo L. Harris	0-5-1-1-2-12	E. T. Hancock	1-5-1-0-0-9
Richd S. Hardesty	0-1-1-0-1-8		
John Hughs	0-0-1-0-0-1	Armstd M. Johnson	0-1-1-0-0-4
Thos Hughs	0-0-1-0-0-1	George Johnston	0-1-1-0-0-2
Armstd Hoof	0-2-1-0-0-1	Herod Jenkins	1-0-1-0-0-1
Mrs. Sarah Hardesty	1-3-0-0-1-8	Solomon R. Jackson	0-0-1-0-0-0
Robt L. Horner	0-0-1-0-0-1	Mathew Jones	1-1-2-0-1-7
Wm B. Harris	0-6-1-0-4-11	John Joliffe	0-7-1-0-1-9
Geo Hansucker	0-1-1-0-0-2	Jacob Islers Est.	0-7-0-0-1-10
Dr. Benjn Harrison	0-7-1-0-0-15	Geo N. Isler	0-0-1-0-0-1
T. B. Heims	0-2-3-0-0-0		

Clarke County, Virginia Personal Property Tax Lists 1854-1870
1854

Jos J. Janney	1-2-1-0-2-7	Wm C. Kennerly	0-6-1-0-1-6
Thos Jenkins	1-0-1-0-0-4	Jos Kline	0-0-1-0-0-1
John Johnson	0-0-1-0-0-0	Jacob Kriser	0-1-1-0-0-3
Alfred Jackson	0-3-1-0-1-9	Jacob Kimmerly	0-0-1-0-0-0
B. H. Jordan	0-1-1-0-0-3	Jno N. Keimmell	1-0-1-0-0-0
Geo W. Joy	0-0-1-0-0-0	James H. Kennan	0-0-1-0-0-0
Wm H. Jones	0-6-1-0-0-7	John Kelly	0-0-1-0-0-0
James Wm Johnson	0-0-1-0-0-1	Wm B. Kennan	0-0-1-0-0-0
Wm A. Jackson	0-4-1-0-2-7	Edward V. Kercheral	0-0-1-0-0-0
Amelia Jordan	0-0-0-0-0-2	James Kile	0-0-1-0-0-0
Wm Johnston	0-0-1-0-0-0	Geo Knight Junr.	0-0-1-0-0-0
George Jenkins	0-0-1-0-0-0		
Thomas Jones	0-3-1-0-0-6	John D. Larue	0-4-1-0-1-9
Leonard Jones	0-0-1-0-0-5	George Lanham	0-0-1-0-0-2
		Wm D. Lee	0-0-1-0-0-1
Franklin Ingle	0-0-1-0-0-0	Dr. James M. Lindsey	0-0-1-0-0-1
Dr. F. J. Kerfoot	0-8-1-0-0-12	Eli Littleton	0-3-1-0-0-4
Dr. C. F. Knight	0-0-1-0-0-1	Enos Lanham	0-0-1-0-0-0
Thomas Kennerlys Est.	0-3-0-0-0-2	Henry Lloyd	1-0-1-0-0-3
Jos McK. Kennerly	0-13-1-0-0-11	John Lock	0-1-1-0-2-7
		James W. Larue	0-8-1-0-1-9
Geo L. Kerfoot & Bro	0-8-0-0-0-10	Wm D. Littleton	0-0-1-0-0-2
Saml G. Kneller	0-6-1-0-0-9	Dr. R. H. Little	0-4-1-0-0-3
Jacob Kretser	0-0-1-0-0-0	John Louthan	1-5-1-0-1-7
Wm C. Kerfoot	0-10-2-0-3-15	John Lee	0-0-1-0-0-0
Geo L. Kerfoot	1-10-1-0-4-13	Lorenzo Lewis Est.	0-22-0-0-5-14
Dr. Randolph Kownslar	0-6-1-0-1-3	Moses Lewin	0-0-1-0-0-0
Wm F. Knight	0-2-2-0-0-15	Col. John B. Larue	0-14-2-0-1-23
John Kable & Cooley	0-1-0-0-0-0	John Lloyd	0-0-1-0-0-1
Henry Kline	0-0-1-0-0-0	James Lloyd Senr.	0-0-1-0-0-0
Charles E. Kimbol	0-5-1-0-0-10	Edgar Lanham	0-0-1-0-0-2
Caleb Kennerly	0-0-1-0-0-0	Abram Longerbeam	0-0-1-0-0-1
Middleton Keeler	0-0-1-0-0-0	Wm Lloyd	0-0-1-0-0-1
		Minor Lanham	0-0-1-0-0-2
		A. L. P. Larue	0-4-1-0-1-9

Clarke County, Virginia Personal Property Tax Lists 1854-1870
1854

Name	Values	Name	Values
Harrison Lloyd	0-0-1-0-0-4	Mason	
Wm Littleton	0-1-2-0-1-4	McCormick	0-0-1-0-0-0
John T. Lindsey	0-4-1-0-1-3	James Mitchell	0-0-1-0-1-5
Rice W. Levi	0-1-1-0-0-3	Dr. Wm D.	
David Lloyd	0-0-1-0-0-0	McGuire	1-12-1-0-0-14
C. C. Larue	0-0-1-0-0-1	Otway	
James Larues heirs		McCormick	0-7-2-0-1-8
or N. Davis	0-0-1-0-0-0	Louisa W. Meade	0-3-0-0-0-1
James Lloyd Junr.	0-0-1-0-0-2	Philip N. Meade	0-7-1-0-3-14
Squire Lee	2-0-1-0-0-2	Wm W. Meade	0-7-1-0-0-9
James Lanham	0-0-1-0-0-0	Saml Morgan	0-0-1-0-0-0
Mrs. E. M. Lewis	0-0-0-0-0-0	Miss Mary	
Richard Lanham	1-0-0-0-0-0	Meade	0-4-0-0-0-0
John W. Littleton	0-0-1-0-0-3	Thomas	
John Longbeam	0-0-1-0-0-0	McCormick	0-8-1-0-2-10
Christopher Lee	0-0-1-0-0-0	John McPhillin	0-3-4-0-2-7
Benjn		Wm Morris	0-0-1-0-0-1
Longerbeam	0-0-1-0-0-4	Alexander	
John W. Luke	0-8-1-0-0-7	Marshall	0-0-1-0-0-1
John A. Lloyd	0-0-1-0-0-0	Col. F.	
James L. Lloyd	0-0-1-0-0-1	McCormick	0-18-1-0-3-20
Geo Langley	0-0-1-0-0-0	Mrs. Susan	
John M. Lupton	0-2-1-0-0-0	Marshall	0-4-0-0-0-6
Saml Lloyd	0-0-1-0-0-0	John Marshall	0-2-1-0-1-4
James T. Louthan	0-0-1-0-0-0	Joseph Moren	0-0-1-0-0-0
John K. Louthan	0-1-1-0-0-0	Jesse McConahay	0-0-1-0-0-0
Wm Levi	0-0-1-0-0-0	John Martz Senr.	1-0-1-0-0-1
Joshua Lanham	0-0-1-0-0-0	Dr. & Saml	
Geo W. Lewis	0-6-1-0-0-7	McCormick	0-22-2-0-1-31
Josiah R. Lock	0-0-1-0-0-9	C. C. McIntyre	0-3-1-0-2-8
		James Maddex	1-0-1-0-0-3
F. B. Meade	0-7-1-1-1-10	Lorenzo D.	
John Morgan	0-6-1-0-2-9	Maddex	0-0-1-0-0-0
Ditto as Guardian		Jesse P. Mercer	0-0-1-0-0-2
for Children		Thos Murphy	0-0-1-0-0-0
Saml McCormick	1-0-1-0-0-0	Col. B. Morgan	2-24-1-0-5-35
Peter McMurray	1-3-1-0-0-8	John G. McCauly	0-0-1-0-1-0
John Maddex	1-2-1-0-0-4	James	
		McCormick	0-2-1-0-0-9

Clarke County, Virginia Personal Property Tax Lists 1854-1870
1854

Name	Values
James Murphy	0-0-1-0-0-1
Stephen Marlow	0-0-0-0-0-0
Ammishaddi Moore	0-4-1-0-3-9
David H. McGuire Do as trustee	1-8-1-0-2-5
Alfred P. Moore	1-0-1-0-0-0
A. Ross Milton	0-5-1-0-0-7
Geo Marple	0-0-1-0-0-1
Edward McCormick	0-12-1-0-4-17
Edwin W. Massey	1-5-1-0-6-8
Jos R. Moore	0-0-1-0-0-0
John Marple	0-0-1-0-0-0
Province McCormick	0-1-1-0-1-3
Harrison McCormick	0-0-1-0-0-5
Moses G. Miley	0-0-1-0-0-3
Richard K. Meade	0-5-1-0-1-8
Wm McCormick	0-0-1-0-0-0
Nathl Mercer	0-0-1-0-0-0
Rev. D. G. Mallory	0-2-1-0-0-0
Henry Mason	0-0-1-0-0-0
Province McCormick	0-7-1-0-0-9
David Meade	0-2-1-0-1-5
Milton H. Moore	0-6-1-0-0-10
Geo W. McCormick	0-0-1-0-0-0
James McClaury	1-0-1-0-0-1
Spencer Marquis	0-0-1-0-0-0
Christian Moren [?]	0-0-1-0-0-0
Saml T. Martz	0-0-1-0-0-1
Bushrod W. Morgan	0-0-1-0-0-0
Nathl B. Meade	0-5-1-0-3-7
Wm B. Morgan	0-0-1-0-0-1
John Mahoney	0-0-1-0-0-0
Andrew J. Maddex	0-0-1-0-0-4
John H. Marker	0-0-1-0-0-1
_____ Morrow	0-0-1-0-0-0
Dr. S. S. Neille	0-7-1-0-0-7
Hugh M. Nelson	0-14-1-0-2-22
Mrs. Sarah Nelson	0-9-0-0-2-7
Thomas F. Nelson	0-10-1-0-3-15
Archie M. Nelson	0-0-1-0-0-2
John Newcomb	0-1-1-0-1-6
James H. Neville	1-2-1-0-0-0
Jos Noble	0-0-1-0-0-0
Miss A. & R. Nelson	0-3-0-0-0-0
John Nessmith	3-0-1-0-0-3
Philip Nelson	0-4-1-0-1-9
John B. Norris	0-5-0-0-0-9
Lewis Neille	0-0-1-0-0-0
John R. Nunn	0-3-1-0-1-6
Wm M. Nelson	0-0-1-0-0-0
Lucy Newman	0-0-1-0-0-0
Elizabeth ORear	0-9-0-0-0-10
Geo ORear	0-2-1-0-1-11
David Osborn	0-0-1-0-0-3
Geo Osborn	0-2-1-0-0-6
Hugh ORourke	0-0-1-0-0-0
Elias Overall	0-3-1-0-0-2
Benjn F. ORear	0-4-1-0-2-5
Overseers of Poor	0-0-0-0-0-5
Mrs. Susan ORear	0-0-0-0-0-0
Wm OCallaghan	0-0-1-0-0-0

Clarke County, Virginia Personal Property Tax Lists 1854-1870
1854

Name	Values	Name	Values
Susan R. Page	0-31-0-0-3-34	Willis Prichard	0-0-1-0-0-0
John Pierc [sic] Junr.	0-4-2-0-0-16	Alexander Parkins	0-3-1-0-1-4
Mathew Pulliam	1-0-0-0-0-1		
John E. Page	0-14-1-0-5-20	James M. Reed	1-0-1-0-0-0
Mrs. E. M. Page	0-5-0-0-1-1	John Rowland	1-0-2-0-0-7
John Page Junr.	0-8-1-0-2-12	Bennett Russell	0-10-2-0-2-11
Mann R. Page	0-12-1-0-0-17	Do as curator for Jno Russells Est.	
Hugh Petitt	0-0-1-0-0-0		
James M. Pine	0-0-1-0-0-0	John Reed	0-0-1-0-0-1
Saml L. Pidgeon	0-0-2-0-0-7	Miss E. W. Royster	0-1-0-0-0-0
Mrs. Mary C. Page	0-5-0-0-0-2	Conrad Ricamore	0-0-0-0-0-0
John Poston	0-0-1-0-0-0	Mathew W. Royston	0-1-1-0-0-10
Paul Pierce	0-7-2-0-2-10	Uriah B. Royston	1-0-1-0-0-4
Mary C. Pages	collateral tax	John Reid	0-0-1-0-0-0
James F. Poole	0-0-1-0-0-0	Jos Ross	1-1-1-0-0-0
John Pierce Senr.	0-5-1-0-1-8	Nancy Redman	0-1-0-0-0-0
Bushrod Puller	0-0-1-0-0-0	Geo W. Rutter	0-0-1-0-0-0
James Puller	0-0-1-0-0-0	Danl B. Richards	0-1-1-0-0-0
Peter McPierce	0-4-1-0-0-6	Saml B. Redman	0-0-1-0-0-1
Richard Parker	0-1-0-0-0-0	Adison Romine	0-2-1-0-0-4
Pendleton & Richardson	0-17-0-1-0-44	James W. Ryan	0-0-1-0-0-1
T. P. Pendleton	0-5-1-0-0-3	Jos F. Ryan	0-1-1-0-0-5
~~Washington F. Padgett~~	~~0-1-1-0-0-2~~	John W. Russell	0-3-1-0-0-4
		Geo Reno	0-0-1-0-0-0
Ben F. Perry	0-0-1-0-0-0	John Russell	1-0-1-0-0-1
Geo R. Page	0-3-1-0-1-5	Thompson Ritt	0-0-1-0-0-0
Michael Pope	0-0-0-0-0-1	Beverly Randolph	0-16-1-0-7-23
Calvin Puller	0-0-1-0-0-0	Dr. R. C. Randolph	2-24-1-0-1-30
John Patterson	2-0-1-0-1-3	John Reynolds	0-0-1-0-0-0
James S. Payne	0-0-1-0-0-2	Charles N. Richards	0-0-1-0-0-0
Barnett Prichard	0-0-1-0-0-0		
Wm Pyle	1-0-1-0-0-0	Michael Russell	0-1-1-0-0-1
Archie C. Page	0-5-1-0-0-13	Jos Richardson	0-0-1-0-0-1
Michael P. Pierce	0-4-1-0-1-12	Wm A. Riely	0-4-1-0-1-8
		J. J. Riely	0-3-1-0-0-5

Clarke County, Virginia Personal Property Tax Lists 1854-1870
1854

Name	Values	Name	Values
P. K. Royston	0-1-1-0-1-0	Parkison D. Shepherd	1-6-2-0-1-13
Dr. R. C. Randolph	collateral tax	Charles Swarts	0-0-1-0-0-0
John Ramey	0-0-1-0-0-0	Dr. Philip Smith	0-20-2-0-2-22
Thos Reradan	0-0-1-0-0-1	John W. Steele	0-0-1-0-0-0
Stephen Reed	0-0-1-0-0-0	Col. T. Smith	0-16-2-0-4-12
Thos W. Russell	0-0-1-0-1-2	Edward Smith	0-0-1-0-0-0
Thos W. Ridings	0-1-1-0-0-0	Charles H. Smith	0-0-1-0-0-0
B. C. Raynolds	0-0-1-0-0-0	Benjn Starkey	0-0-1-0-0-1
Jos P. Riely	0-0-0-0-0-0	Mary C. Shively	0-1-0-0-0-1
Saml Rutter	0-0-1-0-0-0	Mrs. Mary E. Shively	0-4-0-0-1-2
John Riely	0-0-0-0-0-0	Geo K. Sowers Est.	0-4-0-0-1-7
Thos W. Raynolds	0-0-1-0-0-0	James Sowers	0-2-1-0-2-8
Edmund H. Ridings	0-0-1-0-0-0	John Stewart	0-1-1-0-0-3
Wm Riely	0-0-1-0-0-0	L. J. Schooler	0-0-1-0-0-0
John D. Richardson	0-4-1-0-0-1	John Shaffer	0-0-1-0-0-0
		Jackson Shaffer	0-1-1-0-0-0
Champ Shepherd as guardian for son		Burr Smallwood	0-0-1-0-0-2
		Simon Stickles	0-0-1-0-0-1
Champ Shepherd	0-4-1-0-0-5	Hugh T. Swartz	0-3-1-0-1-9
Wm D. & E. J. Smith	0-27-2-0-8-38	Franklin Swartz	0-0-1-0-0-0
		Danl N. Sowers	0-4-1-0-2-11
George Smedley	0-0-1-0-0-1	Wm Strother	0-3-2-0-1-5
Wm Sowers Senr.	1-7-1-0-2-15	John R. Shumate	0-0-1-0-0-0
Jos Shepherd	0-0-1-0-0-0	Henry Shepherd	0-0-1-0-0-0
John O. Snyder	0-1-2-0-1-1	Jos Sprint	0-0-1-0-0-0
Carter Shepherd	0-5-7-0-1-7	John W. Sprint	0-0-1-0-1-0
John W. Sowers	2-11-1-0-1-22	Shedrick Shrout	0-0-1-0-0-0
Thos Shumate	0-3-1-0-1-10	Wm L. Smith	0-0-1-0-0-1
Danl W. Sowers	1-13-1-0-3-21	Erasmus Shackelford	0-0-1-0-0-0
James A. Steele	1-2-1-0-0-1	B. H. Sinnott	0-0-1-0-0-0
Hezekiah Slusher	0-0-1-0-0-0	Wm Stephens	0-0-1-0-0-0
Thomas Sprint	0-0-1-0-0-1	Charles Showers	0-0-1-0-0-1-0
Barnett Smallwood	0-0-1-0-0-2	Emanuel Showers	0-0-3-0-1-0
Fielding L. Sowers	0-3-1-0-4-8	Alexander Sanders	0-0-1-0-1-0

Clarke County, Virginia Personal Property Tax Lists 1854-1870
1854

Paul Smith	1-5-1-0-2-8		Greenbury Thomson	0-0-2-0-0-3
John Shell	0-0-1-0-0-0		James F. Thompson	0-0-1-0-0-1
Geo R. Smith	0-0-1-0-0-0		Geo W. Thompson	0-0-1-0-0-1
Sanders & Ridings	0-0-0-0-0-1		Wm Taylor	0-16-1-0-1-20
Thomas J. Skinker	0-7-1-0-1-15		Saml Tinsman	0-0-1-0-0-1
John H. P. Stone	0-0-1-0-0-0		Benjn Thomson	0-0-2-0-0-9
Robt Stump	0-0-1-0-0-1		Dr. Saml Taylor	0-5-1-0-1-3
Dennis Shehan	0-0-1-0-0-1		Jos Tuley	0-30-1-0-3-21
Stephen Shell	0-0-1-0-0-0		Wm N. Thompson	0-4-1-0-0-1
Isaac Starkey Junr.	0-1-1-0-1-4		Robt Tapscott	0-0-1-0-0-0
John Street	0-0-1-0-0-0		John Trussell	1-2-1-0-3-6
Bushrod Smallwood	0-0-1-0-0-0		Charles H. Taylor	0-0-1-0-1-1
Gipton [?] Smallwood	0-0-1-0-0-0		Wm Trenary	1-3-1-0-0-4
John H. Spots	0-1-1-0-0-0		Adam F. Thomson	0-0-1-0-0-2
Joseph Shipe	0-0-1-0-0-1		Thos Turner	0-0-1-0-0-0
Henry T. Shearer	0-0-1-0-0-0		French Thompson	0-0-1-0-2-4
Wm G. Steele	0-0-1-0-0-0		Andrew J. Thompson	0-0-1-0-0-1
Wm M. Sowers	0-2-1-0-0-4		Howard F. Thornton	0-3-1-0-0-5
Isaac Starkey Senr.	0-0-1-0-0-0		Moses B. Trussell	0-1-1-0-0-3
James F. Shryock	1-0-1-0-0-1		Andrew J. Tinsman	0-0-1-0-0-1
Henry L. Stephens	0-0-1-0-0-0		Calvin Thacker	0-0-1-0-0-0
Conrad Swartz	0-0-1-0-0-0		John B. Taylor	0-4-1-0-1-2
James Swain	0-0-1-0-1-15		Wm D. Timerlake	0-2-1-0-0-6
Geo W. Shimp	0-0-1-0-0-0		Ludwell Tinsman	0-0-1-0-0-1
Mrs. Mary Stribling	0-4-0-0-0-1		Geo F. Tomblin	0-0-1-0-0-0
			Baalis Thompson	0-0-1-0-0-6
Mrs. Sarah Timberlake	0-4-0-0-2-10		Wm Thompson	0-0-1-0-0-0
Addison Timberlake	0-0-1-0-0-0		Charles Thompson	0-0-1-0-0-1
John Turner	0-0-1-0-0-0		Danl Turner	0-0-1-0-0-1
Adam Towner	0-0-1-0-0-0		Dr. Bushrod Taylor	0-0-1-0-0-1

Clarke County, Virginia Personal Property Tax Lists 1854-1870
1854

Jno C. Underwood	1-3-2-0-0-4	Jacob Welch	1-0-1-0-0-4
J. DeLoss Underwood	0-0-1-0-0-0	David Wilcox	0-0-1-0-0-0
		Obed Willingham	0-0-1-0-0-0
		Geo W. Wiley	0-0-1-0-0-1
John Vancleve	0-1-1-0-0-4	Wm Wolfe	1-1-1-0-0-1
Jacob Vanmetre	0-4-0-0-0-7	Jesse Wright	0-0-1-0-0-2
Jos A. Vasse	0-1-2-0-0-2	Robt Whittington	0-0-1-0-0-0
		Alexander Wood	0-0-1-0-0-0
Henry Wilson	1-0-1-0-0-0	Richd B. Welch	1-3-2-0-0-3
Francis H. Whiting	0-3-1-0-0-6	Jos Wood	0-1-1-0-0-5
Wm Willingham	1-0-1-0-0-2	James H. Willis	0-0-1-0-0-1
Allen Williams	0-12-13-0-1-10	Benjn F. Wilson	1-0-1-0-0-2
J. W. Ware & Mrs. Stribling	2-18-1-0-6-20	Bennett Woods	0-0-1-0-0-1
		Walker B. Wilson	0-0-1-0-0-0
Danl Wade & Bro	0-1-2-0-0-3	G. W. Weaver	0-1-1-0-0-3
H. T. Wheat	2-5-3-0-2-5	Lucinda Washington	0-3-0-0-1-0
Hezekiah Wiley	0-0-1-0-0-0		
Saml Wiley's Est.	1-0-0-0-0-1	Francis M. Whittle	0-4-1-0-0-2
Sydnor B. Wyndham	0-0-1-0-0-1	Thos C. Wyndham	0-0-1-0-0-0
John Wilson	0-0-1-0-0-0	Albert Whittington	0-0-1-0-0-0
Leroy P. Williams	0-7-2-0-0-9		
Francis B. Whiting	0-22-2-0-2-16	James Writ [?]	1-0-1-0-0-0
Wm W. Whiting	0-4-1-0-3-6	Wm T. Wharton	0-0-1-0-0-0
Nathl B. Whiting	0-7-1-0-1-9	Wm W. Wood	0-0-1-0-0-0
Wm H. Whiting	0-8-1-0-0-10	Henry Willingham	0-0-1-0-0-0
James V. Weir	0-3-1-0-1-5		
John T. Willingham	0-0-1-0-0-2	Wm Young	1-0-1-0-0-0
James Wiley	0-0-1-0-0-0	Joseph Zeigler	0-0-1-0-0-0
John Wiley	0-0-1-0-0-0		

Clarke County, Virginia Personal Property Tax Lists 1854-1870
1854

Free Negroes

Peter Coats		Sandy Carter	0-0-0-1-0-0
(over age)	0-0-0-0-0-3	John Walker	0-0-0-1-0-0
Wm Howard	0-0-0-1-0-0	Jack Blanham	0-0-0-1-0-0
Wm Parker	0-0-0-1-0-0	John Robinson	
Simeon Parker	0-0-0-1-0-0	(over age)	0-0-0-0-0-0
James Butler	0-0-0-1-0-0	Ralph Bray	0-0-0-1-0-0
Jim Gumby	0-0-0-1-0-0	Wm Toler	0-0-0-2-0-1
Lewis Clifton	0-0-0-1-0-0	John Johnson	0-0-0-1-0-0
Philip B. Martin	0-0-0-1-0-0	Abram Johnson	0-0-0-1-0-0
Wm Allen	0-0-0-2-0-0	Mowen Harris	0-0-0-1-0-0
Alfred Thompson	0-0-0-1-0-0		

Clarke County, Virginia Personal Property Tax Lists 1854-1870

1855

1) Free male persons above 16 years of age, 2) Slaves who have attained the age of 16 years, 3) White male inhabitants who have attained the age of 21 years, except those exempted from taxation on account of bodily infirmity, 4) Male free negroes between the ages of 21 and 55 years, 5) Slaves who have attained the age of 12 years, 6) Horses, mules, asses & jennets

Name	Values	Name	Values
Buckner Ashby	1-8-1-0-1-13	Thos H. Alexander	1-1-1-0-0-6
James M. Allen	0-6-1-0-3-9	Wm Asbury	0-0-1-0-0-0
Mason Anderson	1-4-1-0-1-8	Jno & Nimrod Anderson	0-1-2-0-0-9
Jno H. Anderson	0-2-1-0-0-0	Nimrod F. Anderson	0-0-0-0-0-0
Edgar Allen	0-11-1-0-4-15	Evan P. Anderson	0-1-1-0-0-1
Jesse Allen	0-0-1-0-0-0	D. T. Armstrong	0-0-1-0-0-0
Jno Alexander	0-23-1-0-0-27	Thomas Ashby	0-0-1-0-0-0
Jno W. Anderson of Jos	0-0-0-0-0-0	Mrs. Nancy Allen	0-0-0-0-0-0
James Athey	0-0-1-0-0-0	Elias J. Athey	0-0-1-0-0-0
Levi Athey	0-0-1-0-0-0	Jno W. Anderson, at Bumly's	0-0-1-0-0-0
Robt Ashby Senr.	0-0-1-0-0-1	Jno Avis	0-0-1-0-0-0
Robt Ashby Junr.	0-0-1-0-0-0	Robt O. Allen	0-0-1-0-0-1
Austin C. Ashby	0-0-1-0-0-1	Jno Anderson	0-0-1-0-0-2
Nimrod Ashby	0-0-1-0-0-0	Lewis Ashby	0-0-1-0-0-2
Geo Wm Ashby	0-0-0-0-0-0		
Geo B. Ashby	0-0-1-0-1-0	Geo H. Burwell	0-49-1-0-6-43
Jos E. Anderson	0-0-1-0-0-1	Nathl Burwell	0-13-2-0-2-25
Jos Anderson Senr.	0-0-1-0-0-1	Jno Burchell	0-7-2-0-0-14
Geo Wm Allen	0-4-1-0-1-9	Andrew J. Berlin	0-0-1-0-0-0
Wm T. Allen	0-4-1-0-4-11	Archibald Bowen	2-4-1-0-1-6
A. S. Allen	0-8-1-0-2-14	Hiram O. Bell	0-5-1-0-1-6
Jeremiah Ashby	0-0-1-0-0-0	Strother H. Bell	0-4-3-0-0-5
Jno Ashby	0-0-1-0-0-0	Squire Bell	0-0-1-0-0-1
James Allison	0-0-1-0-0-0	Jno R. Bell	0-0-1-0-0-0
Jno Allison	0-0-1-0-0-0	Geo H. Bell	0-0-1-0-0-0
James Ash	0-0-1-0-0-0		

Clarke County, Virginia Personal Property Tax Lists 1854-1870
1855

Hector Ball	1-0-1-0-0-2	Dr. H. T. Barton	0-1-1-0-0-1
Jessee Bowen	0-2-1-0-1-6	Richd S. Bryarly	0-7-1-0-1-9
Francis O. Byrd	0-9-1-0-0-11	Christian Bowser	0-0-1-0-0-0
Philip Berlin	0-5-1-0-0-5	N. B. Balthrope	3-0-1-0-0-4
Wm Berlin	0-5-1-0-1-0	Mordecai	
Lewis Berlin	0-3-1-0-0-0	Beevers	0-0-0-0-0-1
Geo C.		Abram Beevers	1-0-1-0-0-3
Blakemore	0-6-1-2-13	Peter Bennett	0-0-1-0-0-0
Neille Barnett	0-7-2-0-2-11	Adam Barr	0-0-1-0-0-0
Thos Briggs	0-6-4-0-3-16	A. J. Billmire	0-0-1-0-0-0
Thos Briggs Est.	0-2-0-0-1-6	Jesse Butler	0-0-1-0-0-0
R. W. & Jas C.		Richd Billmire	0-0-1-0-0-0
Briggs	0-5-0-0-1-0	T. T. Byrd's Est.	0-1-0-0-1-0
Arthur Briggs	0-0-1-0-0-2	Richd E. Byrd	0-1-0-0-0-1
Miss Margt		James Brown	0-0-1-0-0-0
Burchell	0-6-0-0-2-7	James J. Board	1-0-2-0-1-1
Jno S. Briggs	0-0-1-0-0-0	Jonas Berkheimer	0-0-1-0-0-1
H. W. Brabham	1-0-1-0-0-0	Benjn F. Boley	0-2-1-0-0-0
John W. Byrd	0-12-1-0-2-10	Geo W. Bradfield	1-1-1-0-0-1
Jno Brumley	1-0-10-0-13	Henry M. Bowen	0-3-1-0-1-10
Geo W. Brumely	0-2-2-0-0-6	Miss Emily Bell	0-0-0-0-0-1
Mrs. Susan R.		Robt Bull	0-1-1-0-0-0
Burwell	0-9-0-0-2-2	Jos C. Bartlett	1-3-2-0-0-8
John C. Bonham	1-0-1-0-2-7	George Board	
Danl S. Bonham	1-1-1-0-1-9	Senr.	0-0-1-0-0-0
Capt. Saml		David Brandt	0-0-1-0-0-0
Bonham	0-5-2-0-4-17	Jas W. Board	0-0-1-0-0-1
Col. S. H. Bowen	0-4-1-0-1-0	Thos Brown	0-0-1-0-0-0
Ann C. Benn	0-0-0-0-0-2	Dr. Wm A.	
John H. Barr	0-0-1-0-0-1	Bradford	0-4-1-0-3-11
Wm Berry	0-0-0-0-0-0	Wm O. H. Brown	0-0-1-0-0-0
Miss Nancy		Geo B. Bradford	0-0-1-0-0-0
Boston	0-0-0-0-0-0	Charles Bales	0-0-1-0-0-1
Miss Juliet Boston	0-0-0-0-0-0	Conrad Bowman	0-0-1-0-0-0
Jno Bussey	0-0-1-0-0-0	Middleton Bowen	0-0-1-0-0-0
James Bell Senr.	0-0-2-0-0-1	Geo W. Board	0-0-1-0-0-1
Jno Bolen	0-0-1-0-0-0	Burr E. Barr	0-0-1-0-0-0
Geo Bolen	0-0-1-0-0-0	Steward J.	
Cornelius Bussey	0-0-1-0-0-0	Brannan	0-2-1-0-0-4

Clarke County, Virginia Personal Property Tax Lists 1854-1870
1855

Jno Beevers	0-0-1-0-0-2	Carper &	
Geo W. Berlin	0-2-1-0-0-0	Marshall	0-0-0-0-0-0
Cornelius		Robt A. Colston	0-5-1-0-2-12
Bussey Jr.	0-0-1-0-0-0	Elizabeth K.	
Philip L. Berlin	0-1-1-0-0-4	Carter	0-3-3-0-0-5
Jno T. Barr	0-0-1-0-0-0	Geo D. Cooper	0-0-1-0-0-0
Wm Briggs	0-0-1-0-0-0	Miss M. Catlett	0-5-1-0-1-7
Jacob Barley	0-0-1-0-0-2	Jno Copenhaver	0-4-2-0-0-9
Bowen &		Jno H. Crebbs	0-1-1-0-1-3
Eberhart	7-1-6-0-1-6	Peter Crain	0-2-2-0-0-6
Mrs. Lucy N.		Dr. R. T. Colston	0-5-0-0-0-12
Buck	0-1-0-0-0-0	Jas H. Clark	1-4-1-0-0-1
Alfred Bishop	0-0-1-0-0-0	Thos H. Crow	2-4-1-0-1-7
		Geo W. Cooper	1-0-1-0-0-0
Alfred Castleman	1-8-1-0-1-16	Jno Cooper	0-0-1-0-0-1
Henry W.		Parkison Corder	0-0-1-0-0-1
Castleman	0-8-1-0-0-12	Thos Carter	0-7-0-0-0-10
Stephen D.		John Carroll Jr.	0-0-1-0-0-0
Castleman	0-4-1-0-0-2	Edwin Cauthorn	0-0-1-0-0-0
Charles D.		Peter Cooley	0-0-1-0-0-1
Castleman	0-4-1-0-0-7	Henry Canniford	0-0-1-0-0-0
Wm A. Castleman		Franklin	
Senr.	0-5-1-0-0-12	Canniford	0-0-1-0-0-0
Mrs. Ury		Jno B. Carter	
Castleman	0-3-0-0-1-1	& Bro	0-6-2-0-0-6
Miss Eloesa		James Carter	0-0-2-0-0-3
Castleman	0-0-0-0-0-0	Wm K. Carter	0-2-1-0-0-6
Geo W.		Jno A. Carter	0-1-1-0-1-8
Castleman	0-0-1-0-0-0	Wm G. Carter	0-0-1-0-1-1
Nathl Castleman	0-0-1-0-0-0	Thos Cornwell	0-0-1-0-0-1
Osborn D.		Aaron Chamblin	0-0-1-0-0-1
Castleman	0-0-1-0-0-0	Isaac Cornwell	0-0-1-0-0-0
Geo F. Calmes	1-5-1-0-0-5	Andrew Cornwell	0-1-1-0-0-0
F. L. Calmes	0-0-1-0-0-0	Michael	
Wm Carper	0-0-1-0-0-3	Copenhaver	0-0-1-0-0-1
Jno Carper	0-5-1-0-1-10	John Carroll Senr.	0-0-1-0-0-0
Jno B. Carper	0-0-1-0-0-1	Jno N. Collier	0-0-1-0-1-2
David Carper	0-3-2-0-0-6	Stephen B. Cooke	0-1-2-0-1-6

Clarke County, Virginia Personal Property Tax Lists 1854-1870
1855

Jno P. Chamberlain	0-0-1-0-0-2	John Donovan	0-0-1-0-0-0
Lewis Carroll	0-0-1-0-0-1	Robt N. Duke	0-4-2-0-1-7
Saml Camel	0-0-1-0-0-0	Saml Dobbins	0-0-1-0-0-3
Mrs. Anne Cooke	0-15-0-0-5-18	Geo W. Diffenderfer	1-0-1-0-1-2
Jacob Clink	0-0-1-0-1-4	Hugh Davis	0-0-1-0-0-0
Jeremiah Cain	0-0-1-0-0-0	John D. Davis	0-0-1-0-0-0
Jno P. Carrigan	0-0-1-0-0-0	James Davis	0-0-1-0-0-0
Jno R. Crockwell	0-0-1-0-1-0	Jno Dow	0-3-1-0-0-3
Wm L. Chipley	1-0-1-0-0-0	Aaron Duble	0-0-2-0-1-1
Fredk Chort	0-0-1-0-0-0	Jos Detter	0-0-0-0-0-0
James L. Carter	0-0-1-0-0-0	John L. Detter	0-0-1-0-0-1
Jno Crim Junr.	0-0-1-0-0-0	Jefferson Dove	0-0-1-0-0-0
Jno S. Cosser	0-0-1-0-0-0	Lewis Dick	0-0-1-1-0-0
Morris Cain	0-0-1-0-0-0	Rev. Mr. Dodge	0-3-1-0-0-1
M. H. Cristy	0-0-1-0-0-0	Geo W. Drish	1-0-0-0-0-0
Robt H. Castleman	0-0-1-0-0-0	Thos Duke	0-0-1-0-0-0
Catharine Castleman	0-3-0-0-0-4	Henry Edwards	1-0-1-0-0-2
Jas W. Conrad	0-2-1-0-2-6	Wm G. Everheart	2-0-2-0-1-7
Humphrey Christian	0-0-1-0-0-0	John Elleyett	0-0-1-0-0-1
H. J. Chamblin	0-0-1-0-0-0	Henson Elliott	0-3-3-0-0-7
		Elliott & Parker	0-1-0-0-0-1
		Hiram P. Evans	1-2-1-0-0-1
		Jacob Enders	0-7-2-0-0-11
Peter Dearmont	0-1-1-0-2-2	A. M. Earle	0-5-1-0-1-13
Michael Dearmont	1-7-1-0-2-13	Wm F. Engle	0-0-1-0-0-0
Washington Dearmont	0-0-1-0-0-3	Jno Eberhart	0-1-1-0-0-0
Moses T. Davis	0-0-1-0-0-0	Jacob W. Everhart	0-0-1-0-0-1
Wm Deahle	1-1-2-0-0-1	Henry Evans	0-1-1-0-0-1
James W. Doran	1-0-1-0-0-0	Edward Eno	0-4-1-0-0-2
Saml Davis	1-0-1-0-0-0	Wm H. Edwards	0-0-1-0-0-2
Jno W. Davis	0-0-1-0-0-0	Isaac N. Elsey	0-0-1-0-0-0
Jas W. Doran	0-0-1-0-0-0	Robt Eddy	0-1-1-1-1-4
John Drish	0-0-1-0-0-2	Robt Evans	0-0-1-0-0-0
Jas Doran Senr.	1-0-1-0-0-3		
Baalis Davis	1-0-1-0-1-1	Washington Ferguson	0-3-1-0-0-3

Clarke County, Virginia Personal Property Tax Lists 1854-1870
1855

Name	Values	Name	Values
Josiah Ferguson	0-1-1-0-0-4	Thos E. Gold	0-7-2-0-2-17
Wm M. Ferguson	0-0-1-0-0-1	Do as guardian	
Edward Franks	0-0-1-0-0-0	for Ben Crampton	
Henry Franks	1-0-1-0-0-0	Geo W. Gordon	0-0-1-0-0-2
Dr. O. R. Funsten	0-13-1-0-3-16	Jno S. Gordon	1-1-1-0-0-6
Dr. Jno F.		Jas J. Gordon	0-3-1-0-0-11
Fauntleroy	0-4-1-0-2-4	Stephen J. Gant	0-4-1-0-0-3
James A. Foster	0-2-1-0-0-5	Henry N. Grigsby	0-6-1-0-1-13
Moses Furr	0-0-1-0-0-0	Saml Grubs	0-0-1-0-0-0
James Furr	0-0-1-0-0-0	Wm Gourley	0-1-1-0-0-4
Enoch Furr	0-0-1-0-0-0	Jno L. Grant	0-0-1-0-0-4
Johnston Furr	1-2-1-0-0-9	Lewis F. Glass	0-6-1-0-1-10
Israel Fiddler	0-0-1-0-0-0	Martin Gant	0-5-1-0-1-9
Ann Farnsworth	1-0-1-0-0-3	Mrs. Isabella	
Mrs. Elizabeth		Glass	0-0-0-0-0-0
Fleming	0-2-0-0-0-2	Wm Gibbs	0-0-1-0-0-0
Jos Fleming Junr.	1-0-1-0-0-7	Thornbury	
Wm Fowler	0-0-1-0-0-3	Grubbs	1-0-1-0-0-0
Everett Fowler	0-0-1-0-0-0	Wm Grubbs Junr.	0-0-1-0-0-1
Martin Feltner	1-0-1-0-0-1	Wm B. Grubbs	0-0-1-0-0-1
Marcus R.		Geo W. Grubb	0-0-1-0-0-0
Feehrer	0-2-2-0-2-2	Jno Gardiner	0-1-1-0-0-1
Christopher		Geo Gardiner	0-0-2-0-0-1
Fonda	0-0-1-0-0-0	Adam Greenwald	0-0-1-0-0-0
Joshua Fellows	0-0-1-0-0-12	Zebide Gray	1-0-1-0-1-0
Thos G. Flagg	0-0-1-0-1-0	Robt Gill	0-0-1-0-0-0
Jno A. Finnell	0-1-0-0-0-0	Jos Gormon	0-0-1-0-0-0
Dennis Fenton	0-0-1-0-0-1	Jno Gill	0-0-1-0-0-0
Meredith Forney	2-0-1-0-0-0	Saml Gruber	0-0-1-0-0-0
		Jefferson Grubb	0-0-1-0-0-0
Emanuel			
Garmong	1-0-2-0-0-2	Geo E. P. Legg	0-0-1-0-0-0
Jas W. Galloway	0-0-1-0-0-0		
Edward Gormon	0-0-1-0-0-2	Jno Grim	0-0-1-0-0-0
James F. Green	0-1-1-0-0-2	Mrs. Mary Green	0-6-0-0-2-5
Geo W. Green	0-6-1-0-1-8	Jno Greenwald	0-0-1-0-0-0
Richd N. Green	0-5-1-0-0-7	Saml Huyett	0-3-1-0-1-9
Jno Green	0-2-1-0-0-8	Abram Huyett	0-0-1-0-0-2
Elias M. Green	0-0-1-0-0-0	Jno Huyett	0-0-1-0-0-0

Clarke County, Virginia Personal Property Tax Lists 1854-1870
1855

James Hamilton	0-0-1-0-0-0	
Whiting Hamilton	2-0-1-0-0-4	
Henry Huyett	0-1-1-0-1-9	
Henry D. Hooe	1-1-2-0-0-4	
Jas H. Hooe	0-0-1-0-0-0	
Jno W. Holland	0-0-1-0-0-0	
Jno W. Hibbard	0-0-1-0-0-0	
Jno Hummer	0-0-1-0-0-1	
E. T. Hancock	0-4-1-0-1-9	
James A. Haynes	0-5-1-0-0-1	
James M. Hite	0-1-1-0-0-5	
C. B. Hancock	0-1-1-0-0-3	
Willoughby Hanvey	1-0-1-0-0-1	
Wm Hummer	0-0-1-0-0-1	
Mason Hummer	0-0-1-0-0-1	
Chas F. Hennis	0-0-1-0-0-1	
Wm Heflin	1-0-1-0-0-0	
Saml Heflebower	0-7-1-0-2-10	
Chas W. Hardesty	0-2-1-0-0-0	
Wm Hay	0-6-1-0-0-3	
Wm G. Hardesty	0-2-1-0-1-9	
Jacob Heflebower	0-7-1-0-1-12	
Wm Holtsclaw Junr.	0-0-1-0-0-1	
Blackwell Holtsclaw	0-0-1-0-0-0	
Wm Holtsclaw Senr.	0-0-1-0-0-0	
Cornelius Hooff	0-0-1-0-0-0	
Philip Hansucker	1-0-1-0-1-0	
George Hansucker	0-1-1-0-0-2	
Geo L. Harris	0-5-1-0-2-15	
A. D. Hardesty	0-1-1-0-0-5	
James M. Hardesty	1-3-1-0-0-8	
Mrs. Sarah Hardesty	0-3-1-0-1-11	
Jno Hughs	0-0-1-0-1-1	
Thos Hughs	0-0-1-0-0-0	
Armstd Huff	0-3-1-0-0-1	
Robt L. Horner	0-0-1-0-0-1	
Wm B. Harris	0-8-1-0-2-12	
Dr. Benjn Harrison	0-6-1-0-0-21	
Abram Hess	0-1-1-0-0-0	
Rev. Jno F. Hoff	0-0-0-0-0-0	
Harrison Hoff	0-0-1-0-0-0	
Jno Hoff	0-0-1-0-0-0	
Nelson E. Hall	0-0-1-0-0-0	
Thos L. Humphry	0-1-1-0-2-3	
Edward E. Hall	0-8-1-0-2-8	
Wm Holland	0-0-1-0-0-1	
Isaac J. Hite	0-8-1-0-1-9	
Henry Horner	0-0-1-0-0-0	
Henry P. Huntsberry	0-2-1-0-0-5	
Jno Hedges	0-0-1-0-0-0	
A. J. Harford	0-2-1-0-0-2	
Henry A. Hibbard	0-0-1-0-0-1	
Jno Henry	0-0-1-0-0-0	
Asbury Hibbard	0-0-1-0-0-0	
Herod Jenkins	1-0-1-0-0-0	
Solomon R. Jackson	0-0-1-0-0-0	
Mathew Jones	0-1-3-1-0-6	
Jno Joliffe	1-6-1-0-1-9	
Geo H. Isler	0-3-1-0-0-4	
Geo Johnston	0-1-1-0-1-3	
Dr. J. J. Janney	0-3-1-0-1-4	
Thos Jenkins	1-0-1-0-0-3	
Alfred Jackson	0-3-1-0-2-7	
Geo W. Joy	0-0-1-0-0-0	
Wm H. Jones	1-5-1-0-2-11	

Clarke County, Virginia Personal Property Tax Lists 1854-1870
1855

Thos Jones	0-2-1-0-2-6	George Lanham	0-0-1-0-0-1
Leonard Jones	0-3-1-0-0-7	Wm D. Lee	0-0-1-0-0-1
Jas W. Johnston	0-0-1-0-0-1	Dr. James M. Lindsey	0-1-1-0-0-2
Wm A. Jackson	0-4-1-0-2-10	Eli Littleton	0-3-1-0-0-7
A. M. Johnson	0-0-1-0-0-4	Enos Lanham	0-0-1-0-0-0
Miss Amelia Jordan	0-0-0-0-0-0	Jno Lee	0-0-1-0-0-1
Wm Johnson	0-0-1-0-0-0	Henry Lloyd	1-0-1-0-0-2
		John Lloyd	1-0-1-0-0-0
Dr. F. J. Kerfoot	0-8-1-0-1-13	Jas Lloyd Junr.	0-0-1-0-0-2
Wm C. Kerfoot	0-12-1-0-1-14	David Lloyd	0-0-1-0-0-0
Geo L. Kerfoot	0-10-1-0-4-13	Jno A. Lloyd	0-0-1-0-0-0
Wm F. Knight	0-7-2-0-2-13	Jno Lock	0-2-1-0-2-8
Dr. C. F. Knight	0-0-1-0-0-0	Wm D. Littleton	0-0-1-0-0-2
Jacob Kriser	0-1-1-0-0-4	Mrs. Mary B. Little	0-0-3-0-1-3
Saml G. Kneller	0-6-1-0-1-8	Moses Lewin	0-0-1-0-0-0
Jos M^cK. Kennerly	0-9-1-0-1-10	Jno Louthan	1-6-1-0-0-7
Dr. R. Kownslar	0-6-1-0-1-3	Mrs. E. M. Lewis	0-2-0-0-0-2
Henry Kline	0-0-1-0-0-0	Lorenzo Lewis' Est.	0-21-0-0-5-16
Chas E. Kimbel	0-5-1-0-1-10	Geo W. Lewis	0-5-1-0-1-5
Wm C. Kennerly	0-6-1-0-1-6	Edgar Lanham	0-0-1-0-0-1
Jos Kline	0-0-1-0-0-0	Abram Longerbeam	0-0-1-0-0-3
Jacob Kimmerly	0-0-1-0-0-0	Jno Longerbeam	0-0-1-0-0-0
Jno N. Keimmell	0-0-2-0-0-0	Benjn Longerbeam	1-0-1-0-0-2
James H. Kennan	0-0-1-0-0-0	Minor Lanham	0-0-1-0-1-2
Jno Kelly	0-0-1-0-0-0	Wm Littleton	0-1-2-0-0-4
Wm B. Kennan	0-0-1-0-0-0	Jno T. Lindsey	0-0-0-0-0-0
E. V. Kercheval	0-0-1-0-0-0	Rice W. Levi	0-0-1-0-0-2
Jas F. Kerfoot	0-3-1-0-1-6	Squire Lee	2-0-0-0-0-2
Judson G. Kerfoot	0-3-1-0-1-5	James Lanham	0-0-1-0-0-0
Jacob Kretzer	0-0-1-0-0-0	Wm Levi	0-0-1-0-0-0
Jno N. Kitchen	1-2-0-0-0-4	Jno W. Littleton	0-0-1-0-0-4
George Knight	0-0-1-0-0-0	Christopher Lee	0-0-1-0-0-0
John D. Larue	0-4-1-0-2-11	Jno W. Luke	0-7-1-0-0-8
Col. Jno B. Larue	0-14-2-0-1-22	Jno M. Lupton	0-1-1-0-0-0
Jas W. Larue	0-6-2-0-0-9		
A. L. P. Larue	0-4-1-0-1-9		
Jas Larues Heirs	0-0-1-0-0-0		

Clarke County, Virginia Personal Property Tax Lists 1854-1870
1855

Jas T. Louthan	0-0-1-0-0-0	Peter McMurray	1-3-1-0-0-7
Jno K. Louthan	0-1-1-0-0-0	Jno Maddex	2-0-1-0-0-7
Josiah Lock	0-0-1-0-0-6	James Maddex	0-1-1-0-0-3
C. C. Larue	0-0-1-0-0-2	Lorenzo D. Maddex	1-0-1-0-0-0
Jno T. Longerbeam	1-0-0-0-0-0	Andrew J. Maddex	0-0-1-0-0-1
Thos Carroll	0-0-1-0-0-0	James Mitchell	1-2-1-0-2-8
Wash^t Lee	0-0-1-0-0-0	Dr. Wm D. McGuire	0-11-1-0-0-15
Jas L. Lloyd	0-0-1-0-0-0	David H. McGuire Do as Trustee	0-8-1-0-1-5
Joshua Lindsey	0-0-1-0-0-0	Mrs. Louisa W. Meade	0-4-0-0-0-2
Jno H. Marker	0-0-1-0-0-1	Thos Murphy	0-0-1-0-0-0
Henry Neville	0-0-1-0-0-0	Philip N. Meade	0-9-1-0-2-15
Francis B. Meade	0-7-1-0-0-11	Wm W. Meade	0-5-1-0-1-9
John Morgan	0-9-1-0-3-17	Nathl B. Meade	0-5-1-0-0-7
Col. Benjn Morgan	1-23-1-0-3-32	David Meade	0-2-1-0-0-7
Dr. C. & Saml McCormick	0-19-2-0-5-36	Miss Mary Meade	0-3-0-0-1-0
Col. Frank McCormick	0-17-1-0-3-24	Richd K. Meade	0-5-1-0-1-10
Thos McCormick	0-9-1-0-1-8	Jno McPhillin	0-5-4-0-1-9
Province McCormick	0-8-2-0-2-10	Wm G. Morris	0-0-1-0-0-0
Saml McCormick	0-0-1-0-0-0	Alexander Marshall	0-0-1-0-0-1
Jno E. McCormick	0-0-1-0-0-1	Jno Marshall	0-2-1-0-1-5
James McCormick	0-3-1-0-0-8	Mrs. Susan Marshall	0-4-0-0-1-6
Geo W. McCormick	0-0-1-0-0-0	Jesse McConahay	0-0-1-0-0-0
Otway McCormick	0-9-2-0-1-6	C. C. McIntyre	0-3-1-0-2-8
Mason McCormick	0-0-1-0-0-0	Nathl Mercer	0-0-1-0-0-2
Chas F. Miller	0-0-1-0-0-0	James Murphy	0-0-1-0-0-0
Province McCormick	0-2-1-0-0-3	Stephen Marlow	0-0-1-0-0-0
		Ammishaddi Moore	0-4-1-0-1-8
		Alfred P. Moore	1-0-1-0-0-0
		Milton H. Moore	0-7-1-0-1-12
		Edward McCormick	0-12-2-0-4-18

Clarke County, Virginia Personal Property Tax Lists 1854-1870
1855

A. Ross Milton	0-5-1-0-1-8		James H.	
George Marple	0-0-1-0-0-1		Newman	1-0-1-0-0-1
Edwin W. Massey	0-6-1-0-3-7		James H. Neville	1-2-1-0-0-0
Richard Morgan	0-0-1-0-1-5			
Moses G. Miley	0-0-1-0-0-4		Mrs. Elizabeth	
Henry Mason	0-0-1-0-0-0		ORear	0-9-0-0-1-9
James McClaury	1-0-1-0-0-2		George ORear	0-3-1-0-0-9
Spencer Marquis	0-0-1-0-0-0		Benjn F. ORear	0-4-1-0-3-5
Saml T. Marts	0-0-1-0-0-0		Mrs. Susan ORear	0-0-0-0-0-0
Jno Mahoney	0-0-1-0-0-0		George Osborn	0-2-1-0-0-6
Jno G. McCauly	1-0-1-0-0-0		David Osborn	0-0-1-0-0-3
Jas W. Morrow	0-0-1-0-0-1		Hugh ORourke	0-0-1-0-0-0
Saml Morgan	0-0-1-0-0-0		Wm OCallaghan	0-0-1-0-0-1
McLean			Overseers of Poor	0-1-1-0-0-6
McClingan	0-0-1-0-0-1			
Jno N. Meade	0-3-1-0-0-2		James Pierson	0-0-1-0-0-0
Patrick Mahoney	0-0-1-0-0-0		Conrad Pope	0-0-1-0-0-0
Sylvanus Moore	1-0-1-0-0-1		Jno E. Page	0-18-1-0-2-22
Albert J. Morris	0-0-1-0-0-1		Mrs. Susan R.	
Bushrod Morgan	0-0-1-0-0-1		Page	0-31-0-0-3-34
			Archie C. Page	0-10-1-0-2-13
Dr. S. S. Neille	0-6-1-0-1-8		Jno Page Junr.	0-13-1-0-2-12
Hugh M. Nelson	0-14-1-0-2-20		Mathew Pulliam	1-1-0-0-0-1
Thos F. Nelson	0-12-1-0-2-13		Jno Pierce Senr.	0-4-1-0-1-8
Archie M. Nelson	0-0-1-0-0-2		Jno Pierce Junr.	0-4-1-0-1-14
Mrs. Sarah Nelson	0-8-0-0-2-4		Michael P. Pierce	1-5-1-0-1-12
Jno Newcomb	0-1-1-0-0-7		Peter McPierce	0-4-1-0-0-7
Miss A. &			Mrs. Eliza M.	
R. Nelson	0-3-0-0-0-0		Page	0-6-0-0-0-7
Jno Nessmith	2-0-1-0-0-2		Paul Pierce	0-8-2-0-2-11
Jno B. Norris	0-5-0-0-1-5		Mann R. Page	0-9-1-0-1-15
Jno R. Nunn	0-5-1-0-1-6		Geo R. Page	0-3-1-0-1-4
Col. Wm N.			Hugh Petitt	0-0-1-0-0-0
Nelson	0-0-3-0-0-0		James M. Pine	1-0-1-0-0-1
Philip Nelson			Saml L. Pidgeon	0-0-2-2-0-7
Senr.	0-4-1-0-1-10		Jno Poston	0-0-1-0-0-0
Philip Nelson			James Pullen	0-0-1-0-0-0
Junr.	1-3-0-0-3-7		Pendleton &	
			Richardson	0-17-0-0-2-45

Clarke County, Virginia Personal Property Tax Lists 1854-1870
1855

T. P. Pendleton	0-5-1-0-1-4		Jno J. Riely	0-3-1-0-0-6
Washington F.			Wm A. Riely	0-4-1-0-1-0
Padgett	0-0-1-0-0-2		Jno Ramey	0-0-1-0-0-0
Benjn F. Perry	0-0-1-0-0-0		Thos Roradan	0-0-1-0-0-1
Michael Pope	0-0-1-0-0-0		Thos W. Ridings	0-1-1-0-0-1
Calvin Puller	0-0-1-0-0-0		Jos P. Riely	0-0-0-0-0-0
Jno Patterson	2-1-1-0-0-4		Saml Rutter	0-0-1-0-0-0
Jas S. Payne	0-0-1-0-0-1		Wm Rousey	0-0-1-0-0-0
Barnett Prichard	0-0-1-0-0-0		Thos W. Raynolds	0-0-1-0-0-0
Wm Pyle	1-0-1-0-0-1		Jno D. Richardson	0-2-1-0-1-2
Willis Prichard	0-0-1-0-0-0		James M. Reed	0-0-1-0-1-0
Alexander Parkins	0-2-2-0-0-5		Archie C.	
			Randolph	0-2-1-0-2-4
Bennett Russell	1-8-2-0-2-13		Jno Rippon	0-0-1-0-0-0
Thos W. Russell	0-0-1-0-1-1		James Rose	0-0-1-0-0-0
Jno W. Russell	0-2-1-0-0-4		Geo W. Rutter	0-0-1-0-0-0
Jno Reed	0-0-1-0-0-1		Jas W. Ryan	0-0-1-0-0-1
Jno Rowland	0-0-3-0-0-7		Patrick Rodgers	0-0-1-0-0-0
Miss E. Royster	0-1-0-0-0-0		Jos F. Ryan	0-1-1-0-0-3
Mathew W.				
Royston	0-1-1-0-0-8		Wm Sowers Senr.	1-7-1-0-2-4
Peter K. Royston	0-5-1-0-0-3		Champ Shepherd	0-4-1-0-0-8
Uriah B. Royston	0-0-1-0-0-4		Do as guardian for son	
Joseph Ross	0-0-1-0-1-1		Wm D. &	
Miss Nancy			E. J. Smith	0-31-2-0-3-39
Redman	0-1-0-0-0-0		Mrs. Mary E.	
Danl B. Richards	0-1-1-0-0-0		Shively	0-4-0-0-1-2
Chas H. Richards	0-0-1-0-0-0		Miss M. C. Shively	0-1-0-0-0-1
Addison Romine	0-2-1-0-0-4		Jno O. Snyder	2-1-1-0-1-1
George Reno	0-0-1-0-0-0		Carter Shepherd	0-7-2-0-2-7
Beverly Randolph	0-16-1-0-5-19		Jno W. Sowers	1-8-2-0-1-14
Thompson Ritt	0-0-1-0-0-0		Thos Shumate	1-3-1-0-1-11
Robt C. Randolph	1-24-1-0-2-30		James A. Steele	0-0-1-0-0-1
Jno Reynolds	0-0-1-0-0-0		Danl W. Sowers	1-13-1-0-1-25
B. C. Reynolds	0-0-1-0-0-0		Thos Sprint	0-0-1-0-0-1
Wm Riely	0-0-1-0-0-0		Geo K. Sowers	
Mathew Rust	0-2-1-0-0-1		Est.	0-4-0-0-0-7
Michael Russell	1-0-1-0-0-2		James Sowers	0-3-1-0-1-6
Jos A. Richardson	0-0-1-0-0-1		Wm M. Sowers	1-1-1-0-0-8

Clarke County, Virginia Personal Property Tax Lists 1854-1870
1855

Fielding L. Sowers	0-4-1-0-3-7	Simon R. Stump	0-0-1-0-0-1
Joseph Sprint	0-0-1-0-0-0	Stephen Shell	0-0-1-0-0-0
Danl H. Sowers	0-5-1-0-1-10	Dennis Shehean	0-0-1-0-0-1
Barnett		Conrad Swarts	0-0-1-0-0-0
Smallwood	0-0-1-0-0-2	Jno S. Street	0-0-1-0-0-0
Burr Smallwood	0-0-1-0-0-2	Jno H. Spots	0-0-1-0-0-0
Bushrod		Jos Shipe	0-0-1-0-0-0
Smallwood	0-0-1-0-0-0	Henry T. Shearer	0-0-1-0-0-0
Gepton		Wm G. Steele	0-0-1-0-0-0
Smallwood	0-0-1-0-0-0	James F. Shryock	1-0-1-0-0-0
Parkison D.		Henry L. Stephens	0-0-1-0-0-0
Shepherd	0-8-2-0-1-14	James Swain	0-0-1-0-0-1
Dr. Philip Smith	0-22-2-0-4-26	Benjn Starkey	0-0-1-0-0-0
Charles Swarts	0-0-1-0-0-0	A. J. Starkey	0-0-1-0-0-0
Col. T. Smith	0-7-2-0-4-21	Mrs. Mary	
Edward C. Smith	0-0-1-0-0-0	Stribling	0-4-0-0-1-1
Wm L. Smith	0-0-1-0-0-1	Mrs. Susan Smith	1-2-0-0-0-0
Chas H. Smith	0-0-1-0-0-0	Jno Stewart	0-0-1-0-0-1
L. J. Schooler	0-0-1-0-0-0	Hezekiah Slusher	0-0-1-0-0-0
Jno Shaffer	0-0-1-0-0-0	Alexander	
Jackson Shaffer	0-0-1-0-0-0	Sinclair	0-0-1-0-0-0
Simon Stickles	0-0-1-0-0-1	Mrs. Nancy Stipe	0-0-0-0-0-0
Hugh T. Swarts	0-4-1-0-2-11	Danl C. Snyder	0-0-1-0-0-1
Franklin Swarts	0-0-1-0-0-0	Timothy Shehean	0-0-1-0-0-0
Wm [?] Strother	0-3-2-0-1-5	Alfred W. Shores	0-0-1-0-0-1
Henry Shepherd	0-0-1-0-0-0	George Smedley	0-0-1-0-0-1
Jno W. Sprint	0-0-1-0-0-1		
Shedrick Shrout	0-0-1-0-0-0	Greenberry	
Erasmus		Thompson	0-0-1-0-0-2
Shackelford	0-0-1-0-0-0	Boston Thompson	0-0-1-0-0-0
Jos Steele Senr.	0-0-1-0-0-0	Adam F.	
Chas Showers	0-0-1-1-0-1	Thompson	0-0-1-0-0-3
Saml Showers	0-1-2-0-1-0	James F.	
Alexander		Thompson	0-0-1-0-0-3
Saunders	0-0-1-0-0-0	French Thompson	2-2-1-0-0-4
Paul Smith	1-4-1-0-2-9	Benjn	
Jno Shell	0-0-1-0-0-0	Thompson Jr.	0-0-1-0-0-6
Geo R. Smith	0-0-1-0-0-0	Baalis Thompson	0-0-1-0-0-4
Jno H. P. Stone	0-0-1-0-0-0	Wm N. Thompson	0-5-1-0-0-1

Clarke County, Virginia Personal Property Tax Lists 1854-1870
1855

Name	Values	Name	Values
Jno F. Thompson	0-0-1-0-0-1	Francis B. Whiting	0-22-2-0-3-16
Wm F. Thompson	0-0-1-0-0-0	Wm H. Whiting	0-8-1-0-0-11
Charles H. Thompson	0-0-1-0-1-1	Wm W. Whiting	0-4-1-0-3-6
Wm Taylor	0-16-2-0-2-18	Nathl B. Whiting	0-6-1-0-5-10
Miss Eliza Taylor	0-0-0-0-0-0	Allen Williams	0-11-3-0-1-16
Robt Tapscott	0-0-1-0-0-0	Wm Willingham	2-0-1-0-0-4
Dr. Saml Taylor	0-5-1-0-0-4	J. W. Ware & Mrs. Stribling	0-17-1-0-2-22
Col. Jos Tuley	0-21-1-0-4-22	Danl Wade & Bro	0-2-2-0-0-3
Jno Trussell	0-2-2-0-4-6	Hezekiah Wiley	0-0-1-0-0-0
Wm Trenary	1-3-1-0-0-3	Cornelius Wiley	0-0-1-0-0-2
Thos Turner	0-0-1-0-0-0	Sydnor B. Wyndham	1-0-1-0-0-2
Howard F. Thornton	0-5-1-0-2-6	Jno Wilson	0-0-1-0-0-0
Moses B. Trussell	0-1-1-0-0-3	Jno T. Willingham	0-0-1-0-0-1
Andrew J. Tinsman	0-0-1-0-0-1	Leroy P. Williams	0-8-2-0-1-8
Calvin Thacher	0-0-1-0-1-5	James V. Weir	0-3-1-1-1-8
Dr. Bush Taylor	0-0-1-0-0-2	James Wiley	0-0-1-0-0-0
Wm D. Timberlake	0-0-1-0-1-0	Jno Wiley	0-0-1-0-0-0
Mrs. Sarah Timberlake	0-4-0-0-3-6	Jacob Welch	1-0-1-0-0-4
David Tristlers Est.	0-0-0-0-0-0	David H. Wilcox	0-0-1-0-0-0
P. G. Taylor	0-0-1-0-0-0	Geo W. Wiley	0-0-1-0-0-0
Isaac Talley	0-0-1-0-0-0	Wm Wolfe	1-1-1-0-0-0
Jno H. Taylor	0-0-1-0-0-0	Jesse Wright	0-0-1-0-0-2
Snowden Tomblin	0-0-1-0-0-0	Robt Whittington	0-0-1-0-0-0
Daniel Turner	0-0-1-0-0-0	Alexander Wood	0-0-1-0-0-0
		Richd B. Welch	0-2-2-0-0-2
Jno C. Underwood	1-1-1-0-0-5	Jos Woods	0-1-1-0-0-7
		Bennett Wood	0-0-1-0-0-0
		Lucinda Washington	0-3-0-0-0-0
		G. W. Weaver	1-3-1-0-0-2
		Rev. F. M. Whittle	0-3-1-0-0-2
Jno Vancleve	0-0-1-0-0-4	Benjn F. Wilson	2-0-1-0-0-1
Jacob Vanmetre	0-4-0-0-1-9	Wm T. Wharton	0-0-1-0-1-0
Jos A. Vasse	1-1-2-0-1-3	Wm W. Wood	0-0-1-0-0-0
Francis H. Whiting	0-2-1-0-0-6	Henry C. Willingham	0-0-1-0-0-0

Clarke County, Virginia Personal Property Tax Lists 1854-1870
1855

Albert		Horatio T. Wheat	2-4-3-0-3-6
Whittington	0-0-1-0-0-0	Lewis Williams	0-0-1-0-0-0
Alexander Webb	0-0-1-0-0-0	Jeremiah Wilson	0-0-1-0-0-0
James T. Wood	0-0-1-0-0-0		
Wm Warden	0-0-1-0-0-0	Wm Young	0-0-1-0-0-0
Thos C. Wyndham	0-0-1-0-0-0		
Welch & Legg	0-0-0-0-0-0	Jos Zeigler	0-0-1-0-0-0

Free Negroes

Wm Parker &		Jacob Johnson	0-0-0-1-0-0
Brother	0-0-0-3-0-1	Sandy Carter	0-0-0-1-0-0
Alfred Thompson	0-0-0-1-0-0	Wm Toler	0-0-0-1-0-1
Shack Johnson	0-0-0-1-0-0	Jack Blanham	0-0-0-1-0-0
Jno Walker	0-0-0-1-0-0	Theophulus	
Jno Johnson	0-0-0-1-0-0	Newman	0-0-0-1-0-0
Peter Coats		Jim Gumby	0-0-0-1-0-0
(over 55)	0-0-0-0-0-3	Jim Butler	0-0-0-1-0-0
Mowen Harris	0-0-0-1-0-0	Burwell Cooke	0-0-0-1-0-0

Clarke County, Virginia Personal Property Tax Lists 1854-1870

1856

1) Free male persons above 16 years of age, 2) Slaves who have attained the age of 16 years, 3) White male inhabitants who have attained the age of 21 years, except those exempted from taxation on account of bodily infirmity, 4) Male free negroes between the ages of 21 and 55 years, 5) Slaves who have attained the age of 12 years, 6) Horses, mules, asses & jennets

Name	Values	Name	Values
Buckner Ashby	0-8-2-0-2-14	Wm Asbury	0-1-1-0-0-0
James M. Allen	0-6-1-0-2-12	Ths Ashby	0-0-1-0-0-1
Mason Anderson	0-4-2-0-1-8	Mrs. Nancy Allen	0-0-0-0-0-0
Jno H. Anderson	0-1-1-1-1-0	Elias J. Athey	1-0-1-0-0-0
Edgar Allen	0-12-1-0-2-17	Jno Avis	0-0-1-0-0-0
Jesse Allen	0-0-1-0-0-1	Robt O. Allen	0-0-1-0-0-1
Jno Alexander	0-25-1-0-2-29	Lewis Ashby	0-0-1-0-0-3
Jno Anderson		Russell W. Ashby	0-0-1-0-0-0
(East of River)	0-0-1-0-0-0	Jno Anderson Est.	0-0-0-0-0-0
Jno Anderson			
(Brumly's)	0-0-1-0-0-0	Geo H. Burwell	0-54-1-0-5-47
James Athey	0-0-1-0-0-0	Do as trustee	
Levi Athey	0-0-1-0-0-0	for Wm Hay	
Robt Ashby Senr.	0-0-1-0-0-1	Nathl Burwell	0-13-1-0-32
Robt Ashby Junr.	0-0-1-0-0-0	Jno Burchell	0-6-2-0-0-12
Nimrod Ashby	0-0-1-0-0-0	A. J. Berlin	0-0-1-0-0-0
George B. Ashby	0-1-1-0-0-1	Wm Brown	0-0-1-0-0-0
Jos E. Anderson	0-0-1-0-1-1	Geo H. Bell	0-0-1-0-0-0
Jno & Nim		Archie Bowen	2-4-1-0-2-8
Anderson	0-1-2-0-1-8	H. O. Bell	0-5-1-0-1-5
Geo W. Ashby	0-0-1-0-0-2	Strother H. Bell	0-4-3-0-0-5
Geo Wm Allen	0-4-1-0-1-9	Squire Bell	0-0-1-0-0-1
Wm T. Allen	0-7-1-0-3-11	Hector Ball	0-0-2-0-0-3
A. S. Allen	1-7-1-0-3-14	Lewis Berlin	1-2-1-0-0-1
Jerimiah Ashby	0-0-1-0-0-0	Geo W. Bolen	0-0-1-0-0-0
John Ashby	0-0-1-0-0-0	Philip Berlin	0-5-1-0-0-5
James Allison	0-0-1-0-0-0	Wm Berlin	0-4-1-0-1-1
John Allison	0-0-1-0-0-0	Geo W. Berlin	0-2-1-1-0-0
Thos H. Alexander	0-1-1-0-0-6	Neille Barnett	0-7-2-0-2-12

Clarke County, Virginia Personal Property Tax Lists 1854-1870
1856

Thos Briggs Senr. Est.	0-12-4-0-1-17	Benjn F. Boley	0-2-1-0-0-0
Thos Briggs Junr. Est.	0-3-0-0-0-5	Geo W. Bradfield	1-2-1-0-1-1
Arthur Briggs	0-0-1-0-0-2	Henry M. Bowen	0-5-1-0-0-8
Miss Margt Burchell	0-5-0-0-0-3	Miss Emily Bell	0-0-0-0-0-1
James Bell Senr.	1-0-1-0-0-2	Jos C. Bartlett	0-3-2-0-1-9
Jno S. Briggs	0-0-1-0-0-0	David Brandt	0-0-1-0-0-0
Jno W. Byrd	0-11-1-0-2-10	Thos Brown	0-1-1-0-0-0
Jno Brumly	1-0-1-0-0-12	Geo B. Bradford	0-0-1-0-0-0
Geo W. Brumly	1-1-2-0-0-6	Conrad Bowman	0-0-1-0-0-0
Mrs. Susan R. Burwell	0-6-0-0-0-2	Middleton Bouen	0-0-1-0-0-0
Danl S. Bonham	1-3-1-0-2-9	Burr E. Barr	0-0-1-0-0-0
Samuel Bonham	0-9-2-0-4-20	Stewart J. Brannan	0-0-1-0-1-2
Col. J. H. Bowen	7-6-3-0-0-0	Philip L. Berlin	0-1-1-0-0-5
Ann C. Benn	0-0-0-0-0-2	Mrs. Lucy N. Buck	?-1-0-0-0-0
Wm H. Brown	0-0-1-0-0-0	Adolphus D. Barr	0-0-1-0-0-0
Jno H. Barr	0-0-1-0-0-1	Geo C. Blakemore	0-7-1-0-1-12
Wm Berry	0-8-2-0-2-9	Robt J. Bean	0-0-1-0-0-0
Miss Juliet Boston	0-1-0-0-0-0	Jno Beattey	0-0-1-0-0-0
Nancy Boston	0-0-0-0-0-0	Alfred Bishop	0-0-1-0-0-0
Jno E. Bradfield	0-1-1-0-0-0	Robt Bull	0-0-1-0-0-0
Dr. H. T. Barton	0-1-1-0-0-1	Jesse Bowen	0-2-1-0-1-6
Richd S. Bryarly	1-8-1-0-0-12	Patrick Brady	0-0-1-0-0-0
Christian Browser	0-0-1-0-1-0	Michael Burgen	0-0-1-0-0-0
N. B. Balthrorpe	2-0-1-0-0-3	H. W. Brabham	2-0-1-0-0-0
Abram Beevers	0-0-1-0-0-3	Richd Billmire	0-0-1-0-0-0
Peter Bennett	0-0-1-0-0-0	Dr. Wm A. Bradford	0-1-1-0-2-10
Adam Barr	0-0-1-0-0-0	Lewis Carroll	0-0-1-0-0-1
A. J. Billmire	0-0-1-0-0-0	Edwin Cauthorn	0-0-1-0-0-0
Jesse Butler	0-0-1-0-0-0	Peter Cooley	0-0-2-0-0-0
T. T. Byrd's Est.	0-1-0-0-1-0	Thos Carroll	0-0-1-0-0-0
R. E. Byrd	0-1-0-0-0-1	Wm K. Carter	0-3-1-0-0-4
James Brown	0-0-1-0-0-0	Jno A. Carter	0-1-1-0-1-8
James J. Board	0-0-1-0-1-1	Wm G. Carter	0-0-1-0-1-1
George Board	0-0-1-0-0-0	Thos Cornwell	0-0-1-0-0-1
Geo W. Board	0-0-1-0-0-2	H. J. Chamblin	0-0-1-0-0-1

Clarke County, Virginia Personal Property Tax Lists 1854-1870
1856

Isaac Cornwell	0-0-1-0-0-0		James W. Doren	0-0-1-0-0-0
Andrew Cornwell	0-0-1-0-0-0		James Doren	0-0-1-0-0-2
Michael			Jno Drish	0-0-1-0-0-2
Copenhaver	0-0-1-0-0-1		Jno Donovan	0-0-1-0-0-0
Jno N. Collier	0-0-1-0-0-2		Thos Duke	0-0-1-0-0-0
Jno P. Carrigan	0-0-1-0-0-0		Samuel Dobbins	0-0-1-0-0-3
Jno P.			Geo W.	
Chamberlain	0-0-1-0-1-2		Diffenderfer	0-0-1-0-0-2
Samuel			Hugh Davis	0-0-1-0-0-0
Canwell [?]	0-0-1-0-0-0		John D. Davis	0-0-1-0-0-0
Mrs. Anne B.			James Davis	0-0-1-0-0-0
Cooke	0-15-0-0-5-19		Jno Dow	0-3-1-0-0-4
Jacob Clink	0-2-2-1-0-4		Jno L. Detter	0-0-1-0-0-1
Jeremiah Cain	0-0-1-0-0-0		Rev. H. W. Dodge	0-3-1-0-0-1
Jos Cavanagh	0-0-1-0-0-0		Lewis Dick	0-0-1-0-0-0
Jno R. Crockwell	0-1-1-0-0-0		Aaron Duble	0-1-3-0-0-0
Fredk Chort	0-0-1-0-0-0		Mrs. Lucy	
James W. Conrad	0-2-1-0-3-8		Dearmont	0-0-0-0-1-2
Catharine			Geo D. Drish	0-0-1-0-0-0
Castleman	0-3-0-0-0-2		Robt Dunn	0-0-1-0-0-0
Jos Carver	0-0-1-0-0-1		Wm Deahl	2-1-1-0-0-1
Robt H.				
Castleman	0-0-1-0-0-1		Henry Edwards	0-0-1-0-0-2
Marshall			Wm G. Everhart	2-4-2-0-1-8
Castleman	0-0-1-0-0-0		Jno Elleyett	0-0-1-0-0-1
Dabney Cauthorn	0-0-1-0-0-0		Henson Elliott	0-2-3-0-1-8
Wm H. Carter	0-2-1-0-1-5		Elliott & Parker	0-0-0-0-0-0
Benjn Crampton	1-0-0-0-0-0		Henry Evans	0-1-1-0-0-1
Henry C. Carr	0-0-1-0-0-0		Hiram P. Evans	0-1-1-0-0-1
Jno Carter	0-0-1-0-0-0		Jacob Enders	0-7-2-0-1-9
Jno P. Crim	0-0-2-0-0-0		A. M. Earle	0-5-1-0-1-14
Franklin			Jacob W.	
Canniford	0-0-1-0-1-0		Everhart	0-0-1-0-0-1
[*Names beginning with C*			Wm F. Engle	0-0-1-0-0-0
continue on page 31]			Edward Eno	0-3-1-0-0-2
Peter Dearmont	0-4-1-0-0-1		Wm H. Edwards	0-0-1-0-0-1
Wash Dearmont	1-5-1-0-0-8		Albert Elsey	0-0-1-0-0-2
Moses T. Davis	0-0-1-0-0-0		Jos W. Edwards	0-0-1-0-0-0
Samuel Davis	1-0-1-0-0-0			

Clarke County, Virginia Personal Property Tax Lists 1854-1870
1856

Name	Values	Name	Values
Robt Evans	0-0-1-0-0-0	Thos Carter	0-11-0-0-1-10
Jos H. Easterday	0-0-1-0-0-1	John Carroll	0-0-1-0-0-0
Alfred Castleman	0-10-1-0-1-15	Dr. O. R. Funsten	0-13-1-0-4-18
Chas D. Castleman	0-4-1-0-0-4	Dr. J. F. Fauntleroy	1-3-1-0-0-3
Wm A. Castleman	0-4-1-0-1-12	James A. Foster	0-2-1-0-1-6
Stephen D. Castleman	0-0-0-0-0-0	Josiah Ferguson	0-1-1-0-0-4
Mrs. Ury Castleman	0-4-0-0-1-2	Wm M. Ferguson	0-0-1-0-0-3
		Edward Franks	0-0-1-0-0-0
Miss E. M. Castleman	0-0-0-0-0-0	Henry Franks	1-0-2-0-0-0
O. D. Castleman	0-0-1-0-0-0	Ephraim Furr	0-0-1-0-0-0
Nathl Castleman	0-0-1-0-0-0	Moses Furr	0-0-1-0-0-0
Wm Carper	0-0-1-0-0-2	James Furr	0-0-1-0-0-2
		Enoch Furr	0-0-1-0-0-0
Mrs. Nancy Carper	0-5-0-0-1-9	Johnston Furr	0-1-1-0-0-8
Jno B. Carper	0-0-1-0-0-0	Israel Fiddler	0-0-1-0-0-0
David Carper	0-3-2-0-1-8	Elizabeth Fleming	0-1-0-0-0-2
Carper & Marshall	0-0-0-0-0-0	Jos Fleming	0-1-1-0-0-6
R. A. Colston	0-5-1-0-0-11	Wm Fowler	0-0-1-0-0-3
Jno Copenhaver	0-5-2-0-0-10	Thos Fowler	0-0-1-0-0-2
Jno H. Crebbs	0-2-1-0-0-2	Robt H. Feltner	0-0-1-0-0-1
		Martin Feltner	1-0-1-0-0-1
Thornton Costello	0-0-1-0-0-0	Dennis Fenton	0-0-1-0-0-0
Jos K. Carter	0-3-1-0-0-4	Marcus R. Feehrer	0-3-1-0-0-3
Jno B. Carter	0-4-1-0-2-3	Thos G. Flagg	0-0-1-0-1-0
Charles Carter	0-2-1-0-0-4	Jno A. Finnell	0-0-1-0-1-0
Miss M. Catlett	0-7-1-0-0-11	Joshua Fellows	0-0-1-0-0-0
Peter Cain	0-1-2-0-0-6	Christopher Fonda	0-0-1-0-0-0
Dr. R. T. Colston	0-6-0-0-0-15	Meredith Forney	0-0-1-0-0-0
James H. Clark	2-4-1-0-0-1	Jeremiah Foley	0-0-1-0-0-0
Thos H. Crow	0-5-2-0-2-7		
Geo W. Cooper	0-0-1-0-0-0	Emanuel Garmong	0-0-2-0-0-2
Benjn Crim	1-0-0-0-0-0	Jas W. Galloway	0-0-1-0-0-0
Parkison Corder	0-0-1-0-0-0	Thos W. Griffith	0-0-1-0-0-0
Jno Cooper	0-0-1-0-0-2		

Clarke County, Virginia Personal Property Tax Lists 1854-1870
1856

Jos Gormon	0-0-1-0-0-0	Wm Hobbs	0-0-1-0-0-0
James F. Green	0-1-1-0-0-3	Whiting Hamilton	2-0-1-0-0-2
Mrs. Mary F. Green	0-5-1-0-1-6	Henry D. Hooe	1-1-2-0-0-5
		Jas H. Hooe	0-1-1-0-0-1
Richd N. Green	0-5-1-0-1-6	Henry A. Hibbard	0-1-1-0-0-0
Jno Green	0-3-1-0-0-8	Asbury Hibbard	0-0-1-0-0-0
Thos E. Gold	0-6-2-0-3-16	Mason Hummer	0-0-1-0-0-2
Geo W. Gordon	0-2-1-0-0-3	Wm Hummer	0-0-1-0-0-1
Jno S. Gordon	1-1-1-0-0-6	Wm A. Holland	0-0-1-0-0-1
James J. Gordon	0-4-1-0-0-11	E. T. Hancock	0-4-1-0-1-9
Philip Gordon	0-1-1-0-0-3	C. B. Hancock	0-1-1-0-0-2
Stephen J. Gant	0-4-1-0-0-3	Dr. Jas A. Haynes	0-5-1-0-0-1
Henry N. Grigsby	0-6-1-0-1-9	James M. Hite	0-1-1-0-0-4
Samuel Grubbs	0-0-1-0-0-0	Isaac J. Hite	0-7-1-0-1-8
Mrs. Isabella Glass	0-0-0-0-1-0	Geo W. Hanvey	0-0-1-0-0-0
		Samuel Heflebower	0-6-1-0-2-10
Lewis F. Glass	0-5-1-0-2-9		
Wm Gourley	0-1-1-0-0-5	Chas W. Hardesty	0-1-1-0-0-0
Jno L. Grant	0-1-1-0-0-4	Wm G. Hardesty	0-3-1-0-0-8
Martin Gant	0-6-1-0-0-7	Adrian D. Hardesty	0-3-1-0-1-9
Wm Gibbs	0-0-1-0-0-0		
Wm Grubbs (of Thornly)	2-0-1-0-0-1	James M. Hardesty	0-2-1-0-0-9
Wm B. Grubbs	0-0-1-0-0-1	Jos R. Hardesty	0-0-1-0-0-0
Geo W. Grubb	0-0-1-0-0-0	Jacob Heflebower	0-7-1-0-2-10
J. Madison Grubb	0-0-1-0-0-0	Wm Holtsclaw	0-0-1-0-0-0
Jno Gruber	0-1-1-1-0-6	Blackwell Holtsclaw	0-0-1-0-0-0
George Gardiner	0-0-1-0-0-0		
Charles S. Grant	0-1-1-0-0-4	Cornelius Hoff	0-0-1-0-0-0
Dr. J. H. Green	0-0-1-0-0-1	Harrison Hoff	0-0-1-0-0-0
Adam Greenwald	0-0-1-0-0-0	Jno Hoff	0-0-1-0-0-0
Jno W. Grim	0-0-1-0-0-0	Rev. Jno F. Hoff	0-4-1-0-0-1
Jno Greenwald	0-0-1-0-0-0	Philip Hansucker	1-0-1-0-0-0
		George Hansucker	0-1-1-0-0-2
Samuel Huyett	0-3-1-0-0-8		
Abram Huyett	0-1-1-0-0-0	George L. Harris	0-3-1-0-2-10
Jno Huyett	0-0-1-0-0-0	Jno Hughs	0-0-1-0-1-1
Henry Huyett	0-2-1-0-2-8	Thos Hughs	0-0-1-0-0-0
A. J. Harford	0-2-1-0-0-1	Robt L. Horner	0-0-1-0-0-2

Clarke County, Virginia Personal Property Tax Lists 1854-1870
1856

Wm B. Harris	0-9-1-0-2-13		A. A. Jordan	0-1-0-0-0-0
Dr. Ben Harrison	0-6-1-0-1-21		Wm Johnson	
Henry Huntsberry	0-2-1-0-0-5		(Berryville)	0-1-1-0-0-1
Thos L. Humphrey	0-1-1-0-2-3		Mrs. Sarah	
Edwd E. Hall	0-8-1-0-2-8		Hardesty	0-3-0-0-1-10
Jno Henry	0-0-1-0-0-0			
Thos S. Hart	0-0-1-0-0-0		Dr. F. J. Kerfoot	0-8-1-0-1-12
James F. Howell	0-0-1-0-0-0		Wm C. Kerfoot	1-10-1-0-0-16
Jno W. Hibbard	0-0-1-0-0-0		James F. Kerfoot	0-5-1-0-1-7
Jno W. Holland	1-0-1-0-0-1		George Knight Junr.	0-0-1-0-0-0
Wm Hay	0-7-1-0-0-3		Wm F. Knight	0-6-3-0-2-15
W. R. Helphinstone	0-0-1-0-0-0		Jacob Kriser	0-1-1-0-0-3
A. T. M. Hough	0-2-1-0-0-1		Saml G. Kneller	0-6-1-0-1-8
Jno Hummer	0-0-1-0-0-1		Wm C. Kennerly	0-2-1-0-0-4
Wm M. Hanvey	0-0-1-0-0-0		Jos McK. Kennerly	0-8-1-0-1-7
Solomon R. Jackson	0-0-1-0-0-0		Henry Kline	0-0-1-0-0-0
Herod Jenkins	1-0-1-0-0-1		Jos Kline	0-0-1-0-0-0
Mathew Jones	0-1-3-0-1-6		D. R. Kownslar	0-6-1-0-1-6
John Joliffe	1-6-1-0-1-9		Charles E. Kimball	0-5-1-0-1-7
Wm H. Jones	0-1-2-0-1-6		Jacob Kimmerly	0-0-1-0-0-0
Leonard Jones	0-2-1-0-0-7		Jno N. Keimmell	1-0-1-0-0-1
Thos Jones	0-0-1-0-1-7		James H. Kennan	0-0-1-1-0-0
Geo H. Isler	0-0-1-0-0-2		Jno Kelly	0-0-1-0-0-0
George Johnston	0-2-1-0-0-3		Edwd V. Kercheral	0-0-1-0-0-0
Dr. J. J. Janney	1-2-1-0-3-5		Wm B. Kennan	0-0-1-0-0-0
Thos Jenkins	1-0-0-0-0-6		Charles H. Kitchen	0-1-1-0-0-0
Jas W. Johnston	0-0-1-0-0-0		Willis F. King	0-0-1-0-0-0
Jno S. Johnston	0-0-1-0-0-0		Jno N. Kitchen	1-0-0-0-0-5
Geo W. Joy	0-0-1-0-0-0		Judson G. Kerfoot	0-3-1-0-1-7
Wm A. Jackson	0-5-1-0-2-11		Jos Kindle	0-0-1-0-0-0
Andrew Jackson	0-0-1-0-0-0		Andrew J. Kerfoot	1-1-1-0-0-1
Wm Johnston (White Post)	0-0-1-0-0-0		Mrs. Lucy Kerfoot	0-5-0-0-2-8
Armstd M. Johnson	0-0-1-0-0-4		Harry Kromling	1-1-1-0-0-0

Clarke County, Virginia Personal Property Tax Lists 1854-1870
1856

Jno D. Larue	0-4-1-0-3-10	Abram	
Jno B. Larue	0-14-2-0-1-27	Longerbeam	0-0-1-0-0-3
James W. Larue	0-6-2-0-1-9	Jno Longerbeam	0-0-1-0-0-0
A. L. P. Larue	0-4-1-0-1-9	Benjn	
C. C. Larue	0-0-1-0-0-1	Longerbeam	0-0-1-0-0-4
Wm D. Lee	0-0-1-0-0-1	Jno T. Lindsey	0-4-1-0-2-4
Squire Lee	1-0-2-0-0-2	Rice W. Levi	0-0-1-0-0-3
Christopher Lee	0-0-1-0-0-1	Jno M. Lupton	0-2-1-0-1-1
Jno Lee	0-0-1-0-0-2	Jno W. Luke	0-7-1-0-0-12
Dr. James M.		Josiah Lock	0-0-1-0-0-6
Lindsey	0-1-1-0-0-2	Jno T.	
Mrs. Emma		Longerbeam	1-0-0-0-0-0
Littleton	0-2-2-0-0-7	Aaron G. Liady	0-0-1-0-0-0
Wm D. Littleton	0-0-1-0-0-2	Richd H. Lee	0-4-0-0-0-6
Wm Littleton	0-1-1-0-1-3	Frank Littleton	0-0-1-0-0-1
Jno W. Littleton	0-0-1-0-0-4	Jno S. Lupton	0-2-1-0-1-12
Enos Lanham	0-0-1-0-0-0	George Lanham	0-0-1-0-0-1
Henry Lloyd	0-1-1-0-0-2		
Jno Lloyd	1-0-1-0-0-0	Francis B. Meade	0-8-1-0-3-10
James Lloyd Junr.	0-0-1-0-0-0	P. N. Meade	0-10-1-0-2-14
James L. Lloyd	0-0-1-0-0-2	Jno N. Meade	0-4-1-0-0-3
David Lloyd	0-0-1-0-0-0	R. R. Meade	0-5-1-0-2-7
Jno A. Lloyd	0-0-1-0-0-1	Wm W. Meade	0-5-1-0-1-8
Saml Lloyd	0-0-1-0-0-0	David Meade	0-2-1-0-1-11
Moses Lewin	0-0-1-0-0-1	Mrs. Louisa W.	
Mrs. Mary B.		Meade	0-4-0-0-0-1
Little	0-5-0-0-1-0	Nathl B. Meade	0-6-1-0-2-8
Jno Luck	0-2-1-0-1-8	Miss Mary	
Jno Louthan	1-6-1-0-1-5	Meade	0-3-0-0-1-0
Jno K. Louthan	0-2-1-0-0-4	Col. B. Morgan	2-26-1-0-5-31
James T. Louthan	0-3-1-0-1-4	Geo Wm Meade	0-0-1-0-0-1
Mrs. E. M. Lewis	0-7-2-0-2-4	Jno Morgan	1-8-1-0-0-9
Lorenzo Lewis'		Do as Guardian	
Est.	0-16-3-0-0-15	Dr. & Saml	
Geo W. Lewis	0-7-2-0-2-0	McCormick	0-21-2-0-2-20
Edgar Lanham	0-0-1-0-0-1	Col. F.	
Minor Lanham	0-0-1-0-1-2	McCormick	0-17-1-0-2-25
James Lanham	0-0-1-0-0-1	Thos McCormick	0-10-1-0-2-9

Clarke County, Virginia Personal Property Tax Lists 1854-1870
1856

Province McCormick	1-7-1-0-3-11	Stephen Marlow	0-0-1-0-0-0
		Ammi Moore	0-4-1-0-1-9
Province McCormick	0-1-1-0-1-3	Alfred P. Moore	1-0-1-0-0-0
		Sylvanus Moore	0-0-1-0-0-1
Saml McCormick	0-0-1-0-0-0	Milton H. Moore	0-4-1-0-1-9
Jno E. McCormick	0-0-1-0-0-1	S. B. Murphy	0-0-1-0-0-0
E. B. Mantor	0-0-1-0-0-0	Saml Moreland	1-0-1-0-0-4
Wm M. McCormick	0-0-1-0-0-1	Geo W. Marple	0-0-1-0-0-1
		Edwin W. Massey	0-6-1-0-2-10
James McCormick	0-3-1-0-0-7	Richd Morgan	0-0-1-0-1-5
		Moses G. Miley	0-0-1-0-0-4
Geo W. McCormick	0-0-1-0-0-0	Henry Mason	0-0-1-0-0-0
		James McClaury	0-0-2-0-0-2
Otway McCormick	0-7-1-0-1-7	Jno McDaniel	0-0-1-0-0-2
		Saml T. Martz	0-0-1-0-0-1
Edwd McCormick	0-12-1-0-4-18	Jno Mahoney	0-0-1-0-0-0
Jno W. McCormick	0-0-1-0-0-0	Jas W. Morrow	0-0-1-0-0-2
		McLean McClingan	0-0-1-0-0-1
Peter McMurray	1-3-1-0-0-7	Saml Morgan	0-0-1-0-0-0
A. Ross Milton	1-5-1-0-0-6	Alfred Martz	1-0-0-0-0-2
Lorenzo D. Maddex	2-1-2-0-0-3	J. W. McGee	0-1-1-0-0-0
James Mitchell	1-2-1-0-0-6	Bush Morgan	0-0-1-0-0-0
Wm D. McGuire	0-11-1-0-0-14	Dr. S. S. Neille	0-5-1-0-1-9
David H. McGuire	0-5-1-0-0-6	Hugh M. Nelson	0-14-1-0-1-21
Thos Murphy	0-0-1-0-0-0	Thos F. Nelson	0-11-1-0-3-15
Jno McPhillin	0-6-1-0-2-8	Archie M. Nelson	0-0-1-0-0-2
Wm G. Morris	0-0-1-0-0-1	Jno Newcomb	0-1-1-0-1-8
Alexander Marshall	0-0-1-0-0-1	Mrs. Sarah Nelson	0-13-0-0-2-3
Jno Marshall	0-3-1-0-1-5	Philip Nelson Senr.	0-4-1-0-1-8
Mrs. Susan Marshall	0-4-0-0-1-6	Philip W. Nelson	0-1-1-0-1-10
Jesse McConahay	0-0-1-0-0-0	Miss A. & R. Nelson	0-3-0-0-0-0
C. C. McIntyre	0-5-1-0-1-9	Col. Wm N. Nelson	0-0-2-0-0-0
Nathl Mercer	0-0-1-0-0-2		
Jno G. McCauley	1-0-1-0-0-0	James H. Neville	1-0-1-0-1-0
James Murphy	2-0-1-0-0-1	Jno Nessmith	2-0-1-0-0-2

Clarke County, Virginia Personal Property Tax Lists 1854-1870
1856

Jno B. Norris	0-4-0-0-1-8	Peter McPierce	0-4-1-0-0-6
Jno R. Nunn	0-4-1-0-2-7	Paul Pierce	0-7-1-0-2-7
James H.		Mrs. E. M. Page	0-6-0-0-0-1
Newman	0-0-1-0-0-0	James M. Pine	1-0-1-0-0-1
Wm Newcomb	0-0-1-0-0-0	Jno Poston	0-0-1-0-0-0
Jno R. Nunn		Wm Puller	0-0-1-0-0-1
Trustee for G. Wm Carter		James Puller	0-0-1-0-0-0
Do as Guardian for		Bush Puller	0-0-1-0-0-0
M. F. Dix		Pendleton &	
		Richardson	0-17-0-0-2-41
Mrs. Elizabeth		T. P. Pendleton	0-4-1-0-0-4
ORear	0-9-0-0-1-12	Wash F. Padgett	0-1-1-0-0-1
Geo ORear	0-3-1-0-1-6	Michael Pope	0-0-1-0-0-1
Benjn F. ORear	0-4-1-0-4-5	Benjn F. Perry	0-0-1-0-0-0
Mrs. Susan ORear	0-0-0-0-0-0	Calvin Puller	0-0-1-0-0-0
Geo Osborn	1-2-1-0-0-6	Jno Patterson	2-1-1-0-0-5
David Osborn	0-0-1-0-0-2	Jas S. Payne	0-0-1-0-0-1
Hugh ORourke	0-0-1-0-0-0	Barnett Prichard	0-0-1-0-0-1
Wm OCallaghan	0-0-1-0-0-1	Wm Pyle	1-0-1-0-0-1
Overseers of Poor	0-1-1-0-01-4	James Pearson	0-0-1-0-0-0
Jno B. Oliver	0-0-1-0-0-0	Conrad Pope	0-0-1-0-0-1
		Richd Parker	0-0-0-0-2-1
Samuel Pidgeon	0-0-1-1-0-7	J. Wm Parkins	0-2-1-0-0-1
Dr. Mat Pages		David T. Pierce	0-0-1-0-0-1
Est.	0-2-0-0-1-0	A. Newton Pierce	0-0-1-0-0-2
Alexander Parkins	0-1-2-0-0-15		
Jno E. Page	0-17-1-0-3-21	Bennett Russell	1-10-2-0-0-13
Mrs. Susan R.		Jno W. Russell	0-2-1-0-0-3
Page	0-29-0-0-8-32	R. E. Robinson	0-3-2-0-1-6
A. C. Page	0-10-1-0-1-14	Thos W. Russell	0-0-1-0-1-2
Dr. Wm M. Page	0-0-1-0-0-1	Michael Russell	0-1-1-0-0-2
Jno Page Junr.	0-11-1-0-2-10	James M. Reed	0-0-1-0-0-1
Mann R. Page	0-10-1-0-1-14	Jno Reed	0-0-1-0-0-1
Miss M. C. Page	0-0-1-0-0-0	Jno Rowland	0-0-2-0-1-8
Geo R. Page	0-4-1-0-0-4	Miss E. Royster	0-1-0-0-1-0
Mathew Pulliam	0-1-1-0-0-1	Mathew W.	
Jno Pierce Senr.	0-4-1-0-2-8	Royston	0-1-1-0-1-6
Jno Pierce Junr.	0-2-1-1-1-11	Peter K. Royston	0-1-1-0-0-1
Michael P. Pierce	0-6-1-0-1-12	Uriah B. Royston	0-0-1-0-0-2

Clarke County, Virginia Personal Property Tax Lists 1854-1870
1856

Geo R. Royston	0-0-1-0-0-0	Carter Shepherd	0-7-2-0-1-7
Miss Nancy		Henry Shepherd	0-0-1-0-0-0
Redman	0-0-0-0-1-0	P. D. Shepherd	0-7-2-0-1-13
Geo W. Rutter	0-0-1-0-1-0	Geo Smedley	0-0-1-0-0-1
Danl B. Richards	0-1-1-0-0-0	Wm D. &	
Chas H. Richards	0-0-1-0-0-0	E. J. Smith	0-28-1-1-6-40
Addison Romine	0-2-1-0-0-4	Miss M. C. Shively	0-0-1-0-0-1
Geo Reno	0-0-1-0-0-0	Mrs. M. E. Shively	0-4-0-0-1-1
Patrick Rogers	0-0-1-0-0-0	Jno O. Snyder	2-1-1-0-1-1
Thompson Ritt	0-0-1-0-0-0	Danl C. Snyder	0-0-1-0-0-0
Beverly Randolph	0-14-1-0-7-21	Thos Shumate	2-3-1-0-1-14
Robt C. Randolph	1-24-1-0-2-32	Jno W. Sowers	0-7-1-0-2-18
A. C. Randolph	0-3-1-0-1-8	James Sowers	0-3-1-0-1-11
Jno Reynolds	0-0-1-0-0-0	Jas W. Sowers	0-5-1-0-1-13
B. C. Reynolds	0-0-1-0-0-0	Wm M. Sowers	0-3-1-0-0-5
Thos W. Reynolds	0-0-1-0-0-1	Danl H. Sowers	0-6-1-0-2-6
Wm Riely	0-0-1-0-0-0	Danl W. Sowers	0-14-1-0-2-27
Mathew Rust	0-2-1-0-0-1	Fielding L. Sowers	0-6-1-0-2-8
Jos A. Richardson	0-0-1-0-0-0	James A. Steele	1-0-1-0-0-1
Jno J. Riely	0-3-1-0-0-5	Wm B. Sowers	0-0-1-0-0-0
Wm A. Riely	0-4-1-0-2-10	Geo K. Sowers	
Jno Ramey	0-0-1-0-0-0	Est.	0-4-1-0-0-9
Thos Roradan	0-0-1-0-0-1	Thos Sprint	0-0-1-0-0-0
Thos W. Ridings	0-1-1-0-0-1	Jos Sprint	0-0-1-0-0-0
Saml Rutter	0-0-1-0-0-0	Geo Sypherd	0-0-1-0-0-0
Jno D. Richardson	0-3-1-0-0-2	Jno W. Sprint	0-0-1-0-0-0
Jno N. Ross	0-0-1-0-0-0	Barnett	
Jno Rippon	0-0-1-0-0-0	Smallwood	0-0-1-0-0-2
James Rose	0-0-1-0-0-0	Burr Smallwood	0-0-1-0-0-2
James W. Ryan	0-0-1-0-0-1	Dr. P. Smith	0-22-2-0-4-25
Moses Riely	0-0-1-0-0-2	Col. T. Smith	0-17-2-0-3-21
Jno M. Reed	0-0-1-0-0-1	D° as Guardian	
Jos W. Riggle	0-0-1-0-0-0	for H. P. Smith	
Chas B. Riely	0-0-1-0-0-0	Wm L. Smith	0-0-1-0-0-0
Cornelius Riely	0-0-1-0-0-0	Paul Smith	0-6-1-0-0-10
Jos F. Ryan	0-1-1-0-0-4	Chas H. Smith	1-0-1-0-0-0
		Edwd Smith	0-0-1-0-0-0
Wm Sowers Senr.	1-7-1-0-2-11	Geo R. Smith	0-0-1-0-0-0
Champ Shepherd	0-4-1-0-0-2	Jno Stewart	0-0-1-0-0-1

Clarke County, Virginia Personal Property Tax Lists 1854-1870
1856

L. J. Schooler	0-0-1-0-0-0		Greenby	
Jno Shaffer	0-1-1-0-0-0		Thompson	0-0-2-0-0-2
Jackson Shaffer	0-0-1-0-0-0		Adam F.	
Simon Stickles	0-0-1-0-0-2		Thompson	0-0-1-0-0-2
Hugh T. Swart	0-5-1-0-2-14		French Thompson	1-3-1-0-0-3
Frank Swarts	0-0-1-0-0-0		Benjn	
Wm Strother	0-3-2-0-1-5		Thompson Jr.	0-0-1-0-0-5
Shedrick Shrout	0-0-1-0-0-0		Jno F. Thompson	0-0-1-0-0-2
Erasmus			Baalis Thompson	0-0-1-0-0-4
Shackelford	0-0-1-0-0-1		Wm N.	
Charles Showers	0-0-1-0-1-0		Thompson	1-3-1-0-0-1
Saml Showers	0-0-3-0-1-0		Wm Taylor	0-16-2-0-2-20
Jno S. Street	0-0-1-0-0-0		Miss Eliza Taylor	0-0-0-0-0-0
Jno Shell	0-0-1-0-0-1		Robt Tapscott	0-0-1-0-0-0
Stephen Shell	0-0-1-0-0-0		Dr. Saml Taylor	0-5-1-0-2-2
Jno H. P. Stone	0-0-1-0-0-0		Col. Jos Tuley	0-27-1-0-5-20
Simon R. Stump	0-0-1-0-0-1		Jno Trussell	0-5-2-0-1-7
Dennis Shehean	0-0-1-0-0-1		Wm Trenary	1-2-1-0-0-3
Jas W.			Daniel Turner	0-0-1-0-0-0
Stephenson	0-4-1-0-0-6		Howard F.	
Jno H. Spotts	0-0-1-0-0-0		Thornton	0-6-1-0-1-6
Jos Shipe	0-0-1-0-0-0		Moses B. Trussell	0-1-1-0-0-4
Henry T. Shearer	0-0-1-0-0-0		Calvin Thacker	0-0-1-0-1-0
Wm G. Steele	0-0-1-0-0-0		Wm F. Thompson	0-0-1-0-0-0
Jas H. Swain	0-0-1-0-0-0		Dr. Bush Taylor	0-2-1-1-0-3
Craven Shell	0-0-1-0-0-0		David Tristlers	
Mrs. Susan Smith	1-2-0-0-0-0		Est.	0-0-0-0-0-0
Hezekiah Slusher	1-0-1-0-1-0		P. Z. Taylor	0-0-1-0-0-1
Braxton D. Smith	0-0-1-0-0-1		Isaac Talley	0-0-1-0-0-0
Timothy Shehean	0-0-1-0-0-0		Jno H. Taylor	0-0-1-0-0-0
Geo Smith	0-0-1-0-0-0		Snowden Tomblin	0-0-1-0-0-1
M. L. Sinclair	0-0-1-0-0-0		Thos W. Trussell	1-0-2-0-0-1
Chas Swarts	0-0-1-0-0-0		Geo W. Taylor	0-0-1-0-0-1
Mrs. M. Swann	0-1-0-0-0-0		French & Isaac	
			Thompson	1-1-1-0-0-3
Mrs. Sarah			Lewis Tapp	0-0-1-0-0-0
Timberlake	0-4-0-0-3-7		Alonza Taylor	0-0-1-0-0-0
James F.			Elizabeth W.	
Thompson	0-0-1-0-0-2		Thomas	0-0-0-0-0-0

Clarke County, Virginia Personal Property Tax Lists 1854-1870
1856

Mason Tinsman	0-0-1-0-0-1	Leroy T. [?] Williams	0-7-1-0-1-9
Isaac Tyson	0-1-1-0-0-7	Jacob Welch	1-0-1-0-0-5
Jno C. Underwood	1-1-1-0-0-4	David H. Wilcox	0-0-1-0-0-0
		Jesse Wright	0-0-1-0-0-1
Jos A. Vasse's Est.	1-1-0-0-1-3	Robt Whittington	0-1-1-0-0-0
Jacob Vanmetre	0-4-1-0-1-11	Alexander Wood	0-0-1-0-0-0
Gerry Vaughn	0-0-2-0-0-0	Jos Wood	0-2-1-0-0-7
Geo Violett	1-0-0-0-0-0	Bennett Wood	1-0-1-0-0-1
		Wm W. Wood	0-0-1-0-0-0
Francis B. Whiting	0-21-2-0-35-15	G. W. Weaver	0-3-2-0-2-5
Wm W. Whiting	0-5-1-0-2-5	Lucinda Washington	0-3-0-0-0-0
Wm H. Whiting	0-6-1-0-0-10	Rev. F. M. Whittle	0-2-1-0-1-2
Francis H. Whiting	0-1-1-0-0-7	Thos C. Wyndham	0-0-1-0-0-0
Benj F. Wilson	2-0-1-0-0-0	Jeremiah Wilson	0-0-1-0-0-0
Allen Williams	0-11-1-0-1-15	Saml G. Wyman	0-9-0-0-1-10
Wm Willingham	1-0-1-0-0-3	N. B. Whiting	0-7-1-0-1-11
J. W. Ware & Mrs. Stribling	0-18-1-0-3-20	Jas W. Whittington	0-0-1-0-0-0
Danl F. Wade & Bro	0-2-2-0-0-3	Jas W. Willingham	1-0-1-0-0-0
H. T. Wheat	2-6-4-0-2-8	Wm Willis	0-0-1-0-0-0
Hezekiah Wiley	0-0-1-0-0-0	E. P. Williams	0-0-1-0-0-0
Cornelius Wiley	0-0-1-0-0-1	Obed Willingham	0-0-1-0-0-0
Jno Wiley	0-0-1-0-0-0	Jackson Wheeler	0-1-1-0-0-6
Geo W. Wiley	0-0-1-0-0-1	A. T. M. Woolford	0-0-1-0-0-0
S. B. Wyndham	0-0-1-0-0-4		
Jno Wilson	0-0-1-0-0-0	Wm H. Young	0-1-1-0-0-0
Jno T. Willingham	0-0-1-0-0-1		
James V. Weir	0-3-1-0-2-9	James Zoney [?]	0-0-1-0-0-0
James Wiley	0-0-1-0-0-0		

Clarke County, Virginia Personal Property Tax Lists 1854-1870
1856

Free Negroes

Wm Toler	0-0-0-1-0-0	Lewis Ransom	0-0-0-1-0-0
Wm Parker	0-0-0-1-0-0	Jno Johnson	0-0-0-1-0-0
Ralph Bray	0-0-0-1-0-0	Shack Johnson	0-0-0-1-0-0
Geo Ransom	0-0-0-1-0-0	Burwell Cooke	0-0-0-1-0-0
Thos Ransom	0-0-0-1-0-0	Jim Butler	0-0-0-1-0-0
		Jack Blanham	0-0-0-1-0-0

Clarke County, Virginia Personal Property Tax Lists 1854-1870

1857

1) Free male persons above the age of 16 years, 2) Slaves who have attained the age of 16 years, 3) White male inhabitants who have attained the age of 21 years, except those exempted from taxation on account of bodily infirmity, 4) Male free negroes between the ages of 21 and 55 years, 5) Slaves who have attained the age of 12 years, 6) Horses, mules, asses & jennets

Buckner Ashby	0-10-2-0-3-18	Dr. Wm A.	
James M. Allen	0-4-1-0-3-10	Bradford	0-0-1-0-7-12
Mason Anderson	0-5-1-0-0-6		
Jno H. Anderson	0-0-1-0-0-0	Margt E.	
Jesse Allen	0-0-1-0-0-1	Alexander	0-1-0-0-0-0
Edgar Allen	0-12-1-0-5-15	Milton B.	
Jno Alexander	0-25-1-0-2-29	Anderson	0-3-1-0-0-5
Jno W. Anderson			
at Brumlys	0-0-1-0-0-0	George H.	
Levi Athey	0-0-1-0-0-0	Burwell	1-55-1-0-5-50
Robt Ashby Senr.	0-0-1-0-0-2	Do as trustee	
Robt Ashby Junr.	0-0-1-0-0-0	for Wm Hay	
Nimrod Ashby	0-0-1-0-0-0	Nathaniel Burwell	0-15-1-0-29
George B. Ashby	0-0-1-0-0-0	Jno Burchell	0-6-2-0-1-11
Thos J. Anderson	0-0-1-0-0-1	Andrew J. Berlin	0-0-1-0-0-0
George W. Ashby	0-0-1-0-0-3	Wm Brown	0-0-1-0-0-0
Jno & N. F.		Geo H. Bell	0-0-1-0-0-2
Anderson	0-1-2-0-1-0	Archibald Bowen	2-0-1-0-0-8
Geo Wm Allen	0-3-1-0-1-6	Jesse Bowen	0-2-1-0-0-5
Wm T. Allen	0-6-1-0-3-10	H. O. Bell	0-4-1-0-1-5
A. S. Allen	0-9-1-1-1-15	Strother H. Bell	0-1-1-0-0-0
James Allison	0-0-1-0-0-0	Squire Bell	0-1-1-0-0-1
Jno Allison	1-0-1-0-0-0	Hector Ball	0-0-1-0-0-4
Thos H.		Lewis Berlin	0-1-1-0-0-1
Alexander	0-0-1-0-0-6	Philip Berlin	0-3-1-0-0-3
Wm Asbury	1-1-1-0-0-0	Wm Berlin	0-4-1-0-1-1
Jno Avis	0-0-1-0-1-0	Geo W. Berlin	0-0-1-0-0-0
Elias J. Athey	1-0-1-0-0-0	George C.	
		Blakemore	0-6-1-0-1-13

Clarke County, Virginia Personal Property Tax Lists 1854-1870
1857

Name	Values	Name	Values
Neille Barnett	0-7-2-0-2-11	James J. Board	0-0-1-0-0-1
James Bell	1-0-1-0-0-3	George Board	0-0-1-0-0-0
James Bell Jr.	0-0-1-0-0-0	Geo W. Board	0-0-1-0-0-3
Thos Briggs Junr. Est.	0-2-0-0-0-5	Geo W. Bradfield	1-2-1-0-1-1
Jno S. Briggs	0-0-1-0-0-0	Maranda Bowen	0-1-1-0-0-3
James C. Briggs	0-6-1-0-0-14	Miss Emily Bell	0-0-0-0-0-1
Miss Margt Burchell	0-4-0-0-0-3	Jno Billmire	0-0-1-0-0-0
John Brumley	0-2-1-0-0-15	Jos C. Bartlett	0-4-1-0-0-8
Jno W. Byrd	0-10-1-0-2-9	James W. Board	0-0-1-0-0-0
George W. Brumley	0-2-1-0-0-8	Jonas P. Bell	0-2-1-0-0-3
Mrs. Susan R. Burwell	0-0-0-0-0-2	Thomas Brown	0-1-1-0-0-0
Jos H. Beevers	0-0-1-0-0-1	George B. Bradford	0-0-1-0-0-0
Ann C. Benn	0-0-0-0-1-2	Conrad Bowman	0-0-1-0-0-0
Danl S. Bonham	1-1-1-0-1-12	Middleton Bowen	0-0-1-0-0-0
Samuel Bonham	0-11-2-0-0-22	Burr E. Barr	0-0-1-0-0-0
Newton Brown	0-0-1-0-0-1	Philip L. Berlin	0-1-1-0-0-3
Wm Berry	0-8-3-0-3-7	Alfred Bishop	0-0-1-0-0-0
Miss Juliet Boyston	0-0-0-0-0-0	Mrs. Lucy N. Buck	0-1-0-0-0-0
Miss Nancy Boyston	0-0-0-0-0-0	~~Robert Bull~~	~~0-0-1-0-0-0~~
Jno E. Bradfield	1-1-2-0-0-1	Patrick Brady	0-0-1-0-0-0
Dr. H. T. Barton	0-1-1-0-0-0	Michael Burgen	0-0-1-0-0-0
Richard S. Bryarly	0-9-1-0-1-11	H. W. Brabham	2-0-1-0-0-0
Christian Browser	0-0-1-0-0-0	George Bolen	0-0-1-0-0-0
Miss Mary Bowser	0-1-0-0-0-0	Thos J. Bragg	0-1-2-0-0-2
Abram Beevers	0-0-1-0-0-3	James B. Ball	0-0-1-0-0-0
N. B. Balthrorpe	0-0-1-0-0-1	Hugh R. Braden	0-0-1-0-0-1
Peter Bennett	0-0-1-0-0-0	Robert Briggs	0-5-2-0-2-5
Adam Barr	0-0-1-0-0-0	J. H. Brewer [?]	1-0-0-0-0-1
Jesse Butler	0-0-1-0-0-2	George S. Bonham	0-1-1-0-1-1
Richard Billmire	0-0-1-0-0-0	Dr. A. M. Bonham	0-0-1-0-0-1
James Brown	0-0-1-0-0-1	Arthur Briggs	0-0-1-0-0-2
		Enos S. Brown	0-0-1-0-0-0
		Jno R. Beuford	0-0-1-0-0-0
		Charles Bales	0-0-1-0-0-0

Clarke County, Virginia Personal Property Tax Lists 1854-1870
1857

Alfred Castleman	2-8-1-0-3-14	Hebron J. Chamblin	0-0-1-0-0-0
Charles D. Castleman	0-0-1-0-1-0	Isaac Cornwell	0-0-1-0-0-0
Wm A. Castleman	0-5-1-0-1-12	Andrew Cornwell	0-1-1-0-0-1
Stephen D. Castleman	0-0-0-0-0-0	Michael Copenhaver	0-0-1-0-0-1
Mrs. Ury Castleman	0-6-0-0-0-3	Jno N. Collier	0-0-1-0-0-4
Osborn Castleman	0-0-1-0-0-0	Jno P. Chamberlain	0-0-1-0-1-2
Nathl Castleman	0-0-1-0-0-0	Samuel Camell	0-0-1-0-0-1
William Carper	0-0-1-0-0-2	Anne B. Cooke	0-15-0-0-2-17
Robt A. Colston	0-4-1-0-0-10	Jacob Clink	0-0-1-0-0-11
Jno Copenhaur	0-5-2-0-0-10	Jeremiah Cain	0-0-1-0-0-0
Jno H. Crebbs	0-2-1-0-0-5	Jno P. Carrigan	0-0-1-0-0-0
Elizabeth K. Carter	0-1-0-0-0-0	Jno R. Crockwell	0-1-1-0-0-0
George K. Cooper	0-0-1-0-0-0	Miss Miriam Catlett	0-6-1-0-2-10
Jos K. Carter	0-2-1-0-0-6	James W. Conrad	0-3-1-0-2-9
Jno B. Carter	0-3-1-0-2-7	Catharine Castleman	0-3-0-0-0-2
Charles Carter	0-2-1-0-0-4	Joseph Carver	0-0-1-0-0-0
Wm K. Carter	0-2-1-0-0-5	Robt H. Castleman	0-3-1-0-1-6
Jno A. Carter	0-1-1-0-1-5	Michael Collins	0-0-1-0-0-0
Jno W. Carter	0-0-1-0-0-0	James N. Corbin	1-0-1-0-0-2
Wm P. Carter	0-11-1-3-11	Benjn Crampton	1-0-0-0-0-1
Wm G. Carter	0-0-1-0-1-1	Bush Crawford	0-0-1-0-0-0
Peter Cain	0-1-2-0-0-8	Jno P. Crim	0-0-2-0-0-0
Dr. R. T. Colston	0-6-0-0-0-15	Franklin Canniford	0-0-1-0-1-0
Parkison Corder	0-0-1-0-0-1	James E. Chamblin	0-0-1-0-0-0
James H. Clark	3-4-1-0-1-1	Miss Sallie Cloud	0-3-0-0-0-0
Thomas H. Crow	1-5-1-0-1-8	Benjn F. Crawford	0-0-1-0-0-0
Jno Cooper	0-0-1-0-0-2	~~Elizabeth Clink~~	~~0-0-0-0-0-0~~
Jno Carroll	0-0-1-0-0-0	Henry Canniford	0-0-1-0-0-0
Lewis Carroll	0-0-1-0-0-1		
Robt Cornwell	0-0-1-0-0-1		
Thos Carroll	0-0-1-0-0-0		
Thos Cornwell	0-0-1-0-0-0		
Aaron Chamblin	0-0-1-0-0-0		

Clarke County, Virginia Personal Property Tax Lists 1854-1870
1857

George W.			Jacob W.	
Castleman	0-0-1-0-0-0		Everhart	0-0-1-0-0-1
Eliza Crim	1-0-0-0-0-1		Edward Eno	0-3-1-0-0-1
			Wm H. Edwards	0-0-1-0-0-1
Col. Wash			Albert Elsey	0-1-1-0-0-2
Dearmont	0-6-2-0-1-11		Jos H. Easterday	0-0-1-0-0-1
William Deahl	2-1-1-0-0-2		Wm G. Everhart Jr.	0-0-1-0-0-0
James W. Doren	0-0-1-0-0-1		Edmund S.	
James Doren	1-0-1-0-0-1		Everhart	0-1-2-0-0-0
Jno Drish	0-0-1-0-0-2		Thos A. Everhart	0-0-1-0-0-0
George D. Drish	0-0-1-0-0-1			
Jno Donovan	0-0-1-0-0-0		Dr. O. R. Funsten	0-14-1-0-4-19
Thos Duke	0-0-1-0-0-1		Dr. J. F.	
Geo W.			Fauntleroy	0-4-1-0-1-4
Diffenderfer	0-1-1-0-0-2		James A. Foster	0-2-1-0-1-6
Hugh Davis	0-0-1-0-0-0		Josiah Ferguson	0-3-1-0-0-3
John D. Davis	0-0-1-0-0-0		Wm M. Ferguson	0-0-1-0-1-2
Jno Dow	0-2-1-0-1-4		Edward Franks	0-0-1-0-0-0
Aaron Duble	0-1-2-0-0-1		Henry Franks	0-0-2-0-0-0
Rev. H. W. Dodge	0-2-1-0-1-1		Wm Franks	0-0-1-0-0-0
Mrs. Lucy			Ephraim Furr	0-0-1-0-0-0
Dearmont	0-0-0-0-1-2		Moses Furr	0-0-1-0-0-0
Robert Dunn	0-0-1-0-0-0		William Fowler	0-0-1-0-0-0
Martin Duble	0-0-1-0-0-0		James Furr	0-0-1-0-0-1
William Donohoe	0-0-1-0-0-0		Johnson Furr	0-1-1-0-1-6
Michael Drislane	0-0-1-0-0-0		Israel Fiddler	0-0-1-0-0-0
			Elizabeth Fleming	0-2-0-0-0-3
Jacob Enders	0-8-1-0-1-12		Jos Fleming	2-0-1-0-0-5
Henry Edwards	0-0-3-0-0-4		William Fowler	0-0-1-0-0-2
Wm G. Everhart			Everett Fowler	0-0-1-0-0-0
Senr.	0-2-1-0-3-9		Thos Fowler	0-0-1-0-0-2
Jno Elleyett	0-0-1-0-0-1		Robt H. Feltner	0-0-1-0-0-4
Wm F. Engle	0-0-1-0-0-0		Martin Feltner	0-0-2-0-0-0
Henson Elliott	0-3-3-0-1-10		Dennis Fenton	0-0-1-0-0-0
Elliott & Millson	0-2-0-0-1-1		Marcus R.	
Henry Evans	0-1-1-0-0-0		Feehrer	0-3-1-0-0-3
Alexander M.			Thos G. Flagg	0-0-1-0-1-0
Earle	0-4-1-0-1-15		Jno A. Finnell	0-1-1-0-0-0
			Joshua Fellows	0-0-1-0-0-1

Clarke County, Virginia Personal Property Tax Lists 1854-1870
1857

Christian Fonda	0-0-1-0-0-0	Charles S. Grant	0-0-1-0-1-4
Jeremiah Foley	0-0-1-0-0-0	Jno W. Grim	0-0-1-0-0-0
James H. Frazier	0-0-1-0-1-0	Jno Greenwald	0-0-1-0-0-0
Abram M. Fry	0-0-1-0-0-0	Robt Gill	0-0-1-0-0-0
Enoch Furr	0-0-1-0-0-0	Jno S. Gibson	0-0-1-0-0-0
~~Enoch Furr~~		T. K. Glover	0-0-1-0-0-0
Abram Fry	1-0-0-0-0-0	Madison Grimes	1-0-1-0-0-2
Jos Fleming Senr.	0-0-1-0-0-0	Jno L. Grant	0-2-1-0-0-4
		Thos E. Gibson	0-0-1-0-0-0
Jas W. Galloway	0-0-1-0-0-0		
Thos W. Griffith	0-0-1-0-0-0	Samuel Huyett	0-2-1-0-2-10
James Chisholm	0-0-1-0-0-0	Jno Huyett	0-0-1-0-0-0
Jos Gormon	0-0-1-0-0-0	Abram Huyett	0-0-1-0-1-1
James F. Green	0-1-1-0-0-3	Henry Huyett	0-1-1-0-2-8
Mrs. Mary Green	0-5-0-0-2-6	Albert Holland	1-0-0-0-0-1
Richd N. Green	0-5-1-0-0-6	Whiting Hamilton	1-0-2-0-0-4
Jno S. Green	0-3-1-0-0-9	Henry D. Hooe	1-1-2-0-1-5
Thos E. Gold	0-7-2-0-3-16	James H. Hooe	0-2-1-0-0-0
Geo W. Gordon	0-2-1-0-0-4	Jno Hummer	0-0-1-0-0-1
Jno S. Gordon	0-2-1-0-1-7	Mason Hummer	0-0-1-0-0-1
Stephen J. Gant	0-2-1-0-0-3	Wm Hummer	0-0-1-0-0-1
Samuel Grubb	0-0-1-0-0-0	Wm A. Holland	0-1-1-0-0-1
Henry N. Grigsby	0-6-1-0-1-8	Jno W. Holland	0-0-1-0-0-0
Mrs. Isabelle Glass	0-1-0-0-0-0	E. T. Hancock	0-5-1-0-2-10
Lewis F. Glass	0-5-1-0-2-11	Charles B. Hancock	0-0-1-0-0-3
Wm Gourley	0-1-1-0-1-5	Wm Heflin	0-0-1-0-0-0
Martin Gant	0-6-1-0-1-7	Dr. James A. Haynes	0-5-1-0-0-1
Wm Gibbs	0-0-1-0-0-0	James M. Hite	0-0-1-0-0-4
Wm Grubbs of Thornly	0-0-1-0-0-1	Isaac J. Hite	0-7-1-0-1-8
Wm B. Grubbs	0-0-1-0-0-2	Geo Wm Hanvey	0-0-1-0-0-0
Samuel Grubbs	0-0-1-0-0-1	Charles F. Hennis	1-1-1-0-0-0
Geo W. Grubb	0-0-1-0-0-0	Samuel Heflebower	0-6-1-0-2-13
J. Madison Grubb	0-0-1-0-0-0	Jacob Heflebower	0-8-2-0-2-9
Nathan Grubb	0-0-1-0-0-0	Charles W. Hardesty	0-1-1-0-0-0
Jno Gruber	0-2-1-0-0-7		
George Gardiner	0-0-1-0-0-0		
Adam Greenwald	0-0-1-0-0-0		

Clarke County, Virginia Personal Property Tax Lists 1854-1870
1857

Name	Values	Name	Values
Adrian D. Hardesty	0-2-1-0-0-4	George Harris Jr.	0-0-1-0-0-0
Wm G. Hardesty	0-2-1-0-0-11	L. S. Hodgsen	0-0-1-0-0-0
James M. Hardesty	0-1-1-0-0-7	Jno W. Hall	0-0-1-0-1-0
Cornelius Hoff	1-0-1-0-0-0	Solomon R. Jackson	0-0-1-0-0-0
Harrison Hoff	0-0-1-0-0-0	Herod Jenkins	0-0-2-0-0-2
Blackwell Holtsclaw	0-0-1-0-0-0	Mathew Jones	0-1-3-0-1-6
Jno Hoff	0-0-1-0-0-0	John Joliffe	1-5-1-0-0-9
Rev. Jno F. Hoff	0-5-1-0-0-1	Leonard Jones	0-1-1-0-0-1
Mrs. Sarah Hardesty	2-0-1-0-0-9	Jno S. Johnston	0-0-1-0-0-0
George Hansucker	0-2-1-0-1-4	Thos Jones	0-1-1-0-0-9
Jno Hughs	0-0-1-0-1-1	George H. Isler	0-0-1-0-0-2
Thomas Hughs	0-0-1-0-0-1	Jacob Islers Est.	0-1-0-0-0-0
Robt L. Horner	0-0-1-0-0-2	George Johnston	0-2-1-0-0-3
Wm B. Harris	0-8-1-0-4-15	J. J. Janney	1-3-1-0-2-6
Henry Horner	0-0-0-0-0-1	Thos Jenkins	0-0-1-0-0-4
Thos S. Hart	0-0-1-0-0-0	James W. Johnston	0-0-1-0-0-0
Geo W. Hooper	0-0-1-0-0-0	George W. Joy	0-0-1-0-0-0
Benjn Harrison	0-6-1-0-1-21	Wm A. Jackson	0-5-1-0-1-11
Henry P. Huntsberry	0-1-1-0-1-6	Wm Johnson (Teacher)	0-0-1-0-0-0
Thos L. Humphrey	0-2-1-0-1-3	Andrew Jackson	0-0-1-0-0-0
Thomas L. Humphry, Exor of D. Tristler Dec'd		A. M. Johnson	0-0-1-0-0-4
Edward E. Hall	0-8-1-0-2-7	Amelia A. Jordan	0-1-0-0-0-0
Jno Henry & Bro	0-0-2-0-0-0	Wm Johnson	0-1-1-0-0-1
James F. Howell	0-0-1-0-0-0	Wm B. Jolliffe	0-0-1-0-0-1
Jno M. Horner	0-0-1-0-0-1	Jones & Lupton	0-2-1-0-0-4
Jos W. Hibbard	0-0-0-0-0-1	Ebin Jenkins	0-0-1-0-0-1
~~Albert Holland~~	~~0-0-0-0-0-0~~	~~Dr. Franklin J. Hoof~~	
W. R. Hevestine	0-0-1-0-0-0	Dr. F. J. Kerfoot	0-8-1-0-2-12
Jno & Thos Heskitt	0-3-2-0-0-7	Wm C. Kerfoot	1-11-1-0-0-17
A. T. M. Hough	0-3-1-0-0-1	James F. Kerfoot	0-5-1-0-0-7
George L. Harris	0-4-0-0-2-11	Judson G. Kerfoot	0-4-1-0-2-7
		George Knight Senr.	0-6-3-0-4-17

Clarke County, Virginia Personal Property Tax Lists 1854-1870
1857

George Knight		C. C. Larue	0-1-1-0-0-3
Junr.	0-0-1-0-0-0	Wm D. Lee	0-0-1-0-0-1
Middleton Keeler	0-0-1-0-0-0	Squire Lee	1-0-2-0-0-1
Jacob Kriser	1-1-1-0-0-4	Christopher Lee	0-0-1-0-0-1
Henry Knight	0-0-1-0-0-0	Jno Lee	0-0-1-0-0-1
Samuel G. Kneller	0-6-1-0-1-9	Dr. James M.	
Jos McK.		Lindsey	0-1-1-0-0-3
Kennerly	0-7-1-0-0-8	Jos B. Lindsey	1-0-0-0-0-1
Wm C. Kennerly	0-4-1-0-1-6	Jno T. Lindsey	0-3-1-0-0-0
Dr. C. B. R.		Mrs. Emily	
Kennerly	0-3-1-0-2-7	Littleton	0-2-1-0-0-6
Thos Kennerly's		Wm D. Littleton	0-0-1-0-0-3
Est.	0-2-0-0-0-0	Wm Littleton	0-1-1-0-0-3
Henry Kline	0-0-1-0-0-0	Jno W. Littleton	0-0-1-0-0-4
Jos Kline	1-0-1-0-0-0	Enos Lanham	0-0-1-0-0-0
Dr. R. Kownslar	0-7-1-0-0-5	Henry Lloyd	0-0-2-0-0-3
Charles E.		Jno Lloyd	0-0-1-0-0-1
Kimball	0-5-1-0-2-7	James Lloyd Jr.	0-0-1-0-0-1
Jacob Kimmerly	0-0-1-0-0-0	James L. Lloyd	0-0-1-0-0-0
Jno N. Keimmell	1-0-1-0-0-1	David Lloyd	0-0-1-0-0-0
Jno Kelly	0-0-1-0-0-0	Jno A. Lloyd	0-0-1-0-0-0
E. V. Kercheral	0-0-1-0-0-0	Samuel Lloyd	0-0-1-0-0-0
Wm Kennan	0-0-1-0-0-0	Moses Lewin	0-0-1-0-0-1
Henry Kennan	0-0-1-0-1-0	Mrs. Mary B.	
Charles H.		Little	0-3-0-0-0-0
Kitchen	0-0-1-0-0-0	Jno Lock	0-3-1-0-0-7
Jno N. Kitchen	1-0-0-0-0-1	Jno Louthan	1-7-1-0-1-7
Mrs. Lucy Kerfoot	0-6-0-0-2-7	Jno K. Louthan	0-1-1-0-1-4
Henry Kromiling	0-1-4-0-0-1	James T. Louthan	0-4-1-0-0-6
James Keyes	0-0-1-0-0-0	Mrs. E. M. Lewis	0-7-2-0-2-4
Harrison Kent	0-0-1-0-0-0	J. R. C. Lewis	0-0-1-0-0-1
Jno Kennedy	0-0-1-0-0-0	Geo W. Lewis	0-4-1-0-0-2
Willis F. King	0-0-1-0-0-0	Edgar Lanham	0-0-1-0-0-1
Bruton Kaufman	0-0-1-0-0-1	Minor Lanham	0-0-1-0-0-2
		James Lanham	0-0-1-0-0-1
Jno B. Larue	0-12-3-0-2-27	Abram	
Jno D. Larue	0-4-1-0-3-10	Longerbeam	0-0-1-0-0-3
A. L. P. Larue	0-5-1-0-0-10	Jno Longerbeam	0-1-1-0-0-0
James W. Larue	0-8-1-0-1-9		

Clarke County, Virginia Personal Property Tax Lists 1854-1870
1857

Name	Values
Benjn Longerbeam	0-0-1-0-0-4
Jno M. Lupton	0-2-1-0-0-0
Jno W. Luke	0-9-1-0-0-14
Josiah Lock	0-0-1-0-0-5
Jno T. Longerbeam	0-0-1-0-0-1
Richd H. Lee	0-5-1-0-1-6
George Lanham	0-0-1-0-0-1
Dr. Jno S. Lupton	0-1-1-0-0-10
Benjn Lock	0-1-1-0-0-6
Huldah C. Lindsey	0-2-0-0-0-3
Francis B. Meade	0-8-1-0-3-12
Philip N. Meade	0-10-2-0-2-13
Jno N. Meade	0-4-1-0-0-9
R. K. Meade	0-5-1-0-1-7
E. B. Mantor	0-0-1-0-0-1
Wm W. Meade	0-4-1-0-2-5
David Meade	1-1-1-0-1-11
Mrs. Louisa W. Meade	0-4-0-0-0-1
Nathl B. Meade	0-9-1-0-2-7
Miss Mary Meade	0-2-0-0-2-0
George W. Meade	0-0-1-0-0-1
Col. Benj Morgan	1-27-2-0-2-32
Jno Morgan Do as Guardian	0-9-1-0-2-9
Dr. Cyrus McCormick & Bro	0-20-2-0-3-26
Col. F. McCormick	0-17-1-0-3-28
Thomas McCormick	0-10-1-0-1-10
Mason McCormick	0-1-1-0-0-3
Province McCormick	0-8-1-0-5-14
Margt A. McCormick	0-0-1-0-1-3
Samuel McCormick	0-1-1-0-0-0
Jno E. McCormick	0-0-1-0-0-0
James McCormick	0-3-1-0-0-7
Geo W. McCormick	0-3-1-0-0-0
Otway McCormick	0-5-1-0-3-8
Edward McCormick	0-13-1-0-3-20
Peter McMurray	1-3-1-0-0-7
A. Ross Milton	1-5-1-0-2-8
Sylvanus Moore	0-0-1-0-0-1
Lorenzo D. Maddex	0-1-4-0-0-5
James Mitchell	3-3-1-0-0-7
Dr. Wm D. McGuire	1-8-1-0-0-14
David H. McGuire	0-6-1-0-1-5
Jno McPhillin	0-3-1-0-1-8
Wm G. Morris	0-0-1-0-0-0
Alexander Marshall	0-2-1-0-1-6
Jno Marshall	0-3-1-0-1-5
Mrs. Susan Marshall	0-4-0-0-2-6
Jesse McConnalay	0-0-1-0-0-0
C. C. McIntyre	0-5-1-0-1-9
Nathl Mercer	0-0-1-0-0-2
Jno G. McCauley	1-0-1-0-0-1
James Murphy	2-0-1-0-0-1
Stephen Marlow	1-0-1-0-0-0
Ammi Moore	0-6-1-0-1-10

Clarke County, Virginia Personal Property Tax Lists 1854-1870
1857

Alfred P. Moore	1-0-1-0-0-0	Jno R. Nunn	0-5-1-0-1-7
Saml Moreland	2-0-1-0-0-6	James H.	
Geo F. Marple	0-0-1-0-0-0	Newman	0-0-1-0-0-1
Moses G. Miley	0-0-1-0-0-4	Wm Newcomb	0-0-1-0-0-0
E. W. Massey	0-9-1-0-1-9	Dr. S. S. Neille	0-6-1-0-1-8
Henry Mason	0-0-1-0-0-0	Wm Nicewarner	0-2-2-0-0-8
James McClaughey	0-0-2-0-0-12	Jno R. [Nunn] Guardian for G. W. Carter	
Saml T. Martz	0-0-1-0-0-1	Do [guardian] for Mary Dix	
Spencer Marquis	0-0-1-0-0-0		
McLean McClingan	0-0-1-0-0-0	Mrs. Elizabeth ORear	0-9-0-0-1-12
Alfred Martz	1-0-0-0-0-1	Geo ORear	0-3-1-0-0-6
Bushrod Morgan	0-0-1-0-0-4	Benjn F. ORear	0-5-1-0-3-4
Geo B. Moore	0-0-1-0-0-0	Mrs. Susan ORear	0-0-0-0-0-0
Richd Morgan	0-0-1-0-0-3	David Osborn	0-0-1-0-0-2
James W. McClelland	0-0-1-0-0-0	Hugh ORourke	0-0-1-0-0-0
Patrick Murray	0-0-1-0-0-0	Wm O. Callaghan	0-0-1-0-0-1
Charles McCormick	0-0-1-0-0-0	Overseers of Poor	0-2-0-0-1-5
Benjn A. May	0-0-1-0-0-0	Jno B. Oliver	0-0-1-0-0-0
_____ Myres	0-1-1-0-0-0	Samuel Pidgeon	0-0-1-1-0-8
Thos McCormick Senr.	0-0-1-0-0-0	Dr. Mat Pages Est.	0-2-0-0-1-2
		Jno E. Page	1-17-1-0-3-27
Hugh M. Nelson	0-13-1-0-2-19	Mrs. Susan R. Page	0-30-0-0-6-40
Thos F. Nelson	0-17-2-0-3-15	Michael Pope Jr.	0-0-1-0-0-0
Jno Newcomb	0-1-1-0-0-7	A. C. Page	0-11-1-0-3-18
Col. Wm N. Nelson	0-0-2-0-0-0	Jno Page Jr.	0-10-1-0-1-10
Philip Nelson of D^r	0-7-1-0-0-9	Mann R. Page	0-9-1-0-4-16
		Miss Mattie C. Page	0-1-0-0-0-0
Philip Nelson of Th^s	0-5-1-0-1-9	Alexander Parkins	0-3-1-0-0-18
Miss A. & R. Nelson	0-3-0-0-0-0	George R. Page	0-3-1-0-0-6
		Mathew Pulliam	0-1-1-0-1-0
James H. Neville	1-1-1-0-0-0	Jno Pierce Senr.	0-5-1-0-1-7
Jno B. Norris	0-3-1-0-0-5	A. Newton Pierce	0-3-1-0-1-9
		Peter McPierce	0-4-1-0-0-7

Clarke County, Virginia Personal Property Tax Lists 1854-1870
1857

Paul Pierce	0-7-1-0-2-8	Miss Nancy		
Mrs. E. M. Page	0-5-0-0-1-1	Redman	0-2-0-0-0-0	
James M. Pine	0-1-1-0-0-2	George W. Rutter	0-1-1-0-0-0	
Jno Poston	0-0-1-0-0-2	Daniel B.		
Wm Puller	0-0-1-0-0-0	Richards	0-1-1-0-0-0	
T. P. Pendleton	0-13-1-0-2-20	Charles H.		
Wash F. Padgett	1-0-1-0-0-1	Richards	0-0-1-0-0-0	
Wm Pyle	1-0-1-0-0-1	James H. Rowland	0-0-1-0-0-2	
Benjn F. Perry	0-0-1-0-0-0	Adison Romine	0-2-1-0-0-5	
Calvin Puller	0-0-1-0-0-5	George Reno	0-0-1-0-0-0	
Jno Patterson	2-1-1-0-0-5	Wesley Russell	1-0-1-0-0-2	
James S. Payne	0-0-1-0-0-1	Beverly Randolph	0-19-1-0-4-24	
Barnett Prichard	0-0-1-0-0-1	James Rouser	0-0-1-0-0-0	
James Pierson	0-0-1-0-0-0	Dr. R. C. Randolph	1-27-1-0-4-28	
Conrad Pope	0-0-1-0-0-1	A. C. Randolph	0-3-1-0-0-6	
J. Wm Parkins	0-1-1-0-0-0	Jno Reynolds	0-0-1-0-0-0	
Pulliam & Howell	0-0-0-0-0-1	Wm Riely	0-0-1-0-0-0	
Michael Pope Sr	0-0-0-0-0-1	Jno Ramey	0-0-1-0-0-0	
Philip H. Powers	0-7-1-0-2-8	Mathew Rust	0-2-1-0-0-1	
		Jno J. Riely	0-3-1-0-0-5	
Miss Mary C.		Wm A. Riely	0-4-1-0-0-12	
Rootes	0-2-0-0-0-0	Thos Reardan	0-0-2-0-0-1	
Bennet Russell	1-10-2-0-0-14	Samuel Rutter	0-0-1-0-0-0	
Jno W. Russell	0-0-1-0-0-4	Jno D. Richardson	0-11-1-0-0-17	
Thos W. Russell	0-1-1-0-1-3	Jno N. Ross	0-0-1-0-0-0	
Michael Russell	1-0-2-0-0-2	Jno Rippon	0-0-1-0-0-1	
Wm H. Robinson	0-3-1-0-0-6	James Rose	0-0-1-0-0-0	
James M. Reed	0-0-1-0-0-0	James W. Ryan	0-2-1-0-0-2	
Jno Reed	0-0-1-0-0-1	Jos F. Ryan	0-2-1-0-0-1	
Jno Rowland	0-0-3-0-0-11	Marcus B. Reed	0-0-1-0-0-1	
Mathew W.		Charles B. Riely	0-0-1-0-0-0	
Royston	0-0-1-0-0-2	Jno Rutter	0-0-1-0-0-7	
Miss E. W.		Richmond &		
Roysten	0-1-0-0-1-0	Stolle	0-1-2-0-0-0	
Patrick Rodgers	0-0-1-0-0-0	Enos Richmond	0-0-0-0-0-0	
Peter K. Royston	0-1-1-0-0-2			
Uriah B. Royston	0-0-1-0-0-2	Col. T. Smith	0-16-2-0-3-24	
George R.		Guardian for		
Royston	0-0-1-0-0-0	H. Smith's heirs		

Clarke County, Virginia Personal Property Tax Lists 1854-1870
1857

Daniel W. Sowers	1-13-1-0-2-31	L. J. Schooler	0-0-1-0-0-0
Jno W. Sprint	0-0-1-0-0-0	Jno Shaffer	0-0-1-0-0-0
Fielding L. Sowers	0-8-1-0-0-5	Jack Shaffer	0-0-1-0-0-0
		Simon Stickles	1-0-1-0-0-2
James F. Reynolds	0-0-1-0-0-1	Franklin Swartz	0-0-1-0-0-0
		Benjn Simmons	0-0-1-0-0-0
		Wm Strother	0-2-1-0-1-5
Mrs. Elizabeth Sowers	0-0-0-0-0-0	Frederick Sh__[illegible]	0-0-1-0-0-0
Jno W. Sowers	0-8-1-0-0-13	Erasmus Shacklefod	0-0-1-0-0-0
Wm B. Sowers	0-0-1-0-0-0		
Wm Sowers Senr.	1-9-1-0-3-12	Charles Showers	0-0-1-0-1-0
Champ Shepherd	1-4-1-0-0-8	Samuel Showers	0-1-2-0-0-0
Carter Shepherd	0-5-1-0-2-7	Jno Stonestreet	0-0-1-0-0-0
Henry Shepherd	0-0-1-0-0-0	James R. Shepherd	0-0-1-0-0-0
P. D. Shepherd	0-5-2-0-1-13		
Geo Smedley	0-0-1-0-0-1	Jno Shell	0-0-1-0-0-1
Wm D. & E. J. Smith	0-23-2-1-4-30	Stephen Shell	0-0-1-0-0-0
		Craven Shell	0-0-1-0-0-0
Dr. Philip Smith	0-20-2-0-4-25	Jno H. P. Stone	0-0-1-0-0-0
Miss M. C. Shively	0-1-0-0-0-1	S. R. Stump	0-0-1-0-0-1
Paul Smith	0-6-1-0-0-9	Dennis Sheheen	0-0-1-0-0-1
Mrs. M. E. Shively	0-4-0-0-1-1	Jas W. Stephenson	0-4-1-0-0-6
Jno O. Snyder	1-2-1-0-1-2		
Daniel C. Snyder	1-1-1-0-0-0	Thos Sprint	0-0-1-0-0-1
Thos Shumate	1-3-1-0-2-10	Jos Shackleford	0-0-1-0-0-0
James W. Sowers	0-2-1-0-1-10	Jos Shipe	0-0-1-0-0-1
James Sowers	0-2-1-0-1-7	Henry T. Shearer	0-0-1-0-0-0
Wm M. Sowers	0-3-1-0-0-6	Wm G. Steele	0-0-1-0-0-0
Mrs. F. E. Sowers	0-5-1-0-0-12	James A. Steele	0-0-1-0-0-0
Danl H. Sowers	0-6-1-0-2-14	James H. Swain	0-0-1-0-0-1
Wm L. Smith	0-0-1-0-0-0	Henry Stickles	0-0-1-0-0-0
Charles K. Smith	0-0-1-0-0-1	Mrs. Susan Smith	1-1-0-0-0-0
Thos Smallwood	0-0-1-0-0-0	Burr Smallwood	1-0-1-0-0-1
Edward C. Smith	0-0-1-0-0-0	James M. Swartz	0-0-1-0-0-0
Geo R. Smith	0-0-1-0-0-0	Hezekiah Slusher	0-0-1-0-1-1
Charles Swart	0-0-1-0-0-0	Mrs. Rebecca S. Smith	2-1-0-0-0-0
James Smallwood	0-0-1-0-0-0		
Jno Stewart Senr.	0-0-1-0-0-1	M. L. Sinclair	0-0-1-0-0-0

Clarke County, Virginia Personal Property Tax Lists 1854-1870
1857

Mrs. Margt Swann	0-1-0-0-0-0	Dr. B. Taylor	0-1-1-0-2-3
Jno H. Stipe	0-0-1-0-0-0	Isaac Talley	0-0-1-0-0-1
George Smith	0-0-1-0-0-0	Snowden Tomblin	0-0-1-0-0-1
George W. Smith	0-0-1-0-0-0	Alonzo Taylor	0-0-1-0-0-0
Geo W. Schultz	0-0-1-0-0-1	Barney Turbeck	0-0-1-0-0-0
		Lewis Tapp	0-0-1-0-0-0
Mrs. Sarah Timberlake	0-4-0-0-5-6	Mrs. U. E. Thomas	0-0-0-0-0-0
Samuel N. Trenary	0-0-1-0-0-2	Mason Tinsman	0-0-1-0-0-1
Adam F. Thompson	0-0-1-0-0-1	Isaac Tyson	0-7-1-0-1-10
James F. Thompson	0-0-1-0-0-0	Ludwell Tinsman	0-0-1-0-0-1
Greenby Thompson	0-0-1-0-0-2	James Vanmetre	0-0-1-0-0-0
French Thompson	0-2-2-0-0-3	Jacob Vanmetre	0-6-0-0-0-11
Baalis Thompson	0-0-1-0-1-4	George Violett	0-0-1-0-0-0
Benjn Thompson Jr.	0-0-1-0-0-4	Gerry Vaughn	1-0-2-0-0-1
Jno F. Thompson	0-0-1-0-0-1	R. C. Wyndeyer	0-0-1-0-0-0
Wm F. Thompson	0-0-1-0-0-1	Horatio T. Wheat	1-5-3-0-2-8
Wm N. Thompson	1-5-1-1-0-3	Benjn F. Wilson	0-0-1-0-0-0
Jno H. Taylor	0-0-1-0-0-0	Jeremiah Wilson	0-0-1-0-0-0
Charles Trussell	0-0-1-0-0-2	Jno Wilson	1-0-1-0-0-0
Boston Thompson	0-0-1-0-0-0	Francis H. Whiting	0-1-1-0-1-0
Isaac Thompson	0-3-2-0-0-7	Wm H. Whiting	0-8-1-0-0-13
Wm Taylor	0-18-1-0-2-19	Francis B. Whiting Sr.	0-20-2-0-5-15
Col. Jos Tuley	0-26-1-0-6-21	Wm W. Whiting	0-5-1-0-1-8
Robt Tapscott	1-0-0-0-0-0	Nathl B. Whiting	0-7-1-0-1-12
Daniel Turner	0-0-1-0-0-0	Allen Williams	0-9-1-0-0-16
Miss Eliza Taylor	0-4-1-0-2-3	Thompson Writ	0-0-1-0-0-1
Jno Trussell	0-5-1-0-1-8	Leroy P. Williams	0-6-1-0-2-10
Moses B. Trussell	0-1-1-0-0-7	E. P. Williams	0-0-1-0-0-1
Wm Trenary	1-2-1-0-0-3	Wm Willingham	2-0-1-0-0-2
Howard F. Thornton	0-0-1-0-0-3	Jno T. Willingham	0-0-1-0-0-1
Calvin Thacker	1-0-1-0-0-2	J. W. Ware & Mrs. Stribling	0-18-1-0-3-20

Clarke County, Virginia Personal Property Tax Lists 1854-1870
1857

Rev. Chas White	0-0-1-0-0-0	Lucinda Washington	0-3-0-0-0-0
Gabriel Williams	0-1-0-0-0-1	Wm T. Wharton	0-0-1-0-0-0
Welch & Funk	0-0-3-0-0-3	Andrew Willingham	0-0-1-0-0-0
Danl F. Wade & Bro	0-2-2-0-0-3	R. B. Welch	0-2-1-0-0-0
Hezekiah Wiley	0-0-1-0-0-0	Rev. F. M. Whittle	0-4-1-0-0-1
Cornelius Wiley	0-0-1-0-0-1	Samuel G. Wyman	0-7-0-0-2-8
Jno Wiley	0-0-1-0-0-0	James W. Whittington	0-0-1-0-0-0
Geo W. Wiley	0-0-1-0-0-2	Jno M. Whittington	0-0-1-0-0-0
Sydnor B. Wyndham	0-2-1-0-0-3	James W. Willingham	0-0-1-0-0-0
Thos C. Windham	0-0-1-0-0-0	Wm Willis	0-0-1-0-0-0
James V. Weir	1-5-1-0-1-9	Jackson Wheeler	0-2-1-0-0-6
James Wiley	0-0-1-0-0-0	R. A. Webb	0-0-1-0-0-0
Jacob Welch	1-0-1-0-0-6	Charles F. Willingham	1-0-0-0-0-0
David H. Wilcox	0-0-1-0-0-0	Isaac Writ	1-0-0-0-0-0
Jesse Wright	0-0-1-0-0-1	James Williams	0-0-1-0-0-1
Robt Whittington	0-1-1-0-0-0	Griffin Ward	0-0-1-0-0-0
Alexander Wood	0-0-1-0-0-0		
Jno C. Wheeler	0-0-1-0-0-0	Wm H. Young	1-0-1-0-0-0
Jos Wood	0-1-1-0-0-7	Wash P. Young	0-0-1-0-0-0
Bennett Wood	1-0-1-0-0-4		
Walker B. Wilson	0-0-1-0-0-0		
Simon Wilcox	0-0-1-0-0-0		
Wm W. Wood	0-0-1-0-0-0		
G. W. Weaver	0-1-1-0-1-10		

[Free Negroes]

Wm Parker	0-0-0-1-0-0	George Ransom	0-0-0-1-0-0
Jim Butler	0-0-0-1-0-0	Thos Ransom	0-0-0-1-0-0
Jno Strother	0-0-0-1-0-0	Lewis Ransom	0-0-0-1-0-0
Mowen Harris	0-0-0-1-0-0	Burwell Cooke	0-0-0-1-0-0

Clarke County, Virginia Personal Property Tax Lists 1854-1870

1858

1) Free male persons above the age of 16 years, 2) Slaves who have attained the age of 16 years, 3) White male inhabitants who have attained the age of 21 years, except those exempted from taxation on account of bodily infirmity, 4) Male free negroes between the ages of 21 and 55 years, 5) Slaves who have attained the age of 12 years, 6) Horses, mules, asses & jennets

Buckner Ashby	0-10-2-0-3-22	Mrs. Nancy Allen	0-0-0-0-0-0
James M. Allen	0-4-1-0-9-9	George D. Adams	0-0-1-0-0-0
Mason Anderson	0-3-1-0-1-6		
John H. Anderson	0-0-1-0-1-0	Dr. Wm A.	
Jesse Allen	0-0-1-0-0-0	Bradford	0-4-1-1-1-4
Edgar Allen	0-10-1-0-4-13		
John Alexander	0-24-1-0-3-28	Margt E.	
John W.		Alexander	0-0-0-0-0-0
Anderson	0-0-1-0-0-1	Milton B.	
Joseph E.		Anderson	0-2-1-0-1-5
Anderson	0-1-1-0-1-6	Austin C. Ashby	0-0-1-0-0-0
Nimrod F.		Mrs. Elizabeth	
Anderson	0-0-1-0-0-1	Ashby	0-0-0-0-0-0
Robert Ashby Jr.	0-0-1-0-0-0	John Amick	0-0-1-0-0-0
Robert Ashby Sr.	0-0-1-0-0-1	Levi Athey	0-0-1-0-0-0
Nimrod Ashby	0-0-1-0-0-0		
Capt C. B. Ashby	0-0-1-0-0-0		
Thos J. Anderson	0-0-1-0-0-1	George H.	
Geo W. Ashby	0-1-1-0-0-4	Burwell	0-52-2-0-4-52
J. W. & N. F.		Do as trustee	0-0-0-0-0-0
Anderson	0-0-0-0-0-2	Nathaniel Burwell	0-14-1-0-2-38
George W. Allen	0-4-1-0-0-6	John Burchell	0-7-2-0-1-12
Wm T. Allen	0-6-1-0-3-10	Andrew J. Berlin	0-0-1-0-0-0
A. S. Allen	0-9-1-0-0-12	Wm O. Brown	0-0-1-0-0-0
James Allison	0-0-1-0-0-0	Henry C. Briggs	0-0-1-0-0-0
John Allison	1-0-1-0-0-0	George H. Bell	0-0-1-0-0-0
Thos H.		Archibald Bowen	1-4-2-0-2-6
Alexander	0-0-1-0-0-8	Jesse Bowen	0-2-1-0-0-5
William Asbury	0-0-1-0-0-0	Hiram O. Bell	0-3-1-0-0-5
John Avis	0-0-1-0-0-0	Squire Bell	0-1-1-0-0-1

Clarke County, Virginia Personal Property Tax Lists 1854-1870
1858

Hector Ball	0-0-1-0-0-3	James Brown	0-0-1-0-0-1
Lewis Berlin	0-1-1-0-1-0	James J. Board	0-0-1-0-0-1
Philip Berlin	0-0-1-0-0-1	George W. Board	0-0-1-0-0-2
William Berlin	0-2-2-0-0-0	George Board	0-0-1-0-0-0
George W. Berlin	0-0-1-0-0-0	Middleton Bowen	0-0-1-0-0-3
George C. Blakemore	0-6-1-0-1-13	Miss Emily Bell	0-0-0-0-0-1
		John Billmyre	0-0-1-0-0-0
Neille Barnett	1-6-1-0-3-12	Joseph C. Bartlett	1-3-2-0-2-9
James Bell Senr.	1-0-2-0-0-3	Jonas P. Bell	0-2-1-0-0-3
Thos Briggs Junr. Est.	0-2-0-0-0-6	A. J. Bradfield	0-0-1-0-0-0
James C. Briggs	0-5-1-0-0-13	George W. Bradfield	0-1-1-0-0-1
Miss Margt Burchell	0-4-0-2-2-3	James W. Board	0-0-1-0-0-0
		Thomas Brown	0-0-1-0-0-0
John S. Briggs	0-0-1-0-0-1	George B. Bradford	0-0-1-0-0-0
Arthur Briggs	0-0-1-0-0-2		
John Bromley	0-0-1-1-0-13	Philip L. Berlin	0-6-1-0-1-9
John W. Byrd	0-10-1-0-2-10	George H. Brown	0-0-1-0-0-0
George W. Bromley	0-4-1-0-0-9	Alfred Bishop	0-0-1-0-0-0
		Mrs. Lucy N. Buck	0-1-0-0-0-0
Susan R. Burwell	0-6-0-0-0-2	Robert Bull	0-0-1-0-1-1
Ann C. Benn	0-0-0-0-1-3	Patrick Brady	0-0-1-0-0-0
Joseph B. Beevers	0-0-1-0-0-1	H. W. Brabham	0-0-1-0-0-0
Daniel S. Bonham	1-0-1-1-0-13	George Bowling	0-0-1-0-0-0
Thomas Byrne	0-0-1-0-0-2	Thomas J. Bragg	0-1-1-0-0-2
Samuel Bonham	0-9-1-0-1-19	Jacob Basore	0-0-1-0-0-0
Jonathan M. Brown	0-0-1-0-0-0	Robert Briggs	0-4-1-0-1-5
		William Briggs	0-0-1-0-1-0
Juliet Boyston	0-1-0-0-0-0	George S. Bonham	0-0-0-0-0-0
William Berry	0-8-1-0-3-7		
Nancy Boyston	0-0-0-0-0-0	Albert Bonham	0-0-1-0-0-1
Dr. H. T. Barton	1-5-1-0-0-3	Enoch L. Brown	0-0-1-0-0-0
Christian Bowser	0-0-1-0-0-0	John R. Buford	0-0-1-0-0-0
R. S. Bryarly	0-8-2-0-1-10	Charles Bayles	0-0-1-0-0-0
Miss Mary C. Bowser	0-0-0-0-0-0	J. H. Bitzer	0-2-1-0-0-7
		Charles H. Brabham	0-0-1-0-0-0
Abraham Beevers	0-0-1-0-0-3		
Adam Barr	0-0-1-0-0-0	Wm Brabham	1-0-0-0-0-0
Jesse Butler	1-0-2-0-0-0	John Brown	0-0-1-0-0-0

Clarke County, Virginia Personal Property Tax Lists 1854-1870
1858

Name	Values
Morgan M. Bowman	0-1-1-0-0-3
Timothy Brisneham [?]	0-0-1-0-0-0
Thomas Barr	0-0-1-0-0-0
Samuel Bromley	0-2-1-0-0-7
F. C. Newton Brown	0-0-1-0-0-1
Mrs. Mary Bowser	0-0-0-0-0-0
Miss Amelia Byrne	0-0-0-0-0-1
Alfred Castleman	1-9-2-0-1-16
Elsey Connor	1-0-1-0-0-0
Charles D. Castleman	0-5-1-0-0-3
Wm A. Castleman	0-6-1-0-0-4
Stephen D. Castleman	0-0-0-0-0-0
Mrs. Ury Castleman	0-0-0-0-0-1
James Chisholm	0-0-1-0-0-0
Nathaniel Castleman	0-0-0-0-0-0
William Carper	0-0-1-0-0-2
Chas M. Castleman	0-0-0-0-0-0
Robert A. Colston	0-4-1-0-0-9
John Copenhaver	0-4-2-0-0-9
John H. Crebbs	0-2-1-0-0-8
George W. Cooper	0-0-1-0-0-0
Joseph K. Carter	0-2-1-0-0-7
Chas J. Carter	0-0-1-0-0-4
John B. Carter	0-2-1-0-0-7
Wm K. Carter	0-2-1-0-0-6
John A. Carter	0-1-1-0-1-8
John W. Carter	0-0-1-0-0-0
William P. Carter	0-11-1-0-4-10
William G. Carter	0-0-1-0-1-1
Peter Cain	0-1-2-0-0-12
Dr. R. T. Colston	1-7-0-0-0-29
William H. Carter	0-1-1-0-0-0
Parkison Corder	1-0-1-0-0-0
James H. Clark	1-4-1-0-1-1
Thomas H. Crow	1-5-1-0-2-8
John Carroll	0-0-1-0-0-0
John Cooper	0-0-1-0-0-2
Lewis Carroll	0-0-1-0-0-1
Robert W. Cornwell	0-0-1-0-0-1
Thomas Cornwell	0-0-1-0-0-0
Aaron Chamblin	0-0-1-0-0-0
Isaac Cornwell	0-0-1-0-0-0
Samuel Campbell	0-0-1-0-0-0
Andrew Cornwell	0-1-1-0-1-1
Michael Copenhaver	0-0-1-0-0-1
John N. Collier	0-0-1-0-0-5
George F. Calmes	0-2-2-0-0-4
Ann B. Cooke	0-18-0-0-1-15
Jacob Clink	0-2-1-0-1-8
John P. Carrigan	0-0-1-0-0-0
Miss Marian Catlett	0-6-1-0-0-11
John R. Crockwell	0-0-1-0-0-0
James W. Conrad	0-4-1-0-2-8
Catharine Castleman	0-3-0-0-1-2
Joseph Carver	0-0-1-0-0-2
Robert H. Castleman	0-3-1-0-1-6
James N. Corbin	0-0-1-0-0-2
Benjamin Crampton	1-0-0-0-0-1
Franklin Caniford	0-0-1-0-1-0

Clarke County, Virginia Personal Property Tax Lists 1854-1870
1858

Name	Values	Name	Values
James E. Chamblin	0-0-1-0-0-0	Matthew H. Doren	0-0-1-0-0-1
John Cooper	1-0-0-0-0-0	Baalis Davis	0-1-0-0-0-0
Miss Sallie Cloud	0-3-0-0-0-0	William Dougherty	0-0-1-0-0-0
Elizabeth Clink	0-0-0-0-0-0	James Dunn	0-0-1-0-0-1
Henry Caniford	0-0-1-0-0-0		
Eliza Crim	0-0-1-0-0-0	Jacob Enders	0-8-1-0-1-10
James E. Cox	0-0-1-0-0-0	Henry Edwards	0-0-1-0-0-3
George W. Corner	0-0-1-0-0-3	Wm G. Everhart	2-2-1-0-0-8
James H. Clarke	0-0-1-0-0-0	Wm F. Engle	0-0-1-0-0-0
Michael Crim	0-0-1-0-0-0	Henson Eliott	0-3-2-0-1-9
Mrs. Hannah Cain	0-0-0-0-0-0	Elliott & Parker	0-0-0-0-0-0
Wm F. Chamblin	1-0-1-0-0-2	Henry Evans	0-1-1-0-0-0
Mrs. Margt Chapman	1-0-0-0-0-0	A. M. Earle	0-5-1-0-1-14
James Carter	0-0-1-0-0-1	Jacob W. Everhart	0-0-1-0-0-1
William Cox	0-0-1-0-0-0	Edward Eno	0-0-1-0-0-0
Hugh Campbell	1-0-1-0-0-1	Wm H. Edwards	1-0-1-0-0-1
Franklin Carter	0-1-1-0-0-4	Albert Elsey	0-2-1-0-0-5
		Joseph W. Edwards	0-0-1-0-0-1
Washington Dearmont	0-5-2-0-2-10	Edwin S. Everhart	1-0-1-0-0-1
William Deahl	1-0-2-0-0-1	Thomas A. Everhart	0-0-1-0-2-0
James W. Doren	0-0-1-0-0-1	John Ellyett	0-0-1-0-0-2
James Doren	1-0-1-0-0-0	J. N. Elsie	0-0-1-0-0-0
John Drish	0-0-1-0-0-2		
George D. Drish	0-0-1-0-0-1	Dr. O. R. Funsten	0-16-1-0-3-20
John Donovan	0-0-1-0-0-0	Dr. J. F. Fauntleroy	0-2-1-0-0-4
Thomas Duke	0-0-1-0-0-1	James A. Foster	0-2-1-0-1-6
George W. Diffenderfer	0-0-1-0-0-1	Josiah Ferguson	0-0-1-0-1-4
Hugh Davis	0-0-1-0-0-0	Wm M. Fergusen	0-1-1-0-0-2
_____ Denney	1-0-0-0-0-0	Edward Franks	1-0-1-0-0-0
Wm Donohue	0-0-1-0-0-0	Ephraim Furr	0-0-1-0-0-0
Michael Drislane	0-0-1-0-0-0	Moses Furr	0-0-1-0-0-1
John D. Davis	0-1-1-0-0-0	Wm Fowler Jr.	0-0-1-0-0-0
John Dow	0-2-1-0-1-5	James Furr	0-0-1-0-0-1
Aaron Duble	0-0-1-0-0-1		
Rev. H. W. Dodge	0-2-1-0-1-1		

Clarke County, Virginia Personal Property Tax Lists 1854-1870
1858

Johnson Furr	0-1-1-0-2-6		Samuel Grubbs	
Israel Fidler	0-0-1-0-0-0		Senr.	0-0-1-0-0-0
Elizabeth			H. N. Grigsby	0-6-1-0-1-9
Fleming	0-1-0-0-0-4		Mrs. Isabella	
Joseph Fleming	1-0-1-0-0-6		Glass	0-1-0-0-0-0
Wm Fowler Senr.	0-0-1-0-0-3		Lewis F. Glass	0-7-1-0-0-10
John Foreman	0-0-1-0-0-0		Wm Gourley	0-0-1-0-0-7
Everett Fowler	0-0-1-0-0-0		Martin Gant	0-6-1-0-0-9
Thomas Fowler	0-0-1-0-0-2		Wm Gibbs	0-0-1-0-0-0
Robert Feltner	0-0-1-0-0-3		Wm B. Grubbs	0-0-1-0-0-1
Martin Feltner	0-0-2-0-0-0		Saml Grubbs Jr.	0-0-1-0-0-1
Dennis Fenton	0-0-1-0-0-1		George W.	
Marquis R.			Grubbs	0-0-1-0-0-0
Feeher	0-2-1-0-2-4		John M. Grubbs	0-0-1-0-0-0
Thomas G. Flagg	0-0-1-0-1-0		John Gruber	0-2-1-0-0-6
George W. Fidler	0-0-1-0-0-0		George Gardiner	0-0-1-0-0-0
John A. Finnell	0-0-1-0-0-1		Adam Greenwald	0-0-1-0-0-1
Joshua Fellows	0-0-1-0-0-1		Andrew E. Gibson	1-0-0-0-0-0
Christian Fonda	0-0-1-0-0-0		Nathan Grubb	0-0-1-0-0-0
Jeremiah Foley	0-0-1-0-0-0		T. K. Glover	0-0-1-0-0-0
Enoch Furr	0-0-1-0-0-0		Madison Grimes	0-0-1-0-0-1
Robert Frazier	0-0-1-0-0-0		John L. Grant	1-1-1-0-0-5
R. R. Foley	0-2-1-0-0-0		Thomas Gibson	0-0-1-0-0-0
Thomas Forrest	0-0-1-0-0-0		Mrs. L. A. Glaize	0-1-1-0-0-0
			Wm C. Gover	0-0-1-0-0-0
James W.			Paul F. Graham	0-0-1-0-0-3
Galloway	0-0-1-0-0-0			
Thomas W.			William	
Griffith	0-0-1-0-0-0		Horseman	0-0-1-0-0-0
Joseph Gorman	0-0-1-0-0-0			
James F. Green	0-4-1-0-0-7		Wm Grubbs	
Mrs. Mary Green	0-3-0-0-0-0		(of Thornly)	1-0-1-0-0-1
Richard N. Green	0-5-1-0-0-8		S. M. Grigsby	1-0-0-0-0-0
John S. Green	0-2-1-0-0-10			
Thomas E. Gold	0-8-2-0-2-19		Samuel Huyett	0-3-1-0-0-9
George W.			John Huyett	0-0-1-0-0-0
Gordon	0-2-1-0-0-6		Abram Huyett	0-0-1-0-1-2
John S. Gordon	0-2-1-0-1-7		Elizabeth	
S. J. [?] Gant	0-2-1-0-0-3		Hansucker	0-0-0-0-0-0

Clarke County, Virginia Personal Property Tax Lists 1854-1870
1858

Whiting Hamilton	0-2-2-0-0-3	Grafton Hilliard	2-0-1-0-0-0
Henry D. Hooe	0-1-3-0-0-6	Edward E. Hall	0-8-1-0-2-8
James H. Hooe	0-0-1-0-0-0	John Henry White P.	0-0-1-0-0-0
John Hummer	0-0-1-0-0-1	James F. Howell	0-0-1-0-0-0
Mason Hummer	0-0-1-0-0-2	John W. Hibbard	0-0-1-0-0-0
Wm Hummer	0-0-1-0-0-1	W. R. Helvestine	0-1-1-0-0-0
Wm A. Holland	0-1-1-0-0-1	Jno & Thos Hiskett	0-3-2-0-0-7
John W. Holland	0-0-1-0-0-0	A. T. M. Hough	0-0-1-0-0-2
E. T. Hancock	0-5-1-0-2-10	Geo Harris Jr.	0-0-1-0-0-0
Chas B. Hancock	0-3-1-0-0-2	Jno W. Hall	0-0-1-0-0-0
Wm Heflin	0-0-1-0-0-0	Jno S. Hummer	0-0-1-0-0-0
Dr. J. A. Haynes	0-4-1-0-0-3	Jacob Heflebower	0-6-1-0-2-12
James M. Hite	0-0-1-0-0-3	Henry Huyett	0-2-1-0-1-9
Isaac J. Hite	1-7-1-0-1-13	Danl Hart	0-0-1-0-0-0
George W. Hanvy	0-0-1-0-0-0	James Henry	0-0-1-0-0-0
Charles F. Hennis	0-0-1-0-0-0	Cornelius Hawks	0-0-1-0-0-0
Saml Heflebower	0-5-1-0-2-12	Thos L. Humphrey	0-2-1-0-1-3
C. W. Hardesty	0-0-1-0-1-3	Do Exr of D. Trislers Est	0-0-0-0-0-0
A. D. Hardesty	0-2-1-0-0-4	Edward C. Harrison	0-1-1-0-0-2
Wm G. Hardesty	0-2-1-0-0-11	Alexander Holtsclaw	0-0-1-0-0-2
James M. Hardesty	0-2-1-0-0-7	Jos R. Hardesty	0-1-1-0-0-4
Cornelius Hoff Blackwell Holtsclaw	0-0-1-0-0-0	James Hayden	0-0-1-0-0-0
John Hoff	0-0-1-0-0-0	George H. Isler	0-0-1-0-0-5
Rev. John F. Hoff	0-4-1-0-1-1	Solomon R. Jackson	0-0-1-0-0-0
Mrs. Sarah Hardesty	0-1-0-0-0-2	Herod Jenkins	1-0-1-0-0-2
Geo Hansucker	0-1-1-0-0-5	Mathew Jones	0-1-1-0-1-2
Geo L. Harris	0-5-0-0-2-9	John Joliffe	1-5-1-0-0-13
Jno Hughs	0-0-1-0-0-1	Leonard Jones	0-2-1-0-0-1
Thos Hughs	0-1-1-0-0-1	John S. Johnston	0-1-1-0-0-5
R. L. Horner	0-3-0-0-0-0	Thomas Jones	0-0-1-0-1-8
Wm B. Harris	0-9-1-0-1-15		
Henry Horner	0-0-0-0-0-1		
John Henry	0-01-0-0-1		
Dr. B. Harrison	0-7-1-0-0-20		
Henry Huntsberry	0-1-1-0-0-6		

Clarke County, Virginia Personal Property Tax Lists 1854-1870
1858

George Johnston			John Kelley	1-0-1-0-0-1
(B. S.)	0-2-1-0-0-1		E. V. Kercheral	0-0-1-0-0-0
Dr. J. J. Janney	0-2-1-0-1-4		William B.	
Thomas Jenkins	0-0-1-0-0-1		Kennan	0-0-1-0-0-0
James W.			James H. Kennan	0-0-1-0-1-0
Johnston	0-0-1-0-0-0		Charles H.	
Wm Johnston	0-0-1-0-0-0		Kitchen	0-0-1-0-0-0
Wm A. Jackson	0-6-1-0-0-12		John N. Kitchen	1-1-0-0-1-7
Andrew Jackson	0-0-1-0-0-0		Mrs. Hannah	
Armstest M.			Kelley	1-0-0-0-0-0
Johnson	0-0-2-0-0-5		Henry Kromling	0-2-2-0-0-1
Amelia A. Jordan	0-1-0-0-0-1		Harrison Kent	0-0-1-0-0-0
Wm Johnston				
(Teacher)	0-3-1-0-0-1		John B. Larue	0-12-3-0-3-32
Wm B. Jolliffe	0-0-1-0-0-0		John D. Larue	0-4-1-0-2-10
George W. Joy	0-0-1-0-0-0			
Ebin Jenkins	0-0-1-0-0-1		John Keen	0-0-1-0-0-0
George Johnson			John W. King	0-0-2-0-1-0
(Miller)	0-0-1-0-0-1			
Edward Jenkins	0-0-1-0-0-0		Edward Lewis	0-3-1-0-0-5
Jones & Lupton	0-0-0-0-0-2		John T.	
Bailey Johnston	0-0-1-0-0-1		Longerbeam	0-0-1-0-0-1
			A. L. P. Larue	0-4-1-0-1-9
John N. Kimmell	1-0-1-0-0-1		James W. Larue	0-6-1-0-0-8
Dr. F. J. Kerfoot	0-8-1-0-2-7		C. C. Larue	0-0-1-0-0-2
Wm C. Kerfoot	0-13-1-0-1-15		Squire Lee	0-0-3-0-0-4
Judson G. Kerfoot	0-5-1-0-0-14		Christopher Lee	0-0-1-0-0-1
George Knight	0-6-3-0-4-18		Dr. J. M. Lindsey	1-1-1-0-0-2
Middleton Keeler	1-0-1-0-0-1		Mrs. Emily	
Jacob Kriser	1-0-1-0-0-2		Littleton	0-2-1-0-0-6
Henry Knight	0-0-1-0-0-0		Wm D. Littleton	0-0-1-0-0-3
Samuel G. Kneller	1-5-1-0-2-9		Wm Littleton	0-0-1-0-0-3
Wm C. Kennerly	0-3-1-0-1-2		John W. Littleton	0-0-1-0-0-4
Jos McK.			Enos Lanham	0-0-1-0-0-0
Kennerly	0-1-1-0-0-8		James W. Lee	0-0-1-0-0-0
Dr. C. B. Kennerly	0-1-1-0-1-6		Henry Lloyd	0-0-1-0-0-3
Joseph Kline	0-0-1-0-0-0		John Lloyd	2-0-1-0-0-2
Dr. R. Kownsler	0-7-1-0-0-5		James L. Lloyd	0-0-1-0-0-1
Charles E. Kimball	0-7-1-0-1-17		David Lloyd	0-0-1-0-0-0

Clarke County, Virginia Personal Property Tax Lists 1854-1870
1858

John A. Lloyd	0-0-1-0-0-0	John N. Meade	0-5-1-0-0-7
Samuel Lloyd	0-0-1-0-0-0	E. B. Manter	0-0-1-0-0-1
Moses Lewin	0-0-1-0-0-0	William W. Meade	0-0-1-0-0-0
John Lock Senr.	0-4-1-0-0-9	R. K. Meade (Trustee)	0-0-0-0-0-2
John Louthan	1-7-1-0-1-7	David Meade	0-4-1-0-1-12
John K. Louthan	0-2-1-0-0-4	Mrs. Louisa W. Meade	0-0-0-0-0-1
James T. Louthan	0-3-1-0-2-7	Nathaniel B. Meade	0-5-1-0-2-7
J. R. C. Lewis	0-0-1-0-0-0	Miss Mary Meade	0-4-0-0-1-1
Mrs. E. M. Lewis	2-2-0-0-3-5	R. K. Meade	0-4-1-0-0-2
George W. Lewis	0-3-1-0-1-2	Col. Benjn Morgan	0-29-2-0-1-35
Edgar Laham	0-0-1-0-0-1	John Morgan Do as Guardian for Children	0-9-1-0-1-8
Minor Laham	0-1-1-0-0-1	Dr. C. & S. McCormick	0-22-2-0-1-31
James Laham	1-0-1-0-0-1	Thomas McCormick	0-12-1-0-1-11
John M. Lupton	0-2-1-0-0-0	Mason McCormick	0-0-1-0-0-0
John W. Luke	0-7-1-0-1-15	Province McCormick Jr.	0-0-1-0-0-0
Josiah R. Lock	0-1-1-0-0-5	Province McCormick Sr.	0-10-1-0-3-16
Joseph B. Lindsey	0-0-1-0-0-1	George W. McCormick	0-0-1-0-0-0
John Longerbeam	0-0-1-0-0-1	Samuel McCormick	0-0-1-0-0-0
R. H. Lee	0-4-0-0-0-7	John E. McCormick	0-0-1-0-0-0
Frank Littleten	0-0-1-0-0-2	James McCormick	0-3-1-0-0-7
George Laham	0-0-1-0-0-1	Dr. Hugh McGuire	0-0-0-0-0-2
Abram Longerbeam	0-0-1-0-0-3		
Benjn Lock	0-1-1-0-0-6		
Miss H. C. Lindsey	0-3-1-0-0-3		
George E. P. Legg	0-0-1-0-0-1		
Benjn Longeream	0-1-1-0-0-4		
F. B. Little	1-3-1-0-1-3		
Emanuel Lahnan	0-0-1-0-0-0		
Richard Lahnan	0-0-1-0-0-0		
Wm Lahan [smeared]	0-0-1-0-0-1		
Charles Lloyd	0-0-1-0-0-0		
William Lloyd	0-0-1-0-0-3		
William D. Lee	0-0-1-0-0-1		
Thomas Laby	0-0-1-0-0-0		
Francis B. Meade	0-8-1-1-1-14		
Philip N. Meade	0-9-1-0-1-16		

Clarke County, Virginia Personal Property Tax Lists 1854-1870
1858

Otway McCormick	0-6-1-0-2-10		McLean McClingan	0-0-1-0-0-1
Edward McCormick	0-13-1-0-5-20		Alfred Martz	0-0-1-0-0-1
John W. McCormick	0-0-1-0-0-0		Bushrod Morgan	0-0-1-0-0-1
Peter McMurray	0-3-1-0-0-7		George B. Moore	0-0-1-0-0-0
A. R. Milton	1-4-1-0-1-8		Richard H. Morgan	0-0-1-0-0-4
S. P. Moore	0-0-1-0-0-1		Patrick Murray	0-0-1-0-0-0
L. D. Maddox & Bro.	0-1-2-0-0-3		Charles McCormick	0-0-1-0-0-0
James Mitchell	0-2-1-0-0-5		Benjamin A. May	0-0-1-0-0-0
Wm D. McGuire	0-13-1-0-1-14		James F. Myers	0-0-1-0-0-0
David H. McGuire	0-6-2-0-2-6		James T. Murphy	0-0-1-0-0-1
John J. McPhillin	0-0-1-0-1-3		S. B. Murphy	0-0-1-0-0-1
Wm G. Morris	0-0-1-0-0-0		Joseph Moore	0-0-1-0-0-0
Alexander Marshall	1-3-1-0-1-8		John McMurray	0-0-1-0-0-0
John Marshall	0-3-1-0-2-4		Samuel J. C. Moore	0-3-1-0-0-1
Mrs. Susan Marshall	0-4-1-0-0-6		John E. Morgan	0-0-1-0-0-1
Jesse McConaha	0-0-1-0-0-1		Col. F. McCormick	0-16-1-0-3-25
C. C. McIntyre	0-7-1-0-1-10		Addison Muntzel	0-0-1-0-0-0
Nathaniel Mercer	0-0-1-0-0-2		A. J. Morris	0-0-1-0-0-0
John G. McCauley	0-0-1-0-0-0		Edward C. Marshall	0-2-1-0-2-5
James Murphy	1-1-1-0-0-1		Garret McDonald	1-1-1-0-0-5
Stephen Marlow	1-0-1-0-0-1		Harvey McDonald	0-0-1-0-0-0
A. M. Moore	0-6-1-0-1-10		Mrs. Jane McDonald	0-0-0-0-0-0
Alfred P. Moore	0-0-1-0-0-0		A. J. Maddex	0-0-1-0-0-1
Samuel Moreland	1-0-3-0-0-5		Hon. [?] John S. Millson	0-1-0-0-0-0
George Marpole	0-0-1-0-0-1		Benjn Morgan Guardian for Miss Alexander	
Moses G. Miley	0-0-1-0-0-4		D° for Jno [&] Wm Alexander	
E. W. Massey	0-8-1-0-1-12			
Henry Mason	0-0-1-0-0-0			
James McClaughey	0-0-1-0-0-2			
Samuel T. Martz	0-0-1-0-0-1			
Spencer Marquis	0-0-1-0-0-0			

Clarke County, Virginia Personal Property Tax Lists 1854-1870
1858

P. McCormick	
Trustee for Edwd McCormick	
D° for Ann Stribling	
D° Guardian for Elizabeth McCormick	
Trustee E. Frost	
Agent for Mrs. Mary Stribling	
William C. Morgan	0-0-1-0-0-0
Hugh M. Nelson	0-13-1-0-0-19
Thomas F. Nelson	0-10-1-0-1-16
John Newcom [sic]	0-0-1-0-0-5
Col. Wm N. Nelson	1-3-1-0-1-6
James H. Neville	0-1-2-0-0-0
Rev. R. W. Nowling	0-2-1-0-0-1
Philip W. Nelson	0-10-1-0-4-17
Miss A. & R. Nelson	0-3-0-0-0-0
John B. Norris	0-3-0-0-0-4
John R. Nunn	1-5-1-0-1-6
James H. Newman	0-0-1-0-1-1
Dr. S. S. Neille	0-4-1-0-1-8
Wm Niswarner	0-0-2-0-0-6
Hamilton Newman	0-0-1-0-0-0
John R. Nunn	
Guardian for M. Dix	
D° Guardian for G. W. Carter	
Mrs. Elizabeth ORear	0-9-0-0-1-10
George ORear	0-2-1-0-1-5
Benjn ORear	0-5-1-0-3-4
Mrs. Susan ORear	0-0-0-0-0-0
Hugh ORoke [sic]	0-0-1-0-0-0
Overseers [of the] Poor	0-2-0-0-1-4
John B. Oliver	0-0-1-0-0-0
Samuel L. Pigeon	0-0-3-0-0-8
Dr. M. Pages Est.	0-3-0-0-1-2
Jno E. Page	0-20-1-0-2-22
S. R. Page	0-30-0-0-6-33
Conrod Pope	1-0-1-0-0-1
A. C. Page	0-8-1-0-2-20
John Page Jr.	0-10-1-0-3-11
Alexander Parkins	1-0-2-0-0-1
Mann R. Page	0-7-1-0-3-16
Geo R. Page	0-3-1-0-0-6
Mathew Pulliam	0-1-1-0-1-0
John Pierce Senr.	0-5-1-0-1-8
A. N. Pierce	0-3-1-0-1-9
Peter Mc Pierce	0-4-1-0-0-9
Paul Pierce	0-8-1-0-2-7
Mrs. E. M. Page	0-5-0-0-1-0
James Pine	1-0-1-0-1-3
John Poston	0-0-1-0-0-2
Wm Puller	0-0-1-0-0-0
T. P. Pendleton	1-12-1-0-2-12
Pendleton & Richardson	0-0-0-0-0-1
W. F. Padgett	1-0-1-0-0-1
Wm Pyle	0-0-1-0-0-1
B. F. Perry	0-0-1-0-0-0
Calvin Puller	0-0-1-0-0-0
Jno Patterson	3-0-1-0-0-5
James S. Payne	0-0-1-0-0-1
Barnett Prichard	0-0-1-0-0-1
James Pearson	0-0-1-0-0-1
Michael Pope	0-0-1-0-0-1
Pulliam & Howell	0-0-0-0-0-1
P. H. Powers	0-7-1-0-2-8

Clarke County, Virginia Personal Property Tax Lists 1854-1870
1858

John M. Pope	0-0-1-0-0-0		Dr. R. C.	
Thos N. Pyle	0-0-1-0-0-1		Randolph	0-17-2-0-4-24
Hon. Richard			A. C. Randolph	0-1-1-0-0-1
Parker	0-1-0-0-0-1		Thos W. Reynolds	0-0-1-0-0-0
Lewis Peacock	0-0-1-0-0-0		John Reynolds	0-0-2-0-1-0
			William Riely	0-0-1-0-0-0
Bennet Russell	2-10-2-0-0-17		John Ramey	0-0-1-0-0-0
Thos W. Russell	0-1-1-0-1-4		John J. Riely	0-3-1-0-1-6
Wm H. Robinson	0-0-1-0-0-5		Do Trustee for	
Robert Robinson	0-3-1-0-0-0		Mrs. Taylor	0-0-0-0-0-0
Miss M. C. Roots	0-2-0-0-0-0		Matthew Rust	0-1-1-0-0-1
John Reed	1-0-1-0-0-1		William A. Riely	0-4-1-0-1-11
John Rowland	0-1-2-0-0-8		Thos Reardan	0-0-2-0-0-1
Miss E. W.			Samuel Rutter	0-0-1-0-0-0
Royster	0-1-0-0-1-0		John D.	
Matthew W.			Richardson	0-11-1-0-1-15
Royston	0-0-1-0-0-3		John N. Ross	0-0-1-0-0-0
Reuben Reins	0-0-1-0-0-0		James Rose	1-0-1-0-0-0
Patrick Rodgers	0-0-1-0-0-0		James W. Ryan	0-2-1-0-0-4
John Rippon	0-0-1-0-0-1		Joseph F. Ryan	1-2-1-0-0-3
Peter K. Royston	0-0-1-0-0-1		Enos Richmond	0-0-0-0-0-0
Uriah B. Royston	0-0-1-0-0-2		Richmond &	
George R. Royston	0-0-1-0-0-0		Stolle	0-1-2-0-0-0
Miss Nancy			James F. Reynolds	0-0-1-0-0-1
Redman	0-1-0-0-0-0		Michael Ramey	1-0-0-0-0-0
George W. Rutter	0-0-1-0-0-0		Matthew T.	
Danl B. Richards	0-1-1-0-0-0		Royston	0-0-1-0-0-1
Charles H.			Bartholomew	
Richards	0-0-1-0-0-0		Russell	0-0-1-0-0-0
James H.			George W.	
Rowland	0-0-1-0-0-1		Rowland	0-0-1-0-0-0
Addison Romine	0-2-1-0-0-4		____ Ross	
George Reno	0-0-1-0-0-0		(Kimball)	0-0-1-0-0-0
Joseph Ross	0-0-1-0-0-0		Richard S.	
John Riely	0-0-1-0-0-2		Ridgeway	0-2-1-0-0-2
Wesley Russell	0-0-1-0-0-2			
Luster Riely	0-0-1-0-0-0		Col. T. Smith	0-15-3-0-2-19
Beverly Randolph	0-17-1-0-3-25		Do as Guardian	1-0-0-0-0-0
			Danl W. Sowers	2-10-1-0-1-26

Clarke County, Virginia Personal Property Tax Lists 1854-1870
1858

John W. Sprint	0-0-1-0-0-0	Saml Showers	0-1-1-0-0-0
F. L. Sowers	0-6-1-0-0-5	John Stonestreet	1-0-1-0-0-1
Mrs. Elizabeth Sowers	0-0-0-0-0-0	James R. Shepherd	0-0-1-0-0-0
John W. Sowers	0-8-1-0-2-18	John Shell	0-0-1-0-0-1
Wm B. Sowers	0-0-1-0-0-0	Stephen Shell	0-0-1-0-0-0
Wm Sowers	1-9-1-0-3-12	Craven Shell	0-0-1-0-0-0
Champ Shepherd	1-3-1-0-4-4	John H. P. Stone	0-0-1-0-0-1
Carter Shepherd	0-6-1-0-1-8	Simon R. Stump	0-0-1-0-0-1
Henry Shepherd	0-0-1-0-0-0	Dennis Sheheen	0-0-1-0-0-1
P. D. Shepherd	0-5-2-0-2-11	James W. Stephenson	0-4-1-0-0-6
Geo Smedley	0-0-1-0-0-0	Thos Sprint	0-0-1-0-0-0
Miss M. C. Shively	0-1-0-0-0-2	James Shackleford	0-0-1-0-0-0
Edwd J. & W. D. Smith	0-24-2-1-5-31	Joseph Shipe	0-0-1-0-0-0
Dr. P. Smith	0-18-2-0-4-25	Henry T. Shearer	1-0-1-0-0-0
Paul Smith	0-6-1-0-0-9	A. J. Shipe	0-0-1-0-0-0
D. C. Snyder	0-0-1-0-0-0	William G. Steel	0-0-1-0-0-0
Thos Shumate	1-4-1-0-1-10	James A. Steel	1-0-1-0-0-1
James W. Sowers	0-4-1-0-0-11	James H. Swain	0-0-1-0-0-2
James Sowers	0-1-1-0-1-7	Henry Stickles	0-0-1-0-0-0
Wm M. Sowers	0-1-1-0-0-8	Mrs. Susan Smith	0-1-0-0-1-0
Mrs. F. E. Sowers	0-5-1-0-0-12	Burr Smallwood	1-0-1-0-0-1
Danl H. Sowers	0-6-1-0-3-14	H. Slusher	0-1-1-0-0-0
Wm L. Smith	0-0-1-0-0-0	Mrs. Rebecca Smith	0-0-2-0-0-0
Charles H. Smith	0-0-1-0-0-2	Marcus L. Sinclair	0-0-1-0-0-0
Thos Smallwood	0-0-1-0-0-1	Mrs. Margt Swann	0-0-0-0-1-0
Geo R. Smith	0-0-1-0-0-0	John H. Stipe	0-0-1-0-0-0
Chas Swarts	0-0-1-0-0-0	George Smith	0-0-1-0-0-0
Wm R. Stewart	0-1-1-0-0-2	George D. Spaulding	0-0-1-0-1-0
L. J. Schooler	0-0-1-0-0-0	George W. Taylor	0-0-1-0-0-1
Jno Shafer	0-0-1-0-0-0	George W. Shultz	0-0-1-0-0-1
Jackson Shaffer	1-0-1-0-0-1	John H. Shoebridge	0-0-1-0-0-0
Simon Stickles	1-0-1-0-0-1		
Franklin Swartz	0-0-1-0-0-0		
James M. Shearer	0-0-1-0-0-0		
Wm Strother	1-2-1-0-2-6		
Kinlin Short [?]	0-0-1-0-0-0		
Charles Showers	0-0-1-0-1-0		

Clarke County, Virginia Personal Property Tax Lists 1854-1870
1858

Christopher H. Swartz	0-0-1-0-0-0		Dr. A. B. Tucker	0-9-1-0-0-9
Benjamin Shipe	0-0-1-0-0-0		Howard F. Thornton	0-0-1-0-0-3
George W. Shimp	0-0-1-0-0-1		Saln[?] M. Trussell	0-0-1-0-0-0
Shepherd & Castleman	0-5-0-0-0-9		Moses B. Trussell	0-4-1-0-0-8
John T. Shores	0-0-1-0-0-0		Wm Trenary	1-3-1-0-0-6
			Calvin Thacker	0-1-1-0-0-0
Mrs. S. Timberlake	0-4-0-0-5-8		Dr. Bushrod Taylor	0-2-1-0-0-3
			Isaac Talley	0-0-1-0-0-0
			Snoden Tomblin	0-0-1-0-0-1
John N. Shepherd	0-3-1-0-0-4		Alonzo Taylor	0-0-1-0-0-0
			Lewis Tapp	0-0-1-0-0-0
Barney Turbeck	0-0-1-0-0-0		Mason Tinsman	0-0-1-0-0-1
Newton Trenary	0-0-1-0-0-2		Isaac Tyson	0-7-1-0-2-10
John Taylor	0-0-1-0-0-0		Griffin Taylor	1-0-1-0-0-1
Adam F. Thompson	0-0-1-0-0-1		Ludwell Tinsman	0-0-1-0-0-1
James F. Thompson	0-0-1-0-0-0		William F. Thompson	0-0-1-0-0-1
Greenberry Thompson	0-0-1-0-0-1		James W. Tanquary	0-0-1-0-1-3
French Thompson	0-2-1-0-0-3		Boston Thompson	0-0-1-0-0-0
Baalis Thompson	0-0-1-0-0-5			
Benjn Thompson Jr.	0-0-1-0-0-0		Jacob Vanmetre	0-4-1-0-0-7
			Gerry Vaughn	1-0-2-0-0-2
Benjn Thompson Senr.	1-0-1-0-0-7		H. T. Wheat	1-5-1-0-2-10
Wm Thompson	0-0-1-0-0-0		B. F. Wilson	0-0-1-0-0-0
Wm N. Thompson	1-1-1-1-0-5		Jeremiah Wilson	0-0-1-0-0-0
John H. Taylor	0-0-1-0-0-0		John Wilson	1-0-1-0-0-0
Charles Trussell	0-2-1-0-0-4		F. B. Whiting	0-21-2-0-4-15
James W. Thompson	0-0-1-0-0-0		Wm H. Whiting	0-9-1-0-0-16
William Taylor	0-16-1-0-2-17		Francis H. Whiting	0-3-1-0-1-8
Robert Tapscott	0-0-1-0-0-0		Wm W. Whiting	0-5-1-0-1-8
Col. Jos Tuley	0-25-1-0-5-20		N. B. Whiting	0-7-1-0-1-14
Daniel Turner	0-0-1-0-0-1		Allen Williams	0-11-1-0-0-17
Mrs. Eliza Taylor	0-4-0-0-2-3		Gabriel Williams	0-0-0-0-0-1

Clarke County, Virginia Personal Property Tax Lists 1854-1870
1858

Thompson Writt	1-0-1-0-0-2	Lucinda	
Leroy P. Williams	0-6-1-0-2-9	Washington	0-2-0-0-0-0
E. P. Williams	0-0-01-0-0-1	Andrew	
Welch & Funk	0-0-0-0-0-3	Willingham	0-0-1-0-0-0
Wm Willingham	1-0-1-0-0-3	Saml G. Wyman	0-7-0-0-2-13
John F.		James W.	
Willingham	0-0-1-0-0-1	Wellington	0-0-1-0-0-1
Mrs. Nancy		Charles F.	
Willingham	0-0-0-0-0-0	Wellingham	0-0-1-0-0-0
Daniel Wade &		Jackson Wheeler	0-0-1-0-0-5
Bro	0-1-2-0-0-3	R. A. Webb	0-0-1-0-0-0
Hezekiah Wiley	0-0-1-0-0-0	Wm H. Young	1-0-1-0-0-1
Cornelius Wiley	0-0-1-0-0-1	Rev. Chas White	0-0-1-0-0-1
John Wiley	0-0-1-0-0-1	James L. Ward	1-0-0-0-0-0
Geo W. Wiley	0-0-1-0-0-2	Joseph H. Wilson	0-0-1-0-0-0
Sydnor B.		George T.	
Wyndham	0-1-1-0-0-3	Willingham	0-0-1-0-0-1
Thos C. Windham	0-0-1-0-0-0	Miss Alice Writt	0-0-0-0-0-0
James V. Weir	0-3-1-0-2-10	Obediah	
James Wiley	0-0-1-0-0-0	Willingham	0-0-1-0-0-0
Jos L. White	0-0-1-0-0-0	T. W. Wheat	0-0-1-0-0-0
Jacob Welch	1-0-1-0-0-5	Col. J. W. Ware	1-12-1-0-6-15
Jesse Wright	0-0-1-0-0-1	James H.	
Robt		Williams	0-0-1-0-0-1
Whittington	0-1-1-0-1-0	G. L. Ward	0-0-1-0-0-0
Alexander Wood	0-0-1-0-0-0	Isaac N. Writt	1-0-0-0-0-0
Jno C. Wheeler	0-0-1-0-0-1	Henry W. Wilson	0-0-2-0-0-0
Bennett Wood	1-0-1-0-0-1	James W.	
Walker B. Wilson	0-0-1-0-0-1	Willingham	
Simon Wilcox	0-0-1-0-0-0	(of Wm)	0-0-1-0-0-0
Wm Wood	0-0-1-0-0-0	James T. Wood	0-0-1-0-0-0
R. B. Welch	0-1-1-0-2-0		

Clarke County, Virginia Personal Property Tax Lists 1854-1870
1858

[Free Negroes]

Burwell Cook	0-0-0-1-0-0	Wm Toler	0-0-0-1-0-1
James Butler	0-0-0-1-0-0	Fielding Banks	0-0-0-1-0-0
Peter Coates	0-0-0-0-0-2	Jacob Webb	0-0-0-1-0-0
Mowen Harris	0-0-0-1-0-0	Wm Parker	0-0-0-1-0-0
Armstest		Nancy Parker	0-0-0-0-0-0
Dickens	0-0-0-1-0-0	George Ranson	0-0-0-1-0-0
Wm Allen	0-0-0-1-0-0	Thomas Ranson	0-0-0-1-0-0
Jack Blanam	0-0-0-1-0-0		

Clarke County, Virginia Personal Property Tax Lists 1854-1870

1859

1) Free male persons above the age of 16 years, 2) Slaves who have attained the age of 16 years, 3) White male inhabitants who have attained the age of 21 years, except those exempted from taxation on account of bodily infirmity, 4) Male free negroes between the ages of 21 and 55 years, 5) Slaves who have attained the age of 12 years, 6) Horses, mules, asses & jennets

Buckner Ashby	0-10-3-0-2-27	Austin C. Ashby	0-0-1-0-0-1
Mason Anderson	0-3-1-0-0-7	Eliz Ashby	1-0-0-0-0-0
John H. Anderson	0-0-1-0-0-0	Levi Athey	0-0-1-0-0-0
Milton B. Anderson	0-2-1-0-0-6	Lewis B. Ashby	0-0-1-0-0-0
James M. Allen	0-4-1-0-2-8	George Anderson	0-0-1-0-0-1
Jesse Allen	0-0-1-0-0-0	Daniel T. Armstrong	0-0-1-0-0-0
Edgar Allen	0-10-1-0-4-14	Walter Anderson	0-0-1-0-0-0
John Alexander	0-21-2-0-3-31		
N. F. & J. E. Anderson	0-2-2-0-0-6	Dr. R. S. Blackburn	0-6-1-0-1-6
N. F. Anderson	0-0-0-0-0-0	H. W. Brabham	0-0-1-0-0-0
Robert Ashby Jr.	0-0-1-0-0-0	George H. Burwell	0-52-2-0-4-52
Robert Ashby Sr.	0-0-1-0-0-1	D° Trustee	
Nimrod Ashby	0-0-1-0-0-0	Wm Hay	0-0-0-0-0-0
Capt. G. B. Ashby	0-0-1-0-0-0	Nathaniel Burwell	0-16-1-0-2-40
James Allison	0-0-1-0-0-0	John Burchell	0-6-2-0-1-12
George W. Ashby	0-1-1-0-0-4	A. J. Berlin	0-0-1-0-0-0
George W. Allen	0-3-1-0-0-6	Wm O. Brown	0-0-1-0-0-0
Wm T. Allen	0-9-1-0-0-10	Henry C. Briggs	0-0-1-0-0-0
A. S. Allen	1-8-2-1-2-13	George H. Bell	0-0-1-0-0-0
John Allison	0-0-1-0-0-0	Hiram O. Bell	0-3-1-0-0-6
Thos H. Alexander	0-1-1-0-0-5	Squire Bell	0-0-1-0-0-1
William Asbury	0-0-1-0-0-0	Hector Ball	0-0-1-0-0-3
John Avis	1-0-1-0-0-0	Lewis Berlin	0-2-1-0-0-0
Mrs. Nancy Allen	0-0-0-0-0-0	Philip Berlin	0-4-1-0-0-6
Margarett E. Alexander	0-0-0-0-0-0	George W. Berlin	0-0-1-0-1-0

Clarke County, Virginia Personal Property Tax Lists 1854-1870
1859

George C.			Peter Bennett	0-0-1-0-0-2
Blakemore	0-7-1-0-1-12		Patrick Brady	0-0-1-0-0-6
James Bell Senr.	0-0-1-0-0-3		George W. Bolen	0-0-1-0-0-0
Thos Briggs Jr.			Thos J. Bragg	0-0-1-0-0-2
Est.	0-2-0-0-0-7		Robert W. Briggs	0-4-1-0-1-5
J. C. & H. C. Briggs	0-7-2-0-0-10		Wm Briggs	0-0-1-0-1-0
Jno S. Briggs	0-0-1-0-0-1		George S. Bonham	0-0-0-0-0-0
Arthur Briggs	0-0-1-0-0-3		Enoch L. Brown	0-0-1-0-0-0
Margarett			Charles Bailes	0-0-1-0-0-0
Burchell	0-4-0-0-2-4		Charles Brabham	0-0-1-0-0-0
Jno Bromley	0-2-2-0-0-10		Wm Brabham	0-0-1-0-0-0
John W. Byrd	0-2-2-0-2-10		John T. Barr	0-0-1-0-0-0
Christian Bowser	0-1-1-0-0-0		Samuel Bromley	0-0-1-0-0-7
George Bromley	0-2-1-0-0-5		A. J. Billmyre	0-0-1-0-0-3
Susan R. Burwell	0-7-0-0-0-2		Mrs. Mary Bowser	0-0-0-0-0-0
Joseph B. Beavers	0-0-1-0-0-1		Miss Amelia Burns	0-0-0-0-0-1
Ann C. Benn	0-1-0-0-0-2		Dr. Wm A.	
Daniel S. Bonham	2-4-1-0-6-9		Bradford	1-6-2-0-3-12
Samuel Bonham	0-3-1-0-0-10		Henry Brown	0-0-1-0-0-0
Wm Berry	0-9-1-0-4-7		Jno W. Benn	0-0-1-0-0-0
Juliett Boyston	1-0-0-0-0-0		James Bell Jr.	0-0-1-0-0-0
Nancy Boyston	0-0-0-0-0-0		J. H. Bitzer	0-1-1-0-0-5
Dr. H. T. Benton	0-3-1-0-0-2		Neill Barnette	1-8-1-0-1-12
Richard S. Bryarly	0-7-2-0-2-11		D° Trustee for	
Miss Mary E.			Wm Berlin	0-2-1-0-0-0
Bouser	0-0-0-0-0-0			
Abraham Beavers	1-0-1-0-0-3		Alfred Castleman	2-8-2-0-1-15
Adam Barr	0-0-1-0-0-0		Chas D.	
Jesse Butler	0-0-1-0-0-0		Castleman	0-1-1-0-0-3
James Brown	0-0-1-0-0-0		Wm A. Castleman	0-5-1-0-0-4
George W. Board	0-0-1-0-0-2		Ury Castleman	0-0-1-0-0-1
George Beard [?]	0-0-1-0-0-0		James Chisholm	0-0-1-0-0-0
Middleton Bowen	0-1-1-0-0-1		Wm Carper	0-0-1-0-0-2
Miss Emily Bell	0-0-0-0-0-1		George W. Cooper	
J. C. Bartlett	1-3-2-0-2-12		(S. Bridge)	0-0-1-0-0-0
Jonah P. Bell	0-2-1-0-0-3		Robt A. Colston	0-5-1-0-0-9
Thomas Brown	0-0-1-0-0-0		John Copenhaver	0-4-2-0-0-12
George H. Brown	0-0-1-0-0-0		John H. Crebs	0-3-1-0-0-8
Alfred Bishop	0-0-1-0-0-0		John K. Carter	0-2-1-0-0-6

Clarke County, Virginia Personal Property Tax Lists 1854-1870
1859

Chas J. Carter	0-2-1-0-1-4	Michael Crim	0-0-1-0-0-0
Jno A. Carter	0-1-1-0-0-6	Mrs. Hannah Cain	0-0-0-0-0-0
John W. Carter	0-0-1-0-0-0	Wm J. Chamblin	1-1-1-0-0-4
Parkerson Corder	0-0-1-0-0-1	Wm M. Chapman	1-0-0-0-0-0
Thomas Carter	0-3-0-0-1-6	James Carter	0-0-1-0-0-1
Wm G. Carter	0-1-1-0-0-1	Franklin B. Carter	0-1-1-0-0-5
Jno H. Crebs Trustee		Charles R. Corder	0-0-1-0-0-0
P. Cain	0-0-2-0-0-5	James Carroll	0-0-1-0-0-0
Wm H. Carter	0-0-1-0-0-1	Wm Carroll	0-0-1-0-0-0
Dr. R. T. Colston	1-7-0-0-1-22	George W.	
James H. Clarke	0-3-1-0-1-1	Cooper	0-0-1-0-0-0
Thomas H. Crow	2-5-1-0-1-8	Elizabeth K.	
John Carroll	0-0-1-0-0-0	Carter	0-0-0-0-0-0
John Cooper	0-0-1-0-0-1	Resin Carroll	0-0-1-0-0-0
Lewis Carroll	0-0-1-0-0-1	James Canter	0-0-1-0-0-5
Thomas Carrell	0-0-1-0-0-1	John B. Carter	0-2-1-0-0-2
Isaac Correll	0-0-1-0-0-0	Benj F. Crawford	0-0-1-0-0-0
Samuel A.		Miss Mariam	
Campbell	0-0-1-0-0-0	Catlet	0-6-1-0-1-12
Andrew Conrell	0-0-1-0-0-1	John R. Crockwell	0-0-1-0-0-0
Michael		Stephen D.	
Copenhaver	0-0-1-0-0-1	Castleman	0-0-0-0-0-0
John N. Collier	0-0-1-0-0-3		
Lucy A. Calmese	0-4-2-0-2-4	Washington	
Ann B. Cooke	0-16-0-0-1-16	Dearmont	1-0-2-0-1-9
John P. Carrigan	0-0-1-0-0-0	William Deahl	0-1-2-0-0-1
Catherine		James W. Doran	0-0-1-0-0-2
Castleman	0-3-0-0-0-2	James Doran	1-0-1-0-0-1
Robt H.		John Drish	1-0-1-0-0-1
Castleman	0-3-1-0-1-10	John Donevan	0-0-1-0-0-0
James N. Corbin	0-0-1-0-0-3	Thomas Duke	0-0-1-0-0-1
Benj Crampton	1-0-0-0-0-0	George W.	
Frank Caniford	0-0-1-0-0-0	Diffendaffer	0-0-1-0-0-1
James E.		Hugh Davis	0-0-1-0-0-0
Chamblin	0-0-1-0-0-0	Aaron Duble	0-0-1-0-0-2
Miss Sallie Cloud	0-3-0-0-0-0	Rev. H. W. Dodge	0-2-1-0-1-1
Miss E. Clink	0-0-0-0-0-0	J. W. Denney	1-0-0-0-0-0
Henry Caniford	0-0-1-0-0-0	John D. Davis	0-1-1-0-0-0
Eliza Crimm	0-0-0-0-0-0		

Clarke County, Virginia Personal Property Tax Lists 1854-1870
1859

Wm		John Foreman	0-0-1-0-0-0
Donodhue [sic]	0-0-1-0-0-0	Thomas Fowler	0-0-1-0-0-3
Michael Drislane	0-1-1-0-0-0	Robert Feltner	0-0-1-0-0-4
L. L. & A. Davis	0-1-0-0-0-0	Martin Feltner	1-0-1-0-0-1
Wm Dorherty	0-0-1-0-0-1	Dennis Fenton	0-0-1-0-0-1
Jeremiah Dailey	0-0-1-0-0-0	Marcus R. Feeher	0-2-1-0-1-3
		Thomas G. Flagg	0-0-1-0-0-0
Jacob Enders	0-8-1-0-1-10	George W. Fiddler	0-0-1-0-0-0
Henry Edwards	0-0-1-0-0-3	John A. Finnell	0-0-1-0-1-0
Wm G. Everhart	1-2-2-0-0-9	Joshua Fellows	0-0-1-0-0-2
Henson Elliott	1-2-2-0-2-10	Christian Fonda	0-0-1-0-0-0
Elliott & Parker	0-0-0-0-0-0	Jerry Foley	0-0-1-0-0-0
A. M. Earle	0-5-1-0-1-14	Enoch Furr	0-0-1-0-0-0
Jacob W.		B. R. Foley	1-1-1-0-0-1
Everhart	0-0-1-0-0-1	Thomas Forest [?]	0-0-1-0-0-0
Wm H. Edwards	0-0-1-0-1-1	Daniel Furr	0-0-1-0-0-0
Albert Elsea	0-0-1-0-0-4	Joseph W. Feltner	0-0-1-0-0-0
Joseph W.		John Franks	0-0-1-0-0-0
Edwards	0-0-1-0-0-0	Barny Fairlack	0-0-1-0-0-0
John Elliott	0-1-1-0-0-6	Franklin Frank	0-0-1-0-0-0
J. N. Elsea	0-0-1-0-0-12		
Thos A. Everhart	0-0-1-0-0-2	John L. Grant	0-2-1-0-0-4
John C. Elliott	0-0-1-0-0-0	J. J. Gordon	0-4-1-0-1-13
		James W.	
Dr. O. R. Funsten	0-19-1-0-4-30	Galloway	0-0-1-0-0-0
D. J. F. Fauntleroy	0-5-1-0-0-6	Thomas W.	
James A. Forster	0-5-1-0-0-6	Griffith	0-0-1-0-0-0
Josiah Ferguson	0-2-1-0-0-4	James F. Green	0-3-1-0-0-7
Wm M. Ferguson	0-0-1-0-0-2	Mary Green	0-3-0-0-1-0
Edward Franks	0-0-1-0-0-0	Richard N. Green	0-5-1-0-0-7
Ephraim Furr	0-0-1-0-0-0	John S. Green	0-2-1-0-0-9
Johnson Furr	0-0-1-0-1-5	Thomas E. Gold	0-10-1-0-2-19
Israel Fiddle	0-0-1-0-0-0	George W.	
Elizabeth Fleming	0-2-0-0-0-4	Gordon	0-1-1-0-0-10
Wm Fowler Junr.	0-0-1-0-0-0	John S. Gordon	1-0-1-0-1-0
James Furr	0-0-1-0-0-1	Mrs. Isabella	
Joseph Fleming	1-0-1-0-0-6	Glass	0-1-0-0-0-0
Wm Fowler Senr.	0-0-1-0-0-2	Stepen [sic] J.	
Everett Fowler	0-0-1-0-0-0	Gant	0-2-1-0-0-3

72

Clarke County, Virginia Personal Property Tax Lists 1854-1870
1859

Samuel Grubbs Sr.	0-0-1-0-0-0	Wm Heflin	0-0-1-0-0-0
Henry N. Grigsby	0-5-1-0-1-11	Dr. J. A. Haines	0-5-1-0-0-4
Lewis F. Glass	0-6-1-0-0-11	Dr. Wm Hay	0-4-1-0-2-2
Martin Gant	0-6-1-0-1-9	J. M. & I. J. Hite	1-8-2-0-0-15
Wm Gibbs	0-0-1-0-0-0	Charles F. Hennis	0-0-1-0-0-0
Wm B. Grubbs	0-0-1-0-0-1	Samuel Heflebower	0-6-1-0-2-14
George W. Grubbs	0-0-1-0-0-0	Charles W. Hardesty	0-2-1-0-1-5
Samuel Grubbs Jr.	0-0-1-0-0-0	A. D. Hardesty	0-2-1-0-0-6
John M. Grubbs	0-0-1-0-0-0	Wm G. Hardesty	0-2-1-0-0-9
John Gruber	0-2-1-0-0-10	James M. Hardesty	0-2-1-0-1-6
George Gardiner	0-0-1-0-0-0	Cornelius Hoff	0-0-1-0-0-0
Andrew E. Gibson	1-0-0-0-0-0	Blackwell Holtsclaw	0-0-1-0-0-0
Thornton K. Glover	0-0-1-0-0-0	Jackson Hoff	0-0-1-0-0-0
Wm Grubbs of Thornberry	0-0-1-0-0-1	George Hansucker	0-1-1-0-0-4
T. M. Grigsby	1-0-0-0-0-0	John Hughes	1-0-1-0-1-1
Matthew Grimes	0-0-1-0-0-1	Thomas Hughes	0-0-1-0-0-1
Thomas E. Gibson	0-0-1-0-0-0	Wm B. Harris	0-10-1-0-0-12
Charles Grubbs	0-0-1-0-0-0	John Henry	0-0-1-0-0-0
Phillip Gorden	0-0-1-0-0-4	Dr. B. Harrison	0-14-1-0-1-24
Curtis Brady	0-0-1-0-0-0	Henry Huntsberry	0-2-1-0-0-6
J. W. & M. L. Grantham	0-2-1-0-0-3	Catherin B. Hall	0-8-0-0-0-12
Elizabeth Glover	0-1-0-0-0-0	John Henry (Wht Post)	0-0-1-0-0-0
Samuel Huyett	0-3-1-0-0-10	James F. Howell	0-0-1-0-0-0
John Huyett	0-0-1-0-0-0	John W. Hibbard	0-0-1-0-0-0
Abraham Huyett	0-0-1-0-0-2	W. R. Helvestine	0-1-1-0-0-0
Elizabeth Hansucker	0-0-0-0-0-0	A. T. M. Hough	0-0-1-0-0-2
Henry D. Hooe	0-1-1-0-0-0	George & J. T. Harris	0-5-2-1-1-8
James H. Hooe	0-0-1-0-0-0	John Hummer	0-0-1-0-0-1
Robt & George Hooe	0-2-2-0-0-5	Jacob Heflebower	0-7-1-0-1-14
Wm Hummer	0-0-0-0-0-1	Henry Huyett	0-2-1-0-0-10
E. T. Hancock	0-5-1-0-2-12	Daniel Hart	0-0-1-0-0-0
		James Henry	0-0-1-0-0-0

Clarke County, Virginia Personal Property Tax Lists 1854-1870
1859

Cornelius Hawk	0-0-1-0-0-0		Andrew Jackson	0-0-1-0-0-0
T. L. Humphrey	0-3-1-0-0-4		Armstead M.	
D° Exr D. Trislers			Johnson	0-1-1-0-0-5
Est	0-0-0-0-0-0		Amelia A. Jordan	0-1-0-0-0-1
Edward C.			Rev. Wm	
Harrison	0-1-1-0-0-2		Johnston	0-3-1-0-0-1
Joseph R.			Wm B. Jolliff	0-0-1-0-0-0
Hardesty	0-1-1-2-0-9		Edward Jenkins	0-0-1-0-0-0
James Hayden	0-0-1-0-0-0		Rev. Joseph R.	
John Heflin	0-0-1-0-0-0		Jones	0-2-1-0-0-1
James W.				
Hummer	0-0-1-0-0-1		John N. Kimmell	0-0-1-0-0-1
Henry A. Hibbard	0-0-1-0-0-0		James F. Kerfoot	0-3-1-0-0-9
J. B. Hawthorn	0-0-1-0-0-3		Dr. F. J. Kerfoot	0-8-1-0-1-12
J. W.			Wm C. Kerfoot	1-10-1-0-3-14
Hudsleth [sic]	0-0-1-0-0-1		Judson J. Kerfoot	0-4-1-0-0-11
John W. Holland	0-0-1-0-0-0		George Knight	0-8-3-0-0-19
John & Thos			Middleton Keeler	0-0-1-0-0-0
Heskitt	0-0-2-0-0-0		Jacob Kriser	1-0-1-0-0-6
Chas B. Hancock	0-0-1-0-0-1		Samuel G. Kneller	1-4-1-0-1-9
			Wm C. Kennerly	0-4-1-0-2-1
George H. Isler	0-0-1-0-0-2		Wm B. Kennan	0-0-1-0-0-0
			Joseph McK.	
Solomon R.			Kennerly	0-7-1-0-2-15
Jackson	0-0-1-0-0-0		Dr. C. B. R.	
Herod Jenkins	1-0-1-0-0-2		Kennerly	0-4-0-0-1-6
Matthew Jones	0-2-1-0-2-3		Joseph Kline	0-0-1-0-0-0
John Joliff	0-5-1-0-0-10		Dr. R. Kownsler	0-6-1-0-0-5
John S. Johnston	0-1-1-0-0-5		John Kelly	1-0-1-0-0-0
Leonard Jones	0-3-1-0-0-4		E. V. Kercheral	0-0-1-0-1-0
Thomas Jones	1-2-1-0-0-8		James H. Kennan	0-0-1-0-0-0
George Johnston	0-2-1-0-0-3		Henry Kromlling	0-2-1-0-0-2
Dr. J. J. Janney	0-3-1-0-0-4		Harrison Kent	0-0-1-0-0-0
Thomas Jenkins	0-0-1-0-0-3		John Kean	0-0-1-0-0-0
James W.			James M. Kiger	0-0-1-0-0-3
Johnston	0-0-1-0-0-0		John N. Kitchen	0-1-1-0-0-7
William Johnston				
W. Post	0-0-1-0-0-0		John B. Laurue	0-13-3-0-2-31
Wm A. Jackson	0-6-1-0-0-12		John D. Laurue	0-6-1-0-1-11

Clarke County, Virginia Personal Property Tax Lists 1854-1870
1859

Edward Lewis	0-4-1-0-0-6	John Morgan	0-9-1-0-2-7
John T.		D° as Guardian	
Longerbeam	0-0-1-0-0-0	for Children	0-0-0-0-0-0
A. L. P. Laurue	0-5-1-0-0-9	Dr. C. & S.	
James W. Laurue	0-7-1-0-2-8	McCormick	1-22-2-0-1-32
C. C. Laurue	0-0-1-0-0-1	Thomas	
Squire Lee	0-0-1-0-0-3	McCormick	0-12-1-0-1-12
Christopher Lee	0-0-1-0-0-2	Samuel	
Dr. James M.		McCormick	0-1-1-0-0-0
Linsey	1-1-1-0-0-2	John A.	
Joseph B. Linsey	0-0-1-0-0-1	McCormick	0-0-1-0-0-0
Miss Emily		James	
Littleton	0-2-1-0-0-4	McCormick	0-3-1-0-0-8
Wm Littleton	0-0-1-0-0-3	Dr. Hugh McGuire	0-0-0-0-0-5
John W. Littleton	0-0-1-0-0-3	Ottaway	
James W. Lee	0-0-1-0-0-2	McCormick	0-6-1-0-1-9
Henry Lloyd	0-0-1-0-0-4	Peter McMurray	0-2-1-0-0-7
John Lloyd	1-0-1-0-0-1	A. R. Milton	1-4-1-0-2-7
James L. Lloyd	0-0-1-0-0-1	Sylvanus P.	
David Lloyd	0-0-1-0-0-0	Moore	0-0-1-0-0-1
John A. Lloyd	0-0-1-0-0-0	L. D. Maddox	0-0-1-0-0-1
Samuel Lloyd	0-0-1-0-0-0	James Mitchell	1-3-1-0-0-7
Moses Lewin	0-0-1-0-0-1	Dr. Wm D.	
John Lock Sr.	0-2-1-0-0-9	McGuire	0-11-1-0-2-9
Howard Lock	0-0-1-0-0-1	David H. McGuire	0-6-2-0-1-6
Thomas Landon	0-0-1-0-0-0	Wm G. Morris	0-0-1-0-0-0
		Alexander	
Francis B. Meade	0-8-1-1-1-16	Marshall	2-2-1-0-0-9
P. N. Meade	0-9-1-0-1-18	John Marshall	0-4-2-0-1-12
John N. Meade	0-4-1-0-0-6	Mrs. Susan	
E. B. Manter	0-1-1-0-0-1	Marshall	0-6-0-0-0-5
W. W. Meade	0-0-1-0-0-0	C. C. McIntyre	0-6-1-0-1-11
R. K. Meade	1-4-1-0-0-2	Nathaniel Mercer	0-0-1-0-0-3
Do as Trustee	0-0-0-0-0-0	James Murphy	0-1-1-0-0-1
David Meade	0-4-1-0-1-9	Stephen Marlow	1-0-1-0-0-2
N. B. Meade	0-4-1-0-3-7	A. M. Moore	2-5-1-0-1-12
Miss Mary		Alfred P. Moore	0-0-1-0-0-0
Meade	0-4-0-0-1-0	Samuel Moreland	1-0-1-0-0-5
Col. B. Morgan	0-28-2-0-1-34	George Marpole	0-0-1-0-0-1

Clarke County, Virginia Personal Property Tax Lists 1854-1870
1859

Moses G. Miley	0-0-1-0-0-5		Joseph E. Mason	0-0-1-0-0-1
E. W. Massey	0-7-1-0-2-12		Joseph R. Moore	0-0-1-0-1-0
Henry Mason	0-0-1-0-0-0		Rev. Wm Meade	0-0-1-0-0-0
James McClaughry	1-0-1-0-0-2		Province McCormick Sr. [?]	0-12-1-0-2-15
Samuel T. Marts	0-0-1-0-0-1		D° Trustee for E. H. McCormick	0-0-0-0-0-0
McLane Mc Clingen	0-0-1-0-0-1		D° " Ann Stribling	
Alfred Marts	0-0-1-0-0-2		D° " Ebin Frost	
Richard Morgan	0-0-1-0-0-4		D° guard for Elijah McCormick	
Patrick Murray	0-0-1-0-0-0		D° Agnt M. Stribling	
Benj A. May	0-0-1-0-0-0		Edward McCormick	0-12-1-0-7-20
J. F. Billmeyer	0-0-1-0-0-0		S. J. C. Moore	0-4-1-0-0-1
James T. Murphy	0-0-1-0-0-0			
Joseph Moore	0-0-1-0-0-0			
John McMurrey	0-0-1-0-0-0		Hugh M. Nelson	0-11-1-0-2-19
Col. Frank McCormick	0-15-1-0-4-18		Thomas F. Nelson	0-10-1-0-2-18
Addison Munsal	0-0-1-0-0-0		Col. Wm N. Nelson	0-4-1-0-0-16
A. J. Morris	0-0-1-0-0-0		James H. Neville	0-1-1-0-0-0
Edward C. Marshall	0-4-1-0-2-7		Philip W. Nelson	0-10-1-0-5-12
			Miss A. & R. Nelson	0-3-0-0-0-0
Garret McDonald	1-1-1-0-0-6			
Henry McDonald	0-0-1-0-0-1		John B. Norris	0-4-1-0-1-4
Mrs. Jane McDonald	0-0-0-0-0-0		John R. Nunn	0-5-1-0-2-6
A. J. Maddex	0-0-1-0-0-1		D° Guard for M. Dix	
Benjn Morgan Guard for Miss Alexander			D° " G. W. Carter	
D° [Gdn for] Jno & Wm Alexander			James H. Neuman	0-0-1-0-0-1
			Dr. S. S. Neille	0-4-1-0-1-6
Charles McDonald	0-0-1-0-0-0		Wm Nicewaner Haden [?] Newman	0-1-2-0-0-6 0-0-1-0-0-0
Thomas Murphy	0-0-1-0-0-0		Matthew Pulliam	0-1-1-0-2-0
John Murphy	0-0-1-0-0-0		George ORear	0-2-1-0-1-4
John G. McCauley	0-0-1-0-0-1		Benjamin ORear	0-8-1-0-0-4
David Meade Trustee	0-3-0-0-0-4		Elizabeth ORear	0-10-0-0-1-9
			Hugh ORouke	0-0-1-0-0-0
John Morgan Jr.	0-3-1-0-0-4		Overseers of Poor	1-0-1-0-0-4

Clarke County, Virginia Personal Property Tax Lists 1854-1870
1859

John B. Oliver	0-0-1-0-0-0	Bennett Russel	2-10-2-0-0-10
David Osburn	0-0-1-0-0-1	S. L. Rose	0-0-1-0-0-0
Wm OFarrell	0-0-1-0-0-1	Thomas W. Russel	0-1-1-0-0-3
Samuel Pigeon	0-0-1-1-0-9	Michael Russel	0-0-1-0-0-1
Dr. M. Pages Est.	0-4-0-0-0-1	Wm H. Robinson	0-2-1-0-0-7
John E. Page	0-19-1-0-1-23	M. C. Root	0-0-0-0-1-0
S. R. Page	0-25-0-0-13-26	John Reed	1-0-1-0-0-1
Conrad Pope	2-0-1-0-0-1	John Roland	0-0-2-0-0-7
Archy C. Page	0-6-1-0-0-15	Miss E. W. Royster	0-0-0-0-1-0
John Page Junr.	0-9-1-0-2-13		
Alexander Parkins	0-0-1-0-0-1	Matthew W. Royston	0-0-1-0-0-3
Mann R. Page	1-8-1-0-3-16		
George R. Page	0-3-1-0-0-7	Reuben Rains	0-0-1-0-0-0
John Pierce Senr.	0-4-1-0-1-9	Patrick Rodgers	0-0-1-0-0-1
A. N. Pierce [?]	0-3-1-0-1-9	John Rippon	0-0-1-0-0-1
Peter McPierce	0-4-1-0-1-11	Peter K. Royston	0-0-1-0-0-1
Paul Pierce	0-8-1-0-1-7	Uriah B. Royston	0-0-1-0-0-2
Mrs. E. M. Page	0-6-0-0-1-0	George R. Royston	0-0-1-0-0-0
James F. Pine	1-0-1-0-0-3		
John Poston	0-0-1-0-0-3	Nancy Redman	0-1-0-0-0-0
Thornton P. Pendleton	0-12-1-0-1-12	George W. Rutter	0-0-1-0-0-0
Pendleton & Richardson	0-0-0-0-0-1	Daniel B. Richards	0-1-1-0-0-0
W. F. Padgett	2-0-1-0-0-0	Chas H. Richards	0-0-1-0-0-0
Wm Pyles	1-0-1-0-0-0	James H. Roland	0-0-1-0-0-1
Benjamin F. Perry	0-0-1-0-0-0	Addison Romaine	0-2-1-0-0-4
John Patterson	2-0-1-0-0-7	George Reno	0-0-1-0-0-0
James F. Payne	0-0-1-0-0-1	John Reily	0-0-1-0-0-0
Barnett Pritchard	0-0-1-0-0-0	Wesley Russel	0-0-1-0-0-2
Michael Pope	0-0-1-0-0-1	Justin Rieley [?]	0-0-1-0-0-0
Pulliam & Howell	0-1-1-0-0-1	Beverly Randolph	0-16-1-0-2-27
Phillip H. Powers	0-7-1-0-2-12	Dr. R. C. Randolph	0-20-1-0-3-31
Thomas N. Pyle	0-0-1-0-0-1	Archy C. Randolph	0-0-1-0-1-2
Richard Parker	0-1-0-0-0-0	Thomas W. Reynolds	0-0-1-0-0-0
Lewis Peacock	0-0-1-0-0-0	John Reynolds	0-1-1-0-0-1-0
John M. Pope	0-0-1-0-0-0	Wm Reiley	0-0-1-0-0-0
		Michael Ramey	0-0-1-0-0-0

Clarke County, Virginia Personal Property Tax Lists 1854-1870
1859

Matthew Rust	0-1-1-0-1-0		George Smedley	0-0-1-0-0-0
John J. Reily	0-4-1-0-1-8		Wm L. Smith	0-0-1-0-0-0
D° Trustee for			Mary C. Shiveley	0-1-0-0-0-3
Mrs. Taylor	0-0-0-0-0-0		E. J. & Wm Smith	0-24-2-1-8-35
Wm A. Reiley	0-4-1-0-2-10		Dr. P. Smith	0-14-1-0-2-22
Thomas Reardon	0-0-2-0-0-1		Paul Smith	1-5-1-0-0-10
Samuel Rutter	0-0-1-0-0-0		Daniel C. Snyder	0-0-1-0-0-0
John D.			Thomas Shumate	1-3-1-0-1-9
Richardson	0-10-1-0-1-17		James Sowers	0-0-1-0-1-7
John N. Ross	0-0-1-0-0-0		James W. Sowers	0-4-1-0-1-12
James W. Ryan	0-2-1-0-0-5		Wm M. Sowers	0-0-1-0-0-10
Aenas Richmond	0-0-0-0-0-0		Francis E. Sowers	0-5-1-0-0-9
J. F. Ryan	1-2-1-0-0-4		Daniel H. Sowers	0-8-1-0-0-14
Richmond & Stale	1-0-2-0-0-0		Charles H. Smith	0-0-1-0-0-1
James F. Reynolds	0-0-1-0-0-2		Thos Smallwood	0-0-1-0-0-1
John Ramey	0-0-1-0-0-0		George R. Smith	0-0-1-0-0-0
M. T. Royston	0-0-1-0-0-1		Charles Swartz	0-0-1-0-0-0
Res. at Kimballs	0-0-1-0-0-0		Wm R. Stewart	0-1-1-0-0-2
Richd S. Ridgeway	0-2-1-0-0-7		L. J. Schuyler	0-0-1-0-0-0
John Rutter	0-0-1-0-0-8		John Shaffer	0-0-1-0-0-0
John Russell	0-0-1-0-0-4		Jackson Shaffer	1-0-1-0-0-1
Jane C. Randolph	0-1-1-0-0-0		Simon Stickle	2-0-1-0-0-2
Samuel Rescer [?]	0-0-1-0-0-0		Franklin Swartz	0-0-1-0-0-0
Daniel T. Richards	0-0-1-0-0-1		James M.	
N. W. Royston	0-0-1-0-0-0		Shearer	0-0-1-0-0-0
			Wm Strother	1-3-1-0-1-5
Col. T. Smith	0-18-3-0-2-24		Chas Showers	0-2-1-0-0-2
D° Guard T.			Samuel Showers	0-0-1-0-0-0
Smith Jr.	0-0-0-0-0-0		James R.	
Daniel W. Sowers	1-13-2-0-1-27		Shepherd	0-0-1-0-0-0
John W. Sprint	0-0-1-0-1-0		John Shell	0-0-1-0-0-1
Fielding J. Sowers	0-6-1-0-0-8		Stephen Shell	0-0-1-0-0-1
Elizabeth Sowers	0-0-0-0-0-0		Craven Shell	0-0-1-0-0-0
John W. Sowers	0-7-1-0-4-19		Simon R. Stump	0-0-1-0-0-2
Wm Sowers	0-9-1-0-3-14		Dennis Shehan	0-0-1-0-0-1
Champ Shepherd	2-3-1-0-3-4		J. W. Stephenson	0-4-1-0-0-9
Carter Shepherd	0-6-1-0-0-9		Thomas Sprint	0-0-1-0-0-0
Henry Shepherd	0-0-1-0-0-0		James	
P. D. Shepherd	0-5-1-0-1-13		Shackleford	0-1-0-0-0-0

Clarke County, Virginia Personal Property Tax Lists 1854-1870
1859

Joseph Shipe	0-0-1-0-0-0		
Henry T. Shearer	0-0-1-0-0-0	George W. Taylor	0-0-1-0-0-1
A. J. Shipe	0-0-1-0-0-0	Mrs. Sarah Timberlake	0-5-0-0-2-12
Wm G. Steel	0-0-1-0-0-0	Newton Trinary	0-0-1-0-0-1
James A. Steel	1-0-1-0-0-1	James Thomas	0-0-1-0-0-0
James H. Swain	0-0-1-0-0-0	Adam Thompson	0-0-1-0-0-1
Henry Stickls [sic]	0-0-1-0-0-0	James F. Thompson	0-0-1-0-0-0
Susan Smith	0-2-0-0-1-0	Greenberry Thompson	0-0-1-0-0-1
Bourbon Smallwood	1-0-1-0-0-1	French Thompson	1-2-1-0-1-3
Henry Slusher	0-1-1-0-0-1	Baylis Thompson	0-0-1-0-0-5
Rebecca A. Smith	0-0-1-0-0-0	Benj Thompson Jr.	0-0-1-0-0-4
Marcus T. Sinclair	0-0-1-0-0-0	Benj Thompson Sr.	0-0-1-0-0-0
Margarette Swann	0-0-0-0-1-0	Wm N. Thompson	2-1-1-0-0-4
John H. Stipe	0-0-1-0-0-0	John H. Taylor	0-0-1-0-0-0
George R. Smith	0-0-1-0-0-0	Wm Taylor	0-15-1-0-4-18
George D. Spaulding	0-0-1-0-0-0	Charles Trussell	0-2-1-0-0-5
Christian H. Swartz	0-0-1-0-0-0	Robert Tapscott	0-0-1-0-1-0
John H. Shoebridge	0-0-1-0-0-1	Col. Joseph Tuley	0-29-1-0-7-22
Benj Shipe	0-0-1-0-1-0	Daniel Turner	0-0-1-0-0-0
George W. Shimp	0-0-1-0-0-1	Mrs. Eliza Taylor	0-4-0-0-2-2
Shepherd & Castleman	0-5-0-0-0-12	Howard F. Thornton	0-3-1-0-1-2
John T. Shores	0-0-1-0-0-0	Samuel M. Trussell	0-2-1-0-0-8
George W. Shultz	0-0-1-0-0-1	Wm Trinary	0-2-2-0-0-3
Mrs. S. E. T. Stribling	0-12-1-0-3-17	Calvin Thatcher	0-1-1-0-0-0
Montgomery Shell	0-0-1-0-0-0	Dr. Bush Taylor	0-2-1-0-0-2
Isaac N. Shepherd	0-0-1-0-0-1	Isaac Tally Snowden	0-0-1-0-0-0
George Sford [sic]	0-0-1-0-0-0	Tumblin	0-0-1-0-0-2
Wm F. Stall	0-0-0-0-0-0	Alonzo Taylor	0-0-1-0-0-0
Treadwell Smith Jr.	1-0-0-0-0-0	Mason Tinsman	0-0-1-0-0-2
Rev. H. Suter	0-3-1-0-0-1	Isaac Tyson	0-0-1-0-0-13
		Griffin Taylor	1-0-1-0-0-0
		Ludwell Tinsman	0-0-1-0-0-1
		Wm F. Thompson	0-0-1-0-0-1

Clarke County, Virginia Personal Property Tax Lists 1854-1870
1859

Name	Values	Name	Values
James W. Tanguary	0-1-1-0-0-4	Cornelius Wiley	0-0-1-0-0-1
Boston Thompson	0-0-1-0-0-0	John Wiley	0-0-1-0-0-1
Wm G. Taylor	0-3-1-0-0-4	George W. Wiley	0-0-1-0-0-2
James Tansil	0-0-1-0-0-0	S. B. Windham	0-1-1-0-0-3
John Tansil	0-0-1-0-0-1	Thos C. Windham	0-0-1-0-0-0
Wm Tansil	0-0-1-0-0-0	James V. Weir	0-3-1-0-2-10
B. F. Thompson	0-0-1-0-0-1	James Wiley	0-0-1-0-0-0
George U. Thompson	0-0-1-0-0-0	Daniel Welch	0-0-1-0-0-4
James F. Trayhern	0-0-1-0-0-1	Jesse Wright	0-0-1-0-0-1
		Robt W. Whittington	0-1-1-0-1-0
John C. Underwood	0-0-0-0-0-0	Alexander Wood	0-0-1-0-0-0
		Bennett Wood	1-0-1-0-0-1
		Walker B. Wilson	0-0-1-0-0-1
Jacob Vanmeter	0-1-1-0-1-7	William Wood	0-0-1-0-0-0
George Vaughn	0-0-1-0-0-1	Richard B. Welch	1-2-1-0-0-0
		Lucinda Washington	0-3-0-0-0-0
Horatio T. Wheat	1-5-1-0-2-10	Andrew Willingham	0-0-1-0-0-0
Benj F. Wilson	0-0-1-0-0-0	Samuel G. Wyman	0-7-2-0-2-18
Jeremiah Wilson	0-0-1-0-0-0	James W. Willingham	0-0-1-0-0-0
John Wilson	1-0-1-0-0-0	Jackson Wheeler	0-2-1-0-1-6
Francis B. Whiting	0-21-2-0-4-15	Rev. Chas White	0-0-1-0-0-1
Francis H. Whiting	0-3-1-0-1-8	Joseph H. Wilson	0-0-1-0-0-0
Wm H. Whiting	0-9-1-0-0-16	Miss Alsea Writt	0-0-0-0-0-0
W. W. Whiting	0-5-1-0-1-8	Obediah Willingham	0-0-1-0-0-0
N. B. Whiting	0-7-1-0-1-14	Francis H. Wheat	0-0-1-0-0-0
Allen Williams	0-11-1-0-0-17	Col. J. W. Ware	0-13-1-0-3-17
Gabriel Williams	0-0-0-0-0-1	James L. Ward	1-0-0-0-0-0
Thompson Writt	1-0-1-0-0-2	Isaac N. Writt	1-0-0-0-0-0
Leroy P. Williams	0-6-1-0-2-9	Henry R. Wilson	0-0-1-0-0-0
Welch & Funk	0-0-0-0-0-3	Robert Wilson	0-0-1-0-0-0
Wm Willingham	1-0-1-0-0-3	Charles Willingham	0-0-1-0-0-0
Nancy Willingham	0-0-0-0-0-0	William Whorten	0-1-1-0-0-0
Hezekiah Wiley	0-0-1-0-0-1		
Daniel Wade & Bro.	0-1-2-0-0-3		

Clarke County, Virginia Personal Property Tax Lists 1854-1870
1859

Lewis Whittington	0-0-1-0-0-0	William H. Young	1-1-1-0-0-1
Joseph White	0-0-1-0-0-0	Simeon Yowell	0-0-1-0-0-0

[Free Negroes]

Burwell Cook	0-0-0-1-0-0	Fielding Banks	0-0-0-1-0-0
James Butler	0-0-0-1-0-0	Jake Webb	0-0-0-1-0-0
Peter Coates	0-0-0-0-0-2	Nancy Parker	0-0-0-0-0-0
Armistead Dickens	0-0-0-1-0-0	Wm Parker	0-0-0-1-0-0
		George Ranson	0-0-0-1-0-0
Wm Allen	0-0-0-1-0-0	Thomas Ranson	0-0-0-1-0-0
Jack Branham	0-0-0-1-0-0	Mowen Harris	0-0-0-1-0-0

Clarke County, Virginia Personal Property Tax Lists 1854-1870

1860

1) Free male persons above 16 years of age, 2) Slaves who have attained the age of 16 years, 3) White male inhabitants who have attained the age of 21 years, except Those exempted from taxation on account of bodily infirmity, 4) Male free negroes between the ages of 21 and 55 years, 5) Slaves who have attained the age of 12 years, 6) Horses, mules, asses & jennets

Name	Values	Name	Values
Buckner Ashby	0-9-4-0-3-24	Geo Anderson	0-0-1-0-0-1
Mason Anderson	0-4-1-0-0-9	D. T. Armstrong	0-0-1-0-0-0
John H. Anderson	0-0-1-0-1-0	Augustine Athey	0-0-1-0-0-0
Milton B. Anderson	0-1-1-0-0-1	Wm Arnold	0-0-1-0-0-0
James M. Allen	0-4-1-0-1-8	Owen Allen	0-0-1-0-0-0
Edgar Allen	0-10-1-0-2-12	Doct. R. S. Blackburn	0-7-1-0-1-7
Jesse Allen	0-0-1-0-0-1	Wesley Bradham	0-0-1-0-0-0
John Alexander	0-19-2-0-4-25	George H. Burwell	0-51-2-0-8-52
N. F. & J. E. Anderson	0-2-2-0-0-7	D° as Trustee	0-0-0-0-0-0
Robert Ashby Jr.	0-0-1-0-0-1	John Burchell's Est.	0-5-1-0-2-9
Robert Ashby Sr.	0-0-1-0-0-1	George H. Bell	0-0-1-0-0-0
Nimrod Ashby	0-0-1-0-0-1	Hiram O. Bell	0-4-1-0-0-6
Capt. Geo B. Ashby	0-0-1-0-0-0	Squire Bell	0-0-1-0-0-1
Geo W. Ashby	0-1-1-0-0-4	Lewis Berlin	0-2-1-0-0-0
Geo W. Allen	0-2-1-0-0-6	Philip Berlin	0-5-1-0-0-6
William T. Allen	0-7-1-0-1-9	George W. Berlin	0-0-1-0-0-0
A. S. Allen	0-8-2-0-1-13	George C. Blakemore	0-7-1-0-1-12
John Allison	0-0-1-0-0-1	James Bell Sr.	1-0-1-0-0-3
Thos H. Alexander	1-0-1-0-0-7	James C. Briggs	0-6-2-0-1-11
John Avis	1-0-1-0-1-0	John S. Briggs	0-0-1-0-0-0
Margt E. Alexander	0-1-0-0-0-0	Arthur Briggs	0-0-1-0-0-2
Austin C. Ashby	0-0-1-0-0-1	Miss Margaret Burchell	0-4-0-0-2-4
Levi Athey	0-0-1-0-0-0	John Bromley	0-1-1-0-0-11
Lewis B. Ashby	0-0-1-0-0-0		

Clarke County, Virginia Personal Property Tax Lists 1854-1870
1860

John W. Byrd	0-10-1-0-1-10	Miranda Bowen	0-0-1-0-0-0
Joseph B. Beavers	0-0-1-0-0-1	Doct. Wm Best	0-1-1-0-0-2
Chris Bouser	0-1-1-0-0-0	Col. S. H. Bowen	0-0-1-0-0-0
George W. Bromley	0-2-2-0-0-9	George Beard	0-0-1-0-0-0
Susan R. Burwell	0-0-6-0-0-2	Alfred Bishop	0-0-1-0-0-0
Ann C. Benn	0-0-1-0-0-2	Charles Bayles	0-0-1-0-0-0
Daniel S. Bonham	1-2-2-0-0-7	William Brabham	0-0-1-0-0-0
Nancy Boyston	0-0-0-0-0-0	Washington Brook	0-0-1-0-0-0
Juliet Boyston	0-1-0-0-0-0	James Bell Jr.	0-0-1-0-0-0
William Berry	0-12-1-0-2-8	A .J. Berlin	0-0-1-0-0-0
R. S. Briarly	0-7-1-0-2-11	Nathaniel Burwell	0-15-1-0-4-43
Miss Mary C. Bowser	0-0-0-0-0-0	Hector Bell	0-0-1-0-0-2
Wm O. Brown	0-0-1-0-0-0	Neill Barnett	1-7-1-0-3-13
Abraham Beavers	0-0-1-0-0-3	Charles H. Brabham	0-0-1-0-0-0
Adam Barr	0-0-1-0-0-0	Curtis Brady	0-0-1-0-0-0
James Brown	1-0-1-0-0-0	John W. Bell	0-0-1-0-0-0
Middleton Bowen	0-0-1-0-0-0		
Miss Emily Bell	0-0-0-0-0-1	Alfred Castleman	1-7-3-0-2-14
Joseph C. Bartlett	0-4-2-0-2-12	Charles D. Castleman	0-0-1-0-0-2
Jonah P. Bell	0-2-1-0-0-5	James Chisholm	0-0-1-0-0-0
Thomas Brown	0-0-1-0-0-0	Wm A. Castleman	1-5-1-0-1-3
Peter Bennett	0-0-1-0-0-2	Mrs. Ury Castleman's Est.	0-0-0-0-0-0
Patrick Brady	0-0-1-0-0-0	William Carper	0-0-1-0-0-4
George W. Bolen	0-0-1-0-0-1	Geo W. Cooper	0-0-1-0-0-0
Thos J. Bragg	0-0-1-0-1-0	Robt A. Colston	0-5-1-0-1-9
Robert Briggs	0-4-1-0-1-4	John Copenhaver	1-5-2-0-1-12
William Briggs	0-0-1-0-0-0	John H. Crebbs	0-2-1-0-0-8
George S. Bonham	0-5-1-0-2-8	Joseph K. Carter	0-2-1-0-0-4
Enos S. Brown	0-1-1-0-0-0	Charles J. Carter	0-1-1-0-1-4
Samuel Bromley	0-0-1-0-0-7	John A. Carter	0-1-1-0-1-6
Miss Amelia Byrn [?]	0-0-0-0-0-1	John W. Carter	0-0-1-0-0-0
Doct. Wm A. Bradford	0-6-2-0-2-12	Parkinson Corder	0-0-1-0-0-1
J. H. Bitzer	0-2-1-0-0-7	Thomas Carter	0-4-0-0-2-5
Geo W. Beard	0-0-1-0-0-2	William G. Carter	0-1-2-0-0-1
		William H. Carter	0-1-1-0-0-2

Clarke County, Virginia Personal Property Tax Lists 1854-1870
1860

Doct. R. T. Colston	0-8-1-0-1-21		Eliza Crim	0-0-1-0-0-0
James H. Clarke	0-3-1-0-1-0		James Canter	0-0-1-0-0-4
Thomas H. Crow	1-6-1-0-1-8		John B. Carter	0-2-1-0-0-1
John Carrell	0-0-1-0-0-1		Benjn F. Crawford	0-0-1-0-0-0
John Cooper	0-0-1-0-0-2		Sarah Chamblin	0-0-0-0-0-1
Lewis Carrell	0-0-1-0-0-1		George W. Castleman	0-0-1-0-0-0
Thos Carrell	0-0-1-0-0-2		John L. Carter	0-0-1-0-0-0
Sam'l A. Campbell	0-0-1-0-0-0		John Cain	0-0-2-0-0-3
Andrew Cornell [?]	0-0-1-0-0-1		Jacob Clink Jr.	0-0-1-0-0-0
Michael Copenhaver	0-0-1-0-0-1		Hanson Cooper	0-0-1-0-0-0
John M. Collier	0-0-1-0-0-5		Michael Cain	0-0-1-0-0-0
Lucy A. Calmese	1-3-2-0-0-4		Joshua R. Crown	0-0-1-0-0-0
Miss Marian Catlett	0-6-1-0-1-13		Wm F. Chamblin	0-0-1-0-0-0
Robert H. Castleman	0-3-1-0-1-10		Wm H. Colston	0-1-1-0-0-5
James N. Corbin	0-0-1-0-0-3		Ann B. Cook	0-15-0-0-1-17
Benjn Crampton	0-1-1-0-0-1		Stephen D. Castleman	0-0-0-0-0-0
Frank Canniford	0-0-1-0-0-0		Washington Dearmont	0-5-1-0-0-8
James E. Chamblin	0-0-1-0-0-0		Wm Deahl	0-1-2-0-0-1
Miss Sally Cloud	0-3-0-0-0-0		James [?] W. Doran	0-0-1-0-0-1
Miss El __[illegible] Clink	0-0-0-0-0-0		John Drish	1-0-1-0-0-1
Henry Canniford	0-0-1-0-0-0		John Donevan	0-0-1-0-0-0
Michael Crim	0-0-1-0-0-0		L. L. & A. Davis	0-1-0-0-0-0
Hannah Cain	0-0-0-0-0-0		Jeremiah Daly	0-0-1-0-0-0
James Carter	0-0-1-0-0-1		Thomas Duke	0-0-1-0-0-0
Franklin B. Carter	0-2-1-0-0-4		Hugh Davis	0-0-1-0-0-0
George D. Cooper	0-0-1-0-0-0		Aaron Duble	0-0-1-0-0-2
Resin Carroll	0-0-1-0-0-1		Michael Drislan	0-1-1-0-0-0
Charles R. Corder	0-0-1-0-0-0		Peter Dearmont	0-2-1-0-1-2
James Carroll	0-0-1-0-0-0		James Doran	0-0-1-0-0-0
Wm Carroll	0-0-1-0-0-0		J. R. Dingle	0-0-1-0-0-0
John P. Carigan	0-0-1-0-0-0		John D. Davis	0-1-1-0-0-1
			Wm Donodhue	0-0-1-0-0-0
			Horace P. Deahl	0-0-1-0-0-0

Clarke County, Virginia Personal Property Tax Lists 1854-1870
1860

Jacob Enders	0-12-1-0-0-10	Marcus R.	
Henry Edwards	0-0-1-0-0-3	Feeher [sic]	0-2-1-0-0-2
Henson Elliott	0-2-2-0-1-8	Thomas G. Flagg	0-0-1-0-0-0
A. M. Earle	0-5-1-0-1-16	Geo W. Fiddler	0-0-1-0-0-0
Jacob W.		Joshua Fellows	0-0-1-0-0-2
Everhart	0-0-1-0-0-1	Enoch Furr	0-0-1-0-0-0
Wm H. Edwards	0-0-1-0-0-1	B. R. Foley	1-1-1-0-0-1
Albert Elsey	0-0-1-0-0-4	Thomas Forrest	0-0-1-0-0-0
John Ellyet	1-1-1-0-1-8	Barney	
Thomas A.		Fairbank [?]	0-0-1-0-0-0
Everhart	0-0-1-0-0-2	Henry S. Fox	0-0-1-0-0-0
William G.		James F. Franks	0-0-1-0-0-0
Everhart Jr.	2-2-3-0-0-8	Ephriam Furr	0-0-1-0-0-0
William G.		Fernando Fox	0-0-1-0-0-0
Everhart Sr.	0-0-1-0-0-0	John W. Fidler	0-0-1-0-0-0
John J. Emory	0-0-1-0-0-0	Uriah Fletcher	0-0-1-0-0-0
John E. Elliott	0-0-1-0-0-0	Everett Fowler	0-0-1-0-0-0
Joseph W.		Joseph W.	
Edwards	0-0-1-0-0-1	Felchner	0-0-1-0-0-0
		John Franks	0-0-1-0-0-0
Dr. O. R. Funsten	0-21-1-0-2-30	Robert Felchner	0-0-0-0-0-3
D. J. F.		Wm M. Ferguson	0-0-1-0-0-1
Fauntleroy	0-5-2-0-0-6	William Fowler Sr.	0-0-1-0-0-2
Josiah Ferguson	0-2-1-0-0-4	Daniel Furr	0-0-1-0-0-0
James A. Forster	0-3-1-0-0-6		
Edward W.		John L. Grant	0-1-1-0-0-3
Franks	0-0-1-0-0-0	James W.	
Johnson Furr	0-0-1-0-1-4	Galloway	0-0-1-0-0-0
Israel Fidler	0-0-1-0-0-0	Thos W. Griffith	0-0-1-0-0-0
Eliz Fleming	0-2-0-0-0-4	James F. Green	0-3-1-0-0-9
Joseph Fleming	0-0-2-0-0-5	Mrs. Mary Green	0-3-0-0-1-2
Wm Fowler Jr.	0-0-1-0-0-1	Mrs. Isabella	
James Furr	0-0-1-0-0-1	Glass	0-0-0-0-0-0
John Foreman	0-0-1-0-0-0	Richard N.	
Thomas Fowler	0-0-1-0-0-2	Green [?]	0-4-1-0-0-7
Martin		Thomas E. Gold	0-10-2-0-1-17
Felchner [sic]	1-0-1-0-0-1	George W.	
Dennis Fenton	0-1-1-0-0-2	Gordon	0-1-2-0-1-10
		Stephen J. Gant	0-1-1-0-0-3

Clarke County, Virginia Personal Property Tax Lists 1854-1870
1860

Samuel Grubb Sr.	0-0-1-0-0-0	Abraham Huyett	0-0-1-0-0-2
Henry N. Grigsby	0-5-1-0-1-11	Henry D. Hooe	0-1-1-0-0-0
Lewis F. Glass	0-6-1-0-2-11	James H. Hooe	0-0-1-0-0-0
Martin Gant	0-6-1-0-1-8	William Hummer	0-0-0-0-0-0
William Gibbs	0-0-1-0-0-2	William Heflin	0-0-1-0-0-0
William B. Grubb	0-0-1-0-0-1	Jackson Hoff	0-0-1-0-0-0
George W. Grubb	0-0-1-0-0-0	Dr. James A.	
Mathew [?]		Haysen [sic]	0-4-1-0-0-4
Grubb Jr.	0-0-1-0-0-0	Dr. Wm Hay	0-4-1-0-2-2
John M. Grubbs	0-0-1-0-0-0	J. M. Hite	0-5-2-0-1-10
John Gruber	0-1-1-0-1-10	Samuel	
George Gardner	0-0-1-0-0-1	Heflebower	0-6-1-0-1-16
Adam		Chas W. Hardesty	0-2-1-0-0-5
Greenwault	0-0-1-0-0-1	A. D. Hardesty	0-0-1-0-0-0
William Grubb	0-0-1-0-0-0	Wm G. Hardesty	0-2-1-0-0-11
T. M. Grigsby	1-0-0-0-0-3	James M.	
Matthew Grimes	0-0-1-0-0-0	Hardesty	0-2-1-0-1-6
Thomas E. Gibson	0-0-1-0-0-0	Cornelius Hoff	0-0-1-0-0-0
L. A. Glaise	0-3-1-0-0-1	Blackwell	
Elias M. Grim	0-0-1-0-0-0	Holtsclaw	0-0-1-0-0-0
Charles Grubb	0-0-1-0-0-1	John Henry	0-0-1-0-0-1
Mrs. E. Glover	0-1-0-0-0-0	John Hughs	1-0-1-0-0-1
Philip Gordon	0-0-1-0-1-4	Thomas Hughes	0-0-1-0-0-1
Sydnor Garrett	1-0-1-0-0-1	William B. Harris	2-10-1-0-1-10
John Greenwault	0-0-1-0-0-0	Dr. B. Harrison	0-15-1-0-1-20
J. R. Grigsby	0-7-1-0-1-5	Henry Huntsberry	0-2-1-0-0-7
Wm Grubb Sr.	0-0-1-0-0-0	James F. Howell	0-0-1-0-0-0
J. W. & J. S.		John W. Hibbard	0-0-1-0-0-0
Grantham	0-1-1-0-0-3	Wm R. Helvestine	0-0-1-0-0-0
H. K. Grigg	0-0-1-0-0-0	A. T. M. Hough	0-1-1-0-0-1
J. J. Gordon	0-3-1-0-1-10	Geo & J. T. Harris	0-5-2-0-1-10
Th K. Glover	0-0-1-0-0-0	John W. Hall	0-0-1-0-0-0
Madison A. Grubb	0-0-1-0-0-0	John Hummer	0-0-1-0-0-3
James T. Grubb	0-0-1-0-0-0	Jacob	
Thomas Guard	0-0-1-0-0-0	Heflebower	0-6-1-0-2-15
John Gilbert	0-0-1-0-0-1	Samuel Huyett	0-3-1-0-0-9
		Cornelius Hawk	0-0-1-0-0-0
Henry Harrison	0-4-1-0-2-4	T. L. Humphrey	0-4-1-0-0-4
Samuel Huyett	0-3-1-0-0-8		

Clarke County, Virginia Personal Property Tax Lists 1854-1870
1860

Edward C. Harrison	0-1-1-0-0-2	Armstead M. Johnson	0-1-1-0-0-5
Alexander Holstclaw	0-0-1-0-0-0	Amelia A. Jordan	0-1-0-0-0-1
Joseph R. Hardesty	0-2-1-0-1-8	Rev. Wm Johnston	0-3-1-0-0-2
James W. Hummer	0-0-1-0-0-1	Edward Jenkins	0-0-1-0-0-0
Henry A. Hibbard	0-0-1-0-0-0	Rev. Joseph R. Jones	0-2-1-0-0-1
J. B. Hawthorn	0-0-1-0-0-3	James W. Johnson	0-0-1-0-0-0
John W. Holland	0-0-1-0-0-0	William Johnson	0-0-1-0-0-0
John & Thos Heskitt	0-0-2-0-0-0	Sol R. Jackson	0-0-1-0-0-0
Solomon Hibbs	0-0-1-0-0-1	Wm B. Jolliff	0-0-1-0-0-0
Geo W. Holtsclaw	0-0-1-0-0-2	M. W. Jones	0-0-1-0-0-0
Humphrey Hoff	0-0-1-0-0-0	Franklin L. Johnson	0-0-1-0-0-0
J. J. Hite Sr.	1-6-1-0-2-11	Frank Ingle	0-0-1-0-0-0
William Hoover [?]	0-0-1-0-0-0	John N. Kimmell	0-0-1-0-0-1
William Hammon [?]	1-0-0-0-0-0	James F. Kerfoot	0-3-1-0-0-9
Geo W. Hanvey	0-0-1-0-0-0	Dr. F. J. Kerfoot	0-9-1-0-1-12
Lewis O. Hunt	0-0-1-0-0-0	Wm C. Kerfoot	1-9-1-0-2-14
James P. Hoff	1-0-0-0-0-0	Judson J. Kerfoot	0-5-1-0-0-11
Norman Howard	1-0-0-0-0-0	Wm & Benjn Knight	0-8-2-0-0-16
Catherine B. Hall	0-7-0-0-0-12	Middleton Keeler	1-0-1-0-0-0
		Jacob Kriser	1-0-1-0-0-4
		Samuel G. Kneller	1-4-1-0-2-8
Herod Jenkins	0-0-1-0-0-2	Wm C. Kennerly	0-4-1-0-2-0
John Joliffe	1-3-1-0-0-6	Wm B. Kennan	0-0-1-0-0-0
Leonard Jones	0-2-1-0-0-5	Joseph McKay Kennerly	0-9-1-0-2-15
Thomas Jones	1-0-1-0-1-8	Dr. C. B. R. Kennerly	0-5-0-0-0-3
Mrs. Moray [*sic*] Janney	1-2-0-0-0-0	Joseph Kline	0-0-1-0-0-0
Thomas Jenkins	0-0-1-0-0-2	Dr. Ran Kownslar	0-6-1-0-0-4
James W. Johnston	0-1-1-0-0-1	John Kelly	0-0-1-0-0-0
Wm A. Jackson	0-6-1-0-0-11	E. V. Kercheral	0-1-1-0-0-0
Andrew Jackson	0-1-1-0-0-0	James H. Kennan	0-0-1-0-0-0
		Henry Kromlling	0-2-1-0-0-1

Clarke County, Virginia Personal Property Tax Lists 1854-1870
1860

James M. Kiger	0-0-2-0-0-4		John T.	
John M. Kitchen	0-3-1-0-0-7		Longerbeam	0-0-1-0-0-0
Reuben Kromling	0-0-1-0-0-0		R. H. Lee	0-3-0-0-1-10
Willie King	0-0-1-0-0-0		Frank Littleton	0-0-1-0-0-2
Henry Knight	0-0-1-0-0-0		George Lanham Albert	0-0-1-0-0-0
John B. Laurue	0-17-3-0-2-33		Longerbeam	0-0-1-0-0-4
John D. Laurue	0-5-1-0-0-10		Benjn Lock	0-0-2-0-0-5
Edwd P. C. Lewis	0-4-1-0-0-6		Benjn	
John Longerbeam	0-1-1-0-0-2		Longerbeam	0-0-1-0-0-3
A. L. P. Laurue	0-5-1-0-1-9		Franklin Little	0-3-1-0-0-5
James W. Laurue	0-5-2-0-1-12		William Lanham	1-0-1-0-0-1
Christopher C. Laurue	0-1-1-0-0-8		William Lloyd	0-0-1-0-0-6
			William D. Lee	0-0-1-0-0-0
Squire Lee	0-0-1-0-0-2		A. J. Lloyd	0-0-1-0-0-1
Christopher Lee	0-0-1-0-0-3		Wm H. Levi	0-0-1-0-0-1
Dr. James M. Lindsay	1-0-1-0-1-1		Rice W. Levi	1-0-1-0-0-7
			John Lee	0-0-1-0-0-3
Eli Littleton	0-2-1-0-2-4		Howard Lock	0-0-1-0-0-0
Wm Littleton	0-0-1-0-0-2		Ludwell Lee	0-0-1-0-0-1
John W. Littleton	0-0-1-0-0-2		John T. Lindsay	0-4-1-0-0-11
Henry Lloyd	0-0-1-0-0-3		Joseph B. Lindsay	0-0-1-0-0-1
John A. Lloyd	0-0-1-0-0-0		James W. Lee	0-0-1-0-0-1
John Lloyd	0-0-1-0-0-3		John M. Lock	0-1-1-0-0-0
David Lloyd	0-0-1-0-0-0		Franklin Lock	0-0-1-0-0-0
James L. Lloyd	0-0-1-0-0-1		William O. Lupton	1-0-0-0-0-1
Moses Lewin	0-0-1-0-0-1		Mrs. Martha Lupton	0-0-0-0-0-0
John Lock Sr.	0-3-1-0-0-9		James W. Lloyd	0-0-1-0-0-0
John Louthan	0-6-1-0-2-7		John D. Lloyd	0-0-1-0-0-0
John K. Louthan	0-2-2-0-0-3		Charles Lloyd	0-0-1-0-0-0
James T. Louthan	0-3-1-0-2-9		Manley Lanham	1-0-1-0-0-0
Mrs. M. Lewis	0-5-0-0-1-3			
George W. Lewis	0-4-1-0-2-0			
Minor Lanham	0-1-1-0-0-1		Francis B. Meade	0-8-1-1-0-14
James Lanham	1-0-1-0-0-1		Philip N. Meade	0-10-1-0-0-16
John M. Lupton	0-1-1-0-0-0		John M. Meade	0-4-1-0-0-6
John W. Luke	0-8-1-1-0-14		Edward M. Mantor [?]	0-2-1-0-0-7
Josiah R. Locke	0-0-1-1-0-6			

Clarke County, Virginia Personal Property Tax Lists 1854-1870
1860

R. K. Meade Trustee	0-0-0-0-0-0	Mrs. Susan Marshall	0-4-0-0-0-5
David Meade	0-4-1-0-0-14	L. D. Maddex	0-1-1-0-0-7
Nathaniel B. Meade	0-5-1-0-2-9	T. C. McIntyre	0-6-1-0-1-9
Miss M. Meade	0-5-1-0-1-1	Nathaniel Mercer	0-0-1-0-0-2
R. K. Meade	1-4-1-0-0-2	James Murphy	0-1-1-0-0-1
Col. Benjn Morgan	0-28-2-0-1-38	Stephen Marlow	1-0-1-0-0-2
D° Guardian for Miss Alexander	0-0-0-0-0-0	A. M. Moore	2-5-1-0-0-10
D° for John & Wm Alexander	0-0-0-0-0-0	D° Trustee for Mrs. Strider	0-0-0-0-0-0
Otway McCormick	0-6-1-0-2-9	Saml Moreland	2-0-1-0-0-5
John Morgan	0-5-1-0-4-9	George Marpole	0-0-1-0-0-1
D° as Guardian for Children	0-0-0-0-0-0	Moses G. Miley	0-0-1-0-0-4
Dr. C. & S. McCormick	0-22-2-0-1-33	E. W. Massey	0-6-1-0-2-11
Thos McCormick	0-12-1-0-1-12	James McClaughry	1-0-1-0-0-2
Saml McCormick	0-0-1-0-0-1	Saml T. Marts	0-0-1-0-0-1
Margt A. McCormick	0-1-1-0-0-2	McLain McClingen	0-0-1-0-0-1
James McCormick	0-3-1-0-0-9	Richard Morgan	0-0-1-0-0-4
Dr. Hugh McGuire	0-0-0-0-0-4	Patrick Murray	0-0-1-0-0-0
Edward McCormick	0-16-1-0-5-19	John McMurray	0-1-1-0-0-2
Peter McMurray	0-2-1-0-0-5	Col. F. M. McCormick	0-15-1-0-2-21
A. Ross Milton	0-2-1-0-0-0	Addison Muntzel	0-0-1-0-0-0
S. P. Moore	0-0-1-0-0-0	E. C. Marshall	0-5-1-0-1-7
James Mitchell	2-2-1-0-0-7	Garret McDonald	1-1-1-0-0-3
Wm D. McGuire	0-13-1-0-2-11	Harry McDonald	0-0-1-0-0-0
Alexander Marshall	2-3-1-0-0-9	Joseph R. Moore	0-0-1-0-0-0
John Marshall	0-4-1-0-1-2	John G. McCauley	0-0-1-0-0-0
		David Meade Trustee	0-2-2-0-1-6
		John Morgan Jr.	0-2-1-0-0-5
		Joseph E. Mason	0-1-1-0-0-1
		Rev. Wm Meade	0-0-1-0-0-0
		Wm T. Milton	0-2-1-0-1-5
		Jessee Mercer	1-0-0-0-0-1
		Joseph Menifee	0-0-1-0-0-0
		Henry Mesmer	0-3-1-0-2-5

Clarke County, Virginia Personal Property Tax Lists 1854-1870
1860

W. W. Meade	0-0-1-0-0-0	Dr. S. S. Neill	0-3-1-0-1-2	
Alfred P. Moore	0-0-1-0-0-0	Hamidhis		
James T. Murphy	0-0-1-0-0-0	Neuman	0-0-1-0-0-0	
Joseph Moore	0-0-1-0-0-0			
Thos Murphy	0-0-1-0-0-0	George ORear	0-2-1-0-0-4	
John Murphy	1-0-0-0-0-0	Mrs. Eliz ORear	0-9-0-0-2-10	
John T. Marts	0-0-1-0-0-0	Benjn O'Rear	0-7-1-0-1-5	
Moses D. Murphy	0-0-1-0-0-0	Overseers of Poor	0-0-1-0-0-4	
Alfred Marts	0-0-1-0-0-0	John B. Oliver	0-0-1-0-0-0	
David H. McGuire	1-5-1-0-2-6	Mrs. Susan		
Saml J. C. Moore	0-3-1-0-1-1	O. Rear	0-0-0-0-0-0	
Provence		Addison O'Rear	0-0-1-0-0-0	
McCormick	0-14-1-0-0-12	John S. Owens	0-0-0-0-0-1	
D° as Trustee		Hughh [sic]		
for Ed McCormick	0-0-0-0-0-0	O'Roke	0-0-1-0-0-0	
D° for Ann Stribling				
	0-0-0-0-0-0	Benjn Perry	0-0-1-0-0-0	
D° for Ebin Frost		James Puller	0-0-1-0-0-0	
	0-0-0-0-0-0	Bushrod Puller	0-0-1-0-0-0	
D° Guardian for		Samuel L. Pigeon	0-0-1-1-0-8	
E. McCormick	0-0-0-0-0-0	Dr. Mat Page's		
D° Agent for Miss. M.		Estate	0-4-0-0-1-2	
Stribling	0-0-0-0-0-0	John E. Page	0-15-1-0-0-15	
		S. R. Page	0-20-0-0-5-31	
Hugh M. Nelson	0-11-1-0-2-20	Conrad Pope	1-0-1-0-0-1	
Thomas F. Nelson	0-6-1-0-1-17	Austin Page	0-1-1-0-0-3	
James H. Neville	0-1-1-0-0-0	John Page	0-10-1-0-4-14	
Philip W. Nelson	0-8-1-0-4-16	Alexander		
Miss A. &		Parkins	0-0-1-0-0-1	
R. Nelson	0-3-0-0-0-0	Mann R. Page	0-9-1-0-4-17	
John B. Norris	0-3-1-0-1-6	George R. Page	0-4-1-0-0-6	
John R. Nunn	0-5-1-0-2-8	Mathew Pulliam	0-1-1-0-3-0	
Ditto Guard for		Mrs. Eliza Peirce	1-3-0-0-1-6	
M. Dix	0-0-0-0-0-0	A. N. Peirce	0-4-1-0-0-9	
D° for G. W.		Peter McPierce	0-5-1-0-0-9	
Carter	0-0-0-0-0-0	Paul Peirce	0-7-1-0-1-6	
Wm Nisewarner	0-1-1-0-0-3	Mrs. E. M. Page	0-6-0-0-1-0	
Thos Nisewarner	0-0-1-0-0-3	James F. Pine	1-0-1-0-0-3	
		John Poston	0-0-1-0-0-3	

Clarke County, Virginia Personal Property Tax Lists 1854-1870
1860

T. P. Pendleton	0-11-1-0-1-15	Addison Romaine	0-2-1-0-1-4
Wm F. Padgett	3-0-1-0-0-0	George Reno	0-0-1-0-0-0
William Pyle	1-0-1-0-0-0	Wesley Russell	1-0-0-0-0-3
John Patterson	3-1-1-0-0-6	Charles Rieley	0-0-1-0-0-1
James S. Payne	0-0-1-0-0-1	Jacob D. Ritter	0-0-1-0-0-0
Barrett Pritchard	0-0-1-0-0-0	Beverly Randolph	0-14-1-0-2-24
Michael Pope	0-0-1-0-0-1	Dr. C. Randolph	1-19-1-0-6-25
Pulliam & Howell	0-2-2-0-0-1	A. C. Randolph	0-1-1-0-0-2
P. H. Powers	0-8-1-0-1-15	John Reynolds	0-1-1-0-1-0
Thomas N. Pyle	0-0-1-0-0-1	John Ramey	0-0-1-0-0-0
Richard Parker	0-1-0-0-0-0	William Rieley	0-0-1-0-0-0
Lewis Peacock	0-0-1-0-0-1	Mathew Rust	0-1-1-0-1-0
John T. Patterson	0-0-1-0-0-0	John J. Rieley	0-3-1-0-2-7
Willis Prichard	0-0-1-0-0-1	D^o Trustee for	
John M. Pope	0-0-1-0-0-0	Mrs. Taylor	0-0-0-0-0-0
William Picket	0-0-1-0-0-0	William A. Reily	0-4-1-0-2-12
		Thos Reardon	0-0-2-0-0-2
Bennett Russell	1-10-3-0-1-14	Samuel Rutter	0-0-1-0-0-0
Thomas W.		John D.	
Russell	0-0-1-0-1-4	Richardson	0-10-1-0-0-17
Michael Russell	0-0-1-0-0-1	John N. Ross	0-1-1-0-0-0
Wm H. Robinson	0-2-1-0-0-7	James W. Ryan	0-4-1-0-0-6
Miss M. P. Root	0-0-0-0-1-0	Enos Richmond	0-0-1-0-0-0
John Reed	0-0-1-0-0-1	Richmond & Stoll	1-0-0-0-0-3
Reh__ Ranse		Joseph F. Ryan	1-1-1-0-0-2
[illegible]	0-0-1-0-0-1	James F. Reynolds	0-0-1-0-0-3
John Rowland	0-1-2-0-0-9	M. T. Royston	0-0-1-0-0-1
M. W. Royston	0-0-1-0-0-2	Richd S.	
John Rippon	0-0-1-0-0-1	Ridgeway	0-1-2-0-0-9
Peter K. Royston	0-0-1-0-0-1	John Ritter	0-0-1-0-0-7
Uriah Royston	0-0-1-0-0-1	Patrick Rogers [?]	0-0-1-0-0-0
Daniel B. Richards	0-1-1-0-0-0	Charles H.	
George R.		Richard	0-0-1-0-0-0
Royston	0-0-1-0-0-0	Thos W. Raynolds	0-0-1-0-0-0
Miss Nancy		Samuel Resser [?]	0-0-1-0-0-0
Redman	0-1-0-0-0-0	John W. Russell	0-0-1-0-0-4
George W. Rutter	0-1-1-0-0-0	Jane C. Randolph	0-1-1-0-0-0
James H. Rowland	0-1-1-0-0-1	Danl T. Richards	0-0-1-0-0-1
		Elisha Romine	0-0-1-0-0-0

Clarke County, Virginia Personal Property Tax Lists 1854-1870
1860

Name	Values	Name	Values
Simon Ross	0-0-1-0-0-0	William Strother	1-2-1-0-1-5
Thomas Ray	0-0-1-0-0-0	John Stonestreet	0-0-1-0-0-0
James Ritter	0-3-1-0-0-9	John Shell	0-0-1-0-0-1
Jackson Roy	0-0-1-0-0-0	Stephen Shell	0-0-1-0-0-1
Miss E. W. Royston	0-1-0-0-0-0	Simon R. Stump	0-0-1-0-0-0
		James Shackleford	0-0-0-0-0-0
Thos Shumate's Estate	2-3-0-0-1-12	Dennis Shehan	0-0-1-0-0-2
Col. Treadwell Smith	0-15-3-0-4-21	John W. Stephenson	0-4-1-0-0-9
John W. Sprint	0-0-1-0-0-0	Thomas Sprint	0-0-1-0-0-1
Eliz Sowers	0-0-0-0-0-0	Joseph Shipe	0-0-1-0-0-0
John W. Sowers	0-6-1-0-4-24	Henry C. Shearer	0-0-1-0-0-0
William Sowers	0-9-1-0-3-16	A. J. Shipe	0-0-1-0-0-0
Champ Shepherd	0-7-1-0-2-18	Wm G. Stull	0-0-1-0-0-0
Carter Shepherd	0-6-1-0-0-9	James Stell	1-0-1-0-0-1
P. D. Shepherd	0-4-1-0-0-12	James H. Swain	0-0-1-0-0-0
Henry Shepherd	0-0-1-0-0-0	Smith & Gibson	0-3-2-0-3-8
E. J. & Wm D. Smith	0-25-2-1-8-36	Burr Smallwood	1-0-1-0-0-2
		Henry Slusher	0-1-1-0-0-0
Paul Smith	1-5-1-0-0-10	Vincent S. Setler [?]	0-1-1-0-0-0
Dr. Philip Smith	0-13-2-0-4-24	Trustee for Nancy Finnell	0-0-0-0-0-0
Daniel C. Snyder	0-0-1-0-0-0	Rebecca A. Smith	0-2-0-0-0-0
James W. Sowers	0-4-1-0-1-12	Mrs. Margt Swann	0-0-0-0-1-0
James Sowers	0-1-1-0-1-6	George Smith	0-0-1-0-0-0
William M. Sowers	0-0-1-0-0-9	George S. Spaulding	0-0-1-0-0-0
Francis E. Sowers	0-5-0-0-0-10	John H. Shubridge	0-0-1-0-0-1
Daniel H. Sowers	1-6-1-0-0-17	Benjn Shipe	0-1-1-0-0-0
Charles H. Smith	0-3-1-0-1-3	George W. Shimp	0-0-1-0-0-0
Thomas Smallwood	0-0-1-0-0-1	Geo W. Shultz	0-0-1-0-0-1
Charles Swartz	0-0-1-0-1-0	Salley E. T. Stribling	0-12-1-0-3-16
John Shaffer	0-0-1-0-0-0	Wm F. Stoll	0-1-1-0-0-0
John J. Shaffer	1-0-1-0-0-3	Rev. H. Suter	0-2-1-0-1-1
Simon Stickel	1-0-1-0-0-1	Jacob Spotts	0-0-1-0-0-0
Franklin Swartz	0-0-1-0-0-0	Henry Stickel Sr.	0-0-1-0-0-0
James M. Shearer	0-0-1-0-0-0		

Clarke County, Virginia Personal Property Tax Lists 1854-1870
1860

Mountjoy Shell	0-0-1-0-0-0	Moses B. Trussell	0-1-1-0-0-8
George Siford	0-0-1-0-0-0	William Trinary	0-2-2-0-0-3
F. L. Sowers	0-2-1-0-1-3	Calin [?] Thacker	1-0-1-0-0-0
Nicholas Sampson	0-0-1-0-0-0	Dr. B. Taylor	2-2-1-0-1-3
Wm. M. Shumate	0-0-1-0-0-0	Snowden Tumblin	0-0-1-0-0-4
Joseph Stuart	0-0-1-0-0-0	Mason Tinsman	0-0-1-0-0-1
Daniel W. Sowers	0-14-2-0-3-26	Ludwell Tinsman	0-0-1-0-0-0
George Smedley	0-0-1-0-0-0	Isaac Tyson Jr.	0-0-1-0-0-10
Wm L. Smith	0-0-1-0-0-0	Griffin Taylor	1-0-0-0-0-1
Wm R. Stuart	0-0-1-0-0-0	Wm F. Thompson	0-0-1-0-0-0
L. J. Schooler	0-0-1-0-0-0	James W. Tanquary	1-1-1-0-0-4
James R. Shepherd	0-0-1-0-0-0	Wm G. Taylor	0-1-1-0-0-1
Marcus L. Sinclair	0-0-1-0-0-0	Benjn F. Thompson	0-0-1-0-0-1
Henry Stickel Jr.	0-0-1-0-0-0	James F. Trayhen	0-0-1-0-0-0
James Smallwood	0-0-1-0-0-0	Geo W. Thompson	0-0-1-0-0-0
Geo R. Smith	0-0-1-0-0-0	John W. Taylor	0-0-1-0-0-0
Susan P. Taylor	0-2-1-0-1-2	Dr. Thomas Turner	0-0-1-0-0-2
John Thompson	0-0-0-0-0-2	Albert Thompson	0-0-1-0-0-0
Mrs. Sarah Timberlake	0-5-0-0-2-10	Thomas Thacker	0-0-1-0-0-0
Saml N. Trinary	0-0-1-0-0-1	Wm H. Thompson	0-0-1-0-0-0
James Thomas	0-0-1-0-0-0	Benjn Thompson Jr.	0-0-1-0-0-0
Adam F. Thompson	0-0-1-0-0-1	John Tanzel	0-0-1-0-0-0
Greenberry Thompson	0-0-1-0-1-1	Wm Tanzel	0-0-1-0-0-0
French Thompson	1-2-1-0-1-3		
Baylis Thompson	0-0-1-0-0-3	Jacob Vanmeter	0-2-1-0-1-9
Benj Thompson Jr.	1-0-1-0-0-3		
John H. Taylor	0-0-1-0-0-0	Horatio T. Wheat	1-6-2-0-0-8
Charles Trussell	0-2-1-0-0-4	Jeremiah Wilson	0-0-1-0-0-0
Wm Taylor	0-12-1-0-2-21	Benjn F. Wilson	0-0-1-0-0-0
Robert Tapscott	1-0-1-0-0-0	F. B. Whiting	0-20-2-0-0-16
Col. Joseph Tuly	0-29-1-0-7-30	Francis H. Whiting	1-1-1-0-0-7
Mrs. Elisa Taylor	0-5-0-0-1-2	Wm H. Whiting	0-9-1-0-1-19
Dr. A. B. Tucker	0-11-1-0-0-10		
Isaac Taley	0-0-1-0-0-0		

Clarke County, Virginia Personal Property Tax Lists 1854-1870
1860

W. W. Whiting	0-5-1-0-0-7	Jackson Wheeler	0-0-2-0-0-7
N. B. Whiting	0-7-1-0-1-14	Rev. Chas White	0-2-1-0-0-1
Allen Williams	0-9-1-0-1-17	Miss Alice Writt	0-0-0-0-0-0
Gabriel Williams	0-0-0-0-0-1	Obediah	
Thompson Writt	0-0-1-0-0-2	Willingham	0-0-1-0-0-0
Leroy P. Williams	0-4-2-0-2-8	Col. J. W. Ware	0-12-1-0-3-17
William		Henry R. Wilson	0-0-1-0-0-0
Willingham	0-1-1-0-0-2	William Wharton	0-1-1-0-0-0
Hezekiah Wiley	0-0-1-0-0-1	Lewis Whittington	0-0-1-0-0-0
Wade & Bro	0-1-2-0-1-3	David	
Cornelius Wiley	0-0-1-0-0-0	Whittington	0-0-1-0-0-0
John Wiley	0-0-1-0-0-0	John T.	
George W. Wiley	0-0-1-0-0-3	Willingham	0-0-1-0-0-0
S. B. Wyndham	0-1-1-0-0-3	George	
Thos C. Windham	0-0-1-0-0-1	Willingham	0-0-1-0-0-0
James Wiley	0-0-1-0-0-0	John Wilson	0-0-1-0-0-0
Daniel Welch	0-0-1-0-0-4	William Wood	0-0-1-0-0-0
James V. Weir	1-6-1-0-1-11	J. W. Willingham	0-0-1-0-0-0
Jesse Wright	0-0-1-0-0-2	Joseph Wilson	0-0-1-0-0-0
Robert		Chas F.	
Whittington	0-2-1-0-0-0	Willingham	0-0-1-0-0-0
Alexander Wood	0-0-1-0-0-1	Robert Wilson	0-0-1-0-0-0
Bennett Wood	2-0-1-0-0-1	Samuel Wilson	0-0-1-0-0-0
Walker B. Wilson	0-0-1-0-0-0	Isaac N. Writt	0-0-1-0-0-0
Lucinda			
Washington	0-3-0-0-1-0	William H. Young	1-1-1-0-0-1
Samuel G.		Simeon Yowell	0-0-1-0-0-1
Wyman	0-8-0-0-2-17	John Yowell	0-0-1-0-0-0

[Free Negroes]

James Butler	0-0-0-1-0-0	Oley Robinson	0-0-0-1-0-0
William Parker	0-0-0-1-0-0	Wm Allen	0-0-0-1-0-0
Spencer Johnson	0-0-0-1-0-0	John Jones	0-0-0-1-0-0
Wesley Hall	0-0-0-1-0-0	Peter Coates	0-0-0-0-0-2
John Walker	0-0-0-1-0-0	Mowing Harris	0-0-0-1-0-0
Burwell Cook	0-0-0-1-0-0	Nancy Parker	0-0-0-0-0-0

Clarke County, Virginia Personal Property Tax Lists 1854-1870

1861

1) White males over 21 years, 2) Male free negroes over 21 years, 3) Male free negroes 21-55 years, 4) Slaves of both sexes who have attained the age of 12 years, 5) Horses, mules, asses, jennets etc.

Buckner Ashby	2-0-0-14-25		
Mason Anderson	1-0-0-4-7	Carter Ambrowse	1-0-0-0-0
John H. Anderson	1-0-0-1-2	William T. Allen	1-0-0-7-11
Milton B. Anderson	1-0-0-1-1	Charles A. Bush	1-0-0-0-7
Edgar Allen	1-0-0-12-15	Mrs. Mary Branson	0-0-0-0-0
Jesse Allen	1-0-0-0-1	R. S. Blackburn	2-0-0-8-7
John Alexander	2-0-0-23-23	Wesley Bradham	1-0-0-0-0
N. F. & J. E. Anderson	2-0-0-2-11	G. H. Burwell	2-0-0-65-53
Robert Ashby Jr.	1-0-0-0-0	D° as Trustee	0-0-0-0-0
Robert Ashby Sr.	1-0-0-0-0	Nathaniel Burwell	1-0-0-16-45
Nimrod Ashby	1-0-0-0-2	John H. Burchell	1-0-0-5-7
George Anderson	1-0-0-0-0	G. H. Bell	1-0-0-0-0
George B. Ashby	1-0-0-0-0	Hiram O. Bell	1-0-0-3-6
George W. Ashby	1-0-0-1-4	Squire Bell	1-0-0-0-2
George W. Allen	1-0-0-3-5	Hector Bell	1-0-0-1-2
A. S. Allen	2-0-0-13-14	Lewis Berlin	1-0-0-2-0
Thomas H. Alexander	1-0-0-0-7	Philip Berlin	1-0-0-5-7
John Allison	1-0-0-0-0	George W. Berlin	1-0-0-1-0
John Avis	1-0-0-1-1	George C. Blakemore	1-0-0-8-11
Margt E. Alexander	0-0-0-0-0	Neill Barnett	1-0-0-8-14
Austin C. Ashby	1-0-0-0-1	James Bell Sr.	1-0-0-0-3
Levi Athey	1-0-0-0-0	James C. Briggs	2-0-0-7-17
Lewis B. Ashby	1-0-0-0-0	John S. Briggs	1-0-0-0-0
D. T. Armstrong	1-0-0-0-0	Miss Margaret Burchell	0-0-0-6-4
Jacob Ambrous	1-0-0-0-0	Arthur Briggs	1-0-0-0-3
James L. Ashby	1-0-0-0-1	John Bromley	1-0-0-1-15
John W. Anderson	1-0-0-0-3	John W. Byrd	1-0-0-11-11
Owen Allen	1-0-0-0-0	Joseph B. Beavers	1-0-0-0-1

Clarke County, Virginia Personal Property Tax Lists 1854-1870
1861

Name	Values	Name	Values
Christian Bowser	1-0-0-2-0	John W. Benn	1-0-0-1-1
Mary C. Bowser	0-0-0-0-0	Thomas M. Broy	0-0-0-0-0
G. W. Bromley	1-1-0-1-10	Mrs. E. M. Baker	0-0-0-1-0
Susan R. Burwell	0-0-0-6-2	George Board	1-0-0-0-0
Ann C. Benn	0-0-0-1-2	Thomas T. Byrd	1-0-0-2-1
William A. Brown	1-0-0-0-0		
A. J. Berlin	1-0-0-0-0	Alfred Castleman	3-0-0-9-14
Alfred Bishop	1-0-0-0-0	C. D. Castleman	1-0-0-0-0
Daniel S. Bonham	2-0-0-2-9	William A.	
Nancy Boyston	0-0-0-0-0	Castleman	1-0-0-4-3
William Berry	1-0-0-12-7	Ury Castleman's	
Mrs. M. C. Bowen	0-0-0-0-2	Est.	0-0-0-0-0
R. S. Briarly	1-0-0-0-8	William Carper	1-0-0-0-2
Abraham Beavers	1-0-0-0-3	Samuel A.	
Adam Barr	1-0-0-0-1	Cambell	1-0-0-0-0
Jesse Butler	1-0-0-0-1	Robert A. Colston	1-0-0-6-8
Miss E. Bell	0-0-0-0-1	John Copenhaver	2-0-0-6-8
James H. Bartlett	1-0-0-6-4	Joseph K. Carter	1-0-0-2-4
Jonah P. Bell	1-0-0-2-6	John A. Carter	1-0-0-2-6
George W.		John W. Carter	1-0-0-0-0
Bowling	1-0-0-0-0	Parkinson Corder	1-10-0-0-0
Thomas Brown	1-0-0-0-0	Thomas Carter	0-0-0-6-5
Peter Bennett	1-0-0-0-0	William G. Carter	1-0-0-1-1
Patrick Brady	1-0-0-0-0	William H. Carter	1-0-0-1-0
Thomas J. Bragg	1-0-0-1-1	James H. Clarke	1-0-0-3-1
Robert W. Briggs	1-0-0-3-3	Thomas H. Crow	1-0-0-8-8
William Briggs	1-0-0-1-0	John Carroll	1-0-0-0-1
George S. Bonham	2-0-0-8-12	John Cooper	1-0-0-0-2
Enos S. Brown	1-0-0-1-0	Lewis Carrell	1-0-0-0-1
Charles H.		Thomas Carrill	1-0-0-0-2
Brabham	1-0-0-0-0	Andrew Cornell	1-0-0-0-1
William Brabham	1-0-0-0-0	Michel	
Samuel Bromley	1-0-0-0-7	Copenhaver	1-0-0-0-0
James M. Berlin	1-0-0-0-0	John N. Collier	1-0-0-1-6
James H. Bitzer	1-0-0-2-11	Lucy A. Calmese	2-0-0-4-4
Joseph Bell	1-0-0-0-0	Ann B. Cook	0-0-0-16-17
Dr. William Best	1-0-0-1-1	John H. Crebbs	1-0-0-2-6
Col. S. H. Bowen	1-0-0-1-1	James Chishome	1-0-0-0-0
G. W. Board	1-0-0-0-2	James Carroll	1-0-0-0-0

Clarke County, Virginia Personal Property Tax Lists 1854-1870
1861

Robert H. Castleman	1-0-0-4-9	Christian DeBow Washington	1-0-0-0-0
Mariam Catlett	1-0-0-8-12	Dearmont	1-0-0-6-10
Benjamine Crampton	1-0-0-1-2	William Deahl	1-0-0-1-1
Frank Caniford	1-0-0-0-0	John Drish	1-0-0-0-1
James E. Chamblin	1-0-0-0-0	John Dannivan	1-0-0-0-0
Sally Cloud	0-0-0-3-0	L. L. & A. Davis	0-0-0-1-0
Elizabeth Clink	0-0-0-0-0	Jerimiah Dailey	1-0-0-0-0
Michael Crim	1-0-0-0-0	Thomas Duke	1-0-0-0-0
Henry Canniford	1-0-0-0-0	George W. Diffandaffer	1-0-0-0-1
William B. Crim	1-0-0-0-0	Hugh Davis	1-0-0-0-0
James Carter	1-0-0-0-4	Aaron Duble	1-0-0-0-0
Hannah Cain	0-0-0-0-0	Peter Dearmont	1-0-0-2-3
Franklin B. Carter	1-0-0-2-4	James Doran	1-0-0-0-1
John [__?] Cooper	1-0-0-0-0	Marcus Dishman	1-0-0-2-4
Resin Carroll	1-0-0-0-1	Joseph Doran	1-0-0-0-1
James Carter	1-0-0-0-1	F. B. Doran	1-0-0-0-0
John B. Carter	1-0-0-3-1	James W. Doran	1-0-0-0-0
B. F. Crawford	1-0-0-0-0	John D. Davis	1-0-0-1-0
Sarah Chamblin	0-0-0-0-1	William Donohooe	1-0-0-0-0
James L. Carter	1-0-0-0-0	H. P. Deahl	1-0-0-0-0
John Cain	2-0-0-0-4		
Harrison Cooper	1-0-0-0-0	Jacob Enders	1-0-0-10-12
James H. Cambell	0-0-0-1-3	Henry Edwards	1-0-0-0-2
John R. Crockerell	1-0-0-0-0	William G. Everhart	2-0-0-2-7
John P. Carrigan	1-0-0-0-0	Henson Elliott	2-0-0-5-10
Charles R. Corder	1-0-0-0-0	Jacob W. Everhart	1-0-0-0-1
William Carwell	1-0-0-0-0	William H. Edwards	1-0-0-0-1
William H. Colston	1-0-0-0-0	Albert Elsea	1-0-0-0-7
Michel Cain	1-0-0-0-0	Joseph W. Edwards	1-0-0-0-1
G. Q. Carper	1-0-0-0-0	John Ellyet	1-0-0-2-9
Jacob Carper	0-0-0-0-0	Thomas A. Everhart	1-0-0-0-4
S. C. Castleman	0-0-0-0-0		
Richard Dulaney	0-0-0-4-6		
H. H. Dunbar	1-0-0-0-0		

Clarke County, Virginia Personal Property Tax Lists 1854-1870
1861

William G.			John L. Grant	1-0-0-1-3
Everhart	1-0-0-0-0		John J. Gordon	1-0-0-4-10
John J. Emory	1-0-0-0-1		James W.	
			Galeway	1-0-0-0-0
O. R. Funston	1-0-0-21-32		Thos W. Griffith	1-0-0-0-0
D. J. F. Fauntleroy	2-0-0-6-5		James F. Green	1-0-0-3-8
James A. Foster	1-0-0-3-7		Mary Green	0-0-0-3-0
Josiah Furguson	1-0-0-2-4		Isabelle Glass	0-0-0-0-0
William A.			Richard N. Green	1-0-0-4-7
Furgerson	1-0-0-0-1		Thomas E. Gold	2-0-0-12-21
Johnston Furr	1-0-0-1-5		George W.	
Israel Fidler	1-0-0-0-0		Gordon	2-0-0-3-10
Elizabeth Fleming	0-0-0-2-3		Samuel Grubb	
Joseph Fleming	2-0-0-0-5		Senr.	1-0-0-0-0
Wm Fowler Jr.	1-0-0-0-1		Henry N. Grigsby	1-0-0-6-9
James Furr	1-0-0-0-1		S. J. Gant	1-0-0-1-0
Wm Fowler Sr.	1-0-0-0-1		Lewis F. Glass	1-0-0-9-11
John Foreman	1-0-0-0-0		Martin Gaunt	1-0-0-7-8
Thomas Fowler	1-0-0-0-2		William Gibbs	1-0-0-0-0
Martin Feltner	1-0-0-0-3		William B. Grubb	1-0-0-0-1
Dennis Fenton	1-0-0-2-2		George W. Grubb	1-0-0-0-0
Marcus R.			Samuel Grubb Jr.	1-0-0-0-0
Feehran [sic]	1-0-0-1-2		John M. Grubb	1-0-0-0-0
Joshua Fellows	1-0-0-0-2		John Gruber	1-0-0-1-4
Enoch Furr	1-0-0-0-0		George Gardner	1-0-0-0-0
Daniel Furr	1-0-0-0-0		Adam	
Joseph W. Feltner	1-0-0-0-1		Greenwauldt	1-0-0-0-1
Barney Fairback	1-0-0-0-0		Mathew Grimes	1-0-0-0-0
Henry S. Fox	1-0-0-0-0		Thomas E. Gibson	1-0-0-0-0
Alexander Finnell	1-0-0-0-1		L. A. Glaze	1-0-0-3-4
John R. Fugett	1-0-0-0-0		Elias M. Green	1-0-0-1-0
Evart Fowler	1-0-0-0-0		Charles Grubb	1-0-0-0-1
George Fiddler	1-0-0-0-0		M. L. Grubb	1-0-0-0-0
John Franks	1-0-0-0-0		Elizabeth Glover	0-0-0-1-0
Ephriam Furr	1-0-0-0-0		Phillip Gordon	1-0-0-4-4
Fernando Fox	1-0-0-0-0		Sydnor Garrett	1-0-0-0-1
John W. Fiddler	1-0-0-0-0		Manen [?] T. Gray	1-0-0-0-0
F. M. Feltner	1-0-0-0-0		J. R. Grigsby	1-0-0-7-25
Christian Fonda	1-0-0-0-0			

Clarke County, Virginia Personal Property Tax Lists 1854-1870
1861

William Grubb	
of Thornbury	1-0-0-0-0
Joseph W. &	
J. L. Grantham	1-0-0-0-9
H. K. Gregg	1-0-0-0-0
John M. Gibson	1-1-0-5-7
James W. Ginnes	1-0-0-0-2
E. Grubb	1-0-0-0-1
Zeb Grey	1-0-0-0-0
T. K. Glover	1-0-0-0-0
James T. Grubb	1-0-0-0-0
Thomas	
Gward [sic]	1-0-0-0-0
William C. Gover	1-0-0-0-0
Henry Harrison	1-1-0-14-13
William Hay	1-0-0-5-2
Samuel	
Heflebower	1-0-0-6-16
C. W. Hardesty	1-0-0-3-7
Samuel Hunt	1-0-0-4-9
Abraham Huyett	1-0-0-0-1
James H. Hooe	1-0-0-0-0
William Heflin	1-0-0-0-0
William G.	
Hardesty	1-0-0-2-4
James M.	
Hardesty	2-0-0-2-6
Cornelius Hoff	1-0-0-0-0
Alexander	
Holtzclaw	1-0-0-0-1
John Hughes	1-0-0-0-1
Thomas Hughes	1-0-0-0-1
William B. Harris	1-0-0-11-13
Dr. B. Harrison	1-0-0-16-20
Henry Huntsbury	1-0-0-2-7
Catharine V. Hall	0-0-0-8-11
James F. Howell	1-0-0-0-0
John W. Hibbard	1-0-0-0-0

W. R. Helvestine	1-0-0-1-0
A. T. M. Hough	1-0-0-2-1
Geo & J. T. Harris	2-0-0-6-12
John W. Hall	1-0-0-1-0
John Hummer	1-0-0-0-2
Jacob Heflebower	1-0-0-8-14
Cornelius Hawks	1-0-0-0-0
Thomas L.	
Humphrey	1-0-0-3-5
Edward R.	
Harrison	1-0-0-1-1
Joseph R.	
Hardesty	1-0-0-3-11
James W.	
Hummer	1-0-0-0-2
Henry A. Hibbard	1-0-0-0-0
J. B. Hawthorn	1-0-0-0-4
John W. Holland	1-0-0-0-0
John & Thomas	
Heskitt	2-0-0-0-0
Solomon Hibs	1-0-0-0-1
Humphrey Hoff	1-0-0-0-0
Mary A. Hooe	0-0-0-0-0
J. M. Hite	1-0-0-6-8
J. J. Hite	1-0-0-5-14
Henry Huyett	1-0-0-3-8
David Hech	1-0-0-0-0
Henry D. Hooe	1-0-0-0-0
William	
Haunam [?]	1-0-0-0-0
John Henry	1-0-0-0-0
Lewis C. Hunt	1-0-0-0-0
James P. Hough	1-0-0-0-0
G. H. Isler	1-0-0-0-1
Herod Jenkins	1-0-0-0-2
Lucy M. Joliffe	0-0-0-4-7
Leonard Jones	1-0-0-3-7

99

Clarke County, Virginia Personal Property Tax Lists 1854-1870
1861

Thomas Jones	1-0-0-1-7	William C. Kennerly	1-0-0-4-1
William B. Joliffe	1-0-0-0-0	Wm B. Kennon	1-0-0-0-0
Maury Janney	0-0-0-2-0	Joseph McK. Kennerly	1-0-0-9-14
Thomas Jenkins	1-0-0-0-2	C. B. R. Kennerly	0-0-0-5-3
James W. Johnston	1-0-0-0-1	Joseph Kline	1-0-0-0-0
William A. Jackson	1-0-0-6-11	Dr. R. Kownslar	1-0-0-6-4
Andrew Jackson	1-0-0-0-0	John Kelley	1-0-0-0-0
A. M. Johnston	1-0-0-1-5	E. V. Kercheval	1-0-0-0-1
Amelia A. Jordan	0-0-0-0-1	James H. Kennon	1-0-0-0-0
Rev. William Johnston	1-0-0-2-1	Henry Krombling	1-0-0-2-1
Edward Jenkins	1-0-0-0-0	Ruben Krombling	1-0-0-0-0
Joseph R. Jones	1-0-0-4-1	James M. Kiger	1-0-0-0-4
James W. Johnston	1-0-0-0-0	George W. Kelly	0-0-0-0-0
William Johnston	1-0-0-0-0	John N. Kitchen	1-0-0-3-12
F. L. Johnston	1-0-0-0-0	Judson J. Kerfoot	1-0-0-8-12
Ebin Jenkins	1-0-0-0-1	Henry Knight	1-0-0-0-0
John S. Johnston	1-0-0-2-5	John B. Larue	3-0-0-19-30
		John D. Larue	1-0-0-5-9
		Edward Lewis	1-0-0-3-0
Martha L. Isler	0-0-0-0-1	John Longerbeam	1-0-0-0-2
		A. L. P. Larue	1-0-0-6-9
Solomon R. Jackson	1-0-0-0-0	James W. Larue	1-0-0-8-10
		C. C. Larue	1-0-0-1-3
George T. Johnston	1-0-0-0-0	Squire Lee	1-0-0-0-1
		Christopher Lee	1-0-0-0-2
		Dr. J. M. Lindsay	1-0-0-0-1
John N. Kimmell	1-0-0-0-1	Eli Littleton	1-0-0-3-4
James F. Kerfoot	1-0-0-5-12	William Littleton	1-0-0-0-3
Dr. F. J. Kerfoot	1-0-0-9-12	John W. Littleton	1-0-0-0-2
William C. Kerfoot	1-0-0-10-13	Henry Lloyd	1-0-0-0-3
		John Lloyd	1-0-0-0-0
W. F. & B. M. Knight	2-0-0-9-16	James L. Lloyd	1-0-0-0-2
		David Lloyd	1-0-0-0-0
Middleton Keeler	1-0-0-0-0	John A. Lloyd	1-0-0-0-0
Samuel G. Kneller	1-0-0-5-8	Moses Lewin	1-0-0-0-1
		John Lock Sr.	1-0-0-3-7

Clarke County, Virginia Personal Property Tax Lists 1854-1870
1861

John Louthan	2-0-0-8-6	F. B. Meade	1-0-0-10-16
John K. Louthan	1-0-0-3-7	John M. Meade	1-0-0-3-12
James T. Louthan	1-0-0-3-9	E. B. Mantor	1-0-0-4-5
Mrs. M. Lewis	0-0-0-4-4	R. K. Meade	1-0-0-3-1
George W. Lewis	1-0-0-6-0	D° Trustee	0-0-0-0-0
Minor Lanham	1-0-0-1-1	Samuel	
James Lanham	1-0-0-0-1	McCormick	1-0-0-0-0
John M. Lupton	1-0-0-1-0	David Meade	1-0-0-3-12
John W. Luke	1-0-0-9-17	Miss Mary	
John R. Locke	1-0-0-0-6	Meade	0-0-0-4-1
R. H. Lee	0-0-0-5-8	Benjamin	
Frank Littleton	1-0-0-0-2	Morgan	2-0-0-26-33
John T.		D° Guardian for	
Longerbeam	1-0-0-0-0	Miss Alexander	0-0-0-0-0
George Lanham	1-0-0-0-1	D° Guardian for	
F. Little	1-0-0-3-8	J. W. Alexander	0-0-0-0-0
Abraham		John Morgan	1-0-0-9-9
Longerbeam	1-0-0-0-2	Dr. C. McCormick's	
Benjamin Lock	1-0-0-0-5	Est.	0-0-0-22-30
Benjamin		Thomas	
Longerbeam	1-0-0-0-3	McCormick	1-0-0-11-10
Charles Loyd	1-0-0-0-1	D° Guardian	0-0-0-7-0
William Lanham	1-0-0-0-1	P. McCormick	1-0-0-13-14
William Loyd	2-0-0-0-6	D° Trustee for	
William D. Lee	1-0-0-0-0	E. McCormick	0-0-0-0-0
James W. Loyd	1-0-0-0-0	D° for Ann	
A. J. Loyd	1-0-0-0-2	Stribling	0-0-0-0-0
William H. Levi	1-0-0-0-1	D° for E. Frost	0-0-0-0-0
Rice W. Levi	1-0-0-2-9	D° Guardian for	
John Lee	1-0-0-0-2	E. McCormick	0-0-0-0-0
Howard Lock	1-0-0-0-0	D° Agent for	
Ludwell Lee	1-0-0-0-2	Mary Stribling	0-0-0-0-0
Joseph B. Lindsey	1-0-0-0-4	Ottoway	
James W. Lee	1-0-0-0-0	McCormick	1-0-0-9-9
John M. Lock	1-0-0-1-0	P. N. Meade	1-0-0-5-18
Dangerfield Lloyd	1-0-0-0-2	R. P. Morgan	1-0-0-0-7
Westley Long	1-0-0-0-1	Margaret A.	
Lewis Lanham	1-0-0-0-1	McCormick	0-0-0-1-0
John D. Lloyd	1-0-0-0-0		

Clarke County, Virginia Personal Property Tax Lists 1854-1870
1861

James			Col. Fr.	
McCormick	1-0-0-3-7		McCormick	1-0-0-26-19
Edward			Addison Muntzel	1-0-0-0-0
McCormick	1-0-0-18-23		E. C. Marshall	1-0-0-6-9
Peter McMurray	1-0-0-2-4		Jarret McDonald	1-0-0-1-3
A. R. Milton	1-0-0-3-1		Harvey McDonald	1-0-0-0-0
S. P. Moore	1-0-0-0-0		John G. McCauley	1-0-0-0-0
W. W. Meade	1-0-0-0-0		John Morgan Jr.	1-0-0-2-7
A. P. Moore	1-0-0-0-0		M. Moore Trustee	
James T. Murphy	1-0-0-0-0		Mrs. Stryder	0-0-0-0-0
L.D. Maddex	1-0-0-0-0		Joseph E. Mason	1-0-0-1-1
James Mitchell	2-0-0-5-6		Bishop W. Meade	1-0-0-0-1
David H. McGuire	1-0-0-8-7		John T.Marts	1-0-0-0-0
William D.			William T. Milton	1-0-0-2-6
McGuire	1-0-0-14-18		Joseph Menifee	1-0-0-0-0
Alexander			Henry Messmer	1-0-0-4-8
Marshall	1-0-0-3-8		Calwell Miley	1-0-0-0-1
John Marshall	1-0-0-4-2		Joseph T. Mitchell	0-0-0-11-9
Miss Susan			David Meade	
Marshall	0-0-0-4-5		Trustee	0-0-0-3-8
C. C. McIntyre	1-0-0-6-8		G. Markell	1-0-0-0-1
Nathaniel Mercer	1-0-0-0-3		Richard F.	
James Murphy	1-0-0-0-0		McPhillan	1-0-0-0-0
Stephen Marlow	1-0-0-0-2		Joseph Moore	1-0-0-0-0
George Marpole	1-0-0-0-1		Thomas Murphy	1-0-0-0-0
A. M. Moore	1-0-0-7-11		John Murphy	1-0-0-0-0
Samuel Moreland	2-0-0-0-6		Moses B. Murphy	1-0-0-0-0
Moses G. Miley	1-0-0-0-4		Jesse Mercer	1-0-0-0-0
E. W. Massey	1-0-0-8-10			
James			Hugh M. Nelson	1-0-0-13-20
McClaughry	1-0-0-0-3		William N. Nelson	1-0-0-7-17
Samuel T. Marts	1-0-0-0-1		James H. Nevill	1-0-0-1-0
Mclain McClingan	1-0-0-0-2		Philip W. Nelson	1-0-0-13-17
Richard Morgan	1-0-0-0-3		Miss A. &	
Patrick Murry	1-0-0-0-0		R. Nelson	0-0-0-3-0
Alfred Marts	1-0-0-0-2		John B. Norris	1-0-0-5-4
John P. McMurry	1-0-0-3-4		John R. Nunn	1-0-0-5-6
S. J. C. Moore	1-0-0-4-0		Dr. S. S. Neill	1-0-0-4-2

Clarke County, Virginia Personal Property Tax Lists 1854-1870
1861

William Nicewarner	1-0-0-1-6		A. N. Pierce	1-0-0-5-8
			Peter Mc Pierce	1-0-0-4-9
Thomas Nicewarner	1-1-0-0-3		Paul Pierce	1-0-0-9-7
			Mrs. E. M. Page	0-0-0-6-0
J. R. Nunn Guard for			James M. Pine	2-0-0-0-2
Miss Dix	0-0-0-0-0		John Poston	1-0-0-0-2
D° for			T. P. Pendleton	1-0-0-11-16
G. W. Carter	0-0-0-0-0		Washington F. Pagett	2-0-0-1-6
George Orear	1-0-0-1-2		William Pyles	1-0-0-0-1
Benjamine Orear	1-0-0-8-6		John Patterson	1-0-0-1-6
Elizabeth Orear	0-0-0-10-11		James S. Payne	1-0-0-0-1
Overseers of Poor	2-0-0-0-5		Barnett Prichard	1-0-0-0-0
Susan Orear	0-0-0-0-0		Michel Pape	1-0-0-0-1
Addison Orear	1-0-0-0-0		Pulliam & Howell	1-0-0-2-1
Hugh Oroke	1-0-0-0-0		Thomas Pyles	1-0-0-0-1
			John T. Patterson	1-0-0-0-0
Phillip Powers	1-0-0-10-14		James Puller	1-0-0-0-0
George Patterson	1-0-0-0-1		Willis Prichard	1-0-0-0-0
Charles H. Payton	1-0-0-0-0		William H. Pape	1-0-0-0-0
William G. Pierce	0-0-0-1-2			
Isaac Pigeon	1-0-0-0-2		Bennett Russell	2-0-0-11-16
John E. Page	1-0-0-15-25		Thomas W. Russell	1-0-0-1-4
R. E. Parker	1-0-0-0-13			
John Pierce	1-0-0-1-0		Michel Russell	1-0-0-0-0
Benjamin Perry	1-0-0-0-0		W. H. Roberson	1-0-0-2-7
Bushrod Puller	1-0-0-0-0		M. C. Rootes	0-0-0-1-0
Samuel Pidgeon	1-0-0-0-9		John Roland	2-0-0-0-9
Dr. Mat Page Est.	0-0-0-3-1		E. W. Royston	0-0-0-2-0
Susan R. Page	0-0-0-23-32		Mathew W. Royston	1-0-0-0-2
Conrad Pope	1-0-0-0-1			
A. C. Page	1-0-0-0-0		John Rippon	1-0-0-0-2
John Page Jr.	1-0-0-15-16		Peter K. Royston	1-0-0-0-3
Alexander Parkins	1-0-0-0-1		Uriah Royston	1-0-0-0-0
Man R. Page	1-0-0-13-17		Daniel B. Richards	1-0-0-1-0
G. R. Page	1-0-0-3-5		G. R. Royston	1-0-0-0-0
John M. Pope	1-0-0-0-0		Nancy Redman	0-0-0-1-0
Mathew Pulliam	1-0-0-4-0		G. W. Rutter	1-0-0-1-0
Elizabeth Pierce	0-0-0-3-5		James H. Roland	1-0-0-0-1

Clarke County, Virginia Personal Property Tax Lists 1854-1870
1861

Addison Romine	1-0-0-3-5		Thomas W. Raynolds	1-0-0-0-0
George Reno	1-0-0-0-0		Samuel Resser	1-0-0-0-0
Westley Russell	0-0-0-0-3			
Rube Rains	1-0-0-0-0			
Patrick Rogers	1-0-0-0-0		Sowers & Grady	2-0-0-7-8
C. H. Richards	1-0-0-0-0		Spilman & Markell	0-0-0-0-0
Jacob B. Ritter	1-0-0-0-0		Waman C. Smith	1-0-0-0-0
Beverly Randolph	1-0-0-14-27		Robert L. Spilman	1-0-0-2-1
Dr. C. Randolph	2-0-0-25-30		Mrs. M. E. Shumate	1-0-0-4-11
A. C. Randolph	1-0-0-0-3		Col. T. Smith	3-0-0-22-19
John Raynolds	1-0-0-1-0		Daniel W. Sowers	1-0-0-14-17
John Ramey	1-0-0-0-0		John W. Sprint	1-0-0-0-0
William Riley	1-0-0-0-0		Elizabeth Sowers	0-0-0-0-0
Mathew Rust	1-0-0-1-1		Henry Shipherd	1-0-0-0-0
John J. Riley	1-0-0-5-7		John W. Sowers	1-0-0-10-24
D° Trustee for Mrs. Taylor	0-0-0-0-0		William Sowers	1-0-0-13-18
William A. Riley	1-0-0-3-12		Champ Shepherd	1-0-0-9-15
Thomas Reardon	2-0-0-0-1		Carter Shepherd	1-0-0-5-10
Samuel Rutter	1-0-0-0-0		P. D. Shepherd	1-0-0-7-9
John D. Richardson	1-0-0-10-19		George Smedley	1-0-0-0-1
Jamees W. Ryan	1-0-0-4-6		Mary C. Shively	0-0-0-0-1
Enos Richmond	1-0-0-0-0		E. J. & W. D. Smith	2-1-0-33-44
Richmond & Stoll	0-0-0-1-3		Paul Smith	1-0-0-5-10
James F. Raynolds	1-0-0-0-2		Dr. Philip Smith	1-0-0-22-24
James Ritter	1-0-0-2-5		Daniel C. Snyder	1-0-0-5-4
Jane C. Randolph	0-0-0-2-0		James Sowers	1-0-0-0-1
Mathew T. Royston	1-0-0-0-1		William M. Sowers	1-0-0-1-12
Richard S. Ridgeway	2-0-0-1-9		F. E. Sowers	1-0-0-6-9
John Ritter	1-0-0-0-5		Daniel H. Sowers	1-0-0-4-9
John W. Russell	1-0-0-0-5		Charles H. Smith	1-0-0-3-7
D. T. Richards	1-0-0-0-1		Thomas Smallwood	1-0-0-0-7
Elisha Romine	1-0-0-0-0		William R. Stewart	1-0-0-1-1
Joseph F. Ryan	1-0-0-2-1		Charles Swarts	1-0-0-0-0
Cyrus Richmond	1-0-0-0-0			

Clarke County, Virginia Personal Property Tax Lists 1854-1870
1861

Name	Values	Name	Values
John Shaffer	1-0-0-0-0	Mrs. S. E. T. Stribling	1-0-0-16-15
George Shumate	1-0-0-0-0	William F. Stoll	1-0-0-1-0
W. L. Smith	1-0-0-0-0	Rev. H. Suter	1-0-0-3-1
G. R. Smith	1-0-0-0-0	Jacob Spotts	1-0-0-0-0
John J. Shaffer	1-0-0-0-3	Henry Stickles Sr.	1-0-0-0-0
Simon Stickle	1-0-0-0-1	Mount Joy Shell	1-0-0-0-1
James M. Shearer	1-0-0-0-0	Henry Stickles Jr.	1-0-0-0-0
Franklin Swarts	1-0-0-0-0	F. L. Sowers	1-0-0-3-3
Charles Showers	1-0-0-0-0	Joseph Stewart	1-0-0-0-0
William Strother	1-0-0-3-7	Silvester Smawlwood [sic]	1-0-0-0-0
John Shell	1-0-0-0-0	B. T. Silman	1-0-0-0-1
Stephen Shell	1-0-0-0-0	Shepherd & Duble	0-1-0-0-2
Simon R. Stump	1-0-0-0-1	G. W. Shuller	1-0-0-0-1
James Shackleford	0-0-0-0-0	Henry T. Shearer	1-0-0-0-0
Dennis Shean	1-0-0-0-1	James L. Showers	2-0-0-2-1
James W. Stephenson	1-0-0-4-7	John Stone Street	1-0-0-0-0
Thomas Sprint	1-0-0-0-2	Craven Sheer	1-0-0-0-0
Joseph Shipe	1-0-0-0-0	Aujustn [sic] Swarts	1-0-0-0-0
A. J. Shipe	1-0-0-0-0	John F. Thompson	0-0-0-0-2
William G. Steel	1-0-0-0-0	Sarah Timberlake	1-0-0-8-10
James Steel	1-0-0-0-0	James Thomas	1-0-0-0-0
James H. Swain [?]	1-0-0-0-0	Adam F. Thompson	1-0-0-0-1
Vincent S. Settle Trustee	1-0-0-1-0	Greenberry Thompson	1-0-0-1-2
Burr Smallwood	1-0-0-0-2	French Thompson	1-0-0-1-2
Hesskiah Slusher	1-0-0-1-0	Bailes Thompson	1-0-0-0-3
Marcus L. Sinclair	1-0-0-0-0	Charles Trussell	1-0-0-1-6
Margaret Swann	0-0-0-0-0	William Taylor	1-0-0-23-18
George Smith	1-0-0-0-0	Robert Tapscott	1-0-0-0-0
George S. Spaulding	1-0-0-0-0	Eliza Taylor	0-0-0-6-2
John H. Shoebridge	1-0-0-1-1	Isaac Tally	1-0-0-0-0
Benjamine Shipe	2-0-0-0-0	Moses B. Trussell	1-0-0-1-7
G. W. Shimp	1-0-0-0-0	William Trenary	2-0-0-2-3

Clarke County, Virginia Personal Property Tax Lists 1854-1870
1861

Calvin Thacker	1-0-0-0-1	H. T. Wheat	1-0-0-0-7
Dr. Bushrod Taylor	1-0-0-4-2	B. F. Wilson	1-0-0-0-0
		Jeremiah Wilson	1-0-0-0-0
Snowden Tumblin	1-0-0-0-0	John Wilson	1-0-0-0-0
Mason Tinsman	1-0-0-0-1	F. B. Whiting	2-0-0-23-17
Ludwell Tinsman	1-0-0-0-0	F. H. Whiting	1-0-0-2-7
Isaac Tyson Jr.	0-0-0-0-11	W. W. Whiting	1-0-0-7-6
John H. Taylor	1-0-0-0-0	N. B. Whiting	1-0-0-9-19
Mrs. Eliza Tucker	0-0-0-0-0	Allen Williams	1-0-0-12-20
Stephen D. Timberlake	0-0-0-0-0	Thompson Writt	1-0-0-0-1
		William Willingham	1-0-0-0-3
William G. Taylor	1-0-0-1-3	L. P. Williams	1-0-0-7-7
Susan Taylor	1-0-0-3-3	John T. Willingham	1-0-0-0-1
Dr. Thomas Turner	1-0-0-1-2	Hezekiah Wiley	1-0-0-0-1
Griffin Taylor	0-0-0-0-1	Daniel Wade & Bro.	2-0-0-1-4
William F. Thompson	1-0-0-0-0	Cornelius Wiley	1-0-0-0-1
James W. Tanquary	1-0-0-1-4	John Wiley	1-0-0-0-0
James F. Trayhern	1-0-0-0-1	G. W. Wiley	1-0-0-0-2
Samuel M. Trussell	1-0-0-0-3	S. B. Windham	1-0-0-0-3
Albert Thompson	1-0-0-0-0	Thomas C. Windham	1-0-0-0-0
Thomas Hatcher	1-0-0-0-0	James Wiley	1-0-0-0-0
Benjamine Thompson Sr.	1-0-0-0-0	Daniel Welch	1-0-0-0-3
		James V. Weir	1-0-0-6-14
William H. Thompson	1-0-0-0-0	Jesse Wright	1-0-0-0-2
Benjamine F. Thompson	1-0-0-0-0	Robert W. Whittington	1-0-0-1-1
		Alexander Wood	1-0-0-0-1
Mrs. Mary Tuley	0-0-0-2-0	Bennett Wood	1-0-0-0-0
		Walker B. Wilson	1-0-0-0-0
Jacob Vanmeter	1-0-0-3-9	Lucinda Washington	0-0-0-4-0
William T. Vaughn	1-0-0-0-0	Samuel G. Wyman	0-0-0-11-15
Jacob B. Vorus	1-0-0-0-5	Revd. Charles White	1-0-0-2-1

Clarke County, Virginia Personal Property Tax Lists 1854-1870
1861

Miss Allice Writt	0-0-0-0-0	John A. Wilson	1-0-0-0-0
Obediah Willingham	1-0-0-0-1	E. P. Williams	1-0-0-3-1
Col. J. W. Ware	1-0-0-16-17	James W. Willingham	1-0-0-0-0
Henry R. Wilson	1-0-0-1-0	Joseph H. Wilson	1-0-0-0-0
William Wharton	1-0-0-0-0	F. W. Wheat	1-0-0-0-0
Lewis Whittington	1-0-0-0-0	C. F. Willingham	1-0-0-0-0
George W. Willingham	1-0-0-0-0	Robert Wilson	1-0-0-0-0
G. F. Willingham	1-0-0-0-0	Lewis Wood	1-0-0-0-0
Robert B. Wood	0-0-0-1-12		
Thornton O. Windham	1-0-0-0-7	John Yowell	1-0-0-0-2
Jackson Wheeler	1-0-0-0-1	William H. Young	1-0-0-1-1
		Simeon Yowell	1-0-0-0-0

[Free Blacks]

Daniel Jenkins	0-1-0-0-0	Peter Coates	0-1-0-0-2
Mowen Harris	0-1-0-0-1	Joseph Brannum [?]	0-1-0-0-0
James Butler	0-1-0-0-0	Charles Clifton	0-1-0-0-0
William Parker	0-1-0-0-0	Nancy Parker	0-0-0-0-0
Spencer Johnston	0-1-0-0-0	[See continuation at end of the year, next page]	
John Walker	0-1-0-0-0		
Burwell Cook	0-1-0-0-0		

Benjamin Thompson Jr.	1-0-0-0-3
Dr. W. A. Bradford	1 white, 8 slaves

Clarke County, Virginia Personal Property Tax Lists 1854-1870
1861

List of Free Negroes in Clarke County for 1861

Names, sex, age, occupation

Name	sex	age	occupation
Jno Osburn	m	22	Labourer
Wm Allen	m	30	Labourer
Peter Dixon	m	23	Labourer
Walter Howard	m	60	Blacksmith
Danl Jenkins	m	24	Labourer
Winaford Thompson	f	70	--
Jane Thornton	f	13	--
Winaford Ranson	f	50	--
Flory Richardson	f	15	--
Richard Ranson	m	15	Labourer
Sarah Ranson	f	11	--
Mowen Harris	m	55	Labourer
Anthony Smith	m	23	Labourer
James Butler	m	51	Labourer
Wm Parker	m	41	Labourer
Spencer Johnson	m	50	Labourer
John Walker	m	30	Labourer
Burwell Cook	m	46	Labourer
Olley Robinson	m	50	Labourer
Peter Coast	m	61	Labourer
Delpha Coats	f	56	--
Nancy Parker	f	70	--
Ann Davis	f	46	--
James Jones	m	31	Labourer
Jefferson Jackson	m	50	Labourer
Jacob Webb	m	24	Barber
Mary Weaver	f	26	--
Julia Weaver	f	27	--
Alfred Ball	m	24	Labourer
John Blantham	m	41	Labourer

Clarke County, Virginia Personal Property Tax Lists 1854-1870

1862

Columns: 1) White males over 21, 2) Male free negroes over 21, 3) Slaves of all ages & both sexes, 4) Horses, mules, asses & jennets

Buckner Ashby	3-0-29-12
Mason Anderson	1-0-9-6
M. B. Anderson	1-0-3-2
Edgar Allen	1-0-29-18
Jesse Allen	1-0-0-1
John Alexander	2-0-31-16
N. F. & J. E. Anderson	2-0-2-12
Robt Ashby Jr.	1-0-0-0
Robt Ashby Sr.	1-0-0-0
Nimrod Ashby	1-0-0-2
Geo Anderson	1-0-0-0
Geo W. Ashby	1-0-1-5
Wm T. Allen	1-0-16-6
Geo W. Allen	1-0-2-5
Thos H. Alexander	1-0-6-4
Jno Allison	1-0-0-0
Margt E. Alexander	0-0-1-0
A. C. Ashby	1-0-0-1
D. T. Armstrong	1-0-0-0
Jno H. Anderson	1-0-2-1
Jacob Ambrose	1-0-0-0
Jno W. Anderson	1-0-0-3
L. B. Ashby	1-0-0-0
Jno W. Anderson of Nimr[d]	1-0-?-4
N. F. Anderson	0-0-0-0
A. S. Allen	1-0-0-0
Owen Allen	1-0-0-0
Dr. R. S. Blackburne	2-0-15-10
W. Brabham	1-0-0-0
Geo H. Burwell	2-0-91-53
D° as Trustee	0-0-0-0
Nathnl Burwell	1-0-26-30
Jno F. Burchwell	1-0-15-10
Geo H. Bell	1-0-0-0
Squire Bell	1-0-1-1
Hector Bell	1-0-2-2
Lewis Berlin	1-0-0-0
Philip Berlin	1-0-9-5
Geo W. Berlin	1-0-0-0
Geo C. Blakemore	1-0-10-7
Neill Barnett	1-0-17-12
Jas Bell Sr.	2-0-0-2
Jas C. Briggs	1-0-12-10
Arthur Briggs	1-0-0-3
Miss Magt Burchwell	1-0-16-3
Jno Bromley	1-0-0-13
Jno W. Byrd	1-0-18-6
Jos B. Beevers	1-0-0-1
C. Bowser	1-0-2-0
Geo W. Bromley	1-1-3-6
S. R. Burwell	0-0-5-0
A. C. Benn	0-0-1-2
D. S. Bonham	1-1-3-6
Miss N. Boston	0-0-6-0
Wm Berry	1-0-23-7
R. S. Bryarley	1-0-15-9
Wm O. Brown	1-0-0-0
A. J. Berlin	1-0-0-0

Clarke County, Virginia Personal Property Tax Lists 1854-1870
1862

Alfred Bishop	1-0-0-0		Alfred Castleman	2-0-15-14
Geo Board	1-0-0-0		Wm A. Castleman	1-0-5-1
Miss Mary			Mrs. Urey Castleman's	
Bowser	0-0-0-0		Est.	0-0-0-0
Abraham Beavers	1-0-0-2		Wm Carper	1-0-0-2
Adam Barr	1-0-0-0		Saml A. Campbell	1-0-0-0
Jesse Butler	1-0-0-1		Robt A. Colston	1-0-12-5
Miss Emily Bell	0-0-0-1		John Copenhaver	1-0-13-4
Jas H. Bartlett	1-0-7-5		Jno H. Crebs	1-0-3-2
Jonah Bell	1-0-1-4		Jos K. Carter	1-0-7-3
Geo W. Bolin	1-0-0-0		Jno A. Carter	1-0-9-4
Thos Brown	1-1-1-0		Jno W. Carter	1-0-0-0
Peter Bennett	1-0-0-0		Parkinson Corder	1-0-0-1
Patrick Brady	1-0-0-0		Thos Carter	1-0-6-7
T. J. Bragg	1-0-2-1		W. G. Carter	1-0-1-2
Robt W. Briggs	1-0-3-0		As Guardian for	
Wm Briggs	1-0-3-0		J. A. Carter	0-0-1-0
Geo S. Bonham	3-1-12-8		Jno Cooper	1-0-0-2
E. S. Brown	1-0-0-0		Wm H. Carter	1-0-1-0
Chas H. Brabham	1-0-0-0		Jas H. Clarke	1-0-6-1
Wm Brabham	1-0-0-0		Thos H. Crow	1-0-11-3
Saml Bromley	1-0-0-4		John Carroll	1-0-0-1
Wm A. Bradford	1-0-0-0		Lewis Carroll	1-0-0-1
Jas M. Berlin	1-0-0-0		Thos Carroll	1-0-0-4
J. H. Bitzer	1-0-3-12		A. Cornwell	1-0-0-0
Dr. Wm Best	1-0-2-1		Michl Copenhaver	1-0-0-0
Geo W. Board	1-0-0-3		Jno N. Collier	1-0-1-5
Chas A. Bush	1-0-0-5		Lucy A. Calamese	2-0-4-1
Miss Mary			Ann B. Cooke	0-0-16-10
Brannon	0-0-0-0		Jas Chisholm	1-0-0-0
Jos Bell	1-0-0-0		Jas Carroll	1-0-0-0
Mrs. E. M. Baker	0-0-1-0		Robt H.	
Francis Bell	0-0-1-2		Castleman	1-0-3-4
Mrs. M. C. Bowen	0-0-0-2		Miss Mariam	
Richd Billmire	1-0-0-0		Catlett	0-0-10-6
Jno W. Bell	1-0-0-0		Frank Caniford	1-0-0-0
Chas Bailes	1-0-0-0		Jas E. Chamblin	1-0-0-0
Chas H. Boxwell	1-0-0-3		Miss S. Cloud	0-0-6-0
			Eliz Clink	0-0-1-0

Clarke County, Virginia Personal Property Tax Lists 1854-1870
1862

Michael Crim	1-0-0-0		H. H. Dunbar	1-0-0-0
Henry Caniford	1-0-0-0		Geo Dick	1-0-0-0
Wm B. Crim	0-0-0-0		Jas W. Doran	1-0-0-0
Mrs. Hannah Cain	0-0-0-0		Peter Dearmont	1-0-0-0
F. B. Carter	1-0-1-2		Jos E. Doran	1-0-0-0
Geo D. Cooper	1-0-0-0		F. B. Doran	1-0-0-0
Raizen Carroll	1-0-0-1			
James Carter	1-0-0-0		Jacob Enders	1-0-15-2
Jno B. Carter	1-0-6-2		Henry Edwards	1-0-0-2
Sarah S. Chamblin	0-0-0-1		Wm G. Everhart	1-0-11-3
Mary A. Colston	1-0-6-3		Henson Eliott	2-0-9-9
Jno Crim	2-0-2-2		Jacob W. Everhart	1-0-0-1
Harrison Cooper	1-0-0-1		Wm H. Edwards	1-0-0-1
Jno R. Crockwell	1-0-0-0		Albert Elsey	1-0-0-7
S. D. Castleman	0-0-0-0		Jos W. Edwards	1-0-0-1
John Cynn	1-0-0-0		Jno Eleyet	1-0-4-8
Geo W. Cooper	1-0-0-0		Thos A. Everhart	1-0-3-2
Jas Carper	1-0-1-4		Jno J. Emory	1-0-0-0
Jno P. Carragan	1-0-0-0		H. P. Evans	1-0-9-4
Wm Carroll	1-0-0-0			
Chas R. Corder	1-0-0-0		Dr. J. F. Fauntleroy	2-0-9-5
Washington Dearmont	1-0-10-7		O. R. Funsten	1-0-27-9
			Jas A. Forster	1-0-9-6
Wm Deahl	1-0-1-0		Josiah Ferguson	1-0-3-3
Jno Drish	1-0-0-1		Wm M. Ferguson	1-0-0-0
Jno Donovan	1-0-0-1		Johnton Furr	1-0-2-6
L. L. & A. Davis	0-0-0-0		Israel Fidler	1-0-0-2
Thos Duke	1-0-0-0		Eliza Fleming	0-0-3-4
Geo W. Diffendefer	1-0-0-1		Jos Fleming	1-0-0-3
			Wm Fowler Jr.	1-0-0-0
Hugh Davis	1-0-0-0		Jas Furr	1-0-0-0
Aaron Duble	1-0-0-0		Wm Fowler Sr.	1-0-0-1
Jno D. Davis	1-0-2-0		John Foreman	1-0-0-0
Jas Doran	1-0-0-1		Thos Fowler	1-0-0-2
H. P. Deahl	1-0-0-0		Martin Feltner	1-0-0-2
Marchus Dishman	1-0-1-4		Dennis Fenton	1-0-2-2
			M. R. Feehrer	1-0-6-4
Richd H. Dulaney	0-0-2-1		Joshua Fellows	1-0-0-4

Clarke County, Virginia Personal Property Tax Lists 1854-1870
1862

Name	Values	Name	Values
Enoch Furr	1-0-0-0	L. A. Glaize	1-0-3-0
Danl Furr	1-0-0-0	Elias M. Green	1-0-1-0
Ramey Fairback	1-0-0-0	Chas Grubb	1-0-0-3
Henry S. Fox	1-0-0-0	Philip Gordon	1-0-1-4
John R. Fuget	1-0-0-0	Warner T. Grey	1-0-0-0
Alx Finnell	1-0-1-1	J. R. Grigsby	1-0-14-22
Wm Fleming	1-0-0-2	Wm Grubb	1-0-0-0
Wasgt Ferguson	1-0-1-2	J. W. & J. S. Grantham	1-0-2-2
Everitt Fowler	1-0-0-0	Wm Gibbs	1-0-0-0
Epriam Furr	1-0-0-0	T. K. Glover	1-0-0-0
Fernando Fox	1-0-0-0	Jas T. Grubb	1-0-0-0
Jno W. Fidler	1-0-0-0	H. K. Gregg	1-0-0-0
F. M. Feltner	1-0-0-0	Jno M. Gibson	1-1-11-7
C. Fondy	1-0-0-0	James W. Grimes	1-0-0-4
John L. Grant	1-0-1-6	Zebede Gray	1-0-0-0
Jas J. Gordon	1-0-9-10	Abraham Grim	1-0-0-0
Jas W. Galeway	1-0-0-0	John S. Green	1-0-1-6
Jas F. Green	1-0-6-9	Mrs. Fanny Grigsby	0-0-0-1
Mrs. Mary Green	0-0-4-0	Thos Guard	1-0-0-0
Thos W. Giffith [sic]	1-0-0-0	Henry Harrison	1-1-23-8
Mrs. Isabella Glass	0-0-0-0	Dr. Wm Hay	1-0-2-2
Richd W. Green	1-0-8-8	Saml Heflybower	1-0-5-6
Thos E. Gold	2-0-14-17	Chas W. Hardesty	1-0-2-7
Geo W. Gordon	1-0-3-7	Saml Huyett	1-0-3-5
Saml Grubb Sr.	1-0-0-0	A. Huyett	1-0-0-1
Lewis F. Glass	1-0-14-11	Jas H. Hooe	1-0-0-0
Martin Gant	1-0-7-5	Wm Hummer	0-0-0-0
Wm B. Grubb	1-0-0-1	Wm Heflin	1-0-0-0
Geo W. Grubb	1-0-0-0	Cornelius Hoff	1-0-0-0
Saml Grubb Jr.	1-0-0-0	Wm G. Hardesty	1-0-1-3
Jno M. Grubb	1-0-0-0	Jas M. Hardesty	1-0-4-11
Jno Gruber	1-0-6-6	Alx Holtsclaw	1-0-0-1
Geo Gardiner	1-0-0-0	John Hughes	1-0-0-1
Adam Greenwald	1-0-0-0	Wm B. Harris	1-0-18-7
Mathew Grimes	1-0-0-0	Henry Huntsberry	1-0-0-7
Thos E. Gibson	1-0-0-0	Catharine N. Hall	0-0-13-10

Clarke County, Virginia Personal Property Tax Lists 1854-1870
1862

Jas F. Howell	1-0-0-0		Thos Jones	1-0-2-5
Jno W. Hibbard	1-0-0-0		Wm B. Jolliffe	1-0-1-0
W. R. Helvestine	1-0-3-0		Mrs. Janney	0-0-3-1
A. T. M. Hough	1-0-1-1		Thos Jenkins	1-0-0-1
Geo & J. P. Harris	2-0-13-8		Jas W. Johnston	1-0-0-1
John W. Hall	1-0-0-0		Wm A. Jackson	1-0-7-8
John Hummer	1-0-0-0		Andrew Jackson	1-0-0-0
Jacob Heflybower	1-0-12-5		A. M. Johnston	1-0-0-1
C. Hawks	1-0-0-0		Amelia A. Jordan	0-0-7-0
Jno & Thos Hesket	2-0-1-0		Rev. J. R. Johnston	1-0-5-1
T. L. Humphrey	1-0-4-4		Edward Jenkins	1-0-0-0
E. R. Harrison	1-0-1-5		James W. Johnston	1-0-0-0
Jos R. Hardesty	1-0-2-10			
H. D. Hooe	1-0-0-0		Ebin Jenkins	1-0-0-0
Jno Henry	1-0-0-0		John S. Johnston	1-0-3-5
Dr. Benj Harrison	1-0-28-11		Mrs. Martha Isler	1-0-2-2
Jas W. Hummer	1-0-0-1		Cathn M. Jones	1-0-3-0
Henry A. Hibbard	1-0-0-0		Geo H. Isler	1-0-0-0
J. B. Hawthorn	1-0-0-11		S. R. Jackson	1-0-0-0
J. W. Holland	1-0-0-0			
S. Hibbs	1-0-0-1		John N. Kimmell	1-0-0-0
Humphrey Hoff	1-0-0-0		F. J. Kerfoot	1-0-15-10
Mary A. Hooe	0-0-0-0		Jas F. Kerfoot	1-0-7-6
James M. Hite	1-0-13-8		Wm C. Kerfoot	1-0-15-10
Henry Huyett	1-0-3-3		Wm & B. F. Knight	2-0-16-11
Wm L. Harris	1-0-0-7		M. Keeler	1-0-0-0
Harrison Hoff	1-0-0-0		Saml G. Kneller	1-0-8-5
Mason Hummer	1-0-0-0		Wm C. Kennerly	1-0-12-1
Edw Hart	1-0-0-1		Wm B. Kennan	1-0-0-0
Thos S. Hart	1-0-0-1		Joseph Kennerly	1-0-20-14
A. D. Hardesty	1-0-4-2		Joseph Kline	1-0-0-0
A. C. Hammond	0-0-0-0		Dr. R. Kownslar	1-0-7-4
Nelson Henry	1-0-0-0		Jno Kelley	1-0-0-0
Lewis B. Helvestine	1-0-0-2		E. V. Kercheral	1-0-0-0
			Jas H. Kennan	1-0-0-0
James P. Hoff	1-0-0-0		Henry Kromling	1-0-3-2
Hend [sic] Jenkins	1-0-0-2		Jno M. Kitchen	1-0-1-2
Lucy M. Jolliffe	0-0-3-5		Judson G. Kerfoot	1-0-5-5
Leonard Jones	1-0-7-4			

Clarke County, Virginia Personal Property Tax Lists 1854-1870
1862

Name	Values	Name	Values
Jaames M. Kiger	1-0-0-3	Abram	
Geo Kitchen	0-0-0-2	Longerbeam	1-0-0-2
Henry Knight	1-0-0-0	Benj Lock	1-0-3-3
		Benj Longerbeam	1-0-0-3
John B. Larue	3-0-21-18	Chas Lloyd	1-0-0-1
John D. Larue	1-0-10-7	Wm Lanham	1-0-0-1
Edward Lewis	1-0-8-11	Wm D. Lee	1-0-0-0
John Longerbeam	1-0-0-2	Jas W. Lloyd	1-0-0-0
A. L. P. Larue	1-0-7-7	A. J. Lloyd	1-0-0-1
Jas W. Larue	1-0-8-9	Wm H. Levi	1-0-1-1
C. C. Larue	1-0-0-0	Rice W. Levi	1-1-1-9
Squire Lee	1-0-0-1	Jno Lee	1-0-0-2
Christopher Lee	1-0-0-0	Howard Lock	1-0-0-0
James M. Lindsey	2-0-1-2	Ludwell Lee	1-0-0-1
Eli Littleton	1-0-4-3	Jos B. Lindsey	1-1-4-6
Wm Littleton	1-0-1-3	James W. Lee	1-0-0-1
John Lloyd	1-0-0-0	Jno M. Lock	1-0-1-1
Henry Lloyd	1-0-0-2	Franklin Lock	1-0-0-0
Jas L. Lloyd	1-0-0-1	Dang Lloyd	1-0-0-2
David Lloyd	1-0-0-0	L. Lanham	1-0-0-0
John A. Lloyd	1-0-0-0	Richd Lanham	0-0-0-0
Moses Lewis	1-0-0-1	Peter Light	1-0-0-3
John Lock Sr.	1-0-3-6	Jno D. Lloyd	1-0-0-0
John Louthan	1-0-16-8		
John K. Louthan	1-0-4-3	F. B. Meade	1-0-16-8
James T. Louthan	1-0-5-5	Jno N. Meade	1-0-6-6
Mrs. L. Lewis	0-0-16-4	C. B. Mauntor	1-0-3-2
Geo W. Lewis	1-0-11-3	David Meade	2-0-6-8
Jas Lanham	1-0-0-0	Miss Mary	
John M. Lupton	1-0-1-0	Meade	0-0-11-1
Josiah R. Locke	1-0-0-7	R. K. Meade	1-0-12-1
John W. Luke	1-0-15-12	Col. Benj Morgan	0-0-0-0
R. H. Lee	0-0-6-5	John Morgan	1-0-16-8
F. Littleton	1-0-1-1	Thos McCormick	1-0-23-10
Geo Lanham	1-0-0-1	D° for Children	0-0-0-0
John T.		Province	
Longerbeam	1-0-0-0	McCormick	1-0-18-11
Franklin Little	1-0-3-6	D° Trustee for Edward McCormick children	

Clarke County, Virginia Personal Property Tax Lists 1854-1870
1862

D° for Ann Stribling	0-0-0-0	Moses G. Miley	1-0-0-4
D° for Ebin Frost	0-0-0-0	James McClaughry	1-0-0-3
D° Gdn for Eliza McCormick	0-0-0-0	McLean McClingan	1-0-0-1
Agent for Mary Stribling	0-0-0-0	Patrick Murray	1-0-0-0
		Alfred Martz	1-0-0-2
		Jos Moore	1-0-0-0
Otway McCormick	1-0-12-6	Jno P. McMurray	1-0-4-0
P. N. Meade	1-0-22-24	Capt. S. J. C. Moore	1-0-2-0
Robt Morgan	1-0-0-0	Col. Frank McCormick	1-0-34-24
James McCormick	1-0-3-5	Edwd C. Marshall	1-0-2-8
Edward McCormick	1-0-28-15	Jarret McDonald	1-0-2-2
Peter McMurry	1-0-5-3	Charles McDonald	1-0-0-0
Sylvanius Moore	1-0-0-0	Thos Murphy	1-0-0-0
L. D. Mattox	1-0-0-1	Jno Murphy	1-0-0-0
James Mitchell	1-0-7-5	Jos E. Mason	1-0-0-1
Geo Marlow	1-0-0-1	Rt. Rev. Wm Meade's Est.	0-0-0-1
D. H. McGuire	1-0-7-4		
Wm D. McGuire	1-0-23-16	Jno T. Martz	1-0-0-0
Alx Marshall	1-0-4-6	Moses B. Murphy	1-0-0-0
John Marshall	1-0-9-2	Wm T. Milton	1-0-6-7
W. W. Meade	1-0-0-0	Jesse Mercer	1-0-0-0
A. P. Moore	1-0-0-0	Henry J. Mesmer	1-0-6-5
Jas F. Murphey	1-0-0-0	Caldwell Miley	1-0-0-1
Mrs. Susan Marshall	0-0-7-4	Jos T. Mitchell	1-0-16-9
C. C. McIntyre	1-0-8-7	David Meade Trustee for W. B. Meade	0-0-5-6
Nathl Mercer	1-0-0-1		
James Murphy	1-0-0-0	George Markell	1-0-0-1
Stephen Marlow	1-0-0-1	R. F. McPhillin	1-0-0-0
Geo Marpole	1-0-0-2	Josiah McDonald	1-0-0-0
Ame Moore	1-0-11-6	Henry Mason	1-0-0-0
D° as Trustee for Mrs. ~~Moreland~~		Dr. Cyrus McCormick's Est.	0-0-0-0
Saml Moreland	2-0-0-4	Jno G. McCauley	1-0-0-0

Clarke County, Virginia Personal Property Tax Lists 1854-1870
1862

James McClellan	1-0-0-0		Paul Peirce	1-0-13-2
Hugh M. Nelson	1-0-19-15		Mrs. E. M. A. Page	0-0-6-1
Wm H. Nelson	1-0-4-10		James M. Pine	2-0-0-2
James H. Neville	1-0-1-0		John Poston	1-0-0-2
Philip W. Nelson	1-0-15-8		T. P. Pendleton	1-0-16-8
Jno B. Nunn	1-0-5-6		Wm Pyle	1-0-0-1
D⁰ as Guardian for Miss Dix			Jno Patterson	1-0-0-6
			James S. Payne	1-0-0-2
D⁰ as Guardian for G. W. Carter			Wm H. Pope	1-0-0-0
			Barrett Prichard	1-0-0-0
Dr. S. S. Neill	1-0-3-2		Michael Pope	1-0-0-1
Thos Nicewarner	1-0-1-3		Pulliam & Howell	0-0-1-0
Wm Nicewarner	1-0-3-2		Thos Pyle	1-0-0-1
			Jno T. Patterson	1-0-0-0
Mrs. Susan ORear	0-0-4-1		Willis Prichard	1-0-0-0
George ORear	1-0-0-2		P. H. Powers	1-0-10-8
Mrs. Eliz ORear	0-0-15-8		Geo W. Patterson	1-0-0-1
Overseers of the Poor	1-0-0-3		Charles H. Peyton	1-0-0-0
			Wm G. Pierce	1-0-1-2
Hugh ORourke	1-0-0-0		Isaac Pidgeon	1-0-0-2
Rowland Osborn	2-0-0-2		Jno E. Page	1-0-22-12
David Osborn	1-0-0-0			
			Bennett Russell	2-0-20-5
James Puller	1-0-0-0		T. W. Russell	1-0-0-2
Bush Puller	1-0-0-0		Michael Russell	1-0-0-1
Conrad Pope	1-0-0-1		Wm H. Robinson	1-0-3-9
Samuel Pidgeon	1-0-0-2		Miss M. C. Roots	0-0-1-0
Dr. Mat Page's Est.	0-0-15-1		Patrick Rodgers	1-0-0-0
			T. W. Reynolds	1-0-0-0
Susan R. Page's Est.	0-0-48-21		Jno Roland	1-0-0-6
			Miss E. W. Royster	0-0-6-0
A. C. Page	1-0-0-0			
Jno Page Jr.	1-0-27-10		M. W. Royston	1-0-1-2
Geo R. Page	1-0-6-3		Jno J. Rippon	1-0-0-1
Mathew Pulliam	1-0-7-0		P. K. Royston	1-0-0-3
Elizth Pierce	0-0-4-2		Geo R. Royston	1-0-0-0
A. N. Pierce	1-0-12-9		Uriah B. Royston	1-0-0-1
Peter McPierce	1-0-12-9		D. B. Richards	1-0-1-0

Clarke County, Virginia Personal Property Tax Lists 1854-1870
1862

Geo W. Rutter	1-0-0-0	Mrs. Elizabeth Sowers	0-0-0-0
C. H. Richards	1-0-0-0	Jno W. Sprint	1-0-0-0
Geo Reno	1-0-0-0	Henry Shepherd	1-0-0-0
A. Romine	1-0-4-5	Jno W. Sowers	1-0-14-18
Beverly Randolph	1-0-22-13	Wm Sowers	1-0-19-9
Jno Reynolds	1-0-1-0	Carter Shepherd	1-0-7-8
Jno Ramey	1-0-0-0	Champ Shepherd	2-0-10-10
Wm Riley	1-0-0-0	P. D. Shepherd	1-0-12-7
Mathew Rust	1-0-1-0	Geo Smedley	1-0-0-1
John J. Riley	1-0-10-8	Wm L. Smith	1-0-0-0
D° Trustee for Mrs. Taylor	0-0-0-0	Miss M. C. Shively	0-0-2-2
Wm A. Riley	1-0-9-7	Ed J. & Wm D. Smith	2-1-55-40
D° as Guardian for P. Swan	0-0-0-0	Paul Smith	1-0-8-4
Thos Reardon	1-0-0-0	Dr. P. Smith	1-0-1-0
John D. Richardson	1-0-17-10	Wm M. Sowers	1-0-0-5
Enos Richmond	1-0-0-0	D. C. Snyder	1-0-6-8
Richmond & Stoll	0-0-1-3	Mrs. F. E. Sowers	1-0-6-7
Cyrus Richmond	1-0-0-0	Danl H. Sowers	1-0-4-10
Jane C. Randolph	0-0-2-0	Chas H. Smith	1-0-2-5
M. T. Royston	1-0-0-0	Geo R. Smith	1-0-0-0
Richd Ridgeway	1-0-1-5	Thos Smallwood	1-0-0-2
Jno Ritter	1-0-0-5	Wm R. Stuart	1-0-1-0
John W. Russell	1-0-2-2	Chas Swartz	1-0-1-0
D. T. Richards	1-0-0-1	Jno Shaffer	1-0-0-0
Elisha Romine	1-0-0-0	Simon Stickels	1-0-0-0
Jos F. Ryan & Bro	2-0-6-8	Jas M. Shearer	1-0-0-0
Jas H. Roland	1-0-1-2	William Strother	1-0-0-0
Jessee N. Russell	1-0-0-0	Jno Stonestreet	1-0-0-0
W. S. Ryland	1-0-0-1	Jno Shell	1-0-0-0
Dr. R. C. Randolph	4-0-30-20	Sephen [sic] Shell	1-0-0-0
		Craven Shell	1-0-0-0
		Simon R. Stump	1-0-0-1
Chas Showers	1-0-0-0	Jas Shackleford	0-0-0-0
Mrs. M. E. Shumate	2-0-7-7	Dennis Shehan	1-0-0-1
Col. T. Smith	2-0-38-16	Dr. J. W. Stephenson	1-0-12-7
Danl W. Sowers	2-0-32-13	Jos Shipe	1-0-0-0

Clarke County, Virginia Personal Property Tax Lists 1854-1870
1862

A. J. Shipe	1-0-0-0		Sylvester	
Wm G. Steele	1-0-0-0		Smallwood	1-0-0-0
Jas A. Steele	1-0-0-1		Geo Sowers	
Jas H. Swain	1-0-0-0		of D. W.	1-0-0-4
Mrs. Mgt Swan	0-0-0-0		Miss A. A. Sowers	1-0-2-0
B. T. Settle			Jas L. Shovers	1-0-2-0
trustee for			Saml Showers	1-0-0-0
Mrs. Finnell	1-0-1-0		Wm B. Sowers	1-0-0-2
T. Smith Jr.	1-0-4-1		Jas W. Sibert	1-0-0-1
Burr Smallwood	1-0-0-1			
H. Slusher	1-0-1-0		Mrs. Sarah	
M. L. Sinclair	1-0-0-0		Timberlake	0-1-15-9
Geo S. Spaulding	1-0-0-0		Thos Thacher	1-0-0-0
John H.			Wm H. Thompson	1-0-0-0
Shoebridge	1-0-0-1		Jas Thomas	1-0-0-0
Benj Shipe	1-0-0-0		A. F. Thompson	1-0-0-1
Geo W. Shimp	1-0-0-0		Greenberry	
Wm F. Stoll	1-0-1-0		Thompson	1-0-0-1
Rev. H. Suter	1-0-4-1		Benj Thompson	
David Spotts	1-0-0-0		Sr.	1-0-0-0
Henry Stickel Sr.	1-0-0-0		French Thompson	1-0-2-1
Mt Joy Shell	1-0-0-0		Balis Thompson	1-0-0-2
Henry Stickles Jr.	1-0-0-0		Benj Thompson	
Jos Stuart	1-0-0-0		Jr.	1-0-0-3
F. L. Sowers	1-0-0-4		Chas Trussell	1-0-1-6
Spilman &			Isaac Talley	1-0-0-0
Markell	0-0-0-0		Wm Taylor	1-0-32-20
R. L. Spilman	1-0-3-2		Robt Tapscott	1-0-0-3
W. C. Smith	1-0-22-8		Mrs. Eliza Taylor	0-0-9-2
C. G. Shumate	1-0-0-0		Moses B. Trussell	1-0-1-3
Geo Sowers	1-0-0-2		Wm Trenary	1-0-6-2
B. T. Silman	1-0-0-1		Calvin Thatcher	1-0-0-1
Shepherd & Duble	0-0-0-0		Dr. B. Taylor	1-0-3-1
Geo W. Schultzs	1-0-0-0		Snowden Tomblin	1-0-0-0
H. T. Shearer	1-0-0-0		Mason Tinsman	1-0-0-2
Augustin Swarts	1-0-0-0		Ludwell Tinsman	1-0-0-1
John J. Shaffer	1-0-0-2		Griffin Taylor	1-0-0-1
Jos Stickles	1-0-0-4		Mrs. Eliza Tucker	0-0-0-0
Wm Strother	1-0-6-8		Wm G. Taylor	1-0-0-3

Clarke County, Virginia Personal Property Tax Lists 1854-1870
1862

Mrs. Susan Taylor	1-0-8-3	Alx Wood	1-0-0-1
Benj F. Thompson	1-0-0-0	Bennett Wood	1-0-0-0
Saml M. Trussell	1-0-0-3	W. B. Wilson	1-0-0-0
Albert Thompson	1-0-0-0	Lucinda Washington	0-0-3-0
Jas W. Tanqeary [*sic*]	1-0-0-4	Saml G. Wyman	0-0-15-10
Jas F. Trayhern	1-0-0-0	Jas W. Willingham of Jno	1-0-0-0
Calvin Thatcher	1-0-0-1	Jos H. Wilson	1-0-0-0
Rufus Timberlake	1-0-0-0	Rev. Chas White	1-0-2-1
Dr. Thos Turner	1-0-1-2	Obed Willingham	1-0-0-1
J. L. E. Vanmeter	1-0-2-5	Miss A. Writ	0-0-0-0
J. B. Vorous	1-0-1-8	Henry R. Wilson	1-0-1-0
H. T. Wheat	1-0-14-8	Chas F. Willingham	1-0-0-0
B. F. Wilson	1-0-0-0	Robt Wilson	1-0-0-0
Jno Wilson	1-0-0-0	Wm T. Whorton	1-0-0-0
F. B. Whiting	1-0-28-9	Lewis Wood	1-0-0-0
F. H. Whiting	1-0-2-5	Geo F. Willingham	1-0-0-0
W. W. Whiting	1-0-19-3	Robt B. Wood	1-0-4-9
Allan Williams	1-0-18-15	T. O. Wyndham	1-0-1-4
Thompson Writ	1-0-0-1	Jackson Wheeler	1-0-0-1
Wm Willingham	1-0-0-3	David Wood	1-0-0-0
Leroy P. Williams	1-0-19-7	Jas W. Willingham of Wm	1-0-0-0
Hezekiah Wiley	1-0-0-1	Jeremiah Wilson	1-0-0-0
Danl Wade & Bro.	2-1-0-2	Richd Whittington	1-0-1-4
Cornelius Wiley	1-0-0-0	Chas Whittington	1-0-0-3
Geo W. Wiley	1-0-0-2	Geo F. Willingham	1-0-0-0
Jas Wiley	1-0-0-0		
S. B. Wyndham	1-0-3-1	John Youwell	1-0-0-0
T. C. Wyndham	1-0-0-0	Wm H. Young	1-0-1-0
Danl Welch	1-0-0-4	Simeon Youwell	1-0-0-0
Jas V. Weir	1-0-11-14		
Jesse Wright	1-0-0-2	Wm Whaley	1-0-0-4
Robt W. Whittington	1-0-2-1		
Mann R. Page	2-0-22-12	Col. Benj. Morgan	3-0-43-24

Clarke County, Virginia Personal Property Tax Lists 1854-1870
1862

Miss A. & R. Nelson 0-0-10-0

Miss Lucy Harrison**Error!**

N. B. Whiting 1-0-11-10 **Bookmark not defined.** 0-0-0-0

Benj Carpenter 1-0-1-1

Free Negroes

Philip Wormley	0-1-0-0		Burwell Cooke	0-1-0-0
Saml Colley	0-1-0-0		Jno Walker	0-1-0-0
Jno Gilkerson	0-1-0-0		Peter Coats	0-1-0-2
Mowen Harris	0-1-0-1		Chas Clifton	0-1-0-0
James Butler	0-1-0-0		Nancy Parker	0-0-0-0
Spencer Johnson	0-1-0-0			

Clarke County, Virginia Personal Property Tax Lists 1854-1870

1865

Columns: 1) White males above 21, for state tax 2) 3Male free negroes above 16, 3) White males above 16, for county levy.
This is the first year free blacks are listed under the initial letter of their surname, along with everyone else; but 5 men are still grouped separately, at the end of this year.

Buckner G. Ashby	1-0-1	Dr. R. S. Blackburn	1-0-1
Mason Anderson	1-0-1	Westley Brabham	1-0-1
Eddgar Allen	1-0-1	Geo H. Burwell	1-0-4
Jno Alexander	1-0-1	Wm O. Brown	1-0-1
J. E. Anderson	1-0-1	Nath Burwell	1-0-3
Robt Ashby Sr.	1-0-1	Jno F. Burchell	1-0-1
Robt Ashby Jr.	1-0-3	Geo H. Bell	1-0-2
Nimrod Ashby	1-0-3	Lewis Berlin	1-0-1
Austin C. Ashby	1-0-1	Philip Berlin	1-0-1
Geo Anderson	1-0-1	Jno Brackett	1-0-3
Wm T. Allen	1-0-1	Geo W. Berlin	1-0-1
A. S. Allen	1-0-1	Geo C. Blakemore	1-0-2
T. H. Alexander	1-0-2	Neille Barnett	2-0-2
Jno Allison	1-0-1	Jas Bell Sr.	1-0-1
Jno Anderson	1-0-1	Arthur Briggs	1-0-1
Edw Alder	1-0-1	Jno Bromley	1-0-1
Owen Allen	1-0-1	Alfard [sic] Bishop	1-0-1
Jacob Ambrose	1-0-1	Dr. D. S. Bonham	2-0-2
Jno W. Anderson	1-0-1	Wm Berry	1-0-1
Philip Affleck	1-0-2	Jno Bell	1-0-1
Wm Ashman	1-0-1	C. Bowser [?]	1-0-1
Wm Asbury	1-0-1	Thos W. Byrne	1-0-2
Warren Anderson	1-0-1	Abraham Beavers	1-0-1
Jno H. Anderson	1-0-1	Adam Barr	1-0-1
Jno F. Allen	1-0-1	Jessee Butler	1-0-1
Jno Albin	1-0-1	R. S. Bryarly	1-0-2
Geo W. Allen	1-0-1	Jas H. Bartlette	1-0-1
Milton B. Anderson	1-0-1	Geo W. Bolin	1-0-2
		Thos Brown	1-0-1
		Patrick Brady	1-0-1

Clarke County, Virginia Personal Property Tax Lists 1854-1870
1865

Geo W. Bromley	1-0-1		Jos K. Carter	1-0-1
Wm H. Billmyre	1-0-2		Jno A. Carter	1-0-3
Jos C. Bartlette	1-0-1		Jno W. Carter	1-0-1
Robt W. Briggs	1-0-1		Jno Conway	1-0-1
Wm Briggs	1-0-1		Timothy Conway [?]	1-0-1
Henry C. Briggs	1-0-1		Jas Chapel	1-0-3
Jas C. Briggs	1-0-1		Jno Chapel	1-0-1
Geo S. Bonham	1-0-2		Prakerson Corder	1-0-1
Enos S. Brown	1-0-2		Thos Carter	1-0-1
Chas Brabham	1-0-1		W. G. Carter	1-0-1
Saml Bromley	1-0-1		Jno Cooper	1-0-1
Beler Bennette	1-0-1		Wm H. Carter	1-0-1
J. H. Bitzer	1-0-1		Lewis Carroll	1-0-1
Dr. Wm J. Best	1-0-1		Geo Castleman	1-0-1
Chas A. Bush	1-0-1		Geo Chapman	1-0-1
Chas H. Boxwell	1-0-1		Andrew Cornell	1-0-1
Chas Bailes	1-0-1		Jno N. Collier	1-0-1
Chas Berry	1-0-1		F. L. Calmes	2-0-2
Conrad R. Pitzer	1-0-1		Henry Catlette	1-0-1
Geo R. Balthrope	1-0-1		Benj Crampton	1-0-1
Chas M. Barrir [?]	1-0-1		Henry Caniford	1-0-1
Wm Bonham	1-0-1		Frank B. Carter	1-0-1
Jno W. Beemer	1-0-2		Geo D. Cooper	1-0-1
T. J. Bragg	1-0-3		Reason Carrrell	1-0-1
Geo W. Belt	1-0-1		Jas Carter	1-0-1
Wm Bush [?]	2-0-2		Jno B. Carter	1-0-1
Bushrod Buckley	1-0-1		Jno Cain	1-0-3
Mary Brannan	1-0-1		Wm B. Conrad	1-0-1
Jno Bailey	1-0-1		Geo W. Copenhaver	1-0-1
Robt Beattey	1-0-1		Jas H. C. Carter	1-0-3
Jno Blackburn	1-0-1		J. R. Crockwell	1-0-1
			Jas W. McClelland	1-0-1
Alfred Castleman	2-0-3		Jas S. Carver	1-0-1
W. A. Castleman	1-0-2		Franklin Carter	1-0-1
Wm Carper	1-0-1		Jno A. Childs	1-0-1
S. A. Campbell	1-0-2		Willis B. Clarke	1-0-1
R. A. Colston	1-0-2		Jas Carrell	1-0-1
Jno Copenhaver	1-0-2		Alfred Carper	1-0-1
Jno H. Crebs	1-0-1		Geo W. Corder	1-0-1

Clarke County, Virginia Personal Property Tax Lists 1854-1870
1865

Geo W. Coonce	1-0-1		Olliver P. Eavans	1-0-1
Jno T. Crow	1-0-1		Jos Edwards	1-0-1
Col. W. Dearmont	1-0-2		Jas J. Foster	1-0-1
Wm Deahl	1-0-1		Josiah Furguson	1-0-1
H. P. Deahl	1-0-1		Wm M. Furguson	1-0-1
Jno Drish	1-0-2		Jonie Fear	2-0-3
Jno Donovan	1-0-1		Israel Fidler	1-0-1
Thos Duke	1-0-1		Joseph Fleming	1-0-2
Geo W. Diffendefer	1-0-3		Wm Fowler Jr.	1-0-1
Hugh Davis	1-0-1		Everit Fowler	1-0-1
Aaron Duble	1-0-1		Thos Fowler	1-0-1
Peter Dearmont	1-0-1		Marti[n] Feltner	1-0-2
Jas W. Dishman	1-0-3		Denis Fenton	1-0-1
Jas Doran	1-0-1		Marcus R. Feehrer	1-0-1
Jos Doran	1-0-1		Geo	
H. H. Dunbar	1-0-1		[Fiddler? erased]	1-0-1
R. F. Doran	1-0-1		Joshua Fellows	1-0-1
Jas W. Doran	1-0-1		Enoch Furr	1-0-1
Jno McDonald	1-0-1		Ebin Frost	1-0-1
R. L. Denny	1-0-3		John H. Ford	1-0-1
Jno Dix	1-0-1		Wm Fowler Sr.	1-0-1
Robert Dunn	1-0-1		Wm Fleming	1-0-1
Geo Dick	1-0-1		Wash Furguson	1-0-1
			Abner Furguson	1-0-1
Jacob Enders	1-0-1		Jno T. Ford	1-0-1
Wm G. Everhart	2-0-2		Andrew B. Fleming	1-0-1
Henson Elliott	1-0-1		Alex Fennell	1-0-1
Jacob W. Everhart	1-0-1		Miner Furr	1-0-1
Albert Elsea	1-0-1		Jas P. Flenster [?]	1-0-1
Jno Eleyet	1-0-3		Dr. O. R. Funston	2-0-2
Thos A. Everhart	1-0-1		Wm Furr	1-0-1
H. P. Evans	1-0-1		Isaac Fletcher	1-0-2
Henry Edwards	1-0-1		Eli Fishpaw	1-0-1
Wm G. Everheart Jr.	1-0-1			
Jno C. Elliott	1-0-1		John L. Grant	1-0-1
Ann G. Ewell [?]	1-0-2		J. J. Gordon	2-0-2
Geo Everitt	1-0-1		Richard N. Green	1-0-2
T. M. Edy [?]	1-0-1		Thos E. Gold	2-0-4

Clarke County, Virginia Personal Property Tax Lists 1854-1870
1865

Geo W. Gordon	2-0-2		Jas W. Hummer	1-0-1
Saml Grubbs	1-0-1		John Hughes	2-0-3
Lewis P. Glass	2-0-3		W. B. Harris	1-0-2
Martin Gant	1-0-1		Dr. B. Harrison	1-0-1
Geo W. Grubb	1-0-1		Jas F. Howell	1-0-1
Jno Gruber	1-0-1		Geo W. Hibbard	1-0-1
Jno Gardner	1-0-1		W. R. Helvestine	1-0-1
T. H. Glover [?]	1-0-1		Thos Hummer	1-0-1
Adam Greenwaldt	1-0-1		Wm Heflin	1-0-2
Madison Grimes	1-0-1		Jno W. Hall	1-0-1
Thos E. Gibson	1-0-2		Jno Hall	1-0-1
L. A. Glaze	1-0-1		Jno Hummer	1-0-1
Elias M. Green	1-0-1		Columbus Hawks	1-0-1
Jas T. Grubb	1-0-1		T. L. Humphrey	1-0-1
Chas Grubb	1-0-1		Edw R. Harrison	1-0-1
Warner T. Gray	1-0-1		Jos R. Hardesty	1-0-1
J. R. Griggsby	1-0-1		J. B. Hawthorn	1-0-2
Wm Grubb	1-0-1		Jno W. Holland	1-0-1
J. L. Grantham	1-0-1		Soloman Hibs	1-0-2
Wm C. Gover [?]	1-0-1		Jas M. Hite	1-0-1
Jno M. Gibson	1-0-1		Henry Huyette	1-0-1
Jas W. Grimes	1-0-1		Wm J. Harris	2-0-2
Zebedee Gray	1-0-1		Geo Hunsucker	1-0-1
John S. Green	1-0-2		Mason Hummer	1-0-1
Philip Grubb	1-0-1		Mrs. Hariett Hough	1-0-2
Israel Green	1-0-1		Saml Huyette	1-0-2
Jas H. Grove	1-0-1		Jno Hodges	2-0-3
Jas W. Green [?]	1-0-1		Jas Heflen	1-0-1
Wm G. Galloway	1-0-1		Lewis B. Helvestine	1-0-1
Kemp Griggsby	1-0-1		Edwin Hart	1-0-1
Geo Grimes	1-0-1		Jno T. Hughs	1-0-1
Benj Galloway	1-0-1		Benj Hutchison	1-0-1
Geo C. Griffin	1-0-1		Geo G. Hooe	1-0-1
Edward Grady	1-0-1		Rev. [?] W. Hedges	1-0-1
Wm G. Hardesty	1-0-2		Macey E.	
A. D. Hardesty	1-0-1		Heflebower	0-0-1
Jas M. Hardesty	1-0-2		Jno Hilyard	1-0-1
Alex Holtsclaw	1-0-1		Nelson Henry	1-0-1
Chas F. Hesser [?]	1-0-1		Chas W. Hardesty	1-0-1

Clarke County, Virginia Personal Property Tax Lists 1854-1870
1865

Thos S. Hart	1-0-1		Jos McK. Kenarly	1-0-1
Wm Horseman	1-0-1		John Kelley	1-0-1
Geo W. Hanway	1-0-1		E. V. Kercheral	1-0-1
			Henry Kromling	2-0-2
Geo H. Isler	1-0-1		Henry Knight	1-0-1
			Jno N. Kitchen	1-0-1
Herod Jenkins	1-0-2		J. G. Kerfoot	1-0-1
Leonard Jones	1-0-2		Jas M. Kiger	1-0-2
Thos Jones	2-0-4		Geo Kitchen	1-0-1
Wm B. Jolliffe	1-0-1		A. J. Kerfoot	1-0-1
Thos Jenkins	1-0-1		Wm Kerfoot	1-0-1
Jas W. Johnston			Danl Knight	0-0-1
Com′ Rev.	1-0-1		J. F. Kerfoot	1-0-1
Wm A. Jackson	3-0-4			
Andrew Jackson	1-0-1		Col. J. B. Larue	2-0-2
Rev. W. Johnston	1-0-1		E. P. C. Lewis	1-0-1
Lafaiette Jones	1-0-1		Jno Longerbean	1-0-1
Edw Jenkins	1-0-1		A. L. B. Larue	1-0-1
Rev. Jos R. Jones	2-0-2		Jas W. Larue	2-0-2
Jas W. Johnston-			Eli Littleton	1-0-1
Montain [sic]	1-0-1		Wm Littleton	1-0-1
Frank Johnston	1-0-1		Jno Lloyd	1-0-1
Jno S. Johnston	1-0-1		Henry Lloyd	1-0-1
Ebin Jenkins	1-0-1		Jas L. Lloyd	1-0-1
Peyton Johns	1-0-1		Jno A. Lloyd	1-0-1
Damph Jackson	1-0-2		Moses Lewin	1-0-1
M. W. Jones	1-0-1		Jno Lock Sr.	1-0-1
Thos C. Janney	1-0-1		Jno Louthan	2-0-2
Alfred Jackson	1-0-1		Jno K. Louthan	1-0-1
Jno Jolliffe	1-0-1		Miner Lanham	1-0-4
			Jno M. Lupton	1-0-2
John M. Kimmell	1-0-1		Jonah R. Lock	1-0-1
Dr. F. J. Kerfoot	1-0-3		Jno W. Luke	1-0-1
W. C. Kerfoot	1-0-1		F. Little	3-0-4
W. F. Knight	1-0-1		Abraham	
Middleton Keeler	1-0-1		Longerbean	1-0-1
S. G. Kneller	2-0-3		Benj Lock	1-0-1
W. C. Kenarly	1-0-2		Benj Longerbean	1-0-1
Wm Kennan	1-0-1		Chas Lloyd	1-0-1

Clarke County, Virginia Personal Property Tax Lists 1854-1870
1865

Wm Lanham	1-0-2		P. N. Meade	2-0-3
Wm D. Lee	1-0-1		Robt P. Morgan	1-0-1
Jas W. Lloyd	1-0-1		Jas McCormick	1-0-1
Wm H. Levi	1-0-1		Edw McCormick	1-0-1
Rice W. Levi	1-0-2		S. P. Moore	1-0-1
Squire Lee	1-0-1		Jas Mitchell	1-0-1
John Lee	1-0-1		A. M. Moore	2-0-3
Ludwell Lee	1-0-1		Moses B. Murphey	1-0-1
J. B. Lindsey	1-0-1		S. B. Murphey	1-0-1
Jas W. Lee	1-0-1		Geo Marpole	2-0-2
Peter Light	1-0-1		Geo Marlow	1-0-1
Jas Lanham	1-0-1		D. H. McGuire	2-0-3
Danl Lanham	1-0-1		Alex Marshall	1-0-2
Remington Lock	1-0-1		Jno Marshall	1-0-1
Jas A. Lawyer	1-0-1		C. C. McIntyre	1-0-1
Dr. E. E. Lippett	1-0-1		Jas Murphey	1-0-1
Robt Lucas	1-0-1		Moses G. Miley	1-0-1
Jno T. Lindsey	1-0-1		E. W. Massey	1-0-1
R. S. Lock	1-0-1		Jas McClaughy	1-0-1
Dangerfield Lewis	1-0-1		McLane McClingan	1-0-1
Jas T. Lay	1-0-1		Patrick Murray	1-0-1
Dr. T. M. Lewis	1-0-1		Jos Moore	1-0-1
Jno W. Lee			Jno P. McMurray	1-0-1
of Wm D.	1-0-1		S. J. C. Moore	1-0-1
Jas W. T. Lewis	0-0-1		Wm McDonald	1-0-1
Geo W. Lewis	1-0-1		Edw McDonald	1-0-1
C. C. Larue	1-0-1		Anglish McDonald	1-0-1
			Henry H. Milton	1-0-1
F. B. Meade	3-0-4		Wm Morris	1-0-1
E. B. Mautan [?]	1-0-1		Alfred Marshall	1-0-1
W. W. Meade	1-0-1		Hezikiah Marpole	1-0-1
David Meade	1-0-1		Jno McClaughey	1-0-1
A. P. Moore	1-0-1		Col. F. McCormick	1-0-2
Jas T. Murphey	1-0-1		E. C. Marshall	1-0-1
Col. B. Morgan	3-0-3		Garrett McDonald	1-0-1
Jno Morgan	1-0-1		Jonah McDonald	1-0-1
Thos McCormick	1-0-2		Henry Mason	1-0-1
P. McCormick	2-0-4		Albert Marshall	1-0-1
Ott McCormick	1-0-2		Thos B. Morehead	1-0-1

Clarke County, Virginia Personal Property Tax Lists 1854-1870
1865

J. S. Mitchell	1-0-1		Conrad Pope	1-0-1
Henry J.			Saml Pidgeon	1-0-1
M [illegible]	2-0-2		A. C. Page	1-0-1
Julius Morales	1-0-1		Jno Page Jr.	1-0-1
Wm T. Milton	1-0-1		Mann R. Page	2-0-2
Jno McCormick	1-0-1		Jno M. Pope	1-0-1
Jos T. Mitchell	1-0-1		M. Pulliam	1-0-1
Wm F. Meade	1-0-1		A. N. Pierce	1-0-1
Mrs. Jane Meade	1-0-3		Peter McPierce	1-0-3
Jas McDonald	1-0-2		Paul Pierce	1-0-1
Joseph S. McDonald	1-0-1		Geo W. Pine	1-0-1
P. McCormick Jr.	1-0-1		T. P. Pendleton	2 1-0-2
Jno G. Morris	1-0-1		Wm Pile	3-0-4
Isaac Manuel	2-0-3		Jno Patterson	1-0-1
Jno G. McCauley	1-0-3		Barnett Prichard	1-0-1
Luther G. Mitchell	1-0-2		Michael Pope	1-0-1
Albert Morris	1-0-1		P. H. Powers	1-0-1
Jesse Mercer	1-0-1		Wm G. Pierce	1-0-1
			Franklin Pope	1-0-1
Col. Wm Nelson	1-0-1		Henry R. Patterson	1-0-1
Jas H. Neville	1-0-1		Jno Pendleton	1-0-1
Hugh Nelson	0-0-0		Killian Pope	1-0-1
Jno R. Nunn	1-0-1		Thos Prichard	1-0-1
Dr. S. S. Niell	1-0-1		Jacob Pierce	1-0-1
Thos Nicewarner	1-0-1		R. C. Priest	1-0-1
Wm Nicewarner	1-0-1		Jno C. Page	1-0-1
Alex Neville	1-0-1			
Jas R. Neville	1-0-1		T. W. Russell	1-0-1
Benj Neuman	1-0-1		Michael Russell	1-0-2
Wm Nelson			Pat Rodgers	1-0-1
(at Jerry Wilsons)	0-0-0		Jno Roland	2-0-3
			P. K. Royston	1-0-2
Geo ORear	1-0-1		Geo R. Royston	1-0-1
Joshua Osburn	2-0-2		Uriah Royston	1-0-1
David Osburn	1-0-1		Jno S. Russell	1-0-1
Edw OBryan	1-0-1		Stephen Reed	1-0-1
			Danl B. Richards	1-0-1
Jas Puller	1-0-1		Geo W. Rutter	1-0-1
Bushrod Puller	1-0-1		Addison Romine	1-0-1

Clarke County, Virginia Personal Property Tax Lists 1854-1870
1865

Wesley Russell	1-0-1		Benj Smith	1-0-1
Beverly Randolph	1-0-1		W. O. Sowers	1-0-1
R. C. Randolph	3-0-4		P. D. Shepherd	3-0-4
Jno Reynolds	1-0-1		Geo Smedley	1-0-1
Wm Riley	1-0-1		C. J. & W. D. Smith	2-0-2
Jno J. Riley	1-0-1		Chas H. Smith	1-0-1
Wm A. Riley			J. A. Steele [?]	1-0-1
Thos Reardon	1-0-3		Geo R. Smith	1-0-1
Jno D. Richardson	1-0-1		Thos Smallwood	1-0-1
Jas W. Ryan	1-0-1		Wm R. Stuart	1-0-2
W. E. Randolph	1-0-1		Chas Swarts	1-0-1
Enos Richmond	1-0-1		John Shaffer	1-0-1
Jno W. Russell	1-0-1		Simon Stickel	1-0-2
D. T. Richards	1-0-1		Peter Stickel	1-0-1
Elish Romine	1-0-1		Jas M. Shearer	1-0-1
Jos F. Ryan	1-0-1		Jno Stonestreet	1-0-1
Marcus B. Reed	2-0-3		Stephen Shell	1-0-1
Dr. J. Philip Smith	1-0-1		Simon R. Stump	1-0-1
Jno Robinson	1-0-1		Denis Shihan	1-0-1
Jesse Russell	1-0-1		J. W. Stephenson	1-0-1
W. Richardson	1-0-2		Jos Shifer [?]	1-0-1
Juster Riley	1-0-1		Moses Shipe	1-0-2
M. T. Royston	1-0-1		A. J. Shipe	1-0-1
T. J. Russell	1-0-1		Burr Smallwood	1-0-1
Jno Riley	1-0-1		Hezekiah Slusher	1-0-1
R. S. T. Russell	1-0-1		Jos Stickel	1-0-1
Jas E. Russell	1-0-1		M. L. Sinclair	1-0-1
Jno Ridenour	1-0-1		Geo S. Spaulding	1-0-1
Elias Rutter	1-0-1		Jno H. Shuebridge	1-0-1
Liman Reynolds	1-0-1		Benj Shipe	1-0-1
W. H. Roberson	1-0-1		Geo W. Shimp	1-0-1
			Mr. S. C. T. Stribling	1-0-1
Chas Showers	1-0-1		Wm F. Stotte	1-0-1
Mrs. M. E. Shumate	1-0-2		Rev. H. Suter	1-0-1
Wm G. Steele	1-0-2		Jacob Spotts	1-0-1
Danl W. Sowers	2-0-3		Henry Stickel Sr.	1-0-1
Jno Sprint	1-0-1		Mount J. Shull	1-0-1
Jno W. Sowers	1-0-2		Geo K. Sowers	1-0-1
Carter Shepherd	1-0-2		Warren C. Smith	1-0-1

Clarke County, Virginia Personal Property Tax Lists 1854-1870
1865

Name	Values	Name	Values
Sylvester Smallwood	1-0-1	French Thompson	1-0-1
Geo Sowers of D. W.	1-0-1	Baalis Thompson Sr.	1-0-1
		Isaac Talley	1-0-2
		Wm Taylor	1-0-1
B. T. Silman	1-0-1	Robert Tapscot	2-0-3
Henry T. Sheaver	2-0-3	Moses B. Trussell	1-0-2
Jno J. Shaffer	1-0-1	Wm Trenary	2-0-2
Jos Stickel Sr.	1-0-2	Calvin Thatcher	1-0-1
Geo Sowers of W^m	1-0-1	Dr. Bush Taylor	1-0-1
Saml Showers	1-0-1	Baalis Thompson Jr.	1-0-1
Wm B. Sowers	1-0-1	Snowden Tumblin	1-0-2
Jos H. Shepherd	2-0-2	Danl Turner	1-0-1
Dr. W. Summerville	1-0-1	Mason Tinsman	1-0-1
Isaac Shipe	1-0-1	Ludwell Tinsman	1-0-1
Richmond & Stolle	3-0-3	Griffin Taylor	1-0-2
Franklin Stine	1-0-1	Wm G. Taylor	1-0-1
Col. T. Smith	1-0-2	Mrs. Susan Taylor	2-0-2
Danl C. Snyder	1-0-1	Saml M. Trussell	1-0-1
Benj Starkey	1-0-1	Jas W. Tanquary	1-0-1
Jno T. Shaffer	1-0-1	Rufus Timberlake	1-0-2
Jas W. Settle	1-0-1	Geo Turner	1-0-1
Craven Shell	1-0-1	Thos Trussell	1-0-2
John Sigafoose	1-0-1	T. Russell Tittille [?]	1-0-1
Jno S. Smith	1-0-1	John Talley Sr.	1-0-1
Thos Smith	1-0-1	Jno Talley Jr.	1-0-1
Geo S. Swarts	1-0-1	Newton Trenary	1-0-1
Jno S. Swarts	1-0-1	John Tayler	1-0-1
Jno R. Stuart	1-0-2	Jas L. Taylor	1-0-1
R. R. Smith	1-0-1	Geo W. Thompson	1-0-1
Geo Shepherd	1-0-1		
Wm L. Smith	1-0-1	J. L. E. Vanmeter	1-0-1
Champ Shepherd	1-0-2	Jacob B. Vorous	1-0-1
Albert Thompson	1-0-1	H. T. Wheat	2-0-2
Wm H. Thompson	1-0-1	B. F. Wilson	1-0-1
Jas Thomas	1-0-1	Jno Wilson	1-0-1
Adam F. Thompson	1-0-1	F. B. Whiting	2-0-2
Greenberry Thompson	1-0-1	W. W. Whiting	1-0-1
		N. B. Whiting	1-0-1

Clarke County, Virginia Personal Property Tax Lists 1854-1870
1865

Allen Williams	1-0-1		J. E. Williams	1-0-1
Thompson Writt	1-0-1		Jackson Wheeler	1-0-1
Wm Willingham	1-0-2		Jas W. Willingham	
Danl Wade	1-0-2		of Wm	1-0-1
Geo W. Wiley	1-0-1		Jeremiah Wilson	1-0-1
Jas Wiley	1-0-2		Richard Whittington	1-0-1
S. B. Wyndham	1-0-1		Wm Whaley	1-0-1
Thos C. Windham	1-0-1		Jno T. Willingham	1-0-1
Danl Welch	1-0-1		Thos Warnax	1-0-2
Jas V. Weir	2-0-3		W. N. C. Wilson	1-0-1
Jesse Wright	1-0-1		Rev. Jno W. Wolfe	1-0-1
Alex Wood	1-0-2		Tobias Waters	1-0-1
Lewis Wood	1-0-1		Jos White	1-0-1
Jas W. Willingham			Jas W. Walker	1-0-1
of Jno	1-0-1		Jas Wiley of (Hez)	1-0-1
Rev. Chas White	1-0-1		Jacob Willingham	1-0-1
Obediah Willingham	1-0-1		Chas L. Willingham	1-0-1
Col. H. W Ware	1-0-2		Fenton Wiley	1-0-1
Wm Whorton	1-0-1			
Geo F. Willingham	1-0-1		Simeon Yowell	1-0-1
Robt B. Wood	1-0-1		Jno Yowell	1-0-1
Thornton O.			Wm H. Young	1-0-2
Wyndham	1-0-1			

Male Free Negroes above the age of 16 years:

Mowen Harris	0-0-1		Peter Coats	0-0-1
Jas Butler	0-0-1		Jas Walker	0-0-1
Burwell Cook	0-0-1			

Clarke County, Virginia Personal Property Tax Lists 1854-1870

1866

Columns: 1) While males above 21 years, 2) Male negroes over 21 years, 3) Horses, mules, mares, & jennets. Column 2 is most often empty. Free black men are still listed separately t the end of the year's list.

Thos H. Alexander	1-0-5	Westley Brabham	1-0-0
Mason Anderson	2-0-6	Dr. Wm J. Best	1-0-3
Jno Alexander	1-4-4	Chas Barr	1-0-2
Edw Alder	1-0-0	Jno F. Burchell	1-0-6
Geo W. Allen	2-0-6	C. Bowser	1-0-1
Robt Atkins	1-0-2	Thos J. Bragg	1-0-2
Wm D. Atkins	1-0-1	Arthur Briggs	1-0-0
Nimrod Ashby	1-0-1	Geo H. Bell	1-0-0
Robt Ashley Sr.	1-0-0	Ann C. Benn	0-0-0
Philip J. Afflick	1-0-0	Neill Barnett	2-0-4
Ann M. Anderson	1-0-1	Henry C. Briggs	1-0-0
Jno W. Anderson		Adam Barr	1-0-1
(of Nimrod)	1-0-1	Enos S. Brown	1-0-0
Arthur Allen	1-0-2	Wm Bush	2-0-5
Edgar Allen	1-3-6	B. B. Bryant	1-0-0
Wm Ashman	1-0-1	Saml Bromley	1-0-6
R. S. Adams	1-0-1	Philip Berlin	1-0-1
Buckner G. Ashby	1-0-7	Chas A. Bush	1-0-1
Milton B. Anderson	1-0-3	Patrick Brady	1-0-1
Jno H. Anderson	1-0-0	Wm Bonham	1-0-5
Jno Anderson	1-0-4	Robt N. Beattey	2-1-5
Robt Ashby Jr.	1-0-1	Jno Bromley	5-0-6
Jos E. Anderson	1-0-5	Geo W. Bromley	1-0-9
Geo Anderson	1-0-0	Bushrod Buckley	2-0-5
Jno Allison	1-0-0	Caroline M. Baker	1-0-2
Jno W. Ashby	1-0-0	Nathl Burwell	1-2-11
Wm T. Allen	1-0-4	J. H. Bitzer	1-0-7
O. R. Allen	2-2-6	J. C. Brown	1-0-0
Jno W. Anderson		R. S. Bryarly	1-0-6
(of Joe)	1-0-5	Jas C. Briggs	1-0-3

Clarke County, Virginia Personal Property Tax Lists 1854-1870
1866

Name	Value	Name	Value
Robt W. Briggs	1-0-2	Jno W. Carpenter	1-0-0
Geo W. Berlin	2-0-0	Parkerson Corder	1-0-2
Wm R. Billmyre	2-0-5	Andrew Cornell	1-1-7
Geo W. Bolin	1-0-0	Jno R. Crockwell	1-1-7
Geo C. Blakemore	1-1-5	Robt Castleman	1-0-1
Wm Berry	2-0-3	Geo W. Copenhaver	1-2-6
Geo H. Burwell	2-0-10	Jno Conway &	
D° Trustee for		Brothers	3-0-5
Mrs. Hay	0-0-0	Wm H. Carter	1-0-0
Jno W. Beemer	1-1-4	Miss Mariam	
Lewis Berlin	1-0-0	Catlette	1-0-3
D. S. Bonham	2-0-6	Lucy A. Calmes	2-1-3
Jno N. Barr	1-0-0	Jno H. Crebs	1-0-2
Jas H. Bartlette	1-2-7	Jos K. Carter	1-0-2
Jas Bell Sr.	1-0-2	Jno A. Carter	2-0-6
Wm P. Briggs	1-0-1	Harrison Cooper	1-0-4
Abraham Beavers	1-0-0	James H. Clark	1-0-1
Frances Ann Brackett	2-0-2	Alfred Carper	1-0-5
Jos B. & Benj Beavers	2-0-4	Benj Crampton	1-0-1
Chas H. Boxwell	1-2-5	Jno Cooper	1-0-4
Thos W. Byrne	2-0-0-	Saml A. Campbell	1-0-1
Peter Bennett	1-0-1	Thos Carrell	1-0-4
Jesse Butler	1-0-2	Geo D. Cooper	1-0-0
Frances E. Bell	"-0-1	Jas Chapel	1-0-1
Mary Brabham	"-0-0	Jno N. Collier	1-0-2
Alfred Bishop	1-0-0	Jno A. Chiles	1-0-4
Geo S. Bennett	1-0-0	Franklin B. Carter	1-0-1
A. J. Berlin	1-0-0	Thos Carter	2-0-7
Chas Bailes	1-0-0	Jno B. Carter	1-0-2
Chas J. Berry	1-0-0	Mann R. P.	
Wm Brown	1-0-0	Castleman	1-0-1
Wm S. Brown	1-0-0	Jno R. Castleman	0-0-2
Geo V. Blake	1-0-0	Jas E. Chamblin	1-0-1
Chas H. Brabham	1-0-0	R. A. Colston	1-0-8
Dr. R. S. Blackburn	2-0-3	James L. Carter	1-0-2
Alfred Castleman	2-0-3	Wm G. Carter	1-0-0
Ann B. Cook	1-1-5	Willis B. Clark	2-0-7
Jno Cain	3-0-3	Wm Carper	2-0-3
Geo Chapman	1-0-1	Geo Chismore	1-0-3

Clarke County, Virginia Personal Property Tax Lists 1854-1870
1866

Jas Correll	1-0-2	Wm G. Everheart Jr.	1-0-2
Jno B. Carper	1-0-2	Geo W. Eagle	1-0-1
Jno W. Carter	1-0-1	Thos A. Everheart	1-0-3
Catharine E. Carter	0-1-4	Christoper Eleyet	1-0-3
Sarah Copenhaver	0-1-2	Jacob Enders	1-0-2
Jno Chapel	1-0-0	T. M. Eddy	1-0-1
Geo W. Corder	1-0-0	Jno & Henson Elliott	2-0-6
Wm T. Chapin	0-0-0	Olliver P. Eavans	1-0-3
Dr. R. T. Colston	1-0-0	Wm G. Everheart	3-0-7
W. Clark	1-0-0	Jacob W. Everheart	1-0-1
Alex Cornell	1-0-0	Henry Edwards	2-0-4
Lewis B. Corder	1-0-0	Geo R. Everett	1-0-0
Jno T. Crow	1-0-6		
Wm A. Castleman	1-0-2	Jos Fleming	2-0-5
		Thos W. Fleming	1-0-3
Jno Drish	1-0-2	Washington Fulgame [?]	1-0-1
Jno M. Dick	1-0-3	Marcus R. Feehrer	1-1-7
Geo W. Diffenderfer	2-0-3	Alexander Finnell	1-0-2
Aaron Duble	1-1-5	James Finnelle	1-0-0
Wm Deahl	1-0-1	Chas F. ~~Fenton~~ Hesser	1-0-3
J. P. Dorsey	1-0-3	Wm Fowler Jr.	1-0-2
Col. W. Dearmont	3-0-9	James Furr	1-0-1
T. J. Dove	1-0-2	Martin Feltner	1-0-4
Jno T. Dove	1-0-3	Denis Fenton	1-1-5
Peter Dearmont	1-0-3	Isaac Fletcher	1-0-5
Jno Donovan	1-0-3	Ewell Fowler	1-0-1
Geo Dick	1-0-1	Israel Fidler	1-0-4
H. H. Dunbar	1-0-0	James A. Foster	1-1-3
Richard Dulany	1-0-5	Johnson Furr	2-0-3
Thos Duke	1-0-1	Wm Furr	1-0-0
Mathew W. Doran	4-0-5	Thos Fowler	1-0-2
Robt L. Denney	1-0-4	Wm Fowler	1-0-1
H. P. Deahl	1-0-0	Joshua G. Fellows	1-0-4
Hugh Davis	1-0-0	Eli L. Fishpaw	1-0-0
Jas W. Doran	1-0-0	Wm M. Furgusen [?]	1-0-1
Albert Elsea	1-0-9	Josiah Furgerson	1-0-4
H. P. Eavans Gdn for children	1-0-6	O. R. Funston	1-2-11

133

Clarke County, Virginia Personal Property Tax Lists 1854-1870
1866

Jno H. Ford	1-0-2		Jas C. Gorrell	1-0-0
Enoch Furr	1-0-0		Geo Gardner	1-0-2
Ephram Furr	1-0-0		Mrs. Fanny Grigsby	0-0-1
Christian Fonda	1-0-0		Jas W. Grimes	1-0-6
Eben Frost	1-0-0		T. K. Glover	1-0-0
Jessee Fellows	1-0-0			
Curtus Fidler	1-0-0		Nelson Henry	1-0-3
J. B. Fleming	1-0-0		Jno W. Hibbard	1-0-2
			Mary E. Heflebower	0-0-3
Jas W. Galloway	1-0-0		James W. Hummer	2-0-7
Richard N. Green	1-0-5		Dr. B. Harrison	1-3-5
Thos W. Griffith	1-0-0		Jas M. Hardesty	1-0-6
Geo W. Grubb	1-0-2		C. Hoff	1-0-0
J. R. Griggsby	1-0-10		Saml Huyette	1-0-9
Adam Greenwaldt	1-0-1		Wm Hareseman	1-0-2
Martin Gaunt	1-0-3		Jno T. Hilliard	2-0-3
Jno & Thos E. Gold	3-2-8		Wm G. Harsdesty	2-0-4
Madison Grimes	1-0-2		Jackson Hoff	1-0-0
Jos W. Grantham	1-0-4		Jno Hensill	1-0-1
Jas H. Grove	1-0-1		Henry Huyette	1-0-5
Jno S. Green	1-0-6		Thos S. Hart	1-0-0
Charles Grubb	1-0-3		Jos R. Hardesty	1-0-7
Jno L. Grant	1-0-3		Jas F. Howell	1-0-0
L. J. Gordon	3-0-11		Jno W. Hall	1-0-0
Warner T. Gray	1-0-0		Wm J. Harris	1-0-8
Galloway & Grubb	0-0-1		Israel G. Hatterly	1-0-0
Geo W. Grimes	1-0-1		James Hamilton	1-0-0
Zebedee Gray	1-0-0		Catharine V. Hall	0-1-1
Wm Galloway	1-0-0		Wm R. Helvestine	1-0-0
Jno Gruber	1-0-3		Bella A. Hughs	1-0-0
Jas V. Green	1-0-3		Lewis Helvestine	1-0-8
B. R. Green	1-0-3		Geo Hansucker	1-0-3
Thos E. Gibson	1-0-1		Soloman Hibbs	1-0-4
Lewis F. Glass	2-0-4		Alfred Haddix	2-0-2
Wm H. Grove	1-0-0		A. D. Hardesty	1-0-3
Saml Grubb	1-0-0		Wm B. Harris	1-3-9
Jno M. Gibson	1-0-12		Jno Hughs	2-0-2
Geo W. Gordon	1-2-5		Thos W. Hesket	1-1-2
Wm C. Gover	1-0-0		J. B. Hawthorne	1-0-5

Clarke County, Virginia Personal Property Tax Lists 1854-1870
1866

Thos B. Hummer	1-0-0		Wm B. Jolliffe	1-0-0
Thos L. Humphrey	1-0-2		Peyton Johns	1-0-0
Jno Hummer	2-0-3		M. W. Jones	1-0-0
Alex Holzclaw	1-0-1		Layfaette Jones	1-0-0
Wm Holzclaw	1-0-1		Jessee Jenkins	1-0-0
A. J. Harford	1-0-1		Jno M. Jolliffe	1-1-4
Jno W. Holland	1-0-0		Geo W. Goy [sic]	1-0-0
Jas W. Haycock	1-0-3		Ebin Jenkins	1-0-0
Jas W. Hite	1-2-6		Jno S. Johnston	7-1-4
Edwd R. Harrison	1-0-4			
Mrs. Harriett Hough	0-0-0		Benj Kite	1-0-1
Jas Heflin	1-0-0		Judson G. Kerfoot	1-0-7
Edwin Hart	1-0-0		Joseph A. Kelso [?]	1-0-4
Wm Heflin	1-0-0		Wm J. Kegar	1-0-1
Wm Hummer	1-0-0		F. J. Kerfoot	1-0-3
Jas Howard	1-0-0		Jas M. Kegar	1-0-3
Rev. Wm Hodges	1-0-3		Dr. R. Kownslar's Est.	"-0-"
C. W. Hardesty	1-0-4		Henry Kromling	2-0-2
			E. V. Kercheval	1-0-1
Jos R. Jones	1-1-7		Geo W. Kitchen	1-0-4
Jas W. Johnston			Geo W. Koonce	1-0-1
(Mountain)	1-0-1		Mrs. E. S. Kownslar	0-1-2
Frank L. Johnson	1-0-0		S. G. Kneller	3-0-2
Benj Johnson	1-0-1		David T. Kerfoot	1-1-3
Wm A. Jackson	1-0-6		Wm F. Knight	1-1-7
O. S. Janney	0-0-3		Wm B. Kennan	1-0-0
Mrs. Martha Isler	0-0-1		Jno N. Kemmill	1-0-1
A. C. Jackson	1-2-6		Wm T. Kerfoot	1-1-3
Jas W. Johnston,			J. R. Kerfoot	1-0-4
Comr. Rev.	1-0-1		Wm. C. Kenarly	1-2-4
Edwd Jenkins	1-0-2		Jos McK. Kenarley	1-1-3
Thos Jones	2-0-4		Jno N. Kitchen	1-0-4
Leonard Jones	1-0-5		Chas H. Kitchen	1-0-2
Rev. Wm Johnston	1-0-0		Middleton Keeler	2-0-1
Thos Jenkins	1-0-3		Wm C. Kerfoot	1-3-8
Geo H. Isler	1-0-1		Henry Knight	1-0-1
Andrew Jackson	1-0-0		A. J. Kerfoot	1-0-0
Herod Jenkins	1-0-2		David Knight	1-0-0
Dennis [?] Jackson	1-0-3		Geo Kitridge	1-0-0

Clarke County, Virginia Personal Property Tax Lists 1854-1870
1866

Jas W. Lloyd	1-0-0		Benj Lock	1-0-6
Franklin Little	3-0-4		Moses Lewis	1-0-1
H. L. D. Lewis	1-1-1		Jno W. Luke	1-1-7
Geo W. Lewis	1-1-2		Wm Lanham	1-0-2
Jno Longerbeam	2-0-2		Jas W. Larue	3-0-5
Eli Littleton	1-0-3		Jas W. Lee	1-0-1
Jas L. Loyd	1-0-2		Wm D. Lee	1-0-1
Jno A. Lloyd	1-0-2		Alexander Lake	1-0-0
James Lanham	1-0-1		Danl J. Lanham	1-0-0
Ludwell Lee	1-0-2		Manly Lanham	1-0-0
Chas A. Lloyd	1-0-2		Benton Lanham	1-0-0
Jno Lee	1-0-2		Jno Louthan	1-0-1
Squire Lee	1-0-3		Jno Lloyd	1-0-1
Henry Lloyd	1-0-2		Jos B. Lindsey	1-1-5
Abraham Longabeam	1-0-0		Mrs. E. M. Lewis	0-0-1
Wm Levi	1-0-3			
Jno Lock Sr.	1-2-6		Jonah McDonald	1-0-2
Jas A. Lawyer	1-0-1		Joseph T. Mitchel	1-2-4
Remington Lock	1-0-5		E. W. Massey	1-0-3
Josiah R. Lock	1-0-6		Patrick Murray	1-0-2
R. W. Levi	1-0-5		Col. B. Morgan	3-2-12
Wm Littleton	1-0-2		Jas McClaughy	1-0-1
Peter Light	1-0-5		Miss Mary Meade	"-0-0
Jno M. Lupton	1-0-1		Jno Marshall	1-2-0
Benj Longabeam	1-0-6		Marshall &	
Jas T. Louthan	1-1-2		Fegurson [?]	1-4-8
R. H. Lee	"-0-5		Jno Morgan	1-0-5
Dr. T. M. Lewis	1-0-1		Wm T. Milton	1-1-3
Jno K. Louthan	1-0-2		Wm Morris	1-0-0
Dr. E. E. Lippett	1-0-1		McLane McCling	1-0-2
Col. J. B. Larue	3-1-9		Henry Mason	1-0-2
Minor Lanham	1-0-3		Jos Minefee	1-0-2
C. S. Lee	1-0-4		James McCormick	1-1-5
Jno F. Lancaster	1-0-0		N. Marshall Monroe	1-0-3
E. P. C. Lewis	1-0-1		P. McCormick Jr.	1-0-3
A. J. Liady	1-0-0		Thos McCormick	1-2-8
C. C. Larue	1-0-1		A. M. Moore	1-0-3
Mrs. Mariah Larue	"-0-0		W. H. H. Mauphin	1-0-1
A. L. P. Larue	1-0-4		S. P. Moore	1-0-1

Clarke County, Virginia Personal Property Tax Lists 1854-1870
1866

McDonald & Brothers	3-1-7		Jno G. McCauly	1-0-0
Geo Marlow	3-0-6		Marshall & Conrad	2-1-6
Sydnor B. Murphey	1-0-1		James Mitchell	"-"-4
S. J. C. Moore	1-0-0		Jno McClaughry	1-0-0
Jas W. McClellan	1-0-0		Jas T. Murphey	1-0-0
C. C. McIntyre	1-1-5		Jos Moore	1-0-0
D. H. McGuire	1-0-1		Robt P. Morgan	1-0-0
Geo Marpole	2-0-2		Jas Murphey	1-0-0
Alex Marshall	1-0-6		J. S. Mitchell	1-0-0
Thos P. Marshall	1-0-1		Justin Morales	1-0-0
Am Moore	2-0-9		Luther Michell	1-0-0
Jos F. McDonald	1-0-3		T. O. Mathews	1-0-0
Jas McDonald	1-0-2		F. M. Mathews	1-0-0
Benj G. McDonald	1-0-1		Dr. Holmes McGuire	1-0-0
Isaac S. Manuel	1-0-11		Jno W. McCormick	2-0-9
Garrett McDonald	1-0-2		Alfred P. Moore	1-0-0
David Meade	1-0-4		Jno G. Morris	1-0-2
D° Admr of			Marshall & Green	2-2-8
Mrs. Washington	"-0-0		E. B. Martin	1-0-0
D° Admr of			Moses B. Murphey	1-0-2
R. K. Meade	0-0-0			
D° Trustee for			Benj Newman	1-0-0
V. W. Meade	1-0-3		Alex V. Neville	1-0-0
David Meade Jr.	2-0-2		Thos C. Nicewarner	1-0-1
Moses G. Miley	1-0-2		Jas H. Neville	1-0-2
W. B. Maddox	1-0-2		Col. Wm Nelson	1-0-5
Col. F. McCormick	1-1-10		Wm Nicewarner	1-1-4
Thos B. Morehead	1-0-0		Mrs. Hugh M. Nelson	2-3-19
P. McCormick	2-1-12		Jno R. Nunn	1-1-3
D° Late Trustee			D° Guardn for	
for Ann Stribling	0-0-0		Geo W. Carter	0-0-0
D° Trustee for			D° Guardian for	
Edw McCormick	0-0-0		May Dix	0-0-0
D° Guardian for			Dr. S. S. Neill	1-0-2
Eliz^a McCormick	0-0-0			
D° Trustee for			Edw McCormick	1-2-10
Ebin Frost	0-0-0			
Dr. Wm D. McGuire	1-2-7		Joshua Osburn	2-0-3
P. N. Meade	2-0-3		Geo ORear	1-0-1

Clarke County, Virginia Personal Property Tax Lists 1854-1870
1866

Elizabeth ORear	"-1-6	Stephen Reed	1-0-0
Edw OBrian	1-0-0	Geo Rutter	1-0-1
Jas H. OBannan	1-0-0	J. B. Robinson	1-0-0
		R. H. Ritter	1-0-0
Killiam [?] Pope	1-0-1	Mrs. Minerva	
Jno E. Page	1-2-5	Royston	"-0-1
Mrs. Henrietta Page	"-0-0	Elisha Romine	1-0-2
Jno Page	1-2-5	R. S. T. Russell	3-1-7
Jos Piper	2-0-6	Marcus Reed	2-0-4
Michael Pope	1-0-1	Jas E. Russell	1-0-6
Paul Pierce	1-0-1	Jno Roland	2-0-7
Geo R. Page	1-0-2	W. Richardson	1-0-0
Conrad Piper	1-0-2	Jos F. Ryan	1-2-6
T. P. Pendleton	2-0-9	Jno D. Richardson	1-0-10
Jno Patterson	1-0-3	Michael Russell	1-0-4
A. N. Pierce	1-0-3	T. W. Russell	1-0-4
Mrs. Eliza Page	0-0-0	Jessee Russell	1-0-3
Wm G. Pierce	1-0-2	Jas W. Ryan	1-1-5
Wm Pile	2-0-5	Wm A. Riley	1-1-8
Pulliam & Howell	"-0-1	Luster Riley	1-0-2
M. Pulliam	1-0-0	J. J. Riley	1-1-4
P. H. Powers	1-0-1	D° Trustee for	
Mann R. Page	2-0-7	Mrs. Susan Taylor	2-1-3
Dr. Wm M. Page	1-0-4	Jas W. Roland	1-0-5
Jno F. Pierce	2-0-6	Jno W. Russell	1-1-5
Thos Prichard	2-0-2	Danl B. Richards	1-0-1
Saml L. Pidgeon	1-0-4	Geo W. Rutter	1-0-0
Peter McPierce	1-2-6	Jno Reynolds	1-0-0
C. M. Parkins	1-1-1	Enos Richmond	1-0-1
W. N. Putman	1-0-0	Dr. R. C. Randolph	4-5-6
Bushrod Puller	1-0-1	D° Guardian for N. P. Page	
Elizabeth Pierce	0-0-0	& Sisters	"-0-5
Richard Perrak	1-0-0	Richmond & Stolle	"-0-2
Jas Puller	1-0-0	Wm H. Robinson	1-0-6
A. C. Page	1-0-0	Westly Russell	1-0-2
Jno M. Pope	1-0-0	Mathew T. Royston	1-0-1
Jacob Pierce	1-0-0	Susan R. Burwell	0-0-0
Saml Polly	1-0-0	Beverly Randolph	1-4-8
		Uriah Royston	1-0-3

Clarke County, Virginia Personal Property Tax Lists 1854-1870
1866

Geo R. Royston	1-0-0		Warner C. Smith	1-2-6
Peter K. Royston	1-0-2		Jno S. Smith	1-0-2
Addison Romine	1-0-0		Jas W. Stephenson	1-0-4
Patrick Rodgers	1-0-0		Jas L. Shower [?]	1-1-3
Thos J. Russell	1-0-0		Dr. J. B. Smith	1-1-4
Leman [?] Reynolds	1-0-0		Carter Shepherd	1-1-5
Saml Rutter	1-0-0		Dr. H. C. Summerville	1-0-0
			Chas H. Smith	1-0-4
Wm D. Smith	1-3-14		Geo T. Shepherd	1-0-2
Simon Stickel	1-0-1		Geo S. Spaulding	1-0-0
Hiram Silman	1-0-1		Wm F. Stolle	1-0-1
Jno Shafer	1-0-0		M. L. Sinclair	1-0-1
Geo Smedley	1-0-0		Benj Starkey	1-0-5
Joseph Stickel	1-0-2		Sylvester Smallwood	1-0-4
Joseph H. Shepherd	1-1-5		Decater J. Shepherd	1-0-1
P. D. Shepherd	2-1-5		Miss Mary Shiveley	"-0-"
Dr. Wm Summerville	1-0-2		Jno W. Steele [?]	1-0-0
Danl W. Sowers	3-0-12		Champ Shepherd	1-3-4
Jno W. Sowers	1-0-7		Rev. H. Suter	1-0-2
Miss Alberter [sic]			Thos Smallwood	1-0-1
Sowers	"-0-2		Henry Stickel Sr.	1-0-0
Wm B. Sowers	1-3-5		Henry Stickel Jr.	1-0-1
Wm R. Stuart	1-0-4		Jos Shipe	1-0-0
Charles Showers	1-0-0		Denis Shehan	1-0-1
Simon R. Stump	1-0-3		R. R. Smith	1-0-0
Geo W. Swartz	1-0-0		Benj T. Silman	1-0-1
Jos B. Shepherd	1-0-3		Peter Stickel	1-0-2
Geo W. Sowers	1-1-3		Jno J. Shaffer	1-0-2
A. J. Shipe	1-0-2		Jno T. Shaffer	1-0-1
Chas Swartz	1-0-0		Wm G. Steel [?]	1-0-1
Lewis Stout	1-0-1		Stephen Stull	1-0-0
Treadwell Smith	1-2-7		Danl C. Snyder	1-2-6
Mount J. Shell	1-0-3		Jno W. Sprint	1-0-0
Mrs. S. E. T. Stribling	1-1-5		Jas A. Steele	1-0-0
Geo W. Shimp	1-0-2		Geo K. Sowers	1-1-6
Jno H. Shubridge	1-0-0		H. Slusher	1-0-0
Philip H. Swann	1-0-2		James M. Sheaver	1-0-1
R. M. Snyder	1-0-1		J. R. Stuart	1-0-5
Geo H. Sowers	1-0-4		Franklin Stine	2-2-9

Clarke County, Virginia Personal Property Tax Lists 1854-1870
1866

Mrs. M. E. Shumate	1-0-6		Wm Trenary	1-0-3
Burboun Smallwood	1-0-2		Dr. Bush Taylor	1-0-1
N. O. Sowers	1-0-0		Henry C. Tapscot	"-0-1
Wm L. Smith	1-0-0		Florinda Tapscot	"-0-1
E. J. Smith	1-0-0		Robt Tapscot	2-0-3
Geo R. Smith	1-0-0		Robt Tharp	1-0-3
Jno Stonestreet	1-0-0		Wm Tharp	1-0-3
Craven Shell	1-0-0		Danl Turner	1-0-0
Thomas Smith	1-0-0		Jno H. Taylor	1-0-0
Geo S. Swarts	1-0-0			
Jno Swarts	1-0-0		Jacob B. Vorours	1-0-9
Jos Stikel Jr.	1-0-0		J. & E. Vanmeter	2-1-3
Moses Shipe	1-0-4			
Mary Stribling	"-"-0		F. W. Wheat	1-0-4
Benj Shipe	1-0-0		F. B. Whiting	2-5-6
			Wm Willingham	1-0-3
Thos W. Trussell	1-0-0		H. T. Wheat	0-1-5
Balis Thompson Sr.	1-0-4		S. B. Wyndham	1-0-2
Jas W. Thomas	1-0-1		Jas V. Wier	2-2-9
Wm F. Thompson	1-0-1		Jno T. Willingham	1-0-2
Jas W. Tavender	1-0-2		N. B. Whiting	1-0-4
Isaac Talley	1-0-3		Chas Whittington	1-0-3
Balis Thompson Jr.	1-0-2		Obediah Willingham	1-0-0
Geo W. Thompson	1-0-1		Thornton O.	
Wm Taylor	1-4-9		Wyndham	1-0-2
Mrs. Eliza Tucker	"-0-0		Lewis Whittington	1-0-1
Adam F. Thompson	2-0-4		Jackson Wheeler	1-0-4
Calvin Thatcher	1-0-0		Frances H. Whiting	1-1-5
Jas L. Taylor	1-0-4		Robt B. Word	1-0-7
Jno W. Taylor	1-0-0		W. Wainsboro	2-0-3
Jas W. Tanquary	1-0-4		Allen Williams	1-2-4
Dr. Thos Turner	1-0-2		Richard Whittington	1-0-4
Snowden Tumblin	1-0-2		Abraham Wilson	1-0-0
Ludwell Tinsman	1-0-0		Jessee Wright	1-0-2
Mason Tinsman	1-0-1		Danl Wade	1-0-2
Saml M. Trussell	1-0-1		Wm T. Wharton	1-0-0
Sarah Timberlake	1-1-7		Alex Wood	1-0-4
Geo Turner	1-0-2		Saml G. Wyman	0-1-6
French Thompson	2-0-3		Geo W. Wiley	1-0-3

Clarke County, Virginia Personal Property Tax Lists 1854-1870
1866

Jas Wiley	1-0-0	Jacob Willingham	1-0-0
Jas W. Whittington	1-0-1	Chas L. Willingham	1-0-0
Walker B. Wilson	1-0-0	Fenton Wiley	1-0-0
Jerry Wilson	1-0-3	Jno Warnax [?]	1-0-0
F. B. Wilson	1-0-3	Danl Whittington	1-0-0
Jas W. Ward [?]	2-0-3	Jno D. Wright	1-0-0
W. N. C. Wilson	0-0-1	Jos White	1-0-0
Eustice Williams	1-0-2	Thos Warnex [?]	1-0-0
W. W. Whiting	1-0-1	Jas W. Willingham	
Rev. Chas White	1-0-2	(of Wm)	1-0-0
Thompson Writt	1-0-0	Geo T. Willingham	1-0-0
Thos C. Wyndham	1-0-0		
Jas W. Willingham		W. H. Young	1-0-0
(of Jno)	1-0-0	Simeon Yowill	1-0-1
Tobias Waters	1-0-0		

[Free blacks]

Peter Mason	0-1-0	Edmond Nueton [?]	0-1-0
Israel Pope	0-1-0	Shelton Walker	0-1-0
Willis Battles	0-1-0	Jno L. Howard	0-1-0
Marcus White	0-1-0	Wm Strange	0-1-0
Edwd Williams	0-1-0	Newman Thompson	0-1-0
Jno Blanham	0-1-0	Jas Thompson	0-1-0
Frank Gordon	0-1-0	Jno Thompson	0-1-0
David Jackson	0-1-0	Peter Jewelle [?]	0-1-0
Nathaniel Carter	0-1-0	Peter Coats	0-1-0
Ralph Laws	0-1-0	Geo Hall	0-1-0
Henry Laton	0-1-0	Levi Williams	0-1-0
Thos Banks	0-1-0	Walter Howard	0-1-0
Hny Strange	0-1-0	Jas Laws	0-1-0
Chas Barbour	0-1-0	Cyrus Burns	0-1-0
Thos Banister	0-1-0	Fenton Conway	0-1-0
Philip Williams	0-1-0	Jas Reed	0-1-0
Jas Butler	0-1-0	Lewis Carter	0-1-0
Chas Strange	0-1-0	Helvy [?] Roy	0-1-0
Hnry Berry	0-1-0	Robt Denmer	0-1-0

Clarke County, Virginia Personal Property Tax Lists 1854-1870
1866

Mowin Harris	0-1-0		Chas Davis	0-1-0
Wm Hall	0-1-0		Franklin Wright	0-1-0
Soloman Holmes	0-1-0		Fairfax Carter	0-1-0
Isaac Webb	0-1-0		Saml Wever	0-1-0
Isaac Bukley	0-1-0		Levi Lewis	0-1-0
Buckley Barbour	0-1-0		Danl Massey	0-1-0
David Jackson	0-1-0		Jno Mills	0-1-0
Top [?]Hite	0-1-0		Wm Field	0-1-0
Jno Howard	0-1-0		Webb Young	0-1-0
Robt Cooper	0-1-0		Robt Hall	0-1-0
Alfred Fox	0-1-0		Heny Slow	0-1-0
Willis Clark	0-1-0		Elsey Wilson	0-1-0
Hny Banks	0-1-0		Joshua Moore	0-1-0
Chas Strange	0-1-0		Sis Dangerfield	0-1-0
Chas Herbert	0-1-0		Jerry Lewis	0-1-0
Geo Washington	0-1-0		Bartlette Miles	0-1-0
Lewis Webb	0-1-0		Henry Harris	0-1-0
Richard Reeno	0-1-0		Geo Fields	0-1-0
Thos Reeno	0-1-0		Chas Johnson	0-1-0
Peter Dorris	0-1-0		Robt Page	0-1-0
Wm Haney	0-1-0		Nelson Reed	0-1-0
Franklin Halter	0-1-0		Saml Sims	0-1-0
Craven Warrick	0-1-0		Jacob Nelson	0-1-0
Geo Blair	0-1-0		Lewis Fletcher	0-1-0
Geo Jones	0-1-0		Chas Bowyer	0-1-0
Chas Sims	0-1-0		Jas Throgmorton	0-1-0
Addison Fox	0-1-0		Jas ~~Williams~~ Wheeler	0-1-0
Franklin Franklin	0-1-0		Geo Jones	0-1-0
Lewis Williams	0-1-0		Robert Tadd	0-1-0

Clarke County, Virginia Personal Property Tax Lists 1854-1870

1867

Columns: 1) White males over 21 years, 2) Male negroess over 21 years, 3) Residence, employer or employment of male negroes listed for taxation. When the third column included a name or place, it is inserted and indented under the tax payer's name. Free blacks are listed under the initial letter of their surname, along with everyone else.

John H. Anderson	1-0	Thos & Adams	
Milton B. Anderson	1-0	Jno Ashby	
D° Trustee for		(of Nimrod)	1-0
M. Anderson	1-0	Frank Acres	1-0
Robt Atkens	1-0	Jas S. Alridge [sic]	1-0
Wm D. Allums	1-0	Robt H. Alexander	1-0
Jno Alexander	1-0	W. F. Anderson	1-0
R. O. Allen	2-0	Wm Alison [?]	1-0
R. S. Adams	1-0	Jno Alison [?]	1-0
Geo W. Allen	1-0	Edmond Adams	0-1
Edgar Allen	1-0	D. C. Snyder	
Philip J. Affleck	1-0	Scot Anderson	0-1
Wm T. Allen	1-0	Island Farm	
Thos H. Alexander	1-0	Carter Alexander	0-1
Jno W. Anderson		D. Funsten	
(of Joe)	1-0	Frank Ashby	0-1
Jno W. Anderson		Geo Hansucker	
(of Nim)	1-0	Jno Anderson	0-1
Jos E. Anderson	1-0	Maj^r Baker	
Jno W. Anderson	1-0	Elija Anderson	0-1
Nimrod Ashby	1-0	Mr. Licklicter	
Geo W. Anderson	1-0	Wm Alexander	0-1
Robt Ashby Jr.	1-0	Dr. Kerfoot's	
Robt Ashby Sr.	1-0		
Wm Ashman	1-0	Jno Bromley	1-0
Geo Ashly	1-0	J. H. Bitzer	1-0
Warren M. Anderson	1-0	Jessee Butler	1-0
Geo. W. Alexander	1-0	Geo Berlin	1-0
Jas R. Ashby	1-0	Chars H. Boxwell	1-0
T. J. Anders	1-0	R. S. Blackburn	1-0

143

Clarke County, Virginia Personal Property Tax Lists 1854-1870
1867

Jno W. Biemer	1-0		R. N. Beattey [?]	2-0
Susan R. Burwell	"		Columbus Brown	1-0
Geo H. Burwell	1-0		Nathl Burwell	1-0
D° trustee for			Arthur [?] S. Briggs	1-0
Mrs. Hay	"		Jno Elliott	2-0
Wm Taylor Burwell	1-0		Jas W. Barton	1-0
Lewis Berlin	2-0		Simon D. Benton	1-0
Saml Bromley	1-0		R. S. Bryarly	1-0
Jno F. Burchell	1-0		Jas T. Bruce	1-0
Danl S. Bonham	2-0		Geo W. Belt	1-0
Wm H. Billmyre	1-0		Jas H. Bartlette	1-0
Wm Bonham	1-0		Wm Berry	1-0
Jas C. Briggs	1-0		Geo W. Bolin	1-0
Neill Barnett	2-0		Zachariach T. Barlow	1-0
Wesley Brabham	1-0		Peter Bennett	1-0
Hny C. Briggs	1-0		Jas Bell Sr.	1-0
Geo C. Blakemore	1-0		Geo W. Bromley	1-0
Geo H. Bell	1-0		Thos W. Byrne	2-0
Philip Berlin	1-0		Francis E. Bell	"-0
H. Beavers	1-0		Wm S. Brown	1-0
Wm P. Briggs	1-0		Jno Brown	1-0
Boyer & Wright	2-0		C. M. Barrer [?]	1-0
R. W. Briggs	1-0		Chas Bailes	1-0
Bushrod Buckley	1-0		Walter F. Bennett	1-0
Chas C. Benn	1-0		A. J. Berlin	1-0
Ann C. Benn	"0		Chas H. Brabham	1-0
Wm H. Brown &			Wm Brown	1-0
A. Romine	2-0		Geo O. Blake	1-0
Mrs. C. M. Baker	1-0		Emanuel Blackburn	0-1
Wm Bush	1-0		Jno Luke	
Wm S. Beattey	1-0		Cyrus Burns	0-1
Miss Margaret			Jacob Enders	
Burchell	1-0		Chas Brawman [?]	0-1
Adam Barr	1-0		Benj Thompson	
A. M. Bradwell	1-0		Wm Brown	0-1
Richard Brown	1-0		Am Moore	
C. Bowser	1-0		Geo Banker	0-1
Patrick Brady	1-0		Mrs. H. Nelson	
Chas A. Bush	1-0			

Clarke County, Virginia Personal Property Tax Lists 1854-1870
1867

Geo Brown	0-1		Thos Brown	0-1
Geo W. Gorden			A. R. Colstin	
Adrew [sic] J. Blanham	0-1		Wm Banks	0-1
Island Farm			Peter Dearmont	
Alfred Ball	0-1		Jas Brown	0-1
Clay Hill			B. Randolph	
Michael Barbour	0-1		Harman Baker	0-1
Clay Hill			B. Randolph	
Jack Bumley	0-1		Thos A. Blackburn	0-1
Jas W. McCormick			Berryville	
Jas Butler	0-1		Wm Brown	0-1
Berrys Ferry			Wm Harris	
Isaac Bickley	0-1		Jas Banks	0-1
Millwood			Geo W. Sowers	
Wm Brown	0-1		Hny Brandy	0-1
No. 2			Berryville	
Chas Barbour	0-1		Heny Bailey	0-1
Jas C. Briggs			Jos Shepherd	
Jas Bird	0-1		Thos Boroman	0-1
Edw Hardesty			Thos McCormick	
Thos Banister [?]	0-1		Jos Blair	0-1
Rev. Jos R. Jones			M. Pulliam	
Robt Banister	0-1		Chas Jackson	0-1
Thos Carter			Berryville	
Jas Bray	0-1		Wilson Brown	0-1
Jno E. Page			D. C. Snyder	
Thos Banks	0-1		Harris Burns	0-1
S. G. Wyman			Edw MCormick	
Alfred Bray	0-1		Geo Blake	0-1
Dr. Harrison			C. Ferry	
Jacob Brooks	0-1		Isaac Bowman	1-0
Dr. Randolph				
Jack Barbour	0-1		Jno W. Carpenter	1-0
Jos McK. Kennerly			Jno N. Collier	1-0
Chas Barbour	0-1		M. R. P. Castleman	1-0
Jos McK. Kennerly			Ann B. Cook	1-0
Andrew Brock	0-1		Alfred Castleman	2-0
Stone Bridge			Jno B. Carter	1-0
			Benj Crampton	1-0

Clarke County, Virginia Personal Property Tax Lists 1854-1870
1867

Jno R. Castleman	"-0	Andrew Cornell	1-0
McLane Cling [sic]	1-0	Geo D. Cooper	1-0
R. A. Colston	1-0	Reason Carrell	1-0
Jas Chapel	1-0	Thos Carrell	1-0
Jos R. Carter	1-0	Jas L. Carter	1-0
Henry Catlette	1-0	Lucy A. Calmes	1-0
Jno H. Crebs	1-0	Thos Carter	2-0
Harrison Cooper	1-0	Hiram Carper	1-0
Alfred Carper	1-0	Geo Carper	1-0
Jno Cain	2-0	J. F. Chismore	1-0
J. N. Cain	1-0	Parkison Corder	1-0
Jacob CrIser	1-0	Jno Cooper	1-0
Mrs. Sarah		D. R. T. Colston	1-0
Copenhaver	"-0	Jno W. Corbin	1-0
W. Carper	2-0	Geo Castleman	1-0
W. J. Carper	1-0	Jno Chapel	1-0
Jas Cornell	1-0	Jas J. W. Clutter	1-0
Willis B. Clark	2-0	Jos Carpenter	1-0
Jno W. Cross	2-0	Mr Cole	1-0
Jno Conway	3-0	E. W. Murry	
Jno A. Carter	2-0	Robt Cooper	0-1
Catharine Castleman	"-0	Martin Gant	
Geo W. Copenhaver	1-0	W. Cooper	0-1
Saml A. Campbell	1-0	T. E. Gold	
Jas H. Clark	1-0	Chas Cooper	0-1
Wm A. Castleman	1-0	No. 2	
Wm H. Carter	1-0	W. H. Clay	0-1
Mrs. C. E. Carter	"-0	Mrs. Irwin	
Mrs. Eliza Carter	"-0	Jacob Coxen	0-1
Amos Cloud	1-0	No. 3	
Jno A. Chiles	1-0	Morgan Coxen	0-1
Jno W. Carter	1-0	No. 3	
Jno R. Crockwell	1-0	Wm Carter	0-1
Geo W. Chismore [sic]	1-0	Wm B. Harris	
Jno B. Carper	1-0	Wm Clayton	0-1
Jno T. Crow	1-0	Clay Hill	
Mrs. F. A. Crow	1-0	Jacob Colston	0-1
Jas E. Chamblin	1-0	Island Farm	
J. Easton Cook	1-0		

Clarke County, Virginia Personal Property Tax Lists 1854-1870
1867

Ed^w Clayton	0-1		Chas Cole	0-1
No. 3			J. L. E. Vanmeter	
Wm Colston	0-1		Nathaniel Carter	0-1
Jno Marshall			Burwell Whiting	
Lewis Carter	0-1		Scot Colburn	0-1
Jas W. Conrad			Millwood	
Abraham Cyrus	0-1		Washington Corder	1-0
Millwood			Nicholas Criser	1-0
Robt Cross^n	0-1			
D. B. Harrison			Chas H. Duvall	1-0
Thos Cook	0-1		Robt Dunn	1-0
No. 3			H. H. Dunbar	1-0
Jno Cook	0-1		Richard Dulany	"-0
Jos F. Ryan			Aaron Duble	1-0
Murray Carter	0-1		Jno M. Dick	1-0
Dr. B. Harrison			Peter Dearmont	1-0
Sandy Carter	0-1		Geo W. Diffendufer	2-0
Jno W. Sowers			Col. W. Dearmont	2-0
Bushrod Cary	0-1		Capt. J. P. Dorsey	1-0
David Kerfoot			Thos J. Dove	1-0
Geo Crictenton [?]	0-1		Jno T. Dove	1-0
White Post			Jas Doran	1-0
Monroe Christian	0-1		Jno Drish	1-0
Dr. J. P. Smith			Geo Dick	1-0
Philip Colston	0-1		Jno Donovan	1-0
Edw Hardesty			Thos Duke	1-0
Rosin Carter	0-1		Robt L. Denney	1-0
Tuleries			Hugh Davis	1-0
Fairfax Carter	0-1		Aron Dunlap	1-0
Edw Lewis			Col. F. McCormick	
Geo Carter	0-1		Geo Dunlap	1-0
Thos McCormick			Col. F. McCormick	
Soloman Carter	0-1		Wm Deahl	1-0
Roger Smith			Cool Spring	
Saml Carter	0-1		H. P. Deahl	1-0
Chas Smith			Jno W. Drish	1-0
Geo Carter	0-1		Franklin Doran	1-0
Berryville			M. H. Doran	1-0
			Lewis Duley	1-0

Clarke County, Virginia Personal Property Tax Lists 1854-1870
1867

Jas W. Doran	1-0		Simon Edwards	0-1
Wm Deahl	1-0		Mrs. H. M. Nelson	
Berryville				
Robt Demmer [?]	0-1		Everett Fowler	1-0
W. H. Robinson			L. H. Fritz	1-0
Ces Dangerfield	0-1		Thos G. Flagg	1-0
Berryville			Geo Fidler	1-0
Danl Doleman	0-1		Israel Fidler	1-0
Jno B. Larue			Jno H. Ford	1-0
Jas Danks	0-1		O. R. Funston Sr.	1-0
Champ Shepherd			Alex Fennell	1-0
Andrew Davis	0-1		Josiah Furgeson	1-0
Neill Barnett			Furgeson & Marshall	1-0
Jas Dunkin	0-1		E. L. Fishpaw	1-0
Dr. Randolph			A. B. Fleming	1-0
Geo Dandridge	0-1		F. M. Feltner	1-0
Saml Bromley			Denis [?] Fenton	1-0
Michael Doctor	0-1		Marcus R. Feehrerr	1-0
Thos Carter			Johnson Furr	1-0
			Thos Fowler	1-0
Jacob W. Everheart	1-0		Wm Fowler Jr.	1-0
Jos Edwards	1-0		Isaac Fletcher [?]	1-0
Henry Edwards	2-0		O. R. Funston Jr.	1-0
O. P. Eavans	1-0		Jas A. Forster	1-0
Jacob Enders	1-0		Joshua G. Fellows	1-0
Thos A. Everheart	1-0		Washington Furgerson	1-0
Wm G. Everheart	4-0		Jno Fleming	1-0
Jno Eavans	1-0		Jessee Finnell	1-0
Geo R. Everett	1-0		Wm Furr	1-0
Benj Edwards	1-0		Is^c Fleming	1-0
Aaron [?] G. Elwell	1-0		Martin Feltner	1-0
Christopher Eleyet	1-0		Jas Furr	1-0
Robt P. Everhart	1-0		Wm Fowler	1-0
Albert Elsea	1-0		Ephraim Furr	1-0
Thos N. Eddy	1-0		Eben Frost	1-0
Jno M. Elwell	1-0		Irvin [?] Feltner	1-0
Benj. Elliott	0-1		Carter Fidler	1-0
Geo H. Isler			Jno Fitzenburger	1-0
			Thos Adams	

Clarke County, Virginia Personal Property Tax Lists 1854-1870
1867

Jno B. Finnell	1-0	Richard N. Green	1-0
Christian Fonda	1-0	Israel Green	1-0
Wm Frank Fowler	1-0	Geo Gardner	1-0
J. T. Freeman	1-0	Martin Gant	1-0
Alfred Fox	0-1	Jno M. Gibson	1-0
J. W. Russell		Maddison Grimm	1-0
Jos Fractious	0-1	Thos W. Griffith	1-0
Mrs. H. Nelson		Jno & Thos E. Gold	2-0
Wm Frontroyal [sic]	0-1	Thos D. Gold	1-0
Robt Frost	0-1	Zebidee Gray	1-0
Wm Fields	0-1	J. R. Grigsby	1-0
Frank Franklin	0-1	Jas W. Galloway	1-0
Augustine Fieud [?]	0-1	Warner T. Gray	1-0
Berryville		Geo W. Grubb	1-0
Wm Fitzhew	0-1	Mrs. Fanny Grigsby	"-0
Edgar Allen		Henry Grim	2-0
Geo Fields	0-1	W. B. Grubb	1-0
Mrs. Stribling		Philip Grubb	1-0
Peyton Fox	0-1	Chas Galloway	1-0
Wm Allen		Os W. Grantham	1-0
Aaron Fields	0-1	Geo W. Grimes	1-0
Kimballs		Wm H. Grove	1-0
Alex Franklin	0-1	Jno L. Grant	1-0
Col. J. B. Larue		Mathew Grubb	1-0
Lewis Fletcher	0-1	Mrs. S. Green	1-0
No. 4		Chas Grubb	1-0
Gurney Fletcher	0-1	Barny Gilbert	1-0
J. W. T. Crow		Wm B. Grubb	1-0
		Jas W. Grimes	1-0
Jno Gruber	1-0	Lewis F. Glass	2-0
Adam Greenwaldt	1-0	Geo W. Gorden [?]	1-0
Maddisan L. Grubb	1-0	J. F. Griffith	1-0
Jno T. Grubb	1-0	J. B. Gohern [?]	1-0
Thos E. Gibson [?]	1-0	Thos & Adams	
B. R. Green	1-0	Jno M. Gill	1-0
Jas F. Green	1-0	Thos & Adams	
Jno S. Grubb	1-0	Saml Grubb	1-0
Jas Grubb	1-0	S. J. Gant	1-0
Casper W. Green	1-0	Geo M. D. Grubb	1-0

Clarke County, Virginia Personal Property Tax Lists 1854-1870
1867

Jack Gage	0-1		Mary E. Heflebower	1-0	
B. Randolph			Philip Hunsucker	1-0	
Albert Green	0-1		Jno W. Hall	1-0	
Wm G. Everheart			Jno T. Hilliard	1-0	
Jas Gumby	0-1		Jos F. Howell	1-0	
Long Branch			T. L. Humphrey	1-0	
Jack Grigsby	0-1		Thos S. Hart	1-0	
Stone Bridge			David Hathaway	1-0	
Robt Green Sr.	0-1		J. W. Ware		
Sommerville			Cornelius Hawks	1-0	
Thornton Gorden	0-1		Geo Hunsicker	1-0	
Tuleries			Thos W. Hesket	1-0	
Frank Gorden	0-1		Henry Harrison	1-0	
Dr. Page			Jas M. Hardesty	1-0	
Ed^d Green	0-1		Jno & Mason Hummer	2-0	
B. Randolph			Jackson Hoff	1-0	
T. K. Glover	0-1		Hummer & Carrell	2-0	
Jas C. Gorrell	0-1		Jno W. Holland	1-0	
Jno Greenwaldt	0-1		Catharine E. Hall	"-0	
Robt Green Jr.	0-1		Burr Hull	1-0	
Sommerville			Jno Hughs	1-0	
			Wm G. Hardesty	1-0	
Edwd R. Harrison	1-0		Wm Harriman	1-0	
Wm J. Harris	1-0		Alex Holtzclaw	1-0	
Mason Hough	1-0		Wm Holtzclaw	1-0	
Jas W. Haycocck	1-0		C. Hoff	1-0	
J. B. Hawthorn	1-0		Wm Hook	2-0	
A. D. Hardesty	1-0		W. R. Helvestine	1-0	
Jos R. Hardesty	1-0		Jacob R. Hilliard	1-0	
C. W. Hardesty	1-0		Jno L. Hughs	1-0	
W. B. Harris	1-0		Jacob C. Hartly	1-0	
Henry Huyett	1-0		Alex Hummer	1-0	
Jas M. Hite	1-0		Jno Henson [?]	1-0	
Lewis B. Helvestein	1-0		Wm Hopkins	1-0	
A. J. Harford	1-0		Thos Haley	1-0	
Jno Hibbard	1-0		Landon L. Hough	1-0	
Soloman Hibs	1-0		Jas P. Hoff	1-0	
Nelson Henry	1-0		Jas Heflin	1-0	
Mrs. Bettie L. Hughs	1-0		Saml Hitchcock	1-0	

Clarke County, Virginia Personal Property Tax Lists 1854-1870
1867

Jno Harris	1-0	Wm Harris	0-1
Wm Hummer	1-0	Dr. Randolph	
Jno Hummer	1-0	Henry Hopper	0-1
Thos & Adams		Page Brook	
W Heflin	1-0	Chas Hubbard	0-1
Robt Hodges	1-0	Millwood	
Jno S. Hardesty	1-0	Jas Harrison	0-1
Preston J. Hamman	1-0	Millwood	
Wm E. Harrison	1-0	Soloman Holmes	0-1
Alex Horner	1-0	Millwood	
Beverly Huntgross	0-1	Adam Hurbert	0-1
Berryville		Jno Jolliffe	
Henry Heaton	0-1	Stepner Helms	0-1
Angus McDonald		Philip Hansucker	
Arche Herbin	0-1	Robt Hall	0-1
Dr. Kerfoot		Berryville	
Danl Huson	0-1	Wesly Hall	0-1
Angus McDonald		Barney Gilbert	
Levi Harris	0-1	Mowin Harris	0-1
P. D. Shepherd		No. 2	
Wm Holmes	0-1	Geo Harris	0-1
Edgar Allen		Jno W. Beemer	
Heny Haris	0-1	Walter Howard	0-1
Berryville		C. Erb	
Buckner Harry	0-1	Sawney Hunter	0-1
Stone Bridge		White Post	
Jno Howard	0-1	Alph Haddex	1-0
J. M. Hite		Chas Huyette	1-0
Geo Helm	0-1		
Millwood		Geo H. Isler	1-0
Danl Haney	0-1	Mrs. Martha Isler	1-0
Tuleries		Marcus B. Irwin	1-0
Maddison Harris	0-1		
Tuleries		Jas W. Johnston	1-0
Fairfax Harris	0-1	Edw Jenkins	1-0
Tuleries		Anders Jackson	1-0
Bennett Hubbard	0-1	Geo W. Joy	1-0
Dr. Randolph		F. L. Johnston	1-0
		Lenard Jones	1-0

Clarke County, Virginia Personal Property Tax Lists 1854-1870
1867

Demst [?] Jackson	1-0		Lewis Jones	0-1
W. B. Jollife	1-0		Jas Shepherds	
Alfred C. Jackson	1-0		Thos Jones	0-1
Thos Jenkins	1-0		T. P. Pendleton	
Peyton T. Johns	1-0		Henry Jackson	0-1
Thos Jones	1-0		Berryville	
Jarvis Jening's	1-0			
Herrod Jenkins	1-0		James Ireland	0-1
Jno S. Johnston	1-0		Col. W. Dearmont	
Rev. Wm Johnston	1-0		Israel Jackson	0-1
Dr. F. Johnson	1-0		Wm Picketts	
Robt Jackson	1-0		Chas Jenison [?]	0-1
Jas W. Johnson	1-0		Tuleries	
Mountain			Jno James	0-1
Wm A. Jackson	1-0		Summerville	
Rev. Jos R. Jones	1-0		Henry Jackson	0-1
Jno M. Jolliffe	1-0		R. S. Adams	
Eben Jenkins	1-0		Geo W. Jackson	0-1
Layfaette Jones	1-0		Wm Pickett	
Jessee Jenkins	1-0		David Jackson	0-1
Jeremiah Jenkins	1-0		White Post	
Herod Jenkins Jr.	1-0		Chas Jackson	0-1
Mathew M. Jones	1-0		Dr. Randolph	
Wm R. Johns	1-0		Jessee Jackson	0-1
Emanuel Jenkins	1-0		Jno E. Page	
Andrew Jefferson	0-1		Gates [?] Jackson	0-1
No home, No. 3			Dr. Randolph	
Archie Jackson	0-1		Everett Jackson	0-1
Berryville			Thos Carter	
Chas Johnson	0-1		Henry Jackson	0-1
No. 3			Jno E. Page	
Jos Jackson	0-"		Jackson Johnson	0-1
Col. F. McCormicks			Heny Harrison	
Robt Jackson	0-1		Chas H. Jackson	0-1
Jno Morgan Jr.			Wm C. Kennerly	
Jas Jackson	0-"		Jno Johnson	0-1
P. D. Shepherds			Geo Chapman	
Fuller Jackson	0-1		Savary Irwin	0-1
Mrs. S. Taylor			Millwood	

Clarke County, Virginia Personal Property Tax Lists 1854-1870
1867

		Henry Knight	1-0
Philip Jackson	0-1	A. J. Kerfoot	1-0
Andrew Cornell		Henry D. Kerfoot	1-0
Harry Johnson	0-1	Koonce & Crow	"-0
Geo W. Gorden		Wm G. Kigar	1-0
Henry Jefferson	0-1	Moses King	"-1
C. H. Boxwell		Capt. Meade	
Thos Johnson	0-1	Middleton Keeler	1-0
Jno Frazer		Mrs. E. S. Kownslar	1-0
Esau Jackson [?]	0-1	Geo W. Koonce	1-0
C. H. Boxwell		Mid Keeler	1-0
Presley Jenkins	0-1		
C. H. Boxwell		Peter Light	1-0
B. F. Johnson	1-0	Jas A. Lawyer	1-0
		Remmington Lock	1-0
Chas L. Kendall	1-0	Jno Lock Sr.	1-0
Jno M. Kitchen	1-0	H. M. Likens	1-0
David T. Kerfoot	1-0	J. M. Laws	1-0
Jos H. Keely	1-0	Frank H. Lock	1-0
W. T. Kerfoot	1-0	Benj Lock	1-0
Thos H. Kerns	1-0	Wm A. Larue	1-0
W. C. Kerfoot	1-0	Col. J. B. Larue	1-0
Jas F. Kerfoot	1-0	Jno Lloyd	1-0
D° Trustee for		Jas W. Lloyd	1-0
Mrs. Adams	"-0	E. P. C. Lewis	1-0
Chas H. Kitchen	1-0	Geo W. Lewis	1-0
Jas M. Kiger	1-0	H. L. D. Lewis	1-0
W. F. Knight	1-0	Mrs. E. M. Lewis	1-0
Judson G. Kerfoot	1-0	Jas W. Larue	1-0
Jos McK. Kenarly	1-0	Benj Longerbeam	1-0
Jos A. Kelso	1-0	Jas F. Louthan	1-0
Wm C. Kenarly	1-0	C. S. Lee	1-0
Jno M. Kimmell	1-0	A. L. P. Larue	1-0
Dr. F. J. Kerfoot	1-0	C. M. Louthan	1-0
S. S. Kneller	2-0	Jno K. Louthan	1-0
F. Howard Kerfoot	"-0	Jno F. Lancaster	1-0
E. O. Kercherval	1-0	Jno M. Lupton	1-0
W. B. Kennan	1-0	Rice W. Levi	1-0
Henry Kromling	1-0	Mrs. Mariah Larue	"-0

Clarke County, Virginia Personal Property Tax Lists 1854-1870
1867

C. C. Larue	1-0		Marshall Lightfoot	0-1
Jos B. Lindey [sic]	1-0		Jos Shepherds	
R. H. Lee	"-0		Frank Lewis	0-1
Dr. T. M. Lewis	1-0		Cool Spring	
A. G. Laidy [smeared]	1-0		Jas Lewis, No. 3	0-1
Frank Littleton	1-0		Robt Lewis	0-1
Jas L. Lloyd	1-0		Berryville	
Jno H. Lauck	3-0		Jno W. Luckley	0-1
Eli Littleton	1-0		Mrs. Copenhaver	
Mose Irwin	1-0		Thos Laws	0-1
Jno Louthan	1-0		Chapel	
Abraham Longerbeam	1-0		Ralph Laws	0-1
Jno L. Lindsey	1-0		White Post	
Squire Lee	1-0		Peter Lavender	0-1
Jno A. Lloyd	1-0		near White Post	
Alex Lake	1-0		Denis Lee	0-1
Wm D. Lee	1-0		near White Post	
Henry F. Licklider	1-0		Benj Lamkins	0-1
Henry Lloyd	1-0		Jno W. Sowers	
Chas A. Lloyd	1-0		Fielding Laws	0-1
Wm Lanham	1-0		Island Farm	
Lippett & Annan	3-0		Thos Lutz	0-1
Jas W. Lee	1-0		Mrs. Cook	
Jno D. Lloyd	1-0		Alex Lewis	0-1
Jas F. Lewis	1-0		Mrs. Betsy ORear	
Jonathan Lupton	1-0		Danl Layton	0-1
Jno S. Laws	1-0		Millwood	
Jas Lanham	1-0		Soloman Lewis	0-1
Danl I. Lanham	1-0		Ashbys Gap	
Manley Lanham	1-0		Jonah Lucas	0-1
Israel Lightfoot	0-1		Jno S. Smith	
Lewis Lightfoot No. 3	0-1		Peter Lurett [?] T. O. Wyndham	0-1
Isaac Lee Champ Shepherds	0-1		Saml Lockley Mann R. Page	0-1
Albert Lightfoot Dr. McGuire	0-1		Benj Lipscomb Jos Gorrell	0-1
___ Lewis ___ Berryville	0-1		Richard Lewis Jos Gorrell	0-1

Clarke County, Virginia Personal Property Tax Lists 1854-1870
1867

Philip Litley	0-1	D° Trustee for	
No. 2		Mrs W. W. Meade	
Peter Lavender	0-1	G. H. McDonald & Bro.	1-0
Mrs. Timberlake		Josiah McDonald	1-0
Rentin [?] Lanham	0-1	Col. F. McCormick	1-0
Benj Lloyd	0-1	Col. B. Morgan	1-0
		Edw McCormick	1-0
Jas McClaughy	1-0	W. W. Meade	1-0
H. M. Moore	1-0	Dr. W. D. McGuire	1-0
Thos B. Morehead	1-0	Hezekiah Marpole	1-0
Jno Morgan Sr.	1-0	E. C. Marshall	1-0
Alex Marshall	1-0	Chas A. Milton	1-0
Moses G. Miley	1-0	Jas W. McClilland	1-0
Wm T. Milton	1-0	Jas F. Milton	1-0
Geo Marpole	1-0	Rev. T. F. Martin	1-0
Jno Morgan	2-0	P. McCormick	1-0
P. McCormick Jr.	1-0	D° guardian for	
Jno G. Morris	1-0	Eliza McCormick	
Jos T. Mitchell	1-0	Jas C. Mason	1-0
Jas ~~W~~ McCormick	1-0	Henry Mason	1-0
Thos McCormick	1-0	Jno G. McCauly	1-0
Jno Marshall	1-0	F. B. Meade	1-0
S. P. Moore	1-0	J. Shep Mildull [?]	1-0
C. C. McIntyre	1-0	E. B. Manter	1-0
W. H. Levi	1-0	Jno W. McCormick	2-0
Alfred Marshall	1-0	Gabriel McDonald	1-0
H. J. Meemore [?]	1-0	G. W. Morris	1-0
Jos A. Mock	1-0	S. B. Murphey	1-0
P. N. Meade	1-0	?. T. Mountjoy	1-0
Garrett McDonald	1-0	W. B. Maddox	1-0
Luther G. [?] Mitchell	1-0	E. W. McEssay [?]	1-0
Angus McDonald	1-0	D. H. McGuire	1-0
Isaac S. Manuel	1-0	S. J. C. Moore	1-0
Casper J. C. Marter [?]	1-0	D° Exor of	
David Meade Jr.	2-0	Dr. Kownslar	1-0
David Mead Sr.	1-0	Hugh McCormack	1-0
D° Admr of R. R. Meade		Jno Miller	1-0
D° Admr of Mrs Washington		Thos & Adams	
		Robert E. McElear [?]	1-0

Clarke County, Virginia Personal Property Tax Lists 1854-1870
1867

Asa Moore	1-0		A. P. Moore	1-0
Patrick Murray	1-0		London Mitchel	0-1
Miss Mary W. Meade	1-0		Berryville	
Jno G. McClaughy	1-0		Chas Myres	0-1
Julius Morales	1-0		D. H. McGuire	
W. F. Meade	1-0		Thos Whiting	0-1
Jno P. McMurray	1-0		Edw Marshall	
Chas E. Moulden	1-0		Wm McAbaugh	1-0
Mr McDonald	1-0		Jesse Mercer	1-0
D. Holmes McGuire	1-0		W. C. Morgan	1-0
Nicholas More	1-0			
Norris Murphey	1-0		Jas H. Neville	1-0
Isaac Mitchil	0-1		Mrs. Hugh M. Nelson	1-0
Jno McIntrie	0-1		D. M. Dickols	1-0
Richard McCard	0-1		Thos Nicewarner	1-0
Jacob L. Murray	0-1		Jno R. Nunn	1-0
Lee Moor	0-1		Alex Neville	1-0
Robt Gill	0-1		Col. Wm Nelson	1-0
Nat Masturn	0-1		Wm Nicewarner	1-0
Jas Morenburg	0-1		Dr. S. S. Neill	1-0
Randle Martin	0-1		Jas N. Nevelle	1-0
Robt Myres	0-1		Elijah G. Nigh	1-0
Geo Moore	0-1		Walker Norris	0-1
Jas Mason	0-1		Millwood	
Rolley Myres	0-1		Henry Norris	0-1
Edgar Miner	0-1		Saratoga	
Henry Mitchel	0-1		Chas Newman	0-1
Joshua Moore	0-1		Cool Spring	
Saml Mildul	0-1			
Jas Murray	0-1		Elizabeth ORear	"-0
Cornelius Miles	0-1		Joshua Osburn	1-0
Jno Mills	0-1		Geo ORear	1-0
Isaac Murray	0-1		Alfred E. Owens	1-0
Jos McCard	0-1		R. K. Ogden	1-0
Danl Massey	0-1		Lewlen [?] Osburn	1-0
Barton Myres	0-1		Edw OBryan	1-0
Geo Mosby	0-1		Jas H. OBannan	1-0
Jas Moore	1-0		Walker Office	0-1
Jas Murphy	1-0		No. 1	

Clarke County, Virginia Personal Property Tax Lists 1854-1870
1867

Bushnell Osburn	0-1		Benj F. Pope	1-0
Clay Hill			Wm H. Pope	1-0
			Jacob Pierce	1-0
Powell Page & Sister	"-0		W. W. Proffett	1-0
Conrad Pope	1-0		Jas Puller	1-0
C. M. Parkins	1-0		Wm Pickett	1-0
A. H. Pitman	2-0		Geo Puller	1-0
Dr. Wm. M. Page	1-0		A. C. Page	1-0
Mrs. Elizabeth Pierce	"-0		Jno M. Pope	1-0
P. H. Powers	1-0		Saml Polley	1-0
Geo C. S. Philips	1-0		Robt Page	0-1
T. P. Pendleton	2-0		Dr. Stephenson	
Peter McPierce	2-0		Edw Pry	0-1
Jno C. Page	1-0		Berryville	
Mrs. Henrietta Page	"-0		Thos Page	0-1
Jno Pickett	1-0		T. McCormick	
Wm Pile	2-0		Wm Philips	0-1
Paul Pierce	1-0		R. W. Briggs	
A. M. Pierce	1-0		Richard Parker	0-1
Jno Page	1-0		Tuleries	
P. D. Shepherd	2-0		Geo G. Potter	0-1
Jno Patterson	1-0		S. G. Wyman	
J. F. Pierce	1-0		Danl Potter	0-1
Mann R. Page	2-0		S. G. Wyman	
Jno Poston	1-0		Jacob Payne	0-1
R. B. Park	1-0		Wm Kerfoot	
Jno F. Perry	1-0		Jno Potter	0-1
Wm. R. Putnam	1-0		Wm Kerfoot	
Jos Pipher	2-0		Baltimore Packer	0-1
Watson Pangle	1-0		Jas V. Weir	
Richard Puller	1-0		Preston Quiler	0-1
Lazaruth Pine	1-0		Jno M. Gibson	
Jno Pine	1-0		Jas W. Quill, No. 1	0-1
Jno B. Patterson	1-0			
Saml Pidgeon	1-0		Jno Roland	3-0
M. Pulliam	1-0		Thos J. Russell	1-0
J. N. Patterson	1-0		Jno W. Russell	1-0
H. R. Patterson	1-0			
Jas B. Patterson	1-0			

Clarke County, Virginia Personal Property Tax Lists 1854-1870
1867

Jno J. Riley	1-0		W. H. Recey	1-0
D° Trustee for			Jas H. Rodrick	1-0
Susan Taylor	2-1		Allan Randoloph	1-0
Thos W. Russell	1-0		Liman Reynolds	1-0
Wm A. Riley	1-0		Geo W. Russell	1-0
Mrs. M. Royston	"-0		E. B. Rossen	1-0
Dr. R. C. Randolph	3-0		M. Pulliam	
Jessee N. Russell	1-0		Jno Reynolds	1-0
Jas E. Russell	2-0		D. H. McGuire	
Stephen Reed	1-0		Frank Randolph	0-1
Wm H. Robinson	1-0		T. P. Pendleton	
Beverly Randolph	1-0		Andrew Robinson	0-1
Wm C. Randolph	1-0		H. L. D. Lewis	
Romancer Rinker	1-0		Saml Robinson	0-1
Marcus B. Reed	2-0		Edgar Allen	
Geo W. Rutter	1-0		Jeffre Runner	0-1
Danl B. Richards	1-0		Alfred Castleman	
Jno D. Richardson	2-0		Harry Robinson	0-1
Jas H. Roland	1-0		C. Fry	
Michael Russell	1-0		Nelson Reed	0-1
Russell & Cross	1-0		Mann R. Castleman	
Geo Rutter	1-0		Buck Robenson	0-1
Isaac A. Reidy	1-0		No. 3	
Moses Riley	1-0		Albert Ranson	0-1
Enos Richmond	1-0		Saratoga	
Jas W. Ryan	1-0		Henry Randolph	0-1
Jos F. Ryan	1-0		Jacob Vorous	
Elisha Romine	1-0		Arche Randolph	0-1
Uriah Royston	1-0		B. Randolph	
Mathew T. Royston	1-0		Harry Randolph	0-1
W. W. Russell	1-0		Saratoga	
Geo R. Royston	1-0		Jno Randolph	0-1
R. H. Ritter	1-0		White Post	
A. Rutherford	1-0		Jas Reynolds	0-1
Cornelius Riley	1-0		White Post	
Luke Riley	1-0		Harry Robinson	0-1
D. T. Richards	1-0		J. W. Byrds Farm	
Ewell Rose	1-0		Jno Robinson	0-1
Elijah J. Roy	1-0		Annfield	

Clarke County, Virginia Personal Property Tax Lists 1854-1870
1867

Nelson Robinson	0-1	Champ Shepherd Jr.	1-0
Millwood		Chas H. Smith	1-0
Geo Richardson	0-1	Geo K. Sowers	1-0
Wm B. Harris		Jno Shafer	1-0
Ambrose Robinson	0-1	Geo S. Spaulding	1-0
T. Hummers Mill		Wm B. Sowers	1-0
Jno Robinson	0-1	Danl W. Sowers	2-0
Berys Ferry		Geo W. Sowers	1-0
Robt Runner	0-1	J. N. Shepherd	1-0
Saratoga		Benj Shipe	1-0
Heny Robinson	0-0	Jno J. Shaffer	1-0
Sam Robinson	0-1	M. L. Sinclair	1-0
T. E. Gold		Danl H. Sowers	1-0
Richard Runner	0-1	Jno F. Sowers	1-0
A. S. Allen		Wm. G. Steel	1-0
Thos Runner	0-1	Jas A. Steel	1-0
A. S. Allen		Peter Stickel	1-0
Saml O. Reed	0-1	Dr. Wm Summerville	1-0
Jas A. Forster		R. M. Snyder	1-0
Jno Thompson	0-1	Geo W. Stillwell	1-0
near S. B. Wyndhams		Jno W. Sowers	1-0
Heny Robinson	0-1	Geo Snyder	2-0
Jas McCormick		Burr Smallwood	1-0
Alph Runer	0-1	Jno W. Steel	1-0
Berryville		Mrs. E. M. Shumate	1-0
Jno Rippen	1-0	Jno G. Snyder	1-0
P. Royston	1-0	Jas S. Sowers	1-0
		Dr. J. P. Smith	1-0
Moses Shipe	1-0	Henry F. Shearer	1-0
Jno S. Smith	1-0	Jas M. Sheaver	1-0
Denis Shehan	1-0	Chas W. Swartz	1-0
R. R. Smith	1-0	Benj Starkey	1-0
E. J. Smith	1-0	A. J. Shipe	1-0
W. D. Smith	1-0	Jno W. Swarts	1-0
Warren C. Smith	1-0	Champ Shepherd	1-0
Danl C. Snyder	1-0	Geo R. Smith	1-0
Jos H. Shepherd	1-0	D. D. Sibold & Son	2-0
S. C. T. Stribling	1-0	Geo W. Shimp	1-0
Sylvester Smallwood	1-0	Wm F. Stolle	1-0

Clarke County, Virginia Personal Property Tax Lists 1854-1870
1867

D. J. Shepherd	1-0		Jos Shipe	1-0
Craven Shell	1-0		G. B. Spekes	"-0
Geo G. Shepherd	1-0		Wadesville	
Mount J. Shell	1-0		Thos Stickel	1-0
J. R. Stuart	1-0		Albert Steel	1-0
Saml McD Shiplett	1-0		Jos B. Shipe	1-0
Nicholas Sweetland	2-0		Stephen Shell	1-0
Carter Shepherd	1-0		Baker [?] Shipe	1-0
Dr. H. C. Summerville	1-0		Doct Shipe	1-0
S. R. F. Stump	1-0		Wm L. Smith	1-0
Thos Smallwood	1-0		Chas Skinner	0-1
Chas Showers	1-0		Mrs. M. Burchell	
Saml Showers	1-0		Wm Smith	0-1
Heny Stickel Jr.	1-0		Berryville	
Hiram Silman	1-0		Henry Stuart	0-1
B. F. Silman	1-0		no house	
Simon Stickel	1-0		Thos Smith	0-1
Jno W. Sprint	1-0		Mrs. M. Burchell	
Jno T. Shaffer	1-0		Chas Johnson	0-1
Frank Stine	2-0		Berryville	
Mary Stribling	"-0		Philip Strange	0-1
Geo Smalley	1-0		Cool Spring	
Geo H. Sowers	1-0		Wm Strange	0-1
T. Smith	1-0		B. Whiting	
H. Slusher	1-0		Heny Smith	0-1
Michael Spencer	1-0		Saratoga	
Chas A. Sigafoose	1-0		Jas Strange	0-1
Thos W. Stickel	1-0		B. Whiting	
Jno Shell	1-0		Wm Strange	0-1
W. R. Stipe	1-0		Peter McPierce	
Edw Smith	1-0		Jas Sanders	0-1
Robt Shearman	1-0		Peter McPierce	
Edison Shumate	1-0		Jas Smith	0-1
Lewis Shrout	1-0		Jas M. Hite	
Timothy Shean [sic]	1-0		Jno Strange	0-1
Augustine Swarts	1-0		Wm C. Kerfoot	
Jas C. Sharp	1-0		Richard Strange	0-1
Jas L. Showers	1-0		Crismore	
W. B. C. Sowers	1-0			

Clarke County, Virginia Personal Property Tax Lists 1854-1870
1867

Peter Strange	0-1		Ludwell Tinsman	1-0
Mrs. Timberlake			Wm Thompson	1-0
Jas Smith	0-1		Mason Tinsman	1-0
Jno E. Page			Saml M. Trussell	1-0
Parkerson Strange	0-1		Robt Tapscot	1-0
J. W. Byrds Farm			H. C. Tapscot	1-0
Andus Stuart	0-1		Mrs. Eliza Tucker	"-0
Neadore [?]			Thomas & Adams	2-0
Richard Smith	0-1		Wm Taylor	1-0
C. H. Boxwell			Danl Turner	1-0
Wm Strother	0-1		Geo W. Thompson	1-0
Mann R. Page			W. F. Thompson & Bro	2-0
Wm Smith	0-1		Bates Thompson Sr.	1-0
Geo W. Gorden			Bates Thompson Jr.	1-0
Stephen Strange	0-1		Fiorinda Tapscot	"-0
Clay Hill			Jno Talley Jr.	1-0
Chas Strange	0-1		Jno Talley Sr.	1-0
Millwood			Albert Thompson	1-0
Revd. [?] Smith	"-0		Jas W. Tumblin	1-0
Dr. J. W. Stephenson	1-0		Frank Thomas	0-1
			D° No. 3	
Sarah Timberlake	1-0		Lee Taylor	0-1
Thos W. Trussell	1-0		D° No. 3	
Jos W. Thomas	1-0		Henry Thomas	0-1
French Thompson	1-0		Frank Shepherd's	
Geo Turner	1-0		Joshua Thomas	0-1
Adam F. Thompson	1-0		Mrs. Stribling	
Wm Trenary	2-0		David Taylor	0-1
Robt Sharp	1-0		Edgar Allen	
Edmond Thomas	1-0		Chas Taylor	0-1
Chas Trussell	1-0		Cool Spring	
Isaac Talley	1-0		Wm Taylor	0-1
Wm. H. Thompson	1-0		Wm Allen	
Dr. B. Taylor	1-0		W. Tracey	0-1
Benj F. Thompson	1-0		Champ Shepherd	
Jas W. Tanquary	1-0		Jno Taylor	0-1
Jas L. Taylor	1-0		Mrs. Fletcher	
Mrs. Eliza Taylor	"-0		Squire Tigney	0-1
Snoden Tumblin	1-0		Casper Green	

161

Clarke County, Virginia Personal Property Tax Lists 1854-1870
1867

Frank Thruston	0-1		Thos C. Wyndham	1-0
French Thompson			S. B. Wyndham	1-0
Harry Taylor	0-1		Jas W. Wiley	1-0
Peter Dearmont			Richard Whittington	1-0
Adamson [?]			Chas L. Whittington	1-0
Townsend	0-1		Jessee Wright	1-0
Mrs. Heflebower			B. F. Wilson	1-0
Jef Tyson	0-1		J. W. Ware	1-0
Russells			Walker B. Wilson	1-0
Jacob Thomas	0-1		N. B. Whiting	1-0
Millwood			Jno W. Whittington	1-0
Hny Thomas	0-1		F. H. Whiting	1-0
Phillip Hansucker			Vance R. Whittington	1-0
Mayberry Thornton	0-1		Geo W. Wiley	1-0
Am Moore			Obed Willingham	1-0
Belford Taylor	0-1		Danl Wade	2-0
A. S. Allen			Jas W. Willingham	1-0
Newman Thompson	0-1		Feo F. Willingham	1-0
near S. B. Wyndhams			T. O. Wyndham	1-0
Levi Twine	0-1		F. B. Whiting	3-0
T. E. Gold			Jas V. Wier	2-0
Mack Thomas	0-1		W. Willingham	1-0
Paul Pierce			Wm Whorton	1-0
Aaron Johnson	0-1		Alex Wood	1-0
T. E. Gold			L. E. Williams	1-0
Taylor Thornton	0-1		Rev. Chas White	1-0
Geo C. Blakemore			W. W. Whiting	1-0
Jas Throgmorton	0-1		Dr. B. Harrison	1-0
A. S. Allen			Allen Williams	2-0
Wm Taylor	0-1		Jacob Willingham	1-0
Jacob Enders			Jerry W. Wilson	1-0
			Jno Wilson	1-0
C. Vandevender	1-0		No. 4	
Jacob B. Vorus	2-0		Jno Warnex [?]	1-0
J. L. E. Vanmeter	1-0		Jno T. Willingham	1-0
			Lewis Whittington	1-0
S. G. Wyman	"-0		Jno W. Wainsburow	1-0
Jno T. Waitright	1-0		Thompson Writt	1-0
Wilson & Johnson	2-0		Fenton Wiley	1-0

162

Clarke County, Virginia Personal Property Tax Lists 1854-1870
1867

J. W. Wainsburrow	1-0	Jas Whiller	0-1
Jno D. Wright	1-0	Edgar Allen	
Richard H. Webster	1-0	Alfred Williams	0-1
F. W. Wheat	1-0	North Hill	
Chas L. Willingham	1-0	Hny Webb	0-1
Uriah Wright	1-0	Thos Heskit	
Saml Weaver	0-1	Craven Warrick	0-1
Berryville		Wm D. Smith	
Elsey Wilson	0-1	Lewis Williams	0-1
Berryville		Wm Larue	
Wm Wright	0-1	Philip Williams	0-1
Jno F. Burchell		Berryville	
Jno Wilson	0-1	Marcus White	0-1
Jno F. Burchell		No. 1	
Geo Williams	0-1	Philip Williams	0-1
C. C. McIntyre		Chapel	
Saml Wilson	0-1	Danl Williams	0-1
R. R. Smith		J. Jennings	
Billy Wilson	0-1	Whilis [?] Wormley	0-1
no home, No. 3		White Post	
Nelson Wright	0-1	Jefferson Ware	0-1
Neill Barnett		M. B. Anderson	
Eddw Williams	0-1	Shelton Walker	0-1
S. E. T. Stribling		M. B. Anderson	
Thos Washington	0-1	Jas W. Williams	0-1
Dr. McGuire		Wm Kerfoot	
Jack Willis	0-1	Edw Williams	0-1
Jno Morgan Jr.		White Post	
Wm White	0-1	Jas H. Withers	0-1
P. McCormick		No. 3	
Franklin Wright	0-1	Jefferson Williams	0-1
J. F. Burchell		J. F. Kerfoot	
Alfred Young	0-1	Frank Withers	0-1
H. L. D. Lewis		Mrs. Eavan's	
Jos Webb	0-1	Geo Washington	0-1
Col. F. McCormick		R. Timberlake	
Robt Williams	0-1	Lewis Walton	0-1
Berryville		Jno Marshall	

Clarke County, Virginia Personal Property Tax Lists 1854-1870
1867

Robt Williams	0-1		Nat Williams	0-1
Jno E. Page			J. R. Grigsby	
Richad Waglon	0-1		Alfred Wildon [?]	0-1
White Post			Berryville	
Top White	0-1		Lewis Webb	0-1
J. H. Baittille			Berryville	
Sidney Williams	0-1		Jas Williams	0-1
Millwood			Mrs. H. M. Nelson	
Geo Williams	0-1		Jos Wilson	0-1
Carter Hall			M. R. Page	
Jno Williams	0-1		Levi Williams	0-1
Bethel			P. McCormick Jr.	
Jno Walker	0-1		Stephen Wilson	0-1
Millwood			Jno W. Beemer	
Isaac Webb	0-1		Jas Williams	0-1
No. 3			Barney Gilbert	
Jno Williams	0-1		Peter Washington	0-1
Millwood			C. H. Boxwell	
Wm Wormley	0-1			
Millwood			Wm H. Young	1-0
Jas Craig Williams	0-1		Simeon Yowill	1-0
J. W. McCormick			Daniel Webster Young	0-1
			Berryville	

Clarke County, Virginia Personal Property Tax Lists 1854-1870

1868

There are several pages in this year where the numbers might be marked in the wrong column. Normally employers were identified for free blacks. In the years that follow, some men who were marked as white also have employers named. Some white males (surnames beginning with K) are marked as free blacks, but without any employer. Researchers are advised to compare all post-war lists to determine the ethnicity of their person of interest.

Columns: 1) No. of white male inhabitants over 21 years, 2) No. of male negroes over 21 years, 3) Residence, employer or employment of male negroes listed for taxation. The third column could be a name or place. It is inserted and indented under the tax payer's name.

John H. Anderson	1-0	Frank Anderson	1-0
Milton B. Anderson	1-0	D. J. Shepherd	
D° Trustee for		T. J. Andrews	1-0
M. Anderson	1-0	Thomas & Adams	
W. Willey Arnett	1-0	Wm Ashman	1-0
Wm T. Allen	1-0	Jno M. Anderson	1-0
Jno W. Anderson (of Nim)	1-0	Jas W. Wiley	
Wm B. Atkins	1-0	Wm Allison	1-0
Geo W. Alexander	1-0	Sil Smallwood	
Geo W. Allen	1-0	Jno Wesley Ashby (of Nim)	1-0
Jno Alexander	3-2	Edgar Allen	1-0
Thos H. Alexander	1-0	Albert Ashby	"-0
Jos E. Anderson	1-0	Edmond Allen	0-1
R. O. Allen	2-0	Dr. F. J. Kerfoot	
Jno W. Anderson (of Joe)	1-0	Wm Alexander	0-1
Robt Ashby Jr.	1-0	Dr. F. J. Kerfoot	
Scot Affleck		Jno Anderson	0-1
Philip J. Affleck	1-0	J. M. Hite	
Robt Atkin	1-0	Scot Anderson	0-1
Nimrod Ashby	1-0	Island Farm	
Roger R. Annan	1-0	Edmon Adams	0-1
R. S. Adams	1-0	Berryville	

Clarke County, Virginia Personal Property Tax Lists 1854-1870
1868

Hny Alexander	0-1	Ann C. Benn	--
Berryville		Jos H. Bartlette	1-0
Frank Allen	0-1	Lewis Berlin	1-0
E. McCormick		Wm P. Briggs	1-0
Jno F. Burchell	1-0	Chas C. Benn	1-0
Chas Brabham	1-0	H. C. Briggs	1-0
J. H. Bitzer	1-0	Patrick Brady	1-0
W. F. Bennett	1-0	A M. Ball	1-0
Jno Bromley	1-1	Geo Bear	1-0
Wm Bush	2-0	Chas A. Bush	1-0
Jno W. Beemer	1-0	Jos A. Broge	-- 1
Wm Bonham	1-0	Miss Milly Jordon	
Arthur S. Briggs	1-0	Wesley Brabham	1-0
Wm H. Brown	2-0	Geo H. Ball	1-0
Jas F. Billmyre	1-0	Richard Beavers	1-0
Wm C. M. Baker	1-0	Robt Briggs	1-0
E.S. Brown	1-0	R. S. Bryarly	1-0
Philip Berlin	1-0	Chas H. Boswell	1-0
Boyce & Wright	3-0	Nath Burwell	1-0
Bushrod Buckley	1-0	Jas C. Briggs	1-0
Wm Taylor Burwell	1-0	Geo C. Blakemore	1-0
Jno Buckner	1-0	Frances E. Bell	--
Geo W. Berlin	1-0	Margaret Burchell	--
Geo H. Burwell	1-0	Adam Barr	1-0
D° Trustee for Mrs. Hay	"-0	Peter Bennett	1-0
Wm H. Billmyre	1-0	Isaac Bowman	1-0
Neill Barnett	2-0	James Bell Sr.	1-0
Geo W. Bromley	2-0	Saml Bromly	1-0
Frances Brackett	"-0	Jos Baker	1-0
Abraham Beavers	1-0	Geo W. Copenhaver	
Geo W. Bolin	1-0	Milton Bowman	1-0
Zachariah T. Baclin	1-0	D. W. Sowers	
Jno D. Bruce	1-0	Armstead Brackett	1-0
Susan R. Burwell	--	Geo C. Blake	1-0
C. Bowser	1-0	W. S. Beatty	1-0
Mrs. Blackburn	-- 1	Wm S. Brown	1-0
Geo W. Belt	1-0	Jno Bitzinburger	1-0
Thos W. Byrne	1-0	Thomas & Adams	
Geo R. Brown	1-0		

Clarke County, Virginia Personal Property Tax Lists 1854-1870
1868

Geo Balar	1-0	Jno Broge	0-1
Thomas & Adams		Miss Milly Jordon	
Alfred Bishop	1-0	Robt Broge	0-1
Robt Barr	1-0	Miss Milly Jordon	
Kimballs		Thos Bowman	0-1
Saml Barr	1-0	F. McCormick	
Kimballs		Geo Brown	0-1
Wm Burnett	1-0	Geo W. Gordon	
Zachariah Bloxton	1-0	Isaac Buckley	0-1
Dr. Wm M. Page		Andrew Cornell	
Frank Burk	1-0	Wm Brown	0-1
Thompson & Ogden		Am Moore	
Jas Butt	1-0	Willis Battes	0-1
Thompson & Ogden		R. W. Briggs	
A. J. Berlin	1-0	Charles Brox	0-1
Chas Bailer	1-0	Wm D. Smith	
Jas E. Robinson	0-1	Jos Berry	0-1
J. H. Bitzer		W. Furgurson	
Jas Brown	0-1	Henry Brandin	0-1
B. Randolph		Berryville	
Alfred Ball	0-1	Horris Burns	0-1
B. Longerbean		Berryville	
Henry Bailey	0-1	Geo Blair	0-1
L. E. Williams		Berryville	
Geo Barnett	0-1	Cyrus Burns	0-1
Jas M. Hite		Berryville	
Wm Banks	0-1	Abraham Bomley	0-1
Peter Dearmont		N. Burwell	
Maddison Brown	0-1	Thos Banister	0-1
Mrs. M. E. Shumate		W. P. Briggs	
Jack Braunan	0-1	Thos Brown	0-1
Island Farm		R. A. Colston	
Jos Butler	0-1	Alfred Bray	0-1
Island Farm		Dr. B. Harrison	
Michael Barbour	0-1	Emanuel Blackburn	0-1
Clay Hill		Dr. B. Harrison	
Jas Byrd	0-1	Jacob Brooks	0-1
A. D. Hardesty		Dr. B. Harrison	

Clarke County, Virginia Personal Property Tax Lists 1854-1870
1868

Danl Burwell	0-1	Thos Carter	1-0
A. W. McDonald		Wm P. Carter	1-0
Chas Butler	0-"	Wesley Carper	1-0
Jno W. McCormick		Willis B. Carr	1-0
Moses [?] ___	0-"	Wm Carper	1-0
Jno W. McCormick		Jno B. Carter	1-0
Chas Baltis [?]	1-0	Lucy A. Calmes	2-0
		Wm A. Castleman	1-0
McLane Clingan	1-0	Alfred Carper	1-0
Jno W. Copenhaver	1-0	J. F. Christmore	1-0
Mann R. P. Castleman	1-0	W. T. Chapin	1-0
Jno T. Crow	1-0	Jno W. Carpenter	1-0
Wm Cremer	1-0	Jno W. Cross	2-0
Mrs. Sarah Copenhaver	"-0	Jas H. Clarke	1-0
Jas L. Carter	1-0	Alfred Castleman	2-0
Jacob Criser	1-0	Mrs. Crow	"-0
Jno Carper	1-0	Jno Conway & Bros	3-0
Jno A. Chiles	1-0	Marian Catlette	1-0
Geo W. Cooper	1-0	Jno A. Carter	2-0
Lewis Carrel	1-0	Jos K. Carter	1-0
Reason Carrell	1-0	Harrison Cooper	2-0
Jno N. Colker	1-0	Jno Cain	2-0
Walter Cirtwell	1-0	Hiram Carper	1-0
Wm Carper	1-0	Jno M. Cobb	1-0
Jas E. Chamblin	1-0	Geo W. Christmore	2-0
Jas Castleman	1-0	Mrs. Catharine Castleman	"-0
Jno H. Crebs	1-0	Jno R. Crockwell	1-0
R. A. Colston	2-0	Parkerson Corder	1-0
Thos Carrell [?]	1-0	Jno Cooper	1-0
Jno R. Castleman	1-0	Dr. R. T. Colston	1-0
Benj Crampton	1-0	Washington Corder	1-0
Jas Carver	1-0	Geo Carper	1-0
Mrs. Eliza Carter	"-0	Robt Caisner [?]	1-0
Mrs.C. C. Carter	"-0	Jas J. W. Cutler	1-0
Jas Chapel	1-0	W. H. Carpenter	1-0
Ann B. Cook	"-0	A. J. Corder	1-0
Andrew Cornell	1-0	Jno W. Campbell	"-0
J. W. Carter	1-0	Robt Cooper	0-1
J. Esten Cooke	1-0	Martin Gant	

Clarke County, Virginia Personal Property Tax Lists 1854-1870
1868

Geo Cole	0-1	Chas R. Cole	0-1
C. Shepherd Sr.		Col. J. B. Larue	
Soloman Carlin	0-1	Nat Carter	0-1
R. R. Smith		Burwell Whiting	
Frank Culler	0-1	Wm Cowell [?]	0-1
D. W. Sowers		W. B. Harris	
Sandy Carter	0-1	Danl Carter	0-1
Stone Bridge		Berryville	
Jno Cook	0-1	Wm Cooper	0-1
Geo W. Copenhaver		Berryville	
Bosen Carter	0-1	Chas Cooper	0-1
Tuleries		Berryville	
Jas H. Carter	0-1	Mifford Cooper	0-1
J. F. Kerfoot		Berryville	
Monroe Christian	0-1	Jos Carter	0-1
Dr. Smith		Berryville	
Robt Cross	0-1	Morgan Coxell	0-1
Dr. Harrison		Berryville	
Wm Carter	0-1	Jack Cyrus	0-1
L. A. Calmes		N. Burwell	
Bushrod Carey	0-1	Lewis Carter	0-1
D. T. Kerfoot		J. H. Bartlette	
Scot Colbert	0-1	Murray Carter	0-1
Jas W. Ryan		D. B. Harrison	
Wm Carter	0-1	Wm Colston	0-1
Mrs. E. M. Shumate		Mrs. E. ORear	
Jacob Colston	0-1		
Island Farm		Capt. J. P. Dorsey	0-1
Fairfax Carter	0-1	Chas H. Duval	1-0
Audley		Thos Duke	1-0
Wm Clayton	0-1	R. L. Denney	1-0
Clay Hill		M. H. Doren	1-0
Edw Clayton	0-1	Jno Donovan	1-0
Clay Hill		T. J. Dove	1-0
Jacob Cooper	0-1	Jno Drish	1-0
J. N. Pierce		Jno W. Drish	1-0
Peter Coats	0-1	Jas Dorren	1-0
Col. J. B. Larue		Wm Deahl & son	2-0
		Aaron Duble	1-0

Clarke County, Virginia Personal Property Tax Lists 1854-1870
1868

Col. W. Dearmont	2-0	Jno S. Eavans	1-0
Richard Dulany	"-0	O. P. Eavans	1-0
H. H. Dunbar	1-0	Wm G. Everheart	3-0
Geo Dick	1-0	Thos A. Everheart	1-0
Peter Dearmont	1-0	Albert Elsea	1-0
Jno T. Dove	1-0	Thos N. Eddy	1-0
Lewis W. Duley	1-0	Hny Edwards	1-0
Jas Thomas		Geo R. Evuilt [?]	1-0
Isaac Debar	1-0	Jno M. Elwell	1-0
J. K. Louthan		Jacob W. Everheart	1-0
Geo Dunlap	1-0	Jacob Enders	1-0
Jos E. Anderson		Christopher Erb	1-0
Robt Dunn	1-0	Jos W. Edwards	1-0
P. P. Deahl	1-0	Benj Edwards	1-0
H. Marpole		Aaron G. Elwell	1-0
Hugh Davis	1-0	Punn [?] Edward	0-1
Jas W. Doren	1-0	Mrs. H. M. Nelson	
Wm Donley	0-1		
J. K. Louthan		Jas A. Forster	1-0
J Dickerson	0-1	Jos P. Fayman	1-0
Benj Longebean		Dr. O. R. Funston	1-0
Jacob Doleman	0-1	M. R. Feehrer	1-0
J. D. Richardson		A. Finchan	1-0
Andrew Davis	0-1	Jno W. Fritz	1-0
Neill Barnett		Isaac Fletcher	1-0
Jonah Dunkin	0-1	O. R. Funston Jr.	1-0
~~Jno Marshall~~ Millwood		Thomas Fowler	1-0
Wm Dorety	0-1	E. L. Fishpaw	1-0
~~Berryville [?]~~ Jno Marshall		Joshua G. Fellows	1-0
S__ Dangerfield	0-1	Israel Fidler	1-0
Berryville		Wm Fowler Jr.	1-0
Geo Dandridge	0-1	Wm Fowler Sr.	1-0
Saml Bromly		Wm Fleming	1-0
Michael Doctor	0-1	Jno Q. Fleming	1-0
Thos Carter		James Furr	1-0
Jas Dank	0-1	Washington Furguson	1-0
Allen Williams		Martin Feltner	1-0
		Wm Furr	1-0
Jno C. Elliott	1-0	Archibald Fleming	2-0

Clarke County, Virginia Personal Property Tax Lists 1854-1870
1868

Sarah A. Fleming	2-0	Geo W. Grubb	1-0
Abner Furguson	1-0	J. R. Grigsby	1-0
T. J. Fritts	1-0	J. T. Griffith	1-0
James T. Freeman	1-0	Martin Gaunt	1-0
Thos G. Flagg	1-0	Jno & Thos Gold	2-0
Denis Fenton	1-0	J. Lee Grant	1-0
Jessee Fennell	1-0	Jno F. Grubb	1-0
Ephram Fur	1-0	Geo Gardner	1-0
Genl. Fauntleroy	1-0	Wm B. Grubb	1-0
Jno Filton	1-0	Mathew Genovan [?]	1-0
H. Mickey		Mrs. Fancy Grigsby	"-0
Saml Fidler	1-0	Henry O. Grim	2-0
Mrs. Copenhaver		Wm H. Grove	1-0
Jessee Fleet	1-0	Thos W. Griffith	1-0
Wm F. Knight		Zebedee Gray	1-0
Frank Fowler	1-0	S. J. Grant	1-0
Curtis Fidler	1-0	Jas W. Galloway	1-0
Eben Frost	1-0	Thos C. Gibson	1-0
Robt Frost	0-1	Geo W. Gordon	1-0
Wm Frontroyal	0-1	Carper W. Green	1-0
Jos Fouley [?]	0-1	Jos W. Granthan	1-0
Peter French	0-1	Jno & Chas W. Grubb	2-0
Austin Ferry	0-1	Adam Grunwaldt	1-0
Albert Fox	0-1	Jno Gruber Agt.	1-0
Alex Franklin	0-1	M. L. Grubb	1-0
Frank Franklin	0-1	Geo M. Grubb	1-0
Wm Fields	0-1	Barney Gilbert	1-0
Wm Fields	0-1	Jno A. Green,	
Aaron Fielding	0-1	Admr of Jno Green	1-0
Adam Field	0-1	B. R. Green	1-0
Jas Fractious	0-1	Richard N. Green	1-0
Lewis Fletcher	0-1	Maj. J. Green	1-0
Geo Fields	0-1	Jas F. Green	2-0
Jas Figgens	0-1	Warner T. Gray	1-0
Peyton Fox	0-1	E. M. Green	1-0
Abraham Fairfax	0-1	Addison Garvin	1-0
Christian Fonda	1-0	Jno M. Gibson	1-0
Everett Fowler	1-0	James Grubb	1-0
		Chas F. Galloway	1-0

Clarke County, Virginia Personal Property Tax Lists 1854-1870
1868

Maddison Grimes	1-0	Wm B. Harris	2-0
Jas W. Grimes	1-0	C. W. Hardesty	1-0
Geo W. Grimes	1-0	Thos S. Hart	1-0
Thos Gorden	1-0	E. T. Hibb	1-0
Jas Gilkerson	1-0	Jno & Mason Hummer	2-0
R. W. Grove	1-0	W. W. Hook	1-0
N. W. Gore	1-0	Jos R. Hardesty	1-0
A. J. Grubb	1-0	J. B. Hawthorn	1-0
Thos Gold	1-0	Jas M. Hite	1-0
J. Louthan		Billie L. Hughs	1-0
J. W. Gohene	1-0	Mary E. Hefflebower	1-0
Thos & Adams		Alex Holtzclaw	1-0
Jno Gill	"-0	Jno W. Holland	1-0
Thos & Adams		Nelson Henry	2-0
David Griffin	1-0	Burr Hull	1-0
J. R. Nunn		Jno Hughs	1-0
Franklin [?] Glover	1-0	A. D. Hardesty	1-0
Philip Grubb	1-0	Jno W. Hibbard	1-0
Chas L. Grubb	1-0	Philip Hansucker	1-0
Robt Green Sr.	0-1	Mrs. C. V. Hall	"-0
Warren C. Smith		Dr. B. Harrison	1-0
Robt Green Jr.	0-1	James Hamilton	1-0
Warren C. Smith		Wm Horseman	1-0
Jack Gray	0-1	Jno W. Hall	1-0
B. Randolph		Heny Harrison	1-0
Alfred Grigsby	0-1	Jas M. Hardesty	1-0
Stone Bridge		Wm G. Hardesty	2-0
Frank Gordon	0-1	Edw R. Harrison	1-0
White Post		C. Hoff	1-0
Edw Green	0-1	Chas F. Hennis	1-0
A. Carrell		W. R. Helvestine	1-0
Heny Green	0-1	Jas W. Haycock	1-0
Berryville		Jackson Hoff	1-0
Sol Gibson	0-"	T. L. Humphrey	1-0
Island Farm		Jas W. Hummer	1-0
L. F. Glass trustee for		Geo W. Hoff	1-0
Mrs. Susan Isler		Wm Holtzclaw	1-0
Lewis F. Glass	2-0	Jas F. Howell	1-0
		Wm J. Harris	1-0

Clarke County, Virginia Personal Property Tax Lists 1854-1870
1868

Alfred Haddock	1-0	Soloman Holmes	0-1
Jno Henry	1-0	Millwood	
Lewis B. Helvestine	1-0	Chas Hubbard	0-1
A. J. Harford	1-0	Millwood	
Geo Hansucker	1-0	Lorenza Harris	0-1
Heny Huyette	1-0	Berryville	
Olliver B. Hibbart	1-0	Heny Harris	0-1
Jno Henry	1-0	Berryville	
Wm E. Hannan	1-0	Geo Harris	0-1
Jas Hefflin	1-0	Berryville	
Wm Hefflin	1-0	Robt Hall	0-1
Wm Hummer	1-0	Berryville	
R. K. Hough	"-0	Baz Hull	0-1
Jno Hummer	"-0	Berryville	
Thomas & Adams		Poston Helmes [?]	0-1
Jas Hooper	"-0	Berryville	
J. M. Kigar		Beverly Hartgrove	0-1
Mount Hefflin	"-0	Berryville	
Archie Hubbard	0-1	Wesley Hall	0-1
B. Randolph		near S. B. Wyndham	
Geo Helm	0-1	Wm Holmes	0-1
B. Randolph		Edward Allen	
Robt Hodges	0-1	Hny Hopper	0-1
Jos K. Carter		Dr. B. Harrison	
Alfred Harris	0-1	Walter Howard	0-1
S. G. Wyman		C. Erb	
Tobe Hite	0-1	Hny Heaton	0-1
J. M. Hite		Angus W. McDonald	
Danl Harris	0-1	Frank Hall	0-0
Tuleries		E. W. Massey	
Maddison Harris	0-1	Jno Hull	0-0
Tuleries		P. McPierce	
Savoney Hunter	0-1	Saml Hitchcock	1-0
White Post		Jno Houpman	1-0
Wm Hull	0-1		
P. M. Pierce		Marcus Irwin	1-0
Geo Hull	0-1	Mrs. Martha Isler	0-0
P. M. Pierce			
		Thos Jenkins	1-0

Clarke County, Virginia Personal Property Tax Lists 1854-1870
1868

Mrs. Kate Jolliffe	1-0	Jno Morgan Jr.	
Wm A. Jackson	1-0	Isaac ___	0-1
M. W. Jones	1-0	T. E. Gold	
Jno M. Jolliffe	1-0	Jackson ___	0-1
Peyton John	1-0	Jno W. Beemer	
F. L. Johnson	1-0	Richard Johnson	0-1
Herrod Jenkins Sr.	1-0	J. M. Hite	
Jessee Jenkins	1-0	Wash Jackson	0-1
Emanuel Jenkins	1-0	Rev. Jno Pickett	
J. Fenton Jackson	1-0	Israel Jackson	0-1
Cornelius Jenkins	1-0	Rev. Jno Pickett	
Osburn A. Jones	1-0	Jno Jackson	0-1
Thos Jones	2-0	Rev. Jno Pickett	
Jas W. Johnson	1-0	Allen Jackson	0-1
Mountain		Rev. Jno Pickett	
C. S. D. Jones	1-0	Chas Jemison	0-1
Andrew Jackson	1-0	Tuleries	
Rev. Jos R. Jones	1-0	Jno Johnson	0-1
Eben Jenkins	1-0	White Post	
Edward Jenkins	1-0	Heny Jackson	0-1
Benj. Johnson	1-0	White Post	
Jno S. Johnston	1-0	David Jackson	0-1
Jas W. Johnston	1-0	White Post	
Lenard Jones	1-0	Edw Johnson	0-1
Denist [?] Jackson	1-0	Col. J. B. Larue	
Alfred C. Jackson	1-0	Everitt Jackson	0-1
Javen Jennings	1-0	Jno Page	
G. W. H. Isler	1-0	Jas Ireland	0-1
Chas Jackson Sr.	0-1	Col. W. Dearmont	
Dr. Randolph		Jno Jenkins	0-1
Chas Jackson Jr.	0-1	Witherspoon	
Dr. Randolph		Jackson Johnson	0-1
Jno James	0-1	Hny Harrison	
Warren C. Smith		Sarey Iverson [?]	0-1
Philip Johnson	0-1	Millwood	
Mann R. Page		Prince Johnson	0-"
Even Jackson	0-1	Millwood	
Dr. Stephenson		Jas Jackson	0-"
Robt Jackson	0-1	Champ Shepherd	

Clarke County, Virginia Personal Property Tax Lists 1854-1870
1868

Geo Jackson	0-"	Jno M. Kimmell	0-1
Rev. Jno Pickett		Judson G. Kerfoot	0-1
Edw Johnson	0-"	Thos H. Kern	0-1
Col. J. B. Larue		David T. Kerfoot	0-1
Jno Johnson	0-1	J. F. Kerfoot	0-1
Geo Chapman		D° Trustee for	
Clay Johnson	0-1	Mrs. Adams	0-"
E. McCormick		Wm C. Kenarly	0-1
Frederick James	0-1	Geo W. Koonce	0-1
Dr. W. M. Page		Hny Knight	0-1
Hny Jefferson Sr.	0-1	Harry D. Kerfoot	0-1
Berryville		Chas L. Kindall	0-1
Chas Johnson	0-1	Jno N. Kitchen	0-0
Berryville		Chas H. Kitchen	1-0
Heny Jefferson Jr.	0-1	E. V. Kercheval	1-0
Berryville		Jas M. Kegar	1-0
Arche Jackson	0-1	Heny Kromling	1-0
Berryville		Wm F. Knight	1-0
Jacob Jackson	0-1	Midl Keeler Sr.	1-0
Berryville		Midl Keeler Jr.	1-0
Hny Jackson Sr.	0-1	Mrs. E. S. Kownslar	0-0
Berryville		Jos H. Kirby	1-0
Hny Jackson Jr.	0-1	S. G. Knight	1-0
Berryville		Wm Kegar	1-0
Geo Jones	0-1	Jesse N. Russell	
C. Fry		Heny Kline	1-0
Geo Johnson	0-"	Danl B. Knight	1-0
Heny Harrison		Geo Kitchen	1-0
Jas Johnson	0-"		
Wm T. Allen		Dr. T. M. Lewis	1-0
Rev. W. Johnston	1-0	Moses Lewin	1-0
		Wm Littleton	1-0
Mrs. E. F. Kownslar,		Jno Lock Sr.	1-0
Guardian for Children		Wm A. Larue	1-0
Chas H. Keeler	0-1	Jas T. Louthan	1-0
Wm T. Kerfoot	0-1	Jno W. Luke	1-0
Jos McK Kenarly	0-1	A G. Laidy	1-0
Dr. F. J. Kerfoot	0-1	Jno Longerbean	1-0
Jos A. Kelso	0-1	Jno K. Louthan	1-0

Clarke County, Virginia Personal Property Tax Lists 1854-1870
1868

Wm Lanham	1-0		Jas L. Loyd	1-0
Armstead S. Lippett	1-0		Frank Little	2-0
Heny Lloyd	1-0		J. N. Laws	1-0
Jas Lanham	1-0		Frank H. Lock	1-0
Jno Lee	1-0		Jas Lloyd	1-0
Squire Lee	1-0		Jno M. Lupton	1-0
Col. R. H. Lee	1-0		Jno D. Lloyd	1-0
Jno T. Lindsey	1-0		Edmond Lake	1-0
Jos B. Lindsey	1-0		Wm T. Kerfoot	
Alex Lake	1-0		Johnathan [sic] Lupton	1-0
Jas W. Lee	1-0		W. Love of R. W.	1-0
Dr. C. E. Lippett	1-0		M. M. Lancaster	1-0
Col. J. B. Larue	2-0		Saml Lanham	1-0
A L. P. Larue	1-0		Chas Trussell	
C. C. Larue	1-0		Frank Lewis	1-0
Mrs. Mariah Larue	"-0		Thompson & Ogdan	
Wm D. Lee	1-0		Geo W. Lawrence	1-0
Peter Light	1-0		Lewis Berlin	
Abraham Longebean	1-0		Benj Lloyd	1-0
Heny Licklider	1-0		Benton Lanham	1-0
Frank Littleton	1-0		Saml Lockley	0-1
Jno F. Lancaster	1-0		M. R. Page	
H. L. D. Lewis	1-0		Benj Lampton	0-1
Geo W. Lewis	1-0		Jno W. Sowers	
Mrs. E. M. Lewis	"-0		Ralph Laws	0-1
E. P. C. Lewis	1-0		White Post	
Jas W. Lewis	1-0		Fielding Lewis	0-1
J. H. Lewis	1-0		Island Farm	
Remington Lock	1-0		Jessee Lovette	0-1
R. W. Levi	2-0		Wm G. Hardesty	
Benj Lock	1-0		Richard Lewis	0-1
Chas H. Lloyd	1-0		Jas McCormick	
Jno A. Lloyd	1-0		Jery Lewis	0-1
Wm H. Love	2-0		Berryville	
Chas H. Lee	1-0		Danl Laton	0-1
Benj Longabean	1-0		Millwood	
Jas W. Larue	1-0		Richard H. Laton	0-1
Jno Louthan	1-0		Millwood	
Josiah R. Lock	1-0			

Clarke County, Virginia Personal Property Tax Lists 1854-1870
1868

Israel Lightfoot	0-1	Mrs. Washington	"
Mrs.Hugh M. Nelson		D° Admr of	
Wm Lewis	0-1	R. K. Meade	"
Jno M. Gibson		W. W. Meade	1-0
Thos Laws	0-1	Jas P. Marshall	1-0
Mrs. Kownslar		P. N. Meade	1-0
Bennett Lipscomb	0-1	Hays Mickey	1-0
J. W. Luke		H. Mason [?] Moore	1-0
Frank Lewis	0-"	S. P. Moore	1-0
Cool Spring		Jas T. Murphey	1-0
Alex Lewis	0-1	E. B. Mantor	1-0
Mrs. E. ORear		Am Moore	1-0
Jno S. Laws	1-0	P. McCormick	1-0
		T. F. Martin	1-0
Edw McCormick	1-0	C. H. McDonald & Bro	2-0
Col. B. Morgan	1-0	Jas McCormick	1-0
Jno Morgan Sr.	1-0	Esom E. Mayhew	1-0
Abraham McDonald	1-0	Col. F. McCormick	1-0
Wm C. Morgan	1-0	Thos McCormick	1-0
Jos Moore	1-0	C. C. McIntyre	1-0
Geo Marpole	1-0	Moses G. Miley	1-0
Jos T. Mitchell	1-0	E. C. Marshall Jr.	1-0
Wm L. Milton	1-0	Jno J. Monroe	1-0
Dr. Wm D. McGuire	1-0	Wm Morris	1-0
Jno G. McCarty	1-0	Jas McClaughey	1-0
D. H. McGuire	1-0	Heny Mason	1-0
Luther G. Mitchel	1-0	Hugh McCormick	1-0
Garrett McDonald	1-0	Saml T. Marts	1-0
F. B. Meade	1-0	Angus W. McDonald	1-0
Jno W. McCormick	2-0	W. B. Maddex	1-0
Isaac Manuel	2-0	Jno Morgan Jr.	1-0
J. Shep Mitchel	1-0	Jno G. Morris	1-0
Miss Mary Meade	"-0	Alfred C. Marshall	1-0
Jno Marshall	1-0	Josiah McDonald	1-0
E. W. Massey	1-0	Jos A. Mock	1-0
David Meade Sr.	1-0	Patrick Brady	1-0
D° Trustee for		Jas W. McClelland	1-0
Mrs. B. Meade	"	Heny J. Mesmer	1-0
D° Admr of		Hezekiah Marpole	1-0

Clarke County, Virginia Personal Property Tax Lists 1854-1870
1868

Jno T. Martin	1-0	Jas McGumby	0-1
Gabriel R. McDonald	1-0	Geo K. Sowers	
J. F. Milton	1-0	Saml Mitchell	0-1
S. J. C. Moore	1-0	Berryville	
Thos B. Morehead	1-0	Isaac Mitchell	0-1
Thos Malony	1-0	Dr. W. D. McGuire	
Jno S. Evans		Isaac Munce	0-1
Wm McAbaugh	1-0	D. W. Sowers	
Jos Moreland	1-0	Algernon Mosby	0-1
Jos W. Granthum		Mrs. Crow	
Jno Miller	1-0	Cornelius Miles	0-1
Thomas & Adams		J. D. Richardson	
Jno L. Morgan	1-0	Robt Mosby	0-1
Chas Moreland	1-0	near Crums Church	
P. McPierce		Jacob L. Murray	0-1
Julian Morales	1-0	A. L. P. Larue	
Frank Malony	1-0	Robt Gill	0-1
G. C. S. Philips		Geo W. Sowers	
Morris Murphey	1-0	Nat Maston	0-1
C. W. Hardesty		Geo W. Sowers	
Nickolas Moore	1-0	Heny Mitchell	0-1
Jno McClaughey	1-0	Edgar Allen	
Holmes McGuire	1-0	Jno McIntree	0-1
Jessee Mercer	1-0	C. Erb	
Robt P. Morgan	1-0	Edward Martin	0-1
Heny J. Miller	1-0	Millwood	
P. McCormick Jr.	1-0	Monroe McCard	0-1
Burwell McGuire	1-0	W. D. Smith	
Richard McCard	0-1	Jno Mills	0-1
Wickliffe		Berryville	
Jos McCard	0-1	Danl Massey	0-1
Berryville		Berryville	
Jacob Mitchel	0-1	Joshua Moore	0-1
B. Randolph		Berryville	
Monroe Mouer [?]	0-1	London Mitchell	0-1
L. B. Helvestine		Berryville	
Lee Moore	0-1	Baittelle Myers	0-1
J. R. Grigsby		Berryville	

Clarke County, Virginia Personal Property Tax Lists 1854-1870
1868

Heny McIntire	0-1	Joshua Osburn	1-0
Berryville		Harriet M. OBannan	1-0
P. McPierce		Lewelen Osburn	1-0
Jas Murray	0-1	Thos Opie Sr.	0-1
Berryville		C. S. Wm Taylor	
Gus Mosby	0-1	Thos Opie Jr.	0-1
Berryville		C. S. Wm Taylor	
Jurney Mosby	0-1		
Berryville		Jno Patterson	1-0
Benj Myres	0-1	Mann R. Page	2-0
Berryville		Jos Pifer	2-0
Chas Myres	0-1	Watson Pangle	1-0
Berryville		Mrs. Henrietta Page	"-0
Geo F. Mann	0-1	Jno E. Page	1-0
Alfred P. Moore	1-0	R. Powell Page	1-0
S. J. C. Moore	"-0	J. F. Pence	1-0
		Jno Page	1-0
Jno A. Nunn	1-0	Geo E. S. Philips	1-0
D° Guardian for		Peter McPierce	1-0
Geo W. Carter		P. H. Powers	1-0
Jas H. Neville	1-0	Michael Pope	1-0
Alex Neville	1-0	Paul Pierce	1-0
Col. Wm N. Nelson	1-0	Saml Pidgeon	1-0
Dr. S. S. Neill	1-0	Susan S. Pine	"-0
Mrs. Hugh M. Nelson	"-0	Conrad Pope	1-0
Jas H. Newcome	1-0	Wm Piles	1-0
Levi Niceley	1-0	Dr. Wm M. Page	1-0
___Nat __	0-1	T. P. Pendleton	1-0
C. S. Lee		Jno Poston	1-0
Walter Norris	0-1	M. Pulliam	1-0
J. W. Sprint		A. H. Pitman	1-0
Hary Norris	0-1	A. N. Pierce	1-0
Saratoga		Rev. Jno Pickett	1-0
Chas Newman	0-1	C. M. Parkins	"-0
Cool Spring		Mrs. Elizabeth Pierce	"-0
Jacob Nelson	0-1	Wm G. Pierce	1-0
Berryville		Richard Puller	1-0
		Geo W. Pine	1-0
Mrs. E. ORear	"-0	W. R. Putman [sic]	1-0

Clarke County, Virginia Personal Property Tax Lists 1854-1870
1868

Wm Pifer	1-0	Jas E. Russell	2-0
Jno F. Piner	1-0	Geo R. Royston	1-0
Wm H. Piner	1-0	Uriah Royston	1-0
Jas Patterson	1-0	Mrs. M. Royston	"-0
Jas Pier [?]	1-0	Marcus B. Reed	1-0
J. R. Grigsby		Thos W. Russell	1-0
J. W. Pince [?]	1-0	Geo Russell	1-0
David T. Piner	1-0	Levi Rose	1-0
Mathew Pine	1-0	D. B. Richards	1-0
Lazareth Pine	1-0	Geo W. Rutter	1-0
Frank Pope	1-0	Patrick Reardon	1-0
Geo Puller	1-0	J. W. Ryan	1-0
Wm Popkins	1-0	Jos F. Ryan	1-0
Wm H. Robinson		Jno D. Richardson	1-0
Jno Pierce Jr.	1-0	Geo Rutter	1-0
Jas Puller	1-0	Jno Roland	3-0
A C. Page	1-0	Esra Routzan	1-0
Jno M. Pope	1-0	Russell & Cross	1-0
Jacob Pane	0-1	Thos J. Russell	1-0
McLane Clingan		Jno J. Riley	1-0
Benj Potter	0-1	D° Trustee for	
S. G. Wynan		Mrs. S. Taylor	2-0
Jno Potter	0-1	Westley Russell	1-0
Jno Pickett		Dr. R. C. Randolph & sons	3-0
Richard Potter	0-1	P. K. Royston	1-0
Berryville		Wm A. Riley	1-0
Jack Papp	0-1	Major B. Randolph	1-0
Berryville		M. T. Royston	1-0
Thos Page	0-1	Jessee N. Russell	1-0
Jno F. Burchel		Enos Richmond	1-0
Jacob Payne	0-1	Wm C. Randolph	1-0
Wm C. Kerfoot		Jno W. Russell	1-0
Jno Porter	0-1	Wm H. Robinson	1-0
Wm C. Kerfoot		Stephen Reed	1-0
		Jno Reynolds	1-0
Preston Quvois [?]	0-1	Jno J. Russell	1-0
Berryville		Jas E. Russell	
		Jno Riggle	1-0
Michael Russell	1-0	Jos S. Hart	

Clarke County, Virginia Personal Property Tax Lists 1854-1870
1868

Patrick Rodgers	1-0	Berryville	
Marshall Randolph	1-0	Richard Reenno [sic]	0-1
D. Sibold		Berryville	
E. D. Rossin	1-0	Thos Reeno	0-1
Pidgeon Hill		Berryville	
Jno Reed	1-0	Harrison Reeves	0-1
Wm D. Smith		Berryville	
Buckner Rose	1-0	Robt Reenno	0-1
Jno S. Johnston		Jno T. Lindsey	
Cornelius Riley	1-0	Jeffry Reenno	0-1
Harry Randolph	0-1	Edgar Allen	
B. Randolph		Wm Rust	0-1
Owen Reed	0-1	C. S. Wm Taylor	
J. A. Forster		Thos Robinson	0-"
Jas Reed	0-1	Thos E. Gold	
Joe R. Hardesty		M. H. Russell	"-0
___Robt___	0-1	White Post	
L. E. Williams		Geo Ricemore [sic]	"-0
Heny Robinson	0-1	Thompson & Ogden	
White Post		R. H. Ritter	1-0
Miles Robinson	0-1	Arche Randolph	1-0
O. R. Funston Jr.		Jacob B. Vorus	
Heny Randolph	0-1		
Saratoga		D. C. Snyder	1-0
Heny Robinson	0-1	Champ Shepherd	1-0
Millwood		Geo R. Sowers	1-0
Hny Robinson	0-1	Dr. J. W. Stephenson	1-0
Jas McCormick		J. R. Stuart	1-0
Jno Robinson	0-1	S. R. Stump	1-0
Chapel		D. W. Sowers	2-0
Nelson Reed	0-1	R. R. Smith	1-0
Cool Spring		Denis Shehan	1-0
Sam Robinson	0-1	Wm B. Sowers	1-0
H. & D. Lewis		Wm G. Steel	1-0
Ambrose Roberts	0-1	Jas A. Steel	1-0
W. B. Harris		Jno W. Sprint	1-0
Martin Redman	0-1	Jno F. Sowers	1-0
Wm D. Smith		Benj Shipe	1-0
Hary Robinson	0-1	Jno W. Sowers	1-0

Clarke County, Virginia Personal Property Tax Lists 1854-1870
1868

H. Slusher	1-0	Hny Stickel Sr.	1-0
Geo H. Sowers	1-0	Thos Smallwood	1-0
Champ Shepherd	1-0	Jas S. Sowers	1-0
Mrs. M. E. Shumate	1-0	Dr. Wm Sommerville	1-0
Edwin Shumate	1-0	Stephen Shell	1-0
Jas M. Shearer	1-0	B. T. Selman	1-0
Dr. H. C. Sommerville	1-0	Jno T. Shaffer	1-0
Jos H. Shepherd	1-0	Syl Smallwood	1-0
P. D. Shepherd	1-0	Wm D. Smith	1-0
D. J. Shepherd	1-0	Moses Shipe	1-0
Geo Snyder	1-0	Joseph H. Stickel	1-0
Jas W. Steel	1-0	Chas H. Smith	1-0
Mount J. Shell	1-0	Geo W. Sowers	1-0
Frank Stine	1-0	Dr. J.P. Smith	1-0
T. M. Smith	1-0	W. C. Smith	1-0
Saml Showers	1-0	Geo W. Shimp	1-0
W. B. C. Sowers	1-0	Jno S. Smith	1-0
Wm F. Stolle	1-0	R. M. Sydnor	1-0
Frank R. Shepherd	1-0	Mary Stribling	"-0
Mrs. S. E. T. Stribling	1-0	T. Smith	1-0
Geo S. Spaulding	1-0	Danl H. Sower [sic]	1-0
Jos B. Shepherd	1-0	Thomas Stickel of Simon	1-0
Danl Sibold & Son	2-0	Wm B. Grubb	
Richard Smithy	1-0	Jno W. Shipe	1-0
M. L. Sinclair	1-0	Geo L. Smithy	1-0
Jno Swarts	1-0	Peter Stickel	1-0
A J. Shipe	1-0	Jos B. Shipe	1-0
Benj Starkey [?]	1-0	Lewis Shrout	1-0
Jno G. Snyder	1-0	Thos Stickel of Hny	1-0
Geo C. Shepherd	1-0	Wm L. Smith	1-0
Chas W. Swarts	1-0	W. C. Smith	"-0
Carter Shepherd	1-0	J. R. Grigsby	
Jos Stickel	1-0	Michael Stickel	"-0
Simon Stickel	1-0	W. H. Robinson	
Burr Smallwood	1-0	Andrew Stuart	0-1
Jno Shaffer	1-0	W. H. Brown	
Henry Stickel Jr.	1-0	Jno Sanders	0-1
Geo Smeadley	1-0	J. M. Gibson	
Jno J. Shaffer	1-0	Wm Strange	0-1

Clarke County, Virginia Personal Property Tax Lists 1854-1870
1868

N. B. Whiting			
Danl Strange	0-1	Nat Shoden	0-1
N. B. Whiting		Wm P. Allen	
Jas Strange	0-1	Jas Smith	0-1
N. B. Whiting		Dr. Harrison	
Parker Strange	0-1	Philip Strange	0-1
N. B. Whiting		Dr. Randolph	
Jas Strange	0-1	Denis Seals	0-1
Wm C. Kerfoot		Jas V. Weir	
Jas Strother	0-1	Frank Shelton	0-0
P. D. Shepherd		Mrs. Hefflebower	
Newton Stuart	0-1	E. J. Smith	1-0
Capt. J. P. Dorsey			
Kemp Steckes	0-1	Magnus S. Thompson	1-0
E. Thomas		Isaac Tally	1-0
Thos Smith	0-1	Saml M. Trussell	1-0
Mrs. M. Burchell		Danl Turner	1-0
Jno Strother	0-1	Wm Trynary	2-0
W. S. Brown		E. S. W. Taylor	"-0
Chas Sims	0-1	Isaac Tyson Jr. Est.	"-0
Col. F. McCormick		Isaac Tyson	"-0
Jno Sprout	0-1	Bales Thompson Sr.	1-0
H. Marpole		French Thompson	1-0
Chas Stuat [sic]	0-1	Robt Tharp	1-0
Cool Spring		Miss Floy Tapscott	"-0
Chas Strange	0-1	Jas B. Tapscot	1-0
Millwood		Robt Tapscot	1-0
Hny Smith	0-1	Heny C. Tapscot	1-0
Millwood		Edmond Thomas	2-0
Hny Smith	0-1	Jas W. Tanquary	1-0
Jno Page		Jas H. Lewis	1-0
___ Stepeney___	0-1	Chas J. Taylor	"-0
P. Hansucker		Bales Thompson Jr.	1-0
Jos Spencer	0-1	Ludwell Tinsman	1-0
J. C. Brown		Frank Tavender	3-0
Wm Smith	0-1	Wm F. Thompson	1-0
Berryville		Albert Thompson	1-0
Richard Smith	0-1	Mrs. Eliza Tucker	"-0
Hny Slow	0-1	Wm Taylor	1-0

Clarke County, Virginia Personal Property Tax Lists 1854-1870
1868

Snoden Tumblin	1-0	Heny Thomas	0-1
Chas Trussell	1-0	Wm Tracey	0-"
Thompson & Ogden	2-0	Stovin Travice [?]	0-1
Thomas & Adams	2-0	Hny Thomas	0-1
Jas L. Taylor	1-0	Love Twine [?]	0-1
Adam F. Thompson	1-0	Geo Taylor	0-1
Albert Thompson	1-0	Thornton Taylor	0-1
Geo W. Thompson	1-0	Newman Thompson	0-1
Jas Thomas	1-0	David Taylor	0-1
Thos W. Trussell	1-0	Hny Taylor	0-1
Geo Turner	1-0	W. Tracey	0-1
Mason Tinsman	1-0	Wm H. Thompson	1-0
Mrs. Eliza Taylor	"-0		
Jas Tally	1-0	J. L. E. Vanmeter	1-0
Thos E. Gold		C. Vandevender	1-0
Benj Thompson	1-0	Jacob B. Vorous	1-0
Jno F. Tumblin	1-0		
Jas W. Tumblin	1-0	L. E. Williams	1-0
Jno Talley Sr.	1-0	W. T. Wharton	1-0
Jno Talley Jr.	1-0	James Wood	1-0
Robt Turley	"-0	Alex Wood	1-0
Thornton Tansy	0-1	S. G. Wyman	"-0
Geo K. Sowers		Thos C. Wyndham	1-0
Andrew Townsend	0-1	Allen Williams	2-1
Jno W. Sowers		Chas L. Willingham	1-0
Jos Thornley	0-1	W. W. Willingham	1-0
Wm A. Jackson		Walker B. Wilson	1-0
Jno Taylor	0-1	F. H. Whiting	1-0
Isaac Fletcher		J. S. Ware	1-0
Jas Thompson	0-1	W. W. Whiting	1-0
Jas W. Ryan		Col. J. W. Ware	1-0
Andrew Turner	0-1	Jno T. Willingham	1-0
Belford Taylor	0-1	B. F. Wilson	1-0
Jas Throgmorton	0-1	Jas W. Willingham	1-0
David Taylor	0-"	Jas W. Wiley	1-0
Guy Taylor	0-"	Geo R. Smith	1-0
Geo Tokas	0-1	Lewis Whittington	1-0
Jno Thompson	0-1	Danl Wade	1-0
Jacob Thomas	0-1	Jessee Wright	1-0

Clarke County, Virginia Personal Property Tax Lists 1854-1870
1868

Jno Witherspoon & Bro	2-0		
Obid Willingham	1-0	Frank Wright	0-1
Jeremiah Wilson	1-0	Jno F. Burchell	
Rev. Chas White	1-0	Monroe Wright	0-"
F. W. Wheat & Co.	"-0	Jno F. Burchell	
F. W. Wheat	1-0	Jerry Williams	0-"
Geo W. Wiley	1-0	R. R. Smith	
Jas V. Wier	1-0	Marcus White	0-1
Thornton O. Wyndham	1-0	J. G. Kerfoot	
Jacob H. Willingham	1-0	Danl Williams	0-1
Mrs. Mary B. Whiting	1-0	Rev. Jno Pickett	
Geo F. Willingham	1-0	Nicholas Word	0-"
Jno W. Whittington	1-0	O. R. Funston	
Chas L. Whittington	1-0	Jefferson William	0-1
Richard Whittington	1-0	J. F. Kerfoot	
Geo W. Writt	1-0	Jno Walker Jr.	0-"
N. B. Whiting	1-0	J. F. Kerfoot	
W. W. Wood	1-0	Jas Williams	0-1
Thos J. Whittington	1-0	W. C. Kerfoot	
White Post		Frank Walker	0-1
Danl Whittington	1-0	Mrs. M. E. Shumate	
D. Sibold		Doreby Williams	0-1
Frank Wooddy	1-0	Jno Marshall	
Thompson & Ogden		Lewis Walden	0-1
Wm Wood Jr.	"-0	Island Farm	
Fenton Wiley	"-0	Edw Wheeller [sic]	0-1
Uriah Wisner	1-0	R. O. Allen	
C. Erb		Jas Washington	0-1
W. W. Wood (Lawyer)	1-0	Witherspoon	
Danl W. Willingham	1-0	Jas Wheeler	0-1
Jos Wilson	0-1	Thos McCormick	
Mann R. Page		Crave Warrick	0-1
Albert Williams	0-1	Haymarket	
Alfred Marshall		Rodney Warrick	0-1
Jas Williams	0-1	Haymarket	
Jno G. Morris		Jas Webb	0-1
Alfred Williams	0-1	C. H. Smith	
Geo W. Copenhaver		Heny Webb	0-1
		C. H. Smith	

Clarke County, Virginia Personal Property Tax Lists 1854-1870
1868

Richard Webb	0-1	Saml Wilson	0-1
C. H. Smith		Berryville	
Wm Watson	0-1	Wm Wilson	0-1
Mrs. C. E. Carter		Berryville	
Lewis Williams	0-1	Elsa Wilson	0-1
Col. J. B. Larue		Berryville	
Geo Williams	0-1	Leve Williams	0-1
C. C. McIntyre		Berryville	
Robt Williams	0-1	Robt Williams	0-1
Thos Carter		Berryville	
Aron Williams	0-1	Marcus White	0-1
Thos Carter		Berryville	
Ellis Willis	0-1	Jas Williams	0-1
R. R. Smith		near S. B. Wyndham	
Shelton Walker	0-1	Albert Williams	0-1
M. B. Anderson		D. H. McGuire	
Jno Williams	0-1	Sidney Williams	0-1
Chapel		Jas H. Bartlette	
Wm Wormley	0-1	~~Levi Williams~~	~~0-1~~
Andrew Cornell		~~C. Erb~~	
Isaac Webb	0-1	Randle Williams	0-1
Millwood		S. B. Wm Taylor	
Thos Wade	0-1	Jas Williams	0-1
Millwood		S. B. Wm Taylor	
Jno Williams	0-1	Edmond Williams	0-1
Millwood		Jno F. Burchell	
Geo Williams	0-1	Jas Jackson	0-1
Millwood		Col. B. Morgan	
Jno Walker	0-1	Jno Jackson	0-1
Wm B. Harris		Col. B. Morgan	
Saml Walker	0-"		
Wm B. Harris		[Ink blotch covers the	
Jackson Walker	0-1	last 3 given names]	
W. D. Smith		____H. Young	1-0
Saml Weaver	0-1	____Yowell	1-0
Berryville		____Yowell	1-0
Geo Weaver	0-1		
Berryville			

Clarke County, Virginia Personal Property Tax Lists 1854-1870
1868

1869

Columns: 1) White males over 21, 2) Male negroes above the age of 21, 3) Residence, employer or employment of male negroes listed for taxation. The third column could be a name or place. It is inserted and indented under the tax payer's name. The surname is listed first this year because that is the way it is written on the tax list.

Alexander, John H.	1-0
Ashley [sic], Nimrod	1-0
Anderson, Mason &	
John H.	2-0
Anderson of Nim, John W.	1-0
Allen, William T.	1-0
Allen, Edgar A.	1-0
Allen, R. O.	2-0
Annan, R. S.	1-0
Arnett, W. Willey	1-0
Afflick, Philip J.	1-0
Atkins, William B.	1-0
Allen, George W.	1-0
Alexander, Thomas H.	1-0
Alexander, John	1-0
Anderson of Joe, John W.	1-0
Anderson, Joseph E.	1-0
Adams, R. S.	1-0
Albin, Joseph	1-0
Ambrows, Page H.	0-0
William Brown	
Anderson, George	1-0
Albert Elsea	
Albin, James	1-0
John S. Russell	
Ashby, George	1-0
Bethel	
Ashby, James R.	1-0
Mountain	
Ashby, John W.	1-0
Mountain	
Afflick, Scott A.	1-0
___ Alfred ___	0-1
Pagebrook	
___ Albert ___	0-1
Audly	
Anderson, Alexander	0-1
George W. Sowes	
Ashby, Frank	0-1
P. Hansucker	
Adams, Edwin	0-1
F. J. Kerfoot	
Alexanderson [sic],	
William	0-1
F. J. Kerfoot	
___ Ambrose ___	0-1
Bethel	
Anderson, John	0-1
Mrs. Hefflebower	
Anderson, Eliga [sic]	0-1
Mountain	
Anderson, Cornelius	0-1
Am Moore	
Burchell, John F.	1-0
Beavers, Abraham	1-0
Benn, M. & Ann C.	0-0
Bartlett, James H.	1-0

Clarke County, Virginia Personal Property Tax Lists 1854-1870
1869

Burns, Thomas W.	1-0	Bradford, W. A.	1-0
Bratham, H. W.	1-0	Bowman, Isaac	1-0
Bell Sr, James	1-0	Berlin, Philip	1-0
Barr, Adam	1-0	Brown, William S.	1-0
Belt, George W.	1-0	Boroser [sic], Christian	1-0
Bell, George H.	1-0	Brown, William	0-1
Beavers, Richard F.	1-0	A. M. Moore	
Brackett, Mrs. Francis	2-0	Byrd, George W.	1-0
Bayliss, Charles H.	1-0	Bromley, John	1-0
Bell, Joseph	1-0	Berlin, Louis	1-0
Bruce, J. Douglas	1-0	Beemer, John W.	2-0
Benn, James H.	1-0	Bratham, Charles H.	1-0
Burwell, Nathaniel	1-0	Blake, George V.	1-0
Barton, Zachariah T.	1-0	Burwell, Susan R.	0-0
Brady, Patrick	1-0	Broy, William A. J.	1-0
Bush, Charles A.	1-0	Bryerly, R. S.	1-0
Baird, George	1-0	Burwell, George H.	1-0
Bonham, William	1-0	D° Trustee for Mrs. Hay	0-0
Baker, Mrs. C. M.	0-0	Billmyre, William H.	3-0
Barr, Robert	1-0	Blakemore, G. C.	1-0
Burchell, Mrs. Margaret	0-0	Briggs, Henry C.	1-0
Blackburn, Mrs. S. A. E.	0-0	Bitzer, James H.	1-0
Brown, William M.	1-0	Boxwell, Charles H.	1-0
Barnett, Nielle	2-0	Balthis, Charles	1-0
Briggs, Arthur S.	1-0	Brown, Jesse	1-0
Briggs, William P.	1-0	John A. Green	
Briggs, Robert W.	1-0	Brisner, P.	1-0
Bell, Mrs. Frances E.	0-0	John D. Richardson	
Briggs, James C.	1-0	Bagley, William	1-0
Brown, William H.	1-0	Broy, William	1-0
Boyce & Wright	4-0	M. R. Feehrer	
Bonham, J. E.	1-0	Bigenberger, John	1-0
Bush, William A.	1-0	Thomas & Adams	
Berlin, George W.	1-0	Blue, Joseph G.	1-0
Brown, E. S.	1-0	Bradford, Erwin	1-0
Bush, William	1-0	C. Erb	
Buckner, J. P.	1-0	Bolton, L. G.	1-0
Bartlett, Thomas D.	1-0	Peter McPierce	
Bard, G. L.	1-0	Buttz, James	1-0

Clarke County, Virginia Personal Property Tax Lists 1854-1870
1869

Thompson & Ogden		Barbour, Buck	0-1
		W. C. Kennerly	
Berlin, Jackson	1-0	Berkely, Isaac	0-1
White Post		A. Cornell	
Blake, Charles	1-0	Brown, James	0-1
Berryville		Millwood	
Blake, John	1-0	Barbour, Charles	0-0
Bolen, George W.	1-0	Rev. J. Pickett	
Mountain		Brown, Thomas	0-1
Bolen, Josiah W.	1-0	Millwood	
Mountain		Brogue, John	0-1
Bell, William C.	1-0	R. R. Smith	
Province McCormick		Brandy, Henry	0-1
Ball, A. M.	1-0	Braxton, Mathew	0-1
Bowles, James A.	1-0	John Bromley	
Blackburn, Bushrod	0-1	Brown, George	0-1
G. C. Blakemore		G. W. Gordan	
Bowman, Thomas	0-1	Burle, William	0-1
T. McCormick		C. Erb	
Barbour, Michael	0-1	Banks, Thomas	0-1
Clay Hill		John Page	
Baltimore, Richard	0-1	Bailey, Henry	0-1
J. W. McCormick		Castlemans Ferry	
Banister, Beverly	0-0	Banister, William	0-1
D. C. Snyder		Saratoga	
Ball, Alfred	0-1	Bray, Joseph	0-1
B. Longerbeam		Page Brook	
___ Bartley ___	0-1	Brooks, Jacob	0-1
T. E. Gold		R. C. Randolph	
Buller, Henry	0-1	Brown, Joseph	0-1
Castlemans Ferry		Henry Harrison	
Bennett	0-1	Burns, Horace	0-1
R. C. Randolph		Champ Shepherd	
Brown, Henry	0-0	Bray, Alfred	0-1
Jarvis Jennings		Dr. Harrison	
Bywater, Nat	0-0	Banister, Thomas	0-1
Mrs. Hefflebower		Eston Randoloph	
Barbour, Charles	0-1	Byrd, James	0-1
Jos McK. Kennerly		R. H. Lee	

Clarke County, Virginia Personal Property Tax Lists 1854-1870
1869

Baltimore, Sam	0-0	Conway & Bro, Michael	2-0
R. L. Denny		Castleman, John R.	1-0
Banister, Bob	0-1	Castleman, Mann, R. P.	1-0
Hugh M. Nelson Jr.		Caqstleman, Alfred	2-0
Baker, Harrison	0-1	Chamblin, James E.	1-0
G. K. Sowers		Cain, Isaac N.	1-0
Bromley, Jack	0-1	Crow, John T.	1-0
Nat Burwell		Cooper, Harrison	1-0
Blair, George	0-1	Copenhaver, Mrs. Sarah	0-0
Dr. McGuire		Carper, Alfred C.	2-0
Bey, Joseph	0-1	Carter, John A.	2-0
Mountain		Cobb, Jacob M.	1-0
Brannan, Jack	0-1	Carver, James	1-0
J. P. Marshall		Chrismore, J. F.	1-0
Butler, James	0-1	Carter, John W.	1-0
J. P. Marshall		Clark & Son, Willis B.	2-0
Butler, Scott	0-0	Cain, John	1-0
J. P. Marshall		Cattlet, Mariam	1-0
Burwell, Thomas	0-0	Chrismore, George W.	1-0
J. P. Marshall		Crockwell, John R.	1-0
Barnes, John	0-1	Carter, Mrs. Sarah E. V.	0-0
C. T. Hebb		Cross, A. F.	1-0
___ Bill ___	0-1	Chrissmore, B. J.	1-0
W. B. C. Sowers		Clingan, McLane	1-0
		Cross, James	1-0
Cook, N. B.	1-0	Cornell, A.	1-0
Chappell, James H.	1-0	Carter, Thomas	2-0
Corder, Parkeson	1-0	Carter, William P.	1-0
Carpenter, John W.	1-0	Cook, J. Eston	1-0
Cooper, John	1-0	Carper, Hiram	1-0
Carroll & Huff, Louis	2-0	Conway, Timothy	1-0
Coffman, Erasmus	1-0	Collier, John N.	1-0
Carroll, Reason	1-0	Calmes, L. A.	2-0
Carroll, Thomas	1-0	Carter, trustee	
Carter, Grafton	1-0	Mrs. E. Carter, J. K.	1-0
Carter, Mrs. C.E.	0-0	Carter, James L.	1-0
Childs, John A.	1-0	Colston, R. A.	1-0
Crow, Mrs. Thomas	0-0	Colston Dr. R. T.	1-0
Castleman, James R.	1-0	Carter, John B.	1-0

Clarke County, Virginia Personal Property Tax Lists 1854-1870
1869

Cook, Ann B.	1-0	Cooper, George	0-1
Copenhaver, George W.	1-0	A. N. Pierce	
Castleman, Thomas	1-0	Cawthorn, J. W.	0-0
Crampton, Benjamin	1-0	D. J. Shepherd	
Cirtwell, Walter	1-0	Christian, Monroe	0-1
Mountain		J. S. Smith	
Carrie, Bushrod	0-0	Carter, Nat	0-1
D. T. Kerfoot		Mrs. B. Whiting	
Crebs, John H.	1-0	Colston, Robert	0-1
Carder, Louis W.	1-0	Jos McK Kennerly	
Stone Bridge		Carter, William	0-1
Castleman, William A.	1-0	William B. Harris	
Chipley, Ludwell	0-0	Crittenden, George	0-1
Thomas & Adams		J. Gilkerson	
Cooper, James	1-0	Commander, James	0-1
Philips & Wiard		Millwood	
Crebs, Gaunt	0-0	Cooper, Robert	0-1
J. W. Kitchen		Martin Gant	
Carmel, John	1-0	Cooper, George	0-0
Castleman, George	1-0	Martin Gant	
Mrs. Burchell		Carter, William	0-1
Chappell, John	1-0	Jos D. Fry	
James Chappell		Crates, Peter	0-1
Carper, John B.	1-0	J. B. Larue	
Carper, Joseph	1-0	Cole Charles	0-1
Carper, Joshua	1-0	Mrs. Blackburn	
A. M. Helper		Cass, Louis	0-0
Carter, William	0-1	Mrs. Burchell	
Thomas Carter		Cooper, William	0-1
Carter, Daniel	0-1	Frank McCormick	
R. R. Smith		Carter, George	0-1
Carter, Albert	0-1	Mrs. Taylor	
R. R. Smith		Carlisle, Albert	0-1
Clayton, William	0-1	R. H. Lee	
Clay Hill		Christian, William	0-1
Clayton, Edward	0-1	Alfred C. Jackson	
Clay Hill		Carter, Bosin	0-1
___ Charles ___	0-1	Boyce & Wright	
John W. Beemer		Cook, John	0-1

Clarke County, Virginia Personal Property Tax Lists 1854-1870
1869

Berrys Ferry		Doleman, Jacob	0-1
		John D. Richardson	
Colston, Jacob	0-1	Duncan, James	0-1
J. R. Marshall		Lancaster Shop	
Cox, Morgan	0-1	Dickenson, Edward	0-1
E. T. Hebb		J. W. Ryan	
Colbert, Richard	0-1	Doctor, Mike	0-1
B. Glover		R. C. Lee	
		Dickenson, Andrew	0-1
Duke, Thomas H.	1-0	H. M. Nelson Jr.	
Deahl, William P.	1-0	Danks, James	0-1
Dove, T. J.	1-0	J. F. Burchell	
Drish, John	1-0	___ Dan ___	0-1
Donovan, John	1-0	G. W. Gordan	
Deck, George	1-0	Dangerfield, Sis	0-1
Dulaney, R. H.	1-0	J. T. Griffith	
Dunbar, H. H.	1-0	Doran, Mathew A.	1-0
Denny, R. L.	1-0		
Dearmont, Peter	1-0	Elliott, John C.	1-0
Dunn, Robert	1-0	Evans, John S.	1-0
Deahl, Horace P.	1-0	Eddy, Thomas M.	1-0
Duble, Aaron	1-0	Everhart, William G.	3-0
Dearmont, Washington	2-0	Evans, O. P.	1-0
Doran, James	1-0	Everhart, Thomas A.	1-0
Doran, James W.	1-0	Elwell, John M.	2-0
Dorsey, J. P.	1-0	Edwards, Henry	1-0
Duvall, C. H.	1-0	Erb, Christopher	3-2
Dooly, John M.	0-0	Elsea, Albert	1-0
Thomas & Adams		Eaton, Philip	1-0
Deck, Frederick A.	1-0	Ed wards, Joseph W.	1-0
Near Salem		Edwards, Benjamin F.	1-0
Denny, John M.	1-0	Epps, John A.	1-0
White Post		Philips & Wiard	
Drish, George	1-0	Estep, Dilman	1-0
Mountain		Millwood	
Danks, Charles	0-1	___ Elick ___	0-1
Wm T. Milton		P. McCormick	
___ David ___	0-0	Edwards, Purnine	0-1
Thomas H. Kerns		Hugh M. Nelson Jr.	

Clarke County, Virginia Personal Property Tax Lists 1854-1870
1869

Foster, James A.	1-0	Millwood	
Fritz, John W.	1-0		
Fellows, Joshua G.	1-0	Fillingains, Frank	1-0
Feehrer, M. R.	1-0	Mountain	
Fayman, Joseph P.	1-0	Freeman, James T.	1-0
Fishpaw, Eli	1-0	Millwood	
Fennell, Jesse	1-0	French, Peter	0-1
Fenton, Dennis	1-0	L. A. Calmes	
Funstan, Dr. O. R.	1-0	Franklin, James	0-1
Fowler, William	1-0	C. S. Lee	
Fry, Joseph D.	1-0	Fields, Adams	0-1
Fletcher, Isaac	1-0	J. S. Ware	
Fidler, H. C.	1-0	Fields, Aaron	0-1
Feltner, Martin	3-0	J. S. Ware	
Fidler, Israel	1-0	Fields, George	0-1
Furr, Johnston	2-0	French, Moses	0-1
Flagg, Thomas G.	1-0	A. F. Cross	
Furr, James	1-0	Fields, W. F.	0-1
Fowler, Thomas	1-0	W. S. Brown	
Fleming, Louisa	0-0	Fox, Alfred J.	0-1
Fleming, Sarah A.	1-0	John W. Russell	
Fowler, Everett	1-0	Fox, Neptune	0-1
Fletcher, Louis	0-1	John W. Russell	
Furr, William	1-0	Fractious, David	0-1
Mountain		E. Marshall	
Furguson, Washington	1-0	Franklin, Elick	0-1
Mountain		J. B. Larue	
Fennell & Son, Alexander	1-0	Franklin, Frank	0-1
Frost, Ebin	1-0	W. A. Larue	
Dr. Cyrus McCormick		Fitzhugh, William	0-1
Furr, Ephraim	1-0	E. Allen	
A. Elsea		Fox, Peyton	0-1
Feltner, George	1-0	W. T. Allen	
W. Pyle		Fox, Jacob	0-0
Fidler, Samuel	1-0	W. T. Allen	
Mrs. Copenhavers		Farril, Austin	0-1
Fry, Joseph	0-0	H. L. D. Lewis	
Thompson & Ogden		___Sam & Alfred ___	0-2
Freeman, Garret C.	1-0	H. L. D. Lewis	

Clarke County, Virginia Personal Property Tax Lists 1854-1870
1869

Fleet, Jesse	0-1	Glass, Louis F.	2-0
W. F. Knight		D° Trustee for	
Ford, Joseph W.	0-0	Mrs. Iceler [sic]	0-0
White Post		Grantham, Joseph W.	1-0
		Grubb, George W.	1-0
Fairfax, Abram	0-1	Grubb, Walter B.	1-0
Col. B. Morgan		Greenwalt, Adam	1-0
___ Frederick ___	0-1	Greenwalt, John	1-0
Dr. W. M. Page		Glover, J. B.	1-1
Fuller, George W.	1-0	Gardiner, Joseph	1-0
B. Longerbeam		Green, Richard N.	2-0
Franks, Madison	1-0	Green, James F.	3-0
W. H. Robinson		Green, E. M.	1-0
		Griffith, Thomas W.	1-0
Garrett, J. Lee	1-0	Gainer, L. W.	1-0
Gruber, John Agt.	1-0	B. T. Kerfoot	
Grove, F. T.	1-0	Glover, T. K.	1-0
Grigsby, Mrs. Bettie	0-0	Gill, John M.	0-0
Gant, S. G.	1-0	Thomas & Adams	
Galloway, Charles F.	1-0	Goheen, John B.	1-0
Gibson, John M.	1-0	Thomas & Adams	
Galloway, James W.	1-0	Gorden, George M.	1-0
Gold, John & Thomas E.	3-0	Berryville	
Grubb, James	1-0	Gordan, Thomas N.	1-0
Gikerson, James	1-0	John Morgan Jr.	
Green, John A.	1-0	Godlover, Isaac	1-0
Grubb, G. M. D.	1-0	J. W. Luke	
Grubb, Mattison L.	1-0	Glycener, George	1-0
Grubb, John & Charles	2-0	Grubb, Philip	1-0
Garthright, Thomas T.	1-0	Bethel	
Gordan, George W.	1-0	Brubb, Mat	1-0
Grubb, William B.	1-0	Bethel	
Grigsby, Mrs. Frances	0-0	Grubb, James T.	1-0
Gardiner, George	1-0	Bethel	
Griffith, J. T.	1-0	Grubb, Samuel	1-0
Gray, Zebedee &		W. B. Sowers	
Warner T.	2-0	Grigsby, Jack	0-1
Gant, Martin	1-0	Gibson, George	0-1
Galloway, Madison	1-0	Pagebrooke	

Clarke County, Virginia Personal Property Tax Lists 1854-1870
1869

Gibson, Thomas	0-1	Hummer, James W.	1-0
Pagebrooke		Harrison, Henry	2-0
Gainer, Jackson	0-1	D° Admr. of	
J. M. Gibson		W. T. Burwell Est.	1-0
Green, Edward	0-1	Huff, Cornelius	1-0
A. Cowell		Houptman, John	1-0
Gray, Jack	0-1	Hall, John W.	1-0
Millwood		Huff, Jackson	1-0
Gardiner, George	0-0	Hughs, John	1-0
Gaskins, John	0-1	Hummer, Alexander	1-0
J. P. Marshall		Hardesty, Kirk	1-0
		Howell, James F.	1-0
Hall, Mrs. C. M.	0-0	Hebb, E. F.	1-0
Huyett, Henry	1-0	Horseman, William	1-0
Hardesty, Joseph R.	1-0	Hummer, John & Mason	2-0
Hardesty, Adrian D.	1-0	Hawkes, Cornelius	1-0
Haycock, James W.	1-0	White Post	
Helvestine, Louis B.	1-0	Humphrey, Thomas L.	1-0
Harris, William G.	1-0	Howard, Walter	0-1
Hibbard, John W.	1-0	C. Erb	
Hansucker, Philip	1-0	Holms, Briscoe	0-1
Hefflebower, Mrs. M. E.	1-0	near T. McCormicks	
Haddox, Alpheus	1-0	Hull, William	0-1
Hansucker, George	1-0	Peter McPierce	
Hawthorn, John B.	1-0	Hunter, Lawrence	0-1
Hite, James M.	1-0	White Post	
Hardesty, James M.	1-0	Holtzclaw, Thomas	1-0
Harrison, Edward R.	2-0	J. M. Gibson	
Holland, John W.	1-0	Hitchcock, George	0-0
Harrison, Dr. Benja^m	1-0	J. P. Dorsey	
Harris, William B.	2-0	Hitchcock, Charles	0-0
Harford, A. J.	1-0	J. P. Dorsey	
Helvestine, W. R.	1-0	Hough, John	0-0
Henry, John C.	1-0	Hummer, James	1-0
Hesser, A. M.	1-0	Hummer, Robert	1-0
Hardesty, William G.	2-0	Hannum, Preston	1-0
Hardesty, Charles W.	1-0	George Marpole	
Hook, William W.	3-0	Hunt, John	1-0
Hart, Thomas S.	1-0	W. C. Smith	

Clarke County, Virginia Personal Property Tax Lists 1854-1870
1869

Henry, John	1-0		E. T. Hebb	
W. F. Knight			Hall, Wesley	0-1
Hefferling, W. G.	1-0		M. Guishelman	
Mountain			Hall, Mrs. C. V.	0-0
Hefferling, James W.	1-0		Irwin, Marcus B.	1-0
Mountain			Iceler, George H.	1-0
Hefferling, Mountjoy	1-0		Iversun, Savory	0-1
Mountain			Millwood	
Hummer, John	0-0			
Berryville			Jennings, Jarvis	1-0
___ Henry ___	0-1		Jenkins, Thomas	1-0
J. Shep Mitchell			Jackson, Deinst [?]	1-0
HarrisOn, Henry	0-1		Jolliffe, J. M.	1-0
J. W. Stephenson			Johnston, F. L.	1-0
Hairis [*sic*] James	0-1		Jones, Leonard	1-0
Carter Hall			Johnston, Benjamin	1-0
Helmes, George	0-1		Jolliffe, Mrs. Kate	1-0
G. R. Royston			Jackson, William A.	1-0
Herbert, Adam	0-1		Jenkins, Herrod Jr.	1-0
Millwood			Jones, Thomas	1-0
Helms, Solomon	0-1		Johnston, James W.	1-0
Millwood			Johnston, John L.	1-0
___ Horace ___	0-1		Jackson, Alfred C.	1-0
William A. Castleman			Jones, Alfred	1-0
Harris, George	0-1		Jenkins, Ebin	1-0
J. T. Crow			Johnston, Rev. William	1-0
Haines, Albert	0-1		Jenkins, Edward	1-0
W. A. Riely			Jenkins, Herrod Sr.	1-0
Holmes, Bill	0-1		Jenkins, Jesse	1-0
E. Allen			Johnston, James W.	1-0
Howard, Joseph	0-1		Mountain	
P. H. Powers			Jones, Rev. Joseph R.	1-0
Harris, Daniel & Mat	2-0		Jackson & son, Robert C.	1-0
Boyce & Wright			Jones, James	1-0
Hall, Frank	0-1		Castlemans Ferry	
White Post			Jackson, George	0-1
Harrison, Reese	0-1		J. W. Ware	
E. T. Hebb			Jackson, John	0-0
Hall, Robert	0-1		J. C. Eliott	

Clarke County, Virginia Personal Property Tax Lists 1854-1870
1869

Jenkins, Presley	0-1	James, John	0-1
C. H. Boxwell		W. C. Smith	
___ Jerry ___	0-1	Jackson, William	0-1
John A. Green		J. B. Larue	
Jackson, Robert	0-1	Johnston, Daniel	0-1
John Morgan Jr.		John Castleman	
Jackson, William	0-1	Jefferson, Thomas	0-1
J. Shep Mitchell		C. C. McIntyre	
___ Josiah ___	0-0	Jackson, Richard	0-1
A. C. Marshall		P. D. Shepherd	
Jackson, Henry	0-0	Jones, Mortimer	0-1
Leonard Jones		P. D. Shepherd	
Jefferson, Henry	0-1	Jones, George	0-1
M. B. Erwin		Champ Shepherd	
Jones, Burr	0-0	Jackson, John	0-1
C. Vandeventer		J. B. Shepherd	
___ Jack ___	0-1	Jackson, Allen	0-1
Mrs. B. Whiting		F. Stine	
Jackson Charles Jr.	0-1	Jackson, Henry	0-1
Dr. R. C. Randolph		R. H. Lee	
Jackson, Henry	0-1	Johnston, Spencer	0-1
Jarvis Jennings		J. A. Kelsoe	
Jackson, David	0-1	Jemmerson, Charles	0-1
W. C. Kennerly		Boyce & Wright	
Jackson, Charles	0-1	Johnston, George	0-1
C. Hull		Wm T. Burwell	
Johnston, Jackson	0-1	Jackson, Daniel	0-1
T. M. Eddy		G. K. Sowers	
Johnston, John	0-1	Jackson, Jesse	0-1
Millwood		Nat Burwell	
Jackson, Wash	0-1	___ Josiah ___	0-1
Millwood		near Mark Miles	
Jackson, Israel	0-1		
Millwood		Kern, Thomas H.	1-0
Johnston, Samuel	0-1	Kennerly, Joseph Mc K.	1-0
Wadesville		Kerfoot, J. F.	
Johnston, Samuel	0-1	trustee Mrs. Adams	0-0
Henry Harrison		Kerfoot, J. G.	1-0
		Kimmel, John M.	1-0

Clarke County, Virginia Personal Property Tax Lists 1854-1870
1869

Kitchen, George	1-0	Little, Frank	1-0
Kerfoot, J. F.	1-0	Laws, N. W.	1-0
Kerfoot, Wm T.	1-0	Laws, J. N.	1-0
Kerfoot, Wm C.	1-0	Longerbeam, Abraham	1-0
Kennerly, Wm C.	1-0	Louthan, John K.	1-0
Knight, D. M.	1-0	Lee, C. S.	1-0
Kiger, James M.	1-0	Laws, J. S.	1-0
Kerfoot, F. J.	1-0	Larue, A. L. P.	1-0
Kennan, James H.	1-0	Littleton, William	1-0
Kindall, Charles L.	1-0	Longerbeam, B.	1-0
Kiger, Wm J.	1-0	Lewis, Mrs. E. M.	0-0
Kirby, Joseph H.	1-0	Lock, Josiah R.	1-0
Kercheral, E. V.	1-0	Lewis, H. L. D.	1-0
Keeler, Middleton	1-0	Lewis, E. P. C.	1-0
Kitchen, John N.	1-0	Lock, John	1-0
Kitchen, Charles H.	1-0	Lee, William D.	2-0
Knight, Henry	1-0	Lewis, Dr. T. M.	1-0
Kerfoot, David T.	1-0	Lock, Remington	1-0
Knight, Wm. F.	1-0	Larue, Wm A.	1-0
Kelso, Joseph A.	1-0	Longerbeam, John	1-0
Kneller, S. G.	1-0	Lloyd, James L.	1-0
Kneller, Jacob & Thomas	2-0	Light, Peter	1-0
Keeler, C. H.	1-0	Levi, George W.	1-0
Kromling, Henry	1-0	Larue, John B.	2-0
Kounslar, Mrs. E. S.	0-0	Lewis, G. W.	1-0
Koonce, G. W.	1-0	Littleton, B. F.	1-0
Kerns, David J. V. Weir	1-0	Lanham, William	1-0
		Lloyd, Henry	1-0
Knight, Abner J. B. Shepherd	1-0	Lippitt, A. S.	1-0
		Lloyd, James W.	1-0
Keeler, J. M. Millwood	1-0	Louthan, James T.	1-0
		Larue, James W.	1-0
Keeler, Joseph W. Millwood	1-0	Liady, A. G.	1-0
		Lee, R. H.	1-0
Kearnsy, James, J. H. Shepherd	1-0	Lewin [sic] Moses	1-0
		Levi, Rice W.	2-0
Kerfoot, A. J. White Post	1-0	Lupton, John M.	1-0
		Lewis, James T.	1-0
		Louthan, John	1-0

Clarke County, Virginia Personal Property Tax Lists 1854-1870
1869

Larue, Christopher C.	1-0	Lloyd, Benjamin	1-0
Luke, John W.	1-0	Mountain	
Lancaster, John F.	1-0	Lee, R. H.	1-0
Lindsey, Joseph B.	1-0	Magnus S. Thompson	
Lloyd, John A.	1-0	Lewis, Richard	0-1
Lanham, George	1-0	T. McCormick	
Lloyd, Charles H.	1-0	Lewis, Levi	0-1
Lee, John	1-0	John Morgan Jr.	
Lee, Squire	1-0	Lee, Other	0-0
Lanham, James	1-0	A. N. Pierce	
Lindsey, John T.	1-0	Lee, Armstead	0-1
Lee, James W.	1-0	D. C. Snyder	
Lloyd, John	1-0	Lampkin, Benjamin	0-0
Lock, F. H.	1-0	G. F. Kerfoot	
Lanham, Benton	1-0	Lee, Isaac	0-1
Mountain		John Alexander	
Laws, Raffe	0-1	Lewis, Jerry	0-1
G. W. Grubbs		Berryville	
Lewis, Fielding	0-1	Lockey, Samuel	0-1
J. P. Marshall		Mann Page	
Land, Joseph	1-0	Lipkins, Benjamin	0-0
Lewis Berlin		John W. Luke	
Lake, Alexander	1-0	Lisles, Charles	0-1
T. A. Keene		J. R. Castleman	
Lanham, Samuel	1-0	Lee, John	0-1
G. W. Wiley		F. McCormick	
Lake, Jordan	1-0	Lavender, Giles	0-0
D. W. Sowers		T. D. Bartlett	
Lancaster, Milton M.	1-0	Laton, Richard H.	0-1
Levi, Henry	0-0	Millwood	
J. B. Shepherd		Lewis, Solomon	0-1
Lakey, A. P.	1-0	Mrs. Susan ORear	
Berryville		Lewis, William H.	0-1
Lake, Vincent	1-0	F. H. Lock	
D. W. Sowers		___ Lee ___	0-1
Lake, Edward	1-0	Millwood	
D. W. Sowers		Laws & Son, Thomas	0-1
Lake, Henry	1-0	Mrs. Kounslar	
D. W. Sowers		Lippitt, Dr. C.E.	1-0

Clarke County, Virginia Personal Property Tax Lists 1854-1870
1869

		McCormick, Otway	1-0
		McCormick, Province	1-0
Meade, David Sr.	1-0	Marpole, George F.	1-0
D° Adm of R. R. Meade	0-0	Moore, S. J. C.	1-0
D° Admr of		McDonald, Garret	1-0
W. M. Washington	0-0	Menefee, Joseph	1-0
D° Trustee of		Meade, Miss Mary	1-0
W. V. Meade	0-0	McDonald, Agnes W.	1-0
Morgan, John Jr.	1-0	McClelland, James W.	1-0
McCormick, James	1-0	McCormick, Dr. Cyrus	1-0
McCormick, Thomas	1-0	Meade, F. B.	1-0
Milton, Wm T.	1-0	McIntyre, C. C.	1-0
Massey, E. W.	2-2	McCune, John T.	1-0
Mason, Joseph	1-0	McDonald, Josiah	1-0
McDonal, A. K.	1-0	McGuire, Dr. W. D.	1-0
Messmer, Henry J.	1-0	Mickey, Hays	1-0
McCauly, John G.	1-0	McClaughry, James	1-0
Marpole, Thomas W.	1-0	Morris, W. G.	1-0
Morgan, John Sr.	2-0	Martz, S. T.	1-0
McGuire, D. H.	2-0	Marpole, Hesekiah	1-0
Marshall, Alexander	2-0	Moore, S. P.	1-0
Monroe, John J.	1-0	McDonald, Charles W.	1-0
Moore, A. M.	1-0	Murphy, James T.	1-0
Moore, Nicholas	1-0	Morgan, Col.B.	1-0
Moore, S. J. C., trustee	0-0	Marshall, J. P.	1-0
Mrs. E. S. Kitchen		Marshall, John	1-0
Mitchell, J. Shep	1-0	Miley, Moses G.	1-0
Marshall, A. C.	1-0	Moore, A. Mason	2-0
McCormick, J. W.	1-0	McNulty, James	1-0
McDonald W. L. & B. J.	3-0	McCormick, Alexander	1-0
Morris, John G.	1-0	Moore, James F.	1-0
Martin, F. T.	1-0	J. T. Murphys	
Meade, Philip N.	1-0	Martin, John T.	1-0
Mills, Mark	1-0	Moseby, Robert	1-0
Marshall, E. C. Jr.	1-1	McCard, Richard	1-0
Miley, Amos D.	1-0	P. H. Powers	
Mason, H. W.	1-0	McAbaugh, William	1-0
McPierce, Peter	1-0	J. E. Russell	
McCormick, Francis	1-0	Myers, George W.	1-0

Clarke County, Virginia Personal Property Tax Lists 1854-1870
1869

C. F. Galloway		Mauser, George	0-1
		R. S. Adams	
McClaughry, J. B.	1-0		
Mountain		Murry, James	0-1
Mock, G. R.	1-0	A. L. P. Larue	
W. C. Kennerly		Moore, Jesse	0-1
Morallis, Julian	1-0	Millwood	
W. H. Young		___ Myers ___	0-1
Moore, Frank	0-0	W. C. Kerfoot	
W. H. Young		Masters, Nat	0-1
Myers, J. B.	1-0	Millwood	
Berryville		McCard, Joseph	0-1
Miller, John	1-0	Col. Smith	
Berryville		Mann, G. F.	0-1
Moore, Alfred	1-0	McIntree, John	0-1
Mountain		C. Erb	
Milton, J. F. Sr.	1-0	McCard, Richard	0-1
Berryville		P. H. Powers	
Milton, C. A.	1-0	Mitchell, Henry	0-1
Berryville		E. Allen	
Milton, J. F. Jr.	1-0	Magill, Frank	0-1
Berryville		W. T. Allen	
Marston, Joseph	1-0	Magill, Robert	0-1
Berryville		W. T. Allen	
McCauly, Robert	1-0	Moseby, Alexander	0-1
F. A. Deck		Berryville	
Meade, W. W.	1-0	Marks, Henry	0-1
White Post		Robert Briggs	
Moore, Joseph	1-0	Mitchell, Isaac	0-1
C. Smallwood		Dr. McGuire	
Mercer, Jesse	1-0	Moss, George	0-1
T. L. Humphrey		Dr. McGuire	
McCormick, Hugh H.	1-0	Mitchell, Isaac	0-1
Moore, Thomas A.	1-0	M. Guishelman	
Dpt. Clerk		Miner, J. Monroe	0-1
Murphy, James	1-0	Berryville	
Col. Morgan		McCormick, Edward	1-0
Marlin, Randall	0-1		
Page Brooke		Neville, Alexander V.	1-0

Clarke County, Virginia Personal Property Tax Lists 1854-1870
1869

Neville, James H.	1-0	H. Whiting	
Nunn, John R.	1-0		
Niff, Hiram	1-0	Pyle, William	1-0
Newcome, James H.	1-0	Page, Thomas D.	1-0
Nelson, William N.	1-0	Patterson, James B.	1-0
Niswanner, Thomas C.	1-0	Page, Dr. William M.	1-0
Nelson, Mrs. Hugh M	1-0	Pidgeon, Samuel L.	1-0
Neille, Dr. S. S.	1-0	Pulliam, Matthew	1-0
Nelson, William A.	1-0	Price, Joseph	1-0
E. McGrady		Pickett, Rev. J.	1-0
Nicklin, James	1-0	Puller, Bushrod	1-0
Berryville		Pitman, A. H.	1-0
Norris, Henry	0-1	Pierce, A. N.	1-0
Saratoga		Page, John E.	1-0
___ Newman ___	0-1	Prichard, Barnett	1-0
M. B. Cork		Patterson, John	2-0
Nelson, Jacob	0-1	Poston, John	1-0
T. E. Gold		Price, Mrs. Susan F.	0-0
Norris, Walker	0-1	Pierce, W. G.	1-0
J. W. Sprint		Page, Mrs. Hannah C.	0-0
Nelson & son, Alfred	0-1	Powers, P. H.	1-0
Mountain		Pierce, Paul	1-0
___ Nelson ___	0-1	Pope, Michael	1-0
J. W. Luke		Arabia	
		Pipher, Joseph	2-0
O,Rear, Mrs. Catharine	0-0	Page, John	1-0
O,Rear, Jesse	2-0	Philips, G. E. S.	1-0
Osborn, Joshua	1-0	Page, R. Powell	1-0
Osborn, Lewellen	1-0	Page, Mann R.	1-0
O,Rear, Mrs. Susan	0-0	Pyle, Robert	1-0
Owen, Alexander W.	1-0	Pyle, William F.	1-0
O,Rear, Mrs. E.	1-0	Pope, John M.	1-0
Owen, Alfred C.	1-0	Pipher, William M.	1-0
J. B. Sowers		Popkins, William	1-0
Owen, James	1-0	G. Bell	
F. Stine		Pope, Conrad	1-0
Osborn, John	1-0	Payne, Jacob	0-1
Mountain		James Grubb	
Osborn, Bushrod	0-1	Parker, Levi	0-1

Clarke County, Virginia Personal Property Tax Lists 1854-1870
1869

P. McPierce		Reynolds, John	1-0
		Randolph, William E.	1-0
Puller, James	1-0	Ritter, G. W.	1-0
Millwood		Reardon, Patrick	1-0
Parkins, C. M.	1-0	Ryan, Joseph F.	1-0
Pope, Franklin	1-0	Ryan, James W.	1-0
Pope, West	1-0	Riely, J. C.	1-0
Page, Dr. Thomas S.	1-0	Russell, James E.	1-0
Pine, George W.	1-0	Richardson, John D.	1-0
Mountain		Ridgely, Samuel	1-0
Pine, Marshall	1-0	Russell, Thomas W.	1-0
Mountain		Riely, Moses	1-0
Pierce, John	1-0	Runner, Robert	0-1
Parker, Daniel	0-1	Mountain	
A. D. Hardesty		Richmond, Enos	1-0
Powers, Josiah	0-1	Royston, M. T.	1-0
C. Vandeventer		Royston, Uriah	1-0
Parker, Baltimore,	0-1	Royston, George R.	1-0
Stone Bridge		Reardon & Bro, Franklin	1-0
Porter, Jack	0-1	Randolph, Beverly	1-0
W. C. Kerfoot		Richards, D. B.	1-0
Pitman, Thomas	0-1	Randolph, Dr. R. C.	1-0
T. Hart		Reed, John R.	1-0
Page, Thomas	0-1	Robertson, W. H.	1-0
F. McCormick		Royston, Mrs. M.	0-0
Page, John & Tom	0-2	Royston, P. K.	1-0
G. W. Lewis		Russell, W. Wesley	1-0
Pray, Charles	0-0	Riely, John J.	1-0
P. H. Powers		Russell, Thomas J.	1-0
		Russell, John W.	1-1
Quince, Robert	0-1	Randolph, Dr. A. C.	1-0
J. M. Hite		Russell, Michael	1-0
		Russell, W. H.	1-0
		Reed, Stephen	1-0
Riley, John J. trustee	3-0	Ritter, R.H.	1-0
Mrs. Taylor, John J.		Roland, John	3-0
Routzan, Ezra	1-0	Riely, William A.	1-0
Russell, John S.	1-0	Reed, Marcus B.	2-0
Russell, Jesse N.	1-0	Royston, Zachariah V.	1-0

Clarke County, Virginia Personal Property Tax Lists 1854-1870
1869

Russell, George B.	1-0	Millwood	
Rippon, John J.	1-0		
Robinson, Samuel	0-1	Robinson, Sol	0-1
Reed, A. J.	1-0	J. Alexander Jr.	
J. D. Richardson		Randolph Henry	0-1
___ Ritter ___	1-0	Millwood	
Millwood		Rittenour, Adam	0-1
Rawlins, James E.	1-0	Rev. J. Pickett	
Berryville		Reed, Samuel O.	0-1
Riggle, John W.	1-0	J. A. Foster	
T. Hart		Reed, Nelson	0-1
Ritter, Harrison	1-0	C. Erd [sic]	
Alfred Carper		Runner, Jeffrey	0-1
Ricamore, George	1-0	C. Allen	
Thompson & Ogden		Robinson, Anthony	0-1
Rose, William	1-0	W. T. Allen	
White Post		Robinson, Scott	0-1
Russell, W. H.	1-0	Mann R. P. Castleman	
Mountain		Robinson, Charles	0-1
Ridenour, Adam	1-0	John Castleman	
Randolph, John	0-1	Rust, William	0-1
Saratoga		Dr. Cyrus McCormick	
Randolph, Henry	0-1	Robinson, Henry	0-1
Saratoga		E. Randolph	
Robinson, Henry	0-1	Rust, Philip	0-1
J. McCormick		Amos D. Miley	
Robinson, Alexander	0-1	Robinson, Henry	0-1
H. J. Mesmer		T. D. Bartlett	
Reid, James	0-1	Robinson, Miles	0-1
J. R. Hardesty		Dr. O. R. Funston	
Robinson, Ambrose	0-1	Richardson, George	0-1
Bethel		Millwood	
Robinson, John	0-1	Randolph, Frank	0-1
John Morgan Sr.		G. W. Lewis	
Randolph, Arche	0-1		
Saratoga		Shipe, Benjamin	1-0
Robinson, William	0-1	Sowers, G. H.	1-0
J. S. Evans		Sowers, W. B.	1-0
Randolph, Jack	0-1	Stuart, J. R.	2-0

Clarke County, Virginia Personal Property Tax Lists 1854-1870
1869

Sommerville, Dr. William	1-0	Shepherd, Joseph H.	1-0
Shipe, Andrew J.	1-0	Stephenson, Dr. J. W.	1-0
Sinclair, M. L.	1-0	Slack, John	1-0
Shipe, Moses W.	1-0	Stine, Frank	1-0
Steele, William G.	1-0	Shepherd, D. J.	1-0
Snyder, George	1-0	Slusher, H.	1-0
Smith, William D.	1-1	Shell, Stephen	1-0
Stribling, Mrs. S. E. T.	1-0	Shell, Mount Joy	1-0
Steele, John W.	1-0	Stickels, Henry Sr.	1-0
Stickel, Joseph	1-0	Silman, Hiram	1-0
Swartz, Charles W.	1-0	Silman, B. F.	1-0
Snyder, D. S.	1-0	Silman, Peter	1-0
Smith, John S.	1-0	Stickels, Joseph H.	1-0
Shearer, Henry T.	2-0	Sowers, G. K.	1-0
Shroud, Louis	1-0	Sowers, Daniel W.	3-0
Shaffer, John T.	1-0	Spaulding, G. S.	1-0
Smithey, Richard	1-0	Shepherd, Champ	1-0
Shimp, G. W.	1-0	Sowers, Robert L.	1-0
Sowers, W. B. C.	1-0	Sowers, James S.	1-0
Smith, George R.	1-0	Sowers, Daniel H.	1-0
Sommerville, Dr. Henry	1-0	Shaffer, J. J.	1-0
Starkey, Benjamin	1-0	Smallwood, T. O.	1-0
Shean, Dennis	1-0	Stump, Simon R.	1-0
Shepherd, Park D.	2-0	Shepherd, Carter	1-0
Strickler, J. S.	1-0	Showers, Samuel	1-0
Shepherd, F. B.	1-0	Smith, Treadwell	1-0
Shepherd, J. N.	1-0	Sowers, George W.	1-0
Shumate, Mrs. M. E.	1-0	Stolle, W. F.	1-0
Stickel, Joseph Jr.	2-0	Smith, Charles H.	1-0
Sowers, J. W.	1-0	Seabold & Son, Daniel D.	1-0
Sowers, John F.	1-0	Shearer, James M.	1-0
Sprint, John W.	1-0	Shepherd, Joseph B.	1-0
Sprought, J. W.	1-0	Stickels, Joseph	1-0
Swartz, J. W.	1-0	Smallwood, Burr	1-0
Snyder, D. C.	1-0	Stickels, Simon	1-0
Smith, Dr. J. P.	1-0	Smallwood, Sylvester	1-0
Stickel, Henry Jr.	1-0	Smith, William C.	1-0
Santmyers, Daniel M.	1-0	Shewalter, W. A.	1-0
Smith, R. R.	1-0	Shiplett, S. M. & R. H.	1-0

Clarke County, Virginia Personal Property Tax Lists 1854-1870
1869

Shipe, John W.	1-0	Millwood	
Sowers, N. O.	1-0	Strange, Reuben	0-1
Smithey, G. L.	1-0	J. W. Larue	
Smith, W. L.	1-0	Strother, John W.	0-1
Berryville		Dennis Fenton	
Shipe, John	1-0	Smith, Thomas	0-1
Spence, Michael	1-0	C. C. Larue	
F. Stine		Stuart, Henry	0-1
Steele, Joseph	1-0	W. T. Allen	
J. S. Strickler		Skinner, Charles	0-1
Shipe, Joseph B.	1-0	Mrs. Burchell	
Moses Shipe		Smith, Filmore	0-1
Struder, William	1-0	C. C. Larue	
Millwood		Scinrus, Charles	0-1
Stickels, Michael	1-0	F. McCormick	
W. H. Robinson		Stepney, John	0-1
Smith, James	1-0	H. H. Dunbar	
J. A. Bartlett		Seals, Dennis	0-1
Stickels, T. W.	1-0	White Post	
H. Edwards		Seals, Lafayett	0-0
Sigafoose, Robt B.	1-0	White Post	
Shackleford, William	1-0	Strange, Philip	0-1
Smeadly, George	1-0	Stephens, Charles	0-1
Mountain		Mrs. Hall	
Shaffer, John	1-0	Smith, Dick	0-1
Mountain		S. J. C. Moore	
Strange, Parker	0-1	Slow, C. H.	0-1
J. W. Byrd		Berryville	
Swift, Warner	0-1		
J. J. Monroe		Thompson, G. W.	1-0
Shelton, Frank	0-1	Trenary, William	1-0
J. G. Kerfoot		Thorp, Robert	1-0
Spencer, Joseph	0-1	Thompson, W. H.	1-0
W. A. Jackson		Thorp, Jonathan	1-0
Strange, Richard	0-1	Thompson, Bayliss Sr.	1-0
R. S. Bryerly		Thomas, James	1-0
Strange, John	0-1	Thompson & Ogden	1-0
W. C. Kerfoot		Taylor, William	1-0
Strange, Charles	0-1	Taylor, Charles J.	1-0

Clarke County, Virginia Personal Property Tax Lists 1854-1870
1869

Thompson, French	1-0	Dr. Randolph	
Taylor, James L.	1-0		
Tanquery, James W.	1-0	Tocas, George	0-1
Tinsman, Mason	1-0	C. H. Boxwell	
Turner, D. J.	1-0	Tabb, James	0-1
Tavenner, J. W.	1-0	T. E. Gold	
Tumblin, Snowden	1-0	Thorton, Mayberry	0-1
Thomas & Adams	1-0	A. M. Moore	
Thompson, John S.	1-0	Townsend, Anderson	0-1
Thompson, Bayliss Jr.	1-0	J. W. Sowers	
Tucker, Mrs. Eliza	1-0	Thompson, Jim	0-1
Tavenner, F. T.	2-0	Kitchen	
Tapscott, Robert	1-0	Thompson, Tasco	0-1
Tapscott & Sister,		Joshua Carters farm	
J. B. & H. C.	2-0	Thompson, Fielding	0-0
Thompson, W. F.	1-0	Philip Berlin	
Trussell, Charles	1-0	Thompson, Baylis	0-0
Tinsman, Ludwell	1-0	Riely & Adams	
Tally, Isaac	1-0	Thornly, Cyrus	0-1
Thompson, A. F.	1-0	C. Erb	
Tyson, Jesse	0-0	Taylor, David	0-1
Baltimore		R. O. Allen	
Tyson Mining & Co.	0-0	Thugmorton [sic] James	0-1
Baltimore		R. O. Allen	
Tanssell, S. J.	1-0	Taylor, David	0-1
Taylor, B. C.	1-0	E. Allen	
Taylor, John H.	1-0	Taylor, John	0-1
Thomas, Mack	0-1	J. Fletcher	
Thompson,		Taylor, Guy	0-1
Mrs. Catharine M.	0-0	J. Fletcher	
Thompson, Magnus S.	1-0	Taylor, Marshall	0-1
Tally, James	1-0	Bethel	
Tumblin, James W.	1-0	Taylor, Jim	0-1
Tumblin, John	1-0	Col. B. Morgan	
Turly, Robert	1-0	Tracy, William	0-1
W. B. C. Sowers		J. Alexander	
Taylor, John	1-0	Thompson, John	0-1
W. C. Kennerly		M. Guishelman	
Tally & Son, John	1-0	Thompson N.	0-1

Clarke County, Virginia Personal Property Tax Lists 1854-1870
1869

M. Guishelman			Wiard, John S.	2-0
			Willingham, Jacob	1-0
Vandeventer, C.	1-0		Wiley, Fenton	1-0
Vandeventer, James H.	1-0		Wright, Jesse	1-0
Vorous, Jacob B.	3-0		Willingham, C. L.	1-0
Vanmeter, J. L. E.	1-0		Wyman, S. G.	1-0
Valantine, Thomas	0-0		Wilt, Henry	1-0
Mrs. Burchel			Whittington, Louis	1-0
Verdy, Robert	0-0		Willingham, Obed	1-0
Jos McK Kennerly			Wilson, Walker B.	1-0
Wyndham, S. B.	2-0		Whittington, Daniel	1-0
Willingham, James W.	1-0		Whittington, John W.	1-0
Willingham, William	1-0		Whittington, Richard	1-0
Wiley, G. W.	1-0		Writt, G. W.	1-0
Whiting, W. W.	1-0		A C. Marshall	
Wharton, W. T.	1-0		Wiley, Moses	1-0
Whiting, Mrs.N. B.	1-0		J. W. Wiley	
Ware, Col. J. W.	1-0		Woodward, John	1-0
Weir, James V.	2-0		W. C. Kennerly	
Ware, J. S.	1-0		Wood, W. T.	1-0
Whittington, C. L.	1-0		John Lloyd	
Wiley, James W.	1-0		White, Edward	1-0
Whiting, F. H.	1-0		Berryville	
Whiting, George	1-0		Wiley, James	1-0
Whiting, Mrs. M. C.	1-0		Mountain	
Wheat, F. W.	1-0		Wyndham, George	0-0
Williams B. & H.	2-0		Berryville	
Wade, Daniel	1-0		Wyndham, John W.	0-0
Williams, E. P.	1-0		Berryville	
Winton, A. J.	1-0		Wade, Robert D.	0-0
Wallenbeck, Reuben	1-0		Wadeville [sic]	
Willingham, G. F.	1-0		Waldron, Francis	1-0
Wilson, Jeremiah	1-0		Berryville	
Whiting, W. H.	1-0		White, James A.	1-0
Wilson, B. F.	1-0		Wadesville	
Wood, Alexander	1-0		Welsh, John	1-0
Wyndham, Y. O.	1-0		J. H. Kirby	
Wright, John D.	1-0		Wisemiller, George A.	0-0
Williams, Allen	2-2		W. A. Riely	

Clarke County, Virginia Personal Property Tax Lists 1854-1870
1869

White, John	1-0	A. Cornwell	
Frank McCormick			
Wammus [?], John	1-0	Williams, Henry	0-1
John Lewis		J. Alexander	
Wood, W. D.	1-0	Webb, Isaac	0-1
Berryville		Millwood	
Wood, James	0-0	Webb, Tom	0-1
Millwood		Millwood	
Webb, Joseph	0-1	Williams, James	0-1
C. Smith		M. Guishelman	
Williams, Nat	0-1	White, William	0-1
Mountain		P. McCormick	
Wood, Nicholas	0-1	Williams, James E.	0-1
O. R. Funston		Joel Lupton	
Williams, Sidney	0-1	Webb, Henry	0-1
J. H. Bartlett		C. Smith	
Williams, William	0-1	Wilson, Taylor	0-1
Berryville		C. Smith	
White, Marcus	0-1	Williams, George	0-1
J. G. Kerfoot		W. N. Nelson	
Willis, Sandy	0-1	Williams, Levi	0-1
Samuel Ridgly		C. Erb	
Williams, George	0-1	Williams, Robert	0-1
Samuel Ridgly		Berryville	
Williams, Edward	0-1	Wilson, Joseph	0-1
R. S. Adams		Mann R. Page	
Wedlock, David	0-0	Wheeler, Edward	0-1
M. R. Feehrer		R. O. Allen	
Walker, John	0-1	Wheeler, James	0-1
Bethel		R. O. Allen	
Wedlock, David	0-1	Williams, Louis	0-1
Stone Bridge		Wm A. Larue	
Webb, Frank	0-0	Warnock, Craven	0-1
R. S. Brierly [sic]		Wm D. Smith	
Walker, Frank	0-1	Walker, Jackson	0-1
Mrs. Shumate		Wm D. Smith	
Washington, George	0-0	White, Tom	0-1
James Cross		Glebe House	
Wormly, William	0-1	Williams, John	0-1

Clarke County, Virginia Personal Property Tax Lists 1854-1870
1869

W. P. Briggs		Williams, Paul	0-1
Williams, Sol	0-1	Young, William H.	1-0
W. P. Briggs		Yowell, Simon	2-0
Walker, Frank	0-1	Young, William A.	1-0
J. F. Chrismore		Young, Alfred	0-1
Williams, James	0-1	Audley	
W. H. Robinson		Young, Isaac	0-1
Williams, Ned	0-1	A. Castleman	
J. F. Burchell		Young, Webb	0-1
Wright, Monroe	0-1	Berryville	
J. F. Burchell		Young, Moses	0-1
Williams, John	0-1	Berryville	
Carter Hall			

Abstract of Errors in Property Book of Clarke County, Virginia
John D. Wright, Commr.

[Eight men were overcharged, eight were undercharged]

Belt, George W.
Briggs, Wm P.
Burwell, Geo H.
Bolen, Geo W.
Conway & Bro., Michael
Furr, William
Hall, Mrs. C. V.
Jones, Rev. Jos R.

Littleton, Wm
Phillips, G. E. S.
Reardon, Patrick
Stribling, Mrs. S. E. T.
Sowers, J. W.
Sowers, Daniel W.
Sowers, Daniel H.
Tapscott, Robert

Clarke County, Virginia Personal Property Tax Lists 1854-1870

1870

Columns: 1) White males over 21, 2) Colored males above the age of 21, 3) Horses, mules etc.
There is no separate *column* for locations & employers this year. Their names are either on the same line, or if too long, follow after the taxable man's name on the next line on the original list. Both styles for employer or place of employment will appear below.

Name	Values	Name	Values
Allen, William T.	1-0-4	Alexander, John	0-1-0
Allen, Edgar	1-0-12	Allen, James	1-0-0
Anderson, John H.W		Anderson, Cornelius	0-1-0
of Joe	1-0-2	Allen, A. Sydney	1-0-0
Anderson, Joseph E.	1-0-6	Ambrose, P. H.	1-0-0
Atkins, William B.	1-0-0	Alexander, James F.	1-0-0
Alexander, John	1-2-18	Alison, Newton	1-0-0
Allen, Geo W.	1-1-7	Abram Fairfax	
Alexander, Thomas	1-0-4	at Reg. Annon [?]	0-1-0
Anderson, Mason &			
John	2-1-6	Barr, Robert & Samuel	2-0-2
Anderson, John W.		Bush, William A.	1-1-3
of Nim	1-0-2	Briggs, Arthur	1-0-3
Ashby, Geo at Mr. Adams	1-0-0	Briggs, William	1-0-3
Albert, Chas		Briggs, Robert W.	1-0-6
at W. H. Whiting's	0-1-0	Briggs, James C.	1-1-4
Addison, Elijah		Beemer, John W.	1-0-5
at J. D. Richardson's	0-1-0	Bromley, John	1-1-11
Aaron at Thomas Carters	0-1-0	Bradford, Philip S.	2-0-4
Allen, R. Owen	1-0-7	Barnett, Neill	2-0-10
Annan, Robert P.	1-0-0	Bruce, James D.	1-0-5
Arnett, W. W.	1-0-0	Bryarly, Richard S.	1-0-6
Anderson, George		Blakemore, George C.	1-0-7
at Albert Elsea's	1-0-0	Bitzer, James H.	1-0-9
Ashley, John R.	1-0-0	Berlin, Sarah	0-1-4
Ashby, Nimrod	1-0-1	Burch, Hilary	2-0-3
Anderson, George W.	1-0-0	Burwell, Nathaniel	1-0-8
Albert at Mr. Browns	0-1-0	Billmire, Wm G.	1-0-5
Alban, James	1-0-0	Beavers, Abraham	1-0-1

Clarke County, Virginia Personal Property Tax Lists 1854-1870
1870

Brady, Patrick	2-0-1	Barber, Michael	
Bennett, Joshua G.	1-0-0	at W. H. Whitings	0-1-0
Bush, Chas A.	1-0-2	Berkley, Isaac at Millwood	0-1-1
Blake, Charles	1-0-0	Brown, George	
Burwell, Chas H.	1-1-1	at Geo Gordon's	0-1-0
Baker, Mrs. Alexander	1-0-1	Bird, James at R. H. Lee's	0-1-0
Berlin, George W.	1-0-0	Bray, James at Pagebrook	0-1-0
Bromley, Samuel	1-0-0	Banks, James	
Brown, Jessee	1-0-0	at F. Burchells	0-1-0
Bell, Geo H.	1-0-2	Banks, Chas	
Barr, Herod H. Dun [sic]	1-0-2	at F. Burchells	0-1-0
Brown, William S.	1-0-0	Brandy, Henry	
Burchell, Foster	1-0-9	at Berryville	0-1-0
Benn, Mrs. Ann C.	0-0-0	Brown, Thomas	
Buckner, John	1-0-0	at Capt. Nelson's	0-1-0
Bishop, Alfred	1-0-0	Brown, William	
Baltimore, Samuel	0-1-0	at Rev. J. Jones	0-1-2
Benn, Chas C.	1-0-0	Brabham, Chas H.	1-0-0
Berlin, A. P.	1-0-0	Brabham, Henry	1-0-0
Buckner, John P.		Brown, Samuel	1-0-0
at Bethel	1-0-0	Bell, James	1-0-3
Blum, Ernest	1-0-0	Brackett, Mrs. Francis	1-0-2
Burch, W. K. at H. Burch's	1-0-0	Beason, Richard	1-0-2
Bell, Isaac at Berryville	0-1-0	Barton, Zachariah	1-0-0
Brooks, Jacob		Bell, Geo W.	1-0-3
at Randolph's	0-1-0	Bayles, Charles	1-0-0
Brown, Robert		Bowling, George W	2-0-0
at J. Doran's	0-1-0	Brown, William	1-0-0
Brown, James		Bartlett, James H.	1-0-6
at Maj. B. Randolphs	0-1-0	Benn, James H.	1-0-0
Blair, George		Brown, Wm H.	1-0-3
at Dr. Wm. McGuire's	0-1-0	Butler, James	0-1-0
Brooks, William		Branham, Jack	0-1-0
at D. Meade's Jr.	0-1-0	Bromley, Jackson	
Ball, Alfred		at M. Wileys	0-1-0
at B. Longerbeam	0-1-1	Butler, Charles	
Barber, Jack at W. Post	0-1-0	at J. Marshalls	0-1-0
Bell, Ben		Bonham, J. E.	1-0-0
at W. H. Whitings	0-1-0	Blake, John	1-0-0

Clarke County, Virginia Personal Property Tax Lists 1854-1870
1870

Ball, A. M.	1-0-0		Barr, Stephen J.	1-0-0
Blackburn, Bushrod	0-1-0		Barry, Henry at Kimball	1-0-0
Banister, Beverly	0-1-0		Bowser, Christian	1-0-0
Banister, William	0-1-0		Brenner [?], Alfred	
Burns, Horace			at Berryville	0-1-0
at D. Snyders	0-1-0		Brown, Spotswood	
Banister, Thomas	0-1-0		at C. Vandeventers	0-1-0
Brown, Thomas E			Beck, Wilson	
at C. Erbs	1-0-0		at L. Scanlands	0-1-0
Burchell, Mrs. Margaret	0-0-2		Bennett, Walter L.	1-0-0
Bell, William T.	1-0-0		Briggs, Henry C.	1-0-4
Blackburn, Emanuel			Burwell, George H.	2-0-14
at Berryville	0-1-0		Brunty, J. H.	1-0-3
Blackburn, Thomas N.			Blackburn, Mrs. S. A. E.	0-0-1
at Berryville	0-1-0		Boyce, W. L. & Wright	2-0-13
Brown, Alfred,			Berlin, Lewis	1-0-1
Battletown	0-1-0		Boson, Carter	
Burwell, William,			at N. L. Boyce's	0-1-0
Battletown	0-1-0			
Blair, Presley, Battletown	0-1-0		Childs, John A.	1-0-6
Bailey, Henry, Battletown	0-1-0		Carter, John B.	1-0-1
Banes, John, Battletown	0-1-0		Copenhaver, Mrs. Sallie	0-2-6
Brown, Albert, Battletown	0-1-0		Cobb, Jacob	1-0-8
Berry, Edmund			Carter, Thomas	1-0-5
at Strothers Farm	0-1-0		Cornwell, Andrew	1-0-8
Bristow, Presley	0-1-0		Cross, A. F.	1-0-6
Brannan, Hugh	1-0-3		Cain, John	2-0-0
Bowman, Isaac	1-0-1		Carpenter, John H.	1-0-0
Burns, Cyrus,			Carter, Mrs. Catherine	0-0-5
Long M. Twp	0-1-0		Carter, Franklin B.	1-0-2
Brown, Tarlton			Cook, Edward	
at Berryville	0-1-0		(Long M. Twp)	0-1-0
Bowman, Thomas,			Carter, John A.	2-0-6
L. M. Twp	0-1-0		Criner, John	1-0-0
Braxton, Matthew,			Castleman, James R.	1-0-4
L. M. Twp	0-1-0		Castleman, Mann R. P.	1-1-3
Broges, John, L. M. Twp	0-1-0		Castleman, Alfred	2-1-0
Bradshaw, Dick	0-1-0		Castleman, Robert H.	1-0-4
Barr, Adam	1-0-0		Chrismore, John F.	1-0-8

Clarke County, Virginia Personal Property Tax Lists 1854-1870
1870

Carter, Mrs. Emily S.	0-0-0	Corder, Parkenson	1-0-2
Cattlette, Miss Miriam	2-1-6	Cirtwell, Walter	1-0-2
Chrismore, Jefferson	1-0-2	Cook, Mrs. Ann B.	1-0-1
Chrismore, G. W.	1-0-5	Cook, N. B.	1-0-5
Crockwell, John R.	1-0-0	Colston, Jacob	0-1-0
Clark, Prince A.	1-0-5	Castleman, George	
Cockey, Thomas D.	2-0-8	at Thos Burchells	1-0-0
Clingan, McLane	1-0-3	Castleman, Wm A.	1-0-0
Copenhaver, Mrs. Mary R.	0-0-0	Carpenter, Joseph	1-0-0
Castleman, Chas M.	1-0-7	Cornwall at P. Meades	1-0-0
Copenhaver, George	1-0-2	Cary, Harry at D. Kerfoots	0-1-0
Chamblin, James E.	1-0-1	Carter, William	
Conway, Michael	1-0-5	at Millwood	0-1-0
Carlyle, John W.	1-0-2	Clayton, William	
Carter, Joseph K.	1-0-4	at Mrs. M. Whiting's	0-1-0
Cooke, John Esten	1-0-2	Clayton, Edward	
Carper, Julia A.	2-0-5	at Mrs. M. Whiting's	0-1-0
Calmes, Miss Lucy A.	2-0-10	Cook, George	
Carper, Hiram	1-0-2	at Mrs. A. B. Cooks	0-1-0
Cooper, Harrison	2-0-2	Colston, William	
Connay, Timothy	1-0-7	at O'Rears	0-1-0
Connay, John	1-0-3	Charley	
Carter, Charles J.	1-0-9	at Maj. Richardson	0-1-0
Carter, James L.	1-0-2	Carter, William at Bethel	0-1-0
Coffman, Erasmus	1-0-0	Cook, Frederick	
Chilcot, Aaron	2-0-1	at F. Stines	0-1-0
Cooper, George	1-0-0	Cooper, Robert	
Collier, John N.	1-0-2	at M. Gant's	0-1-0
Carter, John W.	1-0-1	Carlisle, Albert	
Chapel, James M.	3-0-1	at R. H. Lee's	0-1-0
Carroll, Reason	2-0-3	Carter, Saul	
Carroll, John	1-0-1	at T. McCormicks	0-1-0
Carroll, Thomas	1-0-4	Carter, Shoo Phil	
Carver, James W.	1-0-2	at T. Mccormicks	0-1-0
Carter, Grafton	1-0-3	Compton, Peter	
Crampton, Benjamin	1-0-1	at J. Beemers	0-1-0
Cary, Bushrod		Cook, Thomas at F. Stines	0-1-0
at David Kerfoot	0-1-0	Calvert, Dick	
Corder, Elizabeth	0-0-0	at Maj. B. Randolphs	0-1-0

Clarke County, Virginia Personal Property Tax Lists 1854-1870
1870

Calvert, Thomas		Dove, David	
at Millwood	0-1-0	at Jas V. Weiss	1-0-0
Charles		Doran, Matthew	
at M. M. Burchells	0-1-0	at Millwood	1-0-1
Cox, Morgan		Davis, Hugh	
at C. T. Hebbs	0-1-0	at J. Shepherds	1-0-0
Coates, Peter	0-1-0	Deck, George	1-0-1
Carter, George		Duke, Thomas H.	1-0-2
at Berryville	0-1-0	Donovan, John	1-0-1
Colston, Armistead	1-0-8	Drish, Dock	1-0-2
Carter, Tobe at Berryville	0-1-0	Deahl, William	1-0-1
Carter, Daniel		___ Dan ___	
at Berryville	0-1-0	at J. D. Richardsons	0-1-0
Carter, Samuel		Doctor, Michael	0-1-0
(Long M. Township)	0-1-0	Dove, Thomas J.	1-0-2
Clark, Tucker		Dove, John T.	1-0-0
(Long M. Township)	0-1-0	Dangerfield, Sis	
Carter, Fairfax		at Griffiths	0-1-0
(Long M. Township)	0-1-0	Dick at J. McCormicks	0-1-0
Cooper, Charles		Drish, John	1-0-2
(Long M. Township)	0-1-0	__Davy __ at A. S. Allen's	0-1-0
Clark, James H.	1-0-0	Danks, James	
Cloud, Miss Sallie	1-0-0	at Fos. Burchells	0-1-0
Cain, Isaac W.	1-0-2	Duman, Robert	0-1-0
Crow, John T.	1-0-6	Doleman, Jacob at Clifton	0-1-2
Crow, Mrs. Thomas H.	0-0-1	Doleman, Daniel	
Carter, Capt. Wm P.	1-0-4	at Clifton	0-1-0
Craigbill, John L. [erased]	1-0-1	Duble, Aaron	1-0-8
		Dewer, Joshua J.	1-0-5
Doran, James W.	1-0-0	Dearmont, Thomas	1-0-14
Doran, F. B.	1-0-1	Dearmont, Washington	1-0-1
Dunn, Robert	1-0-0	Davis, Miss Lucy L.	0-0-0
Deahl, Horace P.	1-0-0		
Dorsey, James P.	1-0-4	Evans, Mary E.	0-0-2
Dearmont, Peter	1-0-6	Everhart, Jacob W.	1-0-1
Dicks, John M.	1-0-2	Everhart, William &	
Dulaney, Richard H.	1-0-5	James B.	2-0-7
Denny, Robert L.	1-0-7	Everhart, T. A.	1-0-4
Dumphrey & Spillman	2-0-2	Elliott, Christopher	1-0-3

215

Clarke County, Virginia Personal Property Tax Lists 1854-1870
1870

Edwards, Henry	1-0-4	Furr, James	1-0-0
Eddy, Thomas N.	1-0-1	Furgeson, Washington	1-0-0
Elsea, Albert	1-0-10	Fletcher, Louis	2-0-4
Estep, Dilmon	2-0-1	Furgeson, Abner	1-0-2
Erb, Christopher	1-0-7	Falk, John	1-0-0
Elwell, John M.	2-0-1	Feltner, Geo	2-0-0
Edwards, Joseph W.	1-0-2	Fugitt, Jeremiah	1-0-0
Edwards Benjamin F.	1-0-0	Furr, William	1-0-1
Elsey, Edmund	0-1-0	Fidler, Israel	1-0-4
Ellett, Benj		Freeman, James T.	
at Allen Williams	0-1-0	at Gibsons	1-0-0
Edwards, Pomme		Freeman, Garrett C.	
Greenway Twp	0-1-0	at Gibsons	1-0-0
Everett, George R.	1-0-0	Fuller, Geo H.	
Epps, John		at Benj. Longerbeans	1-0-0
at G. S. Philips	1-0-0	Fidler, Samuel	1-0-0
Evans, O. P.	1-0-0	Fidler, Custins [?]	1-0-0
		French, Peter	
Forster, James A.	1-1-7	at Maj. Calmes	0-1-0
Feehrer, Marcus R.	1-0-6	Fields, George	
Ford, John H.	1-0-1	at Berryville	0-1-0
Finnell, Alexander	1-0-2	Fields, Adam	
Fogg, Elias W.	1-0-0	at Berryville	0-1-0
Fennell, Jessee	1-0-0	Fox, Paton at C. Erbs	0-1-0
Flagg, Thomas G.	1-0-0	Franklin, Frank	
Fletcher, Isaac	1-1-9	at H. A. Larues	0-1-0
Fidler, Hiram K.	1-0-0	Fenton, Dennis	1-0-9
Fellows, Joshua G.	1-0-2	Fryer, M. B.	2-0-1
Fry, Joseph D.	2-0-8	Fields, Aaron	0-1-0
Fishpaw, E. L.	1-0-4	Fractious, Davy	0-1-0
Fillingane, Wm F.	1-0-0		
Fowler, Thomas	1-0-3	Grigsby, William H.	1-0-1
Fowler, Everett	1-0-0	Greene, Israel	1-1-4
Fowler, William	1-0-2	Glass, Lewis F. trustee for	
Fleming, Mrs. Louisa	1-0-3	Mrs. S. M. Isler	0-0-1
Frissell, Charles	1-0-6	Grubb, Walter B.	2-0-4
Fleming, Thomas W.	1-0-3	Green, John A.	1-0-6
Fleming, Mrs. Sarah A.	0-0-3	Grubbs, William B.	1-0-1
Feltner, Martin	1-0-3	Gaunt, Martin	1-1-11

Clarke County, Virginia Personal Property Tax Lists 1854-1870
1870

Grove, F. T.	2-0-0	Gibson, George	
Grant, John L.	1-0-4	at Pagebrook	0-1-0
Galloway, Mason	1-0-1	Greene, Henry	
Gorrell [?] Joseph C.	1-1-2	at Berryville	0-1-0
Gold, Thomas D.	3-0-14	Greene, Ned	
Gordon, George H.	1-1-13	at Millwood	0-1-0
Galloway, Charles	1-0-1	Goshen, J. B. at Thomas	1-0-0
Grubbs, James	1-1-4	Galloway, James	
Glover, Brazier	1-0-2	at Tom Carters	1-0-0
Gearing, William	1-0-0	Garthright, T. J.	1-0-0
Gearing, Franklin	2-0-5	Griffith, J. T.	1-0-0
Gibson, John M.	2-1-13	Gordon, George M.	1-0-0
Gilkerson, James	1-1-4	Gibson, Thomas	0-1-0
Gruber, John	1-0-7	Glass, Lewis F.	2-0-9
Gaunt, Stephen J.	1-0-0	Glass, George	1-0-0
Gardner, George	1-0-3	Grantham, Joseph	2-0-10
Griffy, William	1-0-0	Glover, T. K.	2-0-10
Greene, Richard M.	2-0-5	Grubbs, Geo W.	1-0-2
Grubbs, Samuel	3-0-0	___ George ___	
Garrett, Hamilton	1-0-0	at Lewis Glass's	0-1-0
Greene, James	1-0-3		
Gardner, Joseph	1-0-0	Hawthorn, John B.	1-0-5
Grubb, James	1-0-1	Huyett, Henry	1-0-11
Grady, Edward	1-0-2	Houptman, John	1-0-6
Glassner, George	1-0-3	Hardesty, Adrian	1-2-5
Gray, Zebedee	1-0-0	Hibbard, John W.	1-0-1
Gray, Warner T.	1-0-0	Harrison, Henry	1-0-10
Guiselman, Michael	1-0-0	Hook, W. W.	3-0-5
Grubb, Chas & John W.	2-0-3	Hammer, James W.	1-0-1
Grubbs, Jack	1-0-0	Harrison, Mrs. Edward	0-0-0
Greenwall, Adam	1-0-2	Hardesty, W. G.	1-0-4
Greene, E. Mason	1-0-0	Hardesty, Joseph R.	1-0-8
Gordon, David		Hughes, John	2-0-2
at J. N. Kitchens	0-1-0	Hesser, Mason	2-0-4
Gumby, James		Haycock, James W.	1-0-7
at Millwood	0-1-0	Heflebower, Mary	1-1-5
Grigsby, Jackson		Henry, John C.	1-0-0
at Stone Bridge	0-1-0	Hebb, E. T.	1-1-9
		Harris, Wm B.	2-0-7

Clarke County, Virginia Personal Property Tax Lists 1854-1870
1870

Haddix, Appheus	1-0-6	Hall, Wesley	0-1-0
Hawks, Cornelius	1-0-0	Harris, James	
Hardesty, Charles	1-0-4	at H. H. Dunbars	0-1-0
Harrison, Dr. Benjamin	1-0-9	Harris, Moan	0-1-0
Hoge, Louis N.	1-0-6	Hall, William	
Helvestine, Lewis B.	1-1-10	at P. McPierce's	0-1-4
Hardesty, Joseph M.	1-0-8	Harrison, Reason	
Hinton, Wm. H.	1-0-6	at E. T. Hebbs	0-1-2
Hiskett, Thomas W.	1-0-0	Harris, Lorenzo	
Hansucker, Philip	1-0-6	at Berryville	0-1-0
Hardesty, C. R.	1-0-3	Hubbard, Bennett	
Helvestine, W. R.	1-0-0	at Capt. Nelsons	0-1-0
Hough, John	1-0-0	Hall, Robert	
Hummer, John Mason	2-0-7	at Berryville	0-1-1
Humphrey, Thomas L.	1-0-3	Harris, William	
Horseman, William	1-0-1	at Dr. Randolphs	0-1-0
Hoff, Cornelius	1-0-0	Howard, Walter	
Heflin, William	2-0-0	at Dr. Randolphs	0-1-1
Hunter, Sawney		Holmes, Solomon	
at White Post	0-1-2	at Millwood	0-0-0
Hughes, John		Hansucker, George	1-0-5
at D. J. Kerfoot's	1-0-0	Holmes, Briscoe	0-1-0
Hughes Thomas		Holtsclaw, Thomas J.	1-0-0
at R. S. Adams'	1-0-0	Hannam, Preston	1-0-0
Hannam, Robert		Hardesty, John	
at P. M. Pierce's	1-0-0	at G. W. Sowers	1-0-0
Hesson, Seno at C. Erb's	1-0-0	Hardesty, R. D. at Griffith	1-0-0
Herbert, Archie		Hummer, ~~John~~ Robert	1-0-0
at Marshalls	0-1-0	Howell, James F.	1-0-0
Hubbard, Adam		Hall, John W.	1-0-0
at Millwood	0-1-1	Harris, Henry	
Harrison, Lewis		at Dr. Stephenson	0-1-0
at J. D. Richardson	0-1-0	Hammond, Miss Hattie	0-0-0
Hickman, John		Hansford, Miss A. J.	0-0-2
at J. D. Richardson	0-1-2	Hummer, Sandy	1-0-0
Helm, George		Hennis, Chas F.	1-0-0
at Guiselman's	0-1-0	Harris, George	
Helm, Stephey		at Berryville	0-1-0
at Guiselman's	0-1-0	Hamilton, James	1-0-0

Clarke County, Virginia Personal Property Tax Lists 1854-1870
1870

Hargrove [?], Beverly		Jenkins, David	
at T. F. Martins	0-1-0	at Millwood	1-0-0
Hutcheson, Jacob		Johnson, Richard	
at G. C. Blakemore's	0-1-0	at Wm Meades	0-1-0
Holland, John W.	1-0-0	Jackson, Davy at H. Bank's	0-1-0
Hart, Mrs. Thomas	0-0-3	John at Neill Barnetts	0-1-0
Harrison at J. T. Crows	0-1-0	Jones, George	
Harris, Dan		at Champ Shepherds	0-1-0
at U. L. Boyers	0-1-0	Jones, Burr	
		at Champ Shepherds	0-1-0
Irwin, Marcus B.	1-0-0	Jackson, Jacob	
Isler, Geo. H.	1-0-0	at Berryville	0-1-0
Iverson, Savory		Jackson, Anderson	
at Millwood	0-1-1	at Burwell's	0-1-0
		Jenkins, Presley	
Jones, Leonard	1-0-3	at D. Fentons	0-1-0
Jones, Chas T.	1-0-2	Johnson, Chas	
Jones, James W.	1-0-0	at M. Thompson's	0-1-0
Jones, Thomas	1-0-4	Jackson, Wm	
Jennings, Jarvis	1-1-8	at B. C. Taylor's	0-1-0
Jackson, Demps	1-0-1	Jackson, Charles	
Jolliffe, John M.	1-0-2	at Dr. Randolph's	0-1-0
Jackson, Alfred C.	1-0-7	Jackson, William	
Jones, Alfred	1-0-1	at Col. Larue's	0-1-0
Jenkins, Eben	2-0-1	Joe at Wormley's	
Jenkins, Jessee	1-0-2	near Chapel	0-1-0
Jenkins, Thomas	1-0-3	Jackson, George	0-1-0
Johnson, Benj F.	2-0-1	Johnston, Samuel	
Johnson, James W.	1-0-1	at Wadesville	0-1-0
Johnston, Franklin L.	1-0-0	Jackson, Robert	
Jackson, William		at R. P. Annans	0-1-0
at O'Rear's	0-1-0	Jefferson, Henry	0-1-0
Jenkins, Edward	1-0-1	James, John	0-1-0
Jenkins, Harry	1-0-2	Johnston, Daniel	0-1-0
Jenkins, Herrod	1-0-2	Jones, Rev. Jos K.	1-0-6
Jones, Matthew W.	1-0-2	Johnston, James W.	1-0-2
Jackson, David at W. Post	0-1-0	Jackson Rev. William A.	0-1-0
Johnson, John		Jefferson, Harry	0-2-0
at Millwood	0-1-0	Johnson, Aaron	0-1-0

Clarke County, Virginia Personal Property Tax Lists 1854-1870
1870

Jolliffe, William B.	1-0-0	Killer, Geo H.	1-0-0
Johnson, Jackson	0-1-0	Kercheval, E. V.	1-0-1
Jamisson, Charles		Kromling, Henry	1-0-0
at U. L. Boyce's	0-1-0	Keeler, Joseph W.	1-0-0
Jackson, David	1-0-3	Kownslar, Mrs. E. S.	0-0-6
		Koonce, Geo W.	1-0-1
Kerfoot, Dr. F. J.	1-0-4	Kiner, James M.	1-0-2
Kennon, William B.	1-0-0	Kerns, David	1-0-0
Knight, William	1-1-4		
Kerfoot, A. J.	1-0-0	Larue, Col. John B.	2-0-12
Kerfoot, William T.	2-1-5	Lippitt, Mary F.	0-0-3
Kitchen. Charles	1-0-2	Lewis, H. L. D.	1-0-5
Kerfoot, James F.	1-2-6	Larue, A. L. P.	1-0-3
Kerfoot, Wm C.	1-0-7	Louthan, John	1-0-0
Kern, Thomas H.	1-0-4	Lock, John Sr.	1-0-7
Keeler, Charles H.	2-0-0	Levi, Rice W. [?]	3-0-10
Kerfoot, F. J., Trustee		Levi, G. W.	1-0-2
for Mrs. Adams	2-0-7	Louthan, James T.	1-0-1
Kennerly, William C.	2-0-5	Lock, Josiah	1-0-12
Kerfoot, David T.	1-1-7	Light, Peter	1-0-4
Kerfoot, Judson G.	1-0-7	Lancaster, Milton M.	1-0-0
Kimmell, John N.	1-0-2	Larue, James W.	2-0-7
Kneller, Samuel G.	1-0-2	Lewis, Dr. Thomas M.	1-0-1
Kneller, Thomas G.	1-0-2	Levi, Wm H.	1-0-1
Kitchen, John N.	1-0-11	Longerbean, Benjamin	2-1-7
Kennerly, Joseph McK.	1-1-5	Lanham, T. B.	1-0-0
Knight, Daniel M.	1-0-0	Larue, C. C.	1-0-1
Kearn, Lewis	1-0-3	Lee, Richard H.	1-0-5
Keys, William	1-0-4	Little, Clinton L.	1-0-12
Kiger, William J.	1-0-1	Lewis, James W. T.	1-0-2
Kendall, Charles	1-0-1	Lawyer, James A.	1-0-3
Knight, Henry	1-0-2	Lewis, Washington	1-0-5
Kennon, James H.	1-0-1	Lupton, Joel	2-0-10
Kirby, Joseph H.	1-0-0	Laws, Joel N. Bro & Co.	2-0-0
Kitchen, George		Laws, E. T. & Son	0-0-4
at J. N. Kitchens	1-0-0	Louthan, John K.	1-0-3
Kiger, William		Lee, Charles S.	1-0-5
at Jesse Russells	1-0-0	Lee, William D.	2-0-2
Kline, Henry at Lancaster	1-0-0	Liady, A. G.	1-0-0

Clarke County, Virginia Personal Property Tax Lists 1854-1870
1870

Larue, W. G.	1-0-0	Laupkin, Benj	
Lupton, John L.	1-0-0	at J. S. Mitchell	0-1-0
Longerbean, Abraham	1-0-2	Luets, Thomas	
Lloyd, James W.	1-0-0	at M. H. Fehrer's	0-1-0
Lloyd, Benjamin	1-0-0	Lovett, Wilson	
Lewis, Mrs. E. M.	0-0-1	at Springsbury	0-1-0
Lancaster, John F.	1-0-0	Lee, Ike at F. Lock's	0-1-0
Louthan, Carter M.	1-0-1	Loews, Thomas	
Lee, Mrs. Henrietta	0-0-0	at Mrs. Kounslars	0-1-0
Lock, Franklin H.	1-0-6	Lightfoot, Lewis	
Luin [sic] Moses	2-0-1	at Berryville	0-1-0
Lupton, Silas	1-0-2	Laws, Raphael at W. Post	0-1-0
Lawson, Charles	1-0-2	Lockland, Sam	
Littleton, William	1-0-2	at M. R. Pages	0-1-0
Littleton, B. F.	1-0-4	Ligons, Charley	
Lee, Squire	1-0-2	at F. Burchells	0-1-0
Lee, John	1-0-2	Lewis, Jerry at Berryville	0-1-0
Lloyd, Charles H.	1-0-1	Lippitt, Dr. C. E.	1-0-1
Lloyd, John	1-0-2	Lippitt, Armistead S.	1-0-0
Lanham, Samuel	1-0-0	Lakey, A. P.	1-0-0
Lanham, William	1-0-2	Lake, Edward	1-0-0
Lee, Ludwell	1-0-1	Luke, John W.	2-1-11
Lanham, Thomas B.	1-0-0	Lewis, Jackson	
Lloyd, Henry	2-0-2	at G. H. Sowers	0-1-0
Lannum, James	2-0-1	Lewis, Col. John R. C.	2-1-3
Lloyd, John A.	1-0-2	Lewis, Frank at Berryville	0-1-0
Lennon [?], George	1-0-0		
Lloyd, John W.	1-0-2	McGuire, David H.	2-0-2
Lindsay, John	1-0-5	Menefee, Joseph	1-0-1
Lee, James W.	1-0-2	Massey, E. W.	1-0-6
Lindsay, Joseph B.	1-0-1	Meade, David	1-0-7
Lake, Winston	1-0-0	Meade, Mrs. Jane B.	1-0-0
Lewis, Fielding	0-1-1	McCune, John T.	1-0-3
Lewisburg, Malon		Marshall, James L.	1-0-2
at O'Rears	0-1-0	McCauly, John G.	1-0-3
Leuis, Alexander	0-1-0	Mitchell, J. Ship	1-0-2
Lavender, Giles		Meade, William W.	1-0-2
at M. Catletts	0-1-0	Morris, John G.	1-0-5
		McGuire, Mary W.	0-2-0

Clarke County, Virginia Personal Property Tax Lists 1854-1870
1870

Marshall, Alexander	1-0-7	Moore, Sylvanus	1-0-1
McDonald, Angus	2-0-6	McGuire, Dr. Wm D.	1-0-14
Meade, David Jr.	1-1-0	McCormick, Dr. Cyrus	1-0-7
McCormick, Ottoway	3-0-6	McAtee, W. A.	1-0-3
McCormick, John	1-0-3	Morgan, Wm C.	1-0-3
McCormick, Province Sr.	1-0-4	Myers, Abraham	1-0-0
McCormick, Frank	2-0-18	McCleary, John	2-0-2
Moulden [?], Chas E.	1-0-0	Mason, Henry W.	1-0-1
Moore, A. M. S.	1-0-11	Miley, Moses	1-0-2
McIntyre, C. C.	1-1-5	Morris, Wm. G.	1-0-1
Myers, Geo W.	1-0-0	Murphy, James T.	2-0-2
Monroe, Albert M.	1-0-4	Moore, A. Mason	3-0-6
Milton, William T.	1-0-4	Marshall, John	1-0-9
McCormick, Province Jr. & Sr.	0-0-1	Marshall, James P.	1-0-0
McCormick, Province Jr.	1-2-6	Marston, Nat at Millwood	0-1-0
Marshall, Alfred C.	2-1-5	McIntree, John	0-1-1
Marks, Henry at Mrs. Islers	0-1-1	Miles, Charles at D. H. McGuire	0-1-0
Miles, Amos D.	1-0-1	Minor, James M. at Berryville	0-1-0
Marlow, E.	1-0-3	Mitchell, London	0-1-0
McCauly, Robert	1-0-1	Massey, David	0-1-0
McPierce, Peter	2-0-7	Mills, John at Berryville	0-1-0
Mason, J. C.	1-0-2	Myers [?] Bartlett	0-1-0
McCormick, Thomas	1-0-7	Moore, Lee at Mrs. M. C. Whitings	0-1-0
Martin, Rev. T. F.	1-0-1	Martin, Randall at Page Brook	0-1-0
Morgan, John Jr.	1-0-6	Martin, Glasco at Page Brook	0-1-0
McCormick, John A.	1-0-1	Mitchell, Sam at T. E. Golds	0-1-0
McCormick, James	1-0-7	McCard, Joseph at Col. Smith	0-1-0
McCard, Richard	0-1-6	Mosby, Jonney at Wheat & Glovers	0-1-0
McClellan, James	1-0-0	Mosby, Robert at Thomas' place	0-1-0
Milton, James F. Sr.	3-0-0		
Moore, Ami	1-0-0		
Miller, John at Thomas's	1-0-0		
McNulty, James	1-0-0		
Macebaugh, Wm T.	1-0-0		
Mesmer, Henry J.	1-0-4		
Marple, George F.	2-0-6		
Mason, John M.	1-0-0		

Clarke County, Virginia Personal Property Tax Lists 1854-1870
1870

Mitchell, Isaac		Neill, Dr. S. S.	1-0-2
at Dr. McGuires	0-1-0	Newcombe, James H.	1-0-0
Morallis, J.		Nelson, Alfred	0-1-1
at Wm H. Young	1-0-0	Norris, Harry	
McGuire, D. Holmes	1-0-0	at R. P. Pages	0-1-0
Morgan, John L.	1-0-0	Nelson, Michael	
Moore, Thomas A.	1-0-0	at Berryville	0-1-0
Moore, Eden	1-0-0	Nelson, Jacob	
Moore, S.J. C.	1-0-0	at T. E. Gold's	0-1-0
Marlow, William		Norris, Walker	
at Blakemore's	0-1-0	at J. W. Sprints	0-1-0
Meade, Miss Mary	0-0-0		
Meade, Francis B.	1-0-1	Osbourne, Roland	1-0-0
Meade, Philip C.	1-0-4	Osburn, John	1-0-0
McDonald, Benjamin &		Osburn, Joshua	1-0-0
William	3-0-4	Ogden, Randolph	2-0-0
Marshall, E. C.	1-0-4	O'Rear, Catharine	0-0-1
Manuel, William		O'Rear, Susan	0-0-0
at Granthams	1-0-0	O'Rear, Elizabeth	0-0-5
Marple, Hezekiah	1-0-4	Osburn, Bushrod	0-1-0
Moore, Nicholas	1-0-0	Owen, James	0-1-0
Morgan, John	1-0-1	Owen, Alfred	0-1-0
Morgan Robt P. &		Owens, Alexander	1-0-3
Wm B.	2-0-6	Owens, John S.	1-0-3
Morgan Col. Benjamin	1-0-6	O'Rear, Jessie	2-0-4
McCormick, Mrs. Edward	0-0-17		
Morgan, Col. Benj		Page, John E.	1-0-7
Guar for W. Alexander	0-0-0	Pendleton, Dudley D.	1-0-8
		Page, John	1-0-2
Nelson, Wm. N.	1-0-6	Page, Mann R.	2-0-12
Nunn, John R.	1-0-9	Pendleton, Thornton P.	1-0-0
Nunn, John R.		Powers, Philip	1-1-7
Guardian for W. Carter	0-0-0	Parkins, C. Milton	1-0-1
Neville, James H.	1-0-2	Puller, Bushrod	2-0-0
Nelson, Mrs. A. M. A.	2-2-20	Pierce, A. N.	1-0-6
Neville, Alexander V.	2-0-0	Patterson, James B.	1-0-1
Neff, Hiram A.	1-0-0	Pidgeon, Charles W.	1-0-2
Newcombe, John	1-0-1	Pidgeon, Samuel L.	1-0-9
Nicewanner, Thomas	1-0-0	Potter, Benjamin	0-1-0

Clarke County, Virginia Personal Property Tax Lists 1854-1870
1870

Pope, Michael	1-0-1	Potter, Richard		
Pope, Coonrod [sic]	1-0-1	at Berryville	0-1-0	
Page, R. Powell	1-0-8	Page, Dr. William M.	1-0-5	
Phillips, G. E. S.	1-0-1	Page, Thomas D.	2-0-4	
Pulliam, Matthew	1-0-1			
Pope, John M.	1-0-0	Quinn, Presley		
Popkins, William	1-0-0	at John Morgans	0-1-0	
Poston, John	1-0-0			
Page, Dr. R. P.	1-0-3	Routzong, Ezra	1-0-3	
Peyton, Mrs. Caroline	0-0-0	Randolph, Dr. R. C.	1-0-6	
Pine, Marshall M.	1-0-0	Royston, Peter K.	2-0-4	
Pine, Nathan	1-0-1	Rutter, Geo W.	1-0-0	
Pine, Geo W.	1-0-0	Ryan, James W.	1-0-7	
Price, Joseph	1-0-2	Russell, Thomas	1-0-4	
Patterson, Henry	1-0-0	Riely, Moses	1-0-3	
Pierce, Wm. D.	1-0-2	Russell, John William	2-1-5	
Pierce, John T.	1-0-0	Ritter, Riely H.	2-0-0	
Pipher, William	1-0-2	Russell, Jessee N.	1-0-4	
Pipher, Joseph	1-0-2	Roland, John	3-0-5	
Page, Moses		Riely, John J.	1-0-8	
at Stone Bridge	0-1-0	Robinson, William H.	2-1-8	
Pain, Jacob at J. Grubbs	0-1-1	Russell, John	3-0-4	
Page, Thomas		Russell, William	1-0-2	
at G. W. Lewis'	0-1-1	Russell, Michael	1-0-6	
Porter, Jack at Ragtown	0-1-0	Randolph, Dr. A. C.	1-0-1	
Peterson, Isaac at B.Ville	0-1-0	Richardson, John D.	1-0-16	
Page, Robert		Riely, William A.	1-1-13	
at P. McCormick	0-1-0	Randolph, Eston	1-0-7	
Page, John		Read, Stephen	1-0-1	
at R. Pense Page's	0-1-0	Rippon, John J.	1-0-0	
Phil at R. Pense Page's	0-1-0	Reed, John R.	1-0-1	
Power, Josiah		Reed, Marcus B.	1-0-4	
at C. Vandevanters [?]	0-1-0	Russell, William W.	1-0-2	
Piles, William M.	2-0-2	Romine, Jane	0-0-1	
Patterson, John	1-0-6	Reed, Stanford	1-0-1	
Pope, Franklin	1-0-0	Richmond, Enos	1-0-0	
Pope, West	1-0-0	Riely, J. C.	1-0-0	
Page, Archy	1-0-0	Reynolds, John	1-0-0	
Potter, George	0-1-0	Ryan, Joseph	1-0-1	

Clarke County, Virginia Personal Property Tax Lists 1854-1870
1870

Russell, John W.	1-0-1	Royston, George R.	1-0-0
Reardon, Pat	1-0-0	Royston, Matthew T.	1-0-1
Reily, Cornelius	1-0-0	Russell, George B.	1-0-0
Richards, Daniel B.	1-0-0		
Randolph, Beverly		Smith, Dr. J. P.	1-0-7
Trus For M.C. Randolph	1-0-12	Smith, Robert R.	1-0-2
Royston, M. B.	1-0-3	Steele, John W.	1-0-0
Ricamore, George		Smith, Col. T.	1-0-2
at Thompson & Ogden	1-0-0	Stribling, Mrs. S. E.	1-0-10
Randolph, Frank	0-1-0	Strickler, John S.	1-0-5
Randolph, Harry	0-1-0	Stickle, Henry G.	1-0-2
at Maj. B. Randolph		Smith, Warren C.	1-0-6
Ruffin, Bartlett		Sowers, Geo K.	1-0-6
at J. T. Kerfoot's	0-1-0	Steele, James A.	1-0-2
Rust, William		Smith, William D.	1-1-14
at P. Williams'	0-1-0	Snyder, Daniel C.	1-0-9
Randolph, Henry	0-1-0	Shepherd, Decatur	1-0-1
at R. P. Pages'		Sowers, Daniel H.	1-0-6
Robertson, Ambrose	0-1-0	Shipe, Moses W.	2-0-2
at G. Hansucker		Slusher, Hezekiah	2-0-0
Robertson, Alexander	0-1-0	Steele, Wm. G.	1-0-1
Read, Samuel		Sommerville, Dr. William	1-0-2
at A. Hardesty's	0-1-0	Shipe, Benjamin	1-0-0
Read, James		Sowers, John W.	1-1-15
at A. Hardesty's	0-1-0	Sommerville, Dr. H. C.	1-0-2
Read, Coon at J. Forsters	0-1-0	Stuart, John K.	2-0-9
Robinson, John	0-1-0	Sinclair, J. F.	1-0-2
Robertson, Sam	0-1-2	Starkey, Benjamin	1-0-8
at H. L. D. Lewis's		Sinclair, Marons L.	1-0-1
Ransom, Albert	0-1-0	Smith, George K.	1-0-1
at H. L. D. Lewis's		Seabold, D. D. & Son	2-0-6
Randolph, George	0-1-0	Snyder, Daniel	2-0-11
at Maj. Randolph's		Shepherd, Champ	1-1-5
Read, Nelson	0-1-0	Sillman, Benj F.	2-0-1
Richardson, George	0-1-0	Stine, Frank	1-0-17
Robinson, Anthony	0-1-0	Shumate, Mary E.	1-0-10
Randolph, John	0-1-0	Sowers, William B.	1-0-3
Robinson, Scott	0-1-0	Smith, John S.	1-0-6
Rust, Philip	0-1-0	Stephenson, Dr. James W.	1-1-1

Clarke County, Virginia Personal Property Tax Lists 1854-1870
1870

Sowers, Justin	3-0-10	Shearer, James M.	1-0-1
Shearer, P. H. & Bro.	2-0-0	Swarts, Franklin	1-0-0
Shimp, Mrs. Julia	0-0-1	Swarts, John	1-0-0
Shepherd, Joseph H.	1-0-2	Stump, Robert	1-0-2
Shipe, Andrew J.	1-0-4	Shehan, Dennis	1-0-3
Shearer, Henry T.	1-0-0	Shepherd, Rev. T. B.	1-0-5
Sowers, Robert L.	1-0-3	Scanland, L. A.	1-0-3
Shackleford Mrs. H.	0-0-0	Smith, J. Rice	1-0-1
Shepherd, Carter	1-0-3	Shepherd, George C.	1-0-0
Stolle, Wm F.	1-0-1	Shepherd, Chas C.	1-0-0
Stickels, Joseph	1-0-0	Steele, Albert	
Showers, Samuel	1-0-2	at Jud Kerfoots	1-0-0
Slack, John T.	1-0-0	Shrout, Lewis at M. Popes	1-0-0
Sigafoose, Robert	1-0-0	Smith, William L.	1-0-0
Stickels, Thomas	1-0-0	Stone, Harrison H.	1-0-0
at J. W. Edwards		Shipe, Isaac	1-0-0
Shell, Mrs. Lucinda	0-0-0	Seals, Dennis at J. [?] Weir	0-1-0
Shell, Mountjoy	1-0-1	Stogdell, Andrew	
Stickles, Henry Jr.	1-0-0	at Gorrells'	0-1-0
Spaulding, George S.	1-0-2	Stranger, James	
Sitckler, Henry C.	1-0-2	at Millwood	0-1-0
Stickles, Joseph S.	1-0-1	Strange, John	
Smallwood, Burr	1-0-2	at J. Jennings'	0-1-0
Shaffer, John	1-0-0	Sanders, James	0-1-0
Smallwood, James	1-0-1	at P. McPierce's	
Silman, Peter M.	1-0-1	Strange, Parker	0-1-1
Shipe, William		Strange, William	
at Andersons'	1-0-0	near G. Marple	0-1-0
Silman, Hyram	1-0-1	Slow, Henry at B:Ville	0-1-0
Shipe, ___tby [illegible]	1-0-0	Strother, Jackson	
Shell, Stephen	1-0-0	at Conways	0-1-0
Smedley, George	1-0-0	Stephenson, Bob at B:ville	0-1-0
Snyder, George	1-0-1	Strange, Charles	0-1-1
Snyder, Strauther	1-0-1	at Capt. Nelsons	
Snyder, D.	1-0-0	Smith, William	
Smallwood, Sylvester	1-0-6	at Boxwells	0-1-0
Stickles, Simon P.	1-0-2	Settler, Joseph	
Shaffer, John T.	1-0-2	at D. Jackson	0-1-0
Shaffer, John J.	1-0-2		

Clarke County, Virginia Personal Property Tax Lists 1854-1870
1870

Name		Name	
Smith, Henry		Taylor, John H.	1-0-0
at Thomas Carters	0-1-0	Tinsman, Henry W.	1-0-1
Smith, Harry		Tumberlin, John T.	1-0-0
at R. P. Page's	0-1-0	Thompson, John S.	1-0-0
Simms, Chas	0-1-0	Tinsman, Francis M.	1-0-1
Staples, Bradford	0-1-0	Thompson, Balas	1-0-3
at C. Vandeventers		Tinsman, Ludwell	1-0-0
Scyus [?], Abraham	0-1-0	Tally, John at Haycocks	1-0-0
Sprint, J. W.	1-0-1	Thompson, Magnus	1-0-3
Shackleford, Willie	1-0-0	Thompson,	
Stephney, John	0-1-0	Mrs. Catherine	0-0-0
Smith, James	1-0-0	Thompson, John L.	1-0-0
Strange, Stephen	0-1-0	Thompson, Ogden	0-0-1
Shepherd, Frank R.	1-0-2	Thomas, James W.	1-0-0
Shackleford, Mary L.	0-0-0	Tucker, Mrs. Eliza	0-0-3
Sowers, Geo H.	1-0-4	Thomas, Geo C.	1-0-1
Sowers, John F.	1-0-0	Taylor, James	0-1-0
Shepherd, Parkinson D.	1-0-0	Turner, John at Greens	0-1-0
Smith, E. Jaqueline	1-0-1	Tumberlin, Snowden	1-0-2
Sowers, George W.	1-0-4	Towner, Mrs. Maria	1-0-0
Shepherd, Jos B.	1-0-15	Tapscott, Henry C.	1-0-3
		Tapscott, Joseph B.	1-0-2
Thompson, Balis	1-0-1	Tapscott, Maria L.	0-0-0
Thompson, Adam F.	1-0-5	Tumberlin, James W.	1-0-0
Thompson, French	1-0-3	Talley, Isaac	1-0-0
Tapscott, Robert	3-0-3	Trenary, Robt E.	1-0-0
Tanquary, James W.	1-0-4	Taylor, Griffin	2-0-1
Tavenner, Joseph A.	1-0-3	Turner, Dan at S. S. Mill	1-0-0
Taylor, James L.	1-0-5	Taylor, John B.	1-0-0
Tavenner, Franklin T.	3-0-6	Talley, James	1-0-0
Tyson, Jessee	0-0-9	Townsend, Anderson	
Tyson, Wyman & Co.	0-0-6	at J. W. Sowers	0-1-0
Trenary, John	1-0-2	Taylor, John at Craiglers	0-1-0
Trenary, William	1-0-5	Tyler, Marshall	0-1-0
Thompson, William F.	1-0-1	Turner, Levi	0-1-0
Taylor, William	1-0-17	Tracy, Wm at Locks	0-1-0
Thompson, William H.	1-0-4	Thomas, Harry	
Tharp, Johnathan [sic]	1-0-5	at C. Shepherd's	0-1-0
Taylor, Lindsay	0-1-0	Thornton, Taylor	0-1-0

Clarke County, Virginia Personal Property Tax Lists 1854-1870
1870

Throckmorton, Jim			Williams, Allen	1-0-2
at A. S. Allens	0-1-0		Wiley, George W.	1-0-4
Tabb, James	0-1-0		Whiting, Mrs. Mary B.	1-0-3
Toras, George	0-1-0		Wright, Jessee	1-1-3
Thompson, John	0-1-0		Wallenbeck, Reuben	1-0-2
Thornley, Cyrus	0-1-0		Winton, A. J.	1-0-2
Thornley, Alciada [?]	0-1-0		Willingham, George F.	1-0-0
Taylor, B. C.	1-0-2		Williams, Sydney	0-2-1
Trussell, S. J.	1-0-0		Williams, Nat	
Tharp, Robert	1-0-3		at Maj. Ferguson's	0-1-0
			Williams, George	
Vandeventer, James H.	1-0-1		at Maj. Ferguson's	0-1-0
Vandeventer, C.	1-0-7		Warner, John	1-0-0
Vorous, Jacob	3-1-14		Willson, Walker	1-0-0
Vanmeter, J. L.	1-0-6		Wood, William	1-0-0
			Willson, James A.	1-0-0
Wilson, Abraham	1-0-0		Wigginton, Mrs. Nellie	0-0-0
Wyndham, S. B.	3-0-3		Williams, Edward	
Whiting, Francis H.	1-0-0		at F. Burchells	0-1-0
Whiting, George &			Washington, Mrs. Louisa	0-0-0
Richard H.	0-0-6		Wheat, F. W.	1-0-2
Whiting, Mrs. Mary C.	0-0-4		Wheat, F. W. & Co.	0-0-1
White, Joseph	1-0-0		Wheat & Glover	0-0-0
Wilt, Henry	3-1-8		Whiting, George	1-0-2
Willingham, ____	1-0-2		Williams, James	
Wiley, James W.	2-0-6		at G. Whitings	0-1-1
Whittington, Richard	1-0-4		Willingham, Obedera	1-0-1
Whittington, Chas S.	1-0-1		Wigginton, Jackson	1-0-0
Willingham, John F.	1-0-2		Williams, Lewis	
Whiting, William H.	1-0-13		at Larue's	0-1-0
Willingham, James W.	1-0-2		Wilson, Joe at M. R. Pages	0-1-0
Whittington, Louis	1-0-0		Webb, Henry	0-1-0
Ware, Col. J. W.	1-0-2		Williams, Levi	0-1-1
Williams, E. P.	1-0-1		Wheeler, Jim	
Wharton, William T.	1-0-0		at A. S. Allan's	0-1-0
Weir, Jas V.	2-1-12		Wormley, William	
Wood, Alexander	2-0-3		at Chapel	0-1-0
Willson, Frank	1-0-1		Williams, Sandy	
Williams, Henry A.	1-3-3		at D. Meade's	0-1-0

Clarke County, Virginia Personal Property Tax Lists 1854-1870
1870

Wormley, Philip		Weaver, Sam at B.Ville	0-1-0
at Stone Bridge	0-1-0	Weaver, George	
White, Thomas		at B. Ville	0-1-0
at Wm D. Smiths	0-1-0	Williams, Townsend	
Warric, Craven		at B. Ville	0-1-0
at Wm D. Smiths	0-1-0	Williams, George	
Walter Jackson		at B. Ville	0-1-0
at Wm D. Smiths	0-1-0	White, Williams	
Wyett, John		at P. McCormicks	0-1-0
at Wm Castlemans	0-1-0	Wilson, Taylor	0-1-0
Williams, Geo		Walker, Frank	0-1-0
at E. P. William's	0-1-0	Wheeler, Edward	0-1-0
Ware, Jefferson		Wright, Monroe	0-1-0
at C. R. Hardesty's	0-1-0	Williams, Paul	0-1-0
Walker John Jr.	0-1-0	Welsh, John	1-0-0
Williams, Edmund		Ware, Jaq S.	1-1-7
at Stone Bridge	0-1-0	Wyley, Chas F.	1-0-2
Webb, Isaac at Millwood	0-1-0	Wyndham, T. O.	1-0-6
Walker, Paul at Snyders	0-1-1	Wilson, Jeremiah	1-0-3
Walker, John Sr.	0-1-1	Wiett, George W.	1-0-0
Williams, James	0-1-1	Wade, Daniel	1-0-3
Webb, Joseph	0-1-1	White, Judge Edward	1-0-0
Williams, William		White, Rev. Charles	1-0-0
at B.ville	0-1-1	Waring, William	0-1-0
Wood, Wilson		Whiting, W. W.	1-0-0
at J. Alexander	0-1-0		
Williams, John		Youell, John	1-0-2
at Wm Briggs	0-1-0	Youell, Simeon	1-0-2
Williams, Solomon		Young, William A.	1-0-1
at Wm Briggs	0-1-0	Young, Webb	0-1-2
Wilson, Elsey		Young, Moses	0-1-0
at Maj. Taylors	0-1-0	Young, Alfred at Beamers	0-1-0
Wilson, Billy		Young, Wm H.	1-0-0
at Tom McCormicks	0-1-0		
Willie, Jackson		Zombro, George	2-0-1
at D. Fenton's	0-1-0		

Clarke County, Virginia Personal Property Tax Lists 1854-1870
Index

Index

This index is only for those names that appear out of order in the regular text, and employers; or places of employment.

A

Adams
  Mrs. .153, 175, 197, 220
  R. S...143, 152, 165, 201, 209, 218
  Thomas & 161, 184
  Thos 148
Alexander
  J. 204, 207, 209, 229
  J. W. 101
  John 199
  John & Wm 89
  Miss 62, 89, 101
  W. 223
  Wm 62
Allan's
  A. S. 228
Allen
  A. S...159, 162, 215
  C. 204
  E. 193, 196, 201, 207
  Edgar143, 149, 151, 158, 161, 163, 165, 178, 181
  Edward 173
  R. O.. 143, 165, 185, 207, 209
  W. T. 193, 201, 204, 206
  Wm... 149, 161
  Wm P. 183
  Wm T. 143, 165, 175
Allens
  A. S. 228
Anderson
  Jos E. 143, 165, 170
  M. B.. 163, 186
Andersons' 226
Annan
  Lippett &... 154
Annans
  R. P. 219
Annfield 158
Annon
  Reg. 211
Arabia 202
Ashbys Gap 154
Audley 169, 210
Audly 187

B

B. Ville 229
B.ville............... 229
Baittille
  J. H............. 164
Baker
  Majr.......... 143
Baltimore........ 157, 189, 190, 203, 207, 212
Bank's
  H. 219
Barnett
  Neill. 144, 148, 163, 166, 170
Bartlett
  J. A............. 206
  J. H............. 209
  T. D... 199, 204
Bartlette
  J. H............. 169
  Jas H. 144, 186
Battletown 213
Beamers 229
Beemer
  Jno W. 151, 164, 166, 174
  John W. 191
Beemers

230

Clarke County, Virginia Personal Property Tax Lists 1854-1870
Index

J. 214
Bell
  G. 202
Berlin
  Lewis 144, 166, 176, 199
  Philip 144, 166, 207
Berrys Ferry .. 145, 192
Berryville 145, 147, 148, 149, 151, 152, 154, 156, 157, 159, 160, 163, 164, 165, 166, 167, 169, 170, 172, 173, 175, 176, 178, 179, 180, 181, 183, 186, 189, 194, 196, 199, 201, 202, 204, 206, 208, 209, 210, 212, 213, 215, 216, 217, 218, 219, 221, 222, 223, 224
Berys Ferry 159
Bethel 164, 187, 194, 204, 207, 209, 212, 214
Billmeyer
  J. F. 76
Bitzer
  J. H. ...143, 166, 167
Blackburn
  Mrs. ..166, 191
Blakemore
  Geo C. 144, 162, 166

Blakemore's....223
  G. C. 219
Bolen
  Geo W. 210
Boxwell
  C. H. .. 153, 161, 164, 197, 207
Boxwells 226
Boyce & Wright
  . 191, 196, 197
Boyce's
  N. L. 213
  U. L. 220
Boyers
  U. L. 219
Bradford
  Dr. W. A. 107
  Dr. Wm. A..41, 54
Brady
  Curtis 73
  Patrick 177
Brierly
  R. S.............209
Briggs
  R. W. 144, 157, 167
  Robert 201
  W. P..167, 210
  Wm 229
  Wm P. 210
Bromley
  John 189
  Saml.. 144, 148
Bromly
  Saml.. 166, 170
Brown
  J. C. 183
  W. H..........182
  W. S. ..183, 193

William 187
Bryerly
  R. S. 206
Bumly's............. 15
Burchel
  Jno F. 180
  Mrs. 208
Burchell
  J. F.163, 192, 210
  Jno F.144, 163, 166, 185, 186
  Mrs... 191, 206
  Mrs. M..... 160, 183
Burchells
  F. 212, 221, 228
  Fos 215
  M. M. 215
  Thos 214
Burwell
  Geo H. 210
  George H. ... 41
  N. 167, 169
  Nat 190, 197
  Susan R..... 138
  W. T.......... 195
  Wm T........ 197
Burwell's......... 219
Butler
  Jas 130
Byrd
  J. W. 206
Byrds
  J. W. . 158, 161

C

Callaghan

Clarke County, Virginia Personal Property Tax Lists 1854-1870
Index

Wm O 49
Calmes
   L. A. ...169, 193
   Maj 216
Carpenter
   Benj 121
Carper
   Alfred 146, 168, 204
Carrell
   A. 172
   Hummer & 150
Carroll
   Thos 22
Carter
   G. W. 49, 63, 90, 103, 116
   G. Wm 36
   Geo W. 179
   Jos K. ..168, 173
   Mrs. C. E.. 146, 186
   Thomas 191
   Thos .145, 146, 148, 152, 170, 186
   W. 223
Carter Hall 164, 196, 210
Carter, J. K.
   Mrs. E 190
Carters
   Joshua 207
   Thomas ... 211, 227
   Tom 217
Castleman
   A. 146, 168, 210
   Alfred 145, 158

J. R. 199
   John .. 197, 204
   Mann R. 158
   Mann R. P.168, 204
   Shepherd &66, 79
   William A. ..196
Castlemans
   Wm 229
Castlemans Ferry
   .... 189, 196
Castleman's Ferry
   145
Catletts
   M. 221
Chapel 146, 154, 163, 181, 186, 214, 219, 228
Chapman
   Geo ... 152, 175
Chappell
   James 191
Chrismore
   J. F.210
Clay Hill .. 145, 146, 157, 161, 167, 169, 189, 191
Clifton 215
Clingan
   McLane 168, 180
Coats
   Peter 130
Colstin
   A. R. 145
Conrad
   Jas W. 147
   Mashall & .137
Conway & Bro.210
Conways 226

Cook
   Burwell 130
   Mrs. 154
Cooks
   Mrs. A. B... 214
Cool Spring 147, 154, 156, 160, 161, 177, 179, 181, 183
Cooley
   Kable & 7
Copenhaver
   Geo W. 146, 166, 169, 185
   Mrs ... 154, 171
Copenhavers
   Mrs. 193
Cork
   M. B. 202
Cornell
   A. 189
   Andrew 146, 153, 167, 186
Cowell
   A. 195
Crampton
   B. 5
   Ben 19
Crismore 160
Cross
   A. F. 193
   James 209
   Russell & . 158, 180
Crow
   J. T.196
   J. W. T 149
   Koonce & .. 153
Crums Church. 178

Clarke County, Virginia Personal Property Tax Lists 1854-1870
Index

D

Davis
 N 8
Dearmont
 Col. W. 147, 152, 174
 Peter 145, 147, 162, 167
Deck
 F. A. 201
Denny
 R. L. 190
Dix
 M. 63, 76, 90
 M. F. 36
 Mary ...49, 137
 Miss ..103, 116
Doran's
 J. 212
Dorsey
 Capt. J. P. 147, 169, 183
 J. P. 195
Duble
 Shepherd & 105, 118
Dunbar
 H. H. ..147, 170, 206
Dunbars
 H. H. 218

E

E. T. Hebb 192, 196
Eavan's
 Mrs. 163
Eberhart
 Bowen & 17
Eddy
 T. M. 197
Edwards
 H. 206
 J. W. 226
Eliott
 J. C. 196
Elsea
 A. 193
 Albert 148, 170, 187, 211
Enders
 Jacob 144, 148, 162
 L. 2
Erb
 C. 151, 173, 178, 185, 186, 188, 189, 195, 201, 207, 209, 218
Erbs
 C. 213, 216
Erd
 C. 204
Erwin
 M. B. 197
Evans
 J. S. 204
 Jno S. 178
Everheart
 Bowen & 1
 Wm G. 148, 150

F

Fairfax
 Abram 211
Feehrer
 M. R. 170, 188, 209
Fegurson
 Marshall & 136
Fehrer's
 M. H. 221
Fenton
 Dennis 206
Fenton's
 D. 229
Fentons
 D. 219
Ferguson's
 Maj. 228
Finnell
 Mrs. 118
 Nancy 92
Fletcher
 Isaac 148, 170, 184
 J. 207
 Mrs. 161
Forster
 J. A. 181
 Jas A. 148, 159
Foster
 J. A. 204
Frazer
 Jno 153
Frost
 E. 63, 101
 Eben 76
 Ebin ... 90, 115, 137
Fry
 C. 158, 175
 Jos D. 191
Funk
 Welch & 53, 67, 80
Funsten

Clarke County, Virginia Personal Property Tax Lists 1854-1870
Index

D. 143
Funston
  O. R. .148, 170,
    181, 185,
    204, 209
  O. R. Jr..... 148,
    170, 181
Furgurson
  W. 167
Furr
  William..... 210

G

Galloway
  C. F. 201
Gant
  Martin..... 146,
    149, 168,
    191
Gant's
  M. 214
Gibson
  J. M. ..182, 195
  Jno M. 149,
    157, 177
  Smith &...... 92
Gibsons 216
Gilbert
  Barney..... 151,
    164
Gilkerson
  J. 191
Gill
  Robt ..156, 178
Glass's
  Lewis........ 217
Glebe House .. 209
Glover
  B. 192
  Wheat & .. 228

Gold
  T. E... 146, 159,
    162, 174,
    189, 202,
    207, 223
  Thos E. 149,
    181, 184
Golds
  T. E. 222
Gordan
  G. W.. 189, 192
Gorden
  Geo W. 145,
    149, 153,
    161
Gordon
  Geo W. 167
Gordon's
  Geo 212
Gorrell
  Jos 154
Gorrells' 226
Goy
  Geo 135
Grady
  Sowers & ..104
Grantham
  J. L.99
Granthams...... 223
Granthum
  Jos W. 178
Green
  Casper 161
  John A...... 188,
    197
  Marshall & 137
Greenway Twp 216
Griffith ... 149, 171,
  194, 217, 218
  J. T.171, 192
Griffiths........... 215

Grigsby
  J. R... 149, 164,
    178, 180,
    182
Grubb
  James 171, 202
  Wm B. 149,
    171, 182
Grubbs
  G. W. 199
  J. 224
Guiselman's.... 218
Guishelman
  M. 196, 201,
    207, 208,
    209

H

Hall
  Mrs. 206
  Mrs. C. V... 210
Hansucker
  G. 225
  Geo........... 143
  P. 183, 187
  Philip 151
  Phillip 162
Hardesty
  A. D.. 150, 167,
    203
  C. W. 150, 172,
    178
  Edw .. 145, 147
  J. R. 204
  Joe R. 181
  Mrs. Sarah.. 33
  Wm G. 150,
    172, 176
Hardesty's
  A. 225

Clarke County, Virginia Personal Property Tax Lists 1854-1870
Index

C. R........... 229
Harris
  Mowen 130
  W. B. 150, 169, 181
  William B.. 191
  Wm ...145, 151
  Wm B. 146, 159, 186
Harrison
  D. B. ...147, 169
  Dr. 145, 169, 183, 189
  Dr. B. 147, 162, 167, 173
  Henry 150, 189, 197
  Heny .152, 175
  Hny 174
  Lucy.......... 121
Hart
  Jos S. 180
  T. 203, 204
Hay
  Mrs. .132, 144, 166
  Wm .28, 41, 69
Haycocks 227
Haymarket 185
Hebb
  C. T............ 190
Hebbs
  C. T............ 215
  E. T. 218
Hefflebower
  Mrs. .183, 187, 189
Heflebower
  Mrs. 162
Helper
  A. M. 191

Heskit
  Thos 163
Hesser
  Chas F. 133
Hite
  J. M.. 151, 165, 173, 174, 203
  Jas M. 150, 160, 167
~~Hoof~~
  Franklin J. ...46
Horseman
  William 58
Howell
  Pulliam & ... 50, 63, 77, 91, 116, 138
  PUlliam &.. 103
Huff,
  Carroll & Louis 190
Hull
  C. 197
Humphrey
  T. L... 150, 172, 201

I

Iceler
  Mrs. 194
Irwin
  Mrs. 146
Island Farm 143, 145, 146, 154, 165, 167, 169, 172, 176, 185
Isler
  Geo H....... 148, 151

Mrs. S. M.. 216
  Susan 172
Islers
  Mrs. 222

J

Jackson
  Alfred C. .. 152, 174, 191
  Chas 145
  D. 226
  Jas 186
  Jno 186
  W. A. 206
  Wm A. 152, 174, 184
Jennings
  J. 163, 226
  Jarvis 189, 197
Johnson
  Aaron 162
  Wilson &... 162
Johnston
  Jno S. 152, 174, 181
Jolliffe
  Jno 151
Jones
  Leonard 197
  Rev. J. 212
  Rev. Jos R. 145, 152, 210
Jordon
  Miss Milly 166, 167

K

Keene
  T. A. 199

Clarke County, Virginia Personal Property Tax Lists 1854-1870
Index

Kelsoe
  J. A. 197
Kennerly
  Jos McK... 189, 191, 208
  Jos McK.... 145
  W. C. 189, 197, 201, 207, 208
  Wm C. 152
Kerfoot
  B. T. 194
  D. T. ...169, 191
  David.147, 214
  Dr. 143, 151
  Dr. F. J. 153, 165
  F. J.175, 187
  G. F. 199
  J. F.163, 169, 185
  J. G. ...185, 206, 209
  W. C. 153, 185, 201, 203, 206
  Wm ...157, 163
  Wm C. 160, 180, 183
  Wm T.175, 176
Kerfoot's
  D. J. 218
  J. T.225
Kerfoots
  D. 214
  Jud 226
Kerns
  Thomas H. 192
Kigar
  J. M. 173
Kimballs ..149, 167

[residence] .78
Kirby
  J. H. 208
Kitchen... 153, 175, 198, 207
  J. W. 191
  Mrs. E. S. ...200
Kitchens
  J. N. ...217, 220
Knight
  W. F. 153, 194, 196
  Wm F. 171
Kounslar
  Mrs. 199
Kounslars
  Mrs. 221
Kownslar
  Dr. 155
  Mrs. 177

L

L. M. Twp 213
Lancaster Shop192
Larue
  A. L. P. 153, 178, 201
  C. C. .154, 176, 206
  Col. J. B. ...149, 153, 169, 174, 175, 186
  J. B. ...176, 191, 193, 197
  J. W. 206
  Jno B. 148
  John B. 60
  John D. 60
  W. A. 193

Wm 163
Wm A. 153, 175, 209
Larue's 228
  Col.219
Larues
  H. A. 216
Lee
  C. S. . . 153, 179, 193
  R. C. 192
  R. H.. 154, 176, 189, 191, 197, 212, 214
Legg
  Geo E. P. 19
  Welch & 27
Lewis
  Edw 147
  G. W. 203, 204, 224
  H. & D. 181
  H. L. D. 153, 158, 163, 193, 225
  John 209
Licklicter
  Mr. 143
Littleton
  Wm 210
Lloyd
  John 208
Lock
  F. H. 199
Long Branch ... 150
Long M. Township 215
Long M. Twp... 213
Longebean
  Benj 170

Clarke County, Virginia Personal Property Tax Lists 1854-1870
Index

Longerbeam
  B. 189, 194, 212
Longerbean
  B. 167
Longerbeans
  Benj 216
Louthan
  J. 172
  J. K 170
Luke
  J. W .. 177, 194, 202
  Jno 144
  John W 199
Lupton
  Joel 209
  Jones & . 46, 60

M

Markell
  Spilman & 104, 118
Marple
  G. 226
Marpole
  George 195
  H. 170, 183
Marshall
  A. C. .. 197, 208
  Alfred 155, 185
  Carper & 17, 31
  E. 193
  Ferguson & 148
  J. P 190, 195, 199
  J. R. 192
  Jno 147, 155, 163, 170, 185

Marshalls 218
  J. 212
Martins
  T. F. 219
Massey
  E. W. 173
Mc K. Kennerly,
  Joseph 197
McClelland
  Jas W. 122
McCormick
  Col. F 147, 155, 163, 183
  Dr. Cyrus .. 193, 204
  E. 166, 175
  F. 167, 199, 203, 206
  Frank 191, 209
  J. 204
  J. W ... 164, 189
  Jas 159, 176, 181
  Jas W. 145
  Jno W 155, 168
  P. 155, 163, 164, 178, 192, 209, 224
  Province 189
  T. 157, 189, 199
  Thos. 145, 147, 155, 185
Mccormicks
  T. 214
McCormicks
  Col. F 152
  J. 215

P. 229
T. 195, 214
Tom 229
McDonald
  A. W. 168
  Angus 151, 155
  Angus W ... 173
McGrady
  E. 202
McGuire
  D. H. 155, 156, 158, 186, 222
  Dr. 154, 163, 190, 201
  Dr. W. D ... 155, 178
McGuire's
  Dr. Wm 212
McGuires
  Dr. 223
McIntyre
  C. C. .. 155, 163, 186, 197
MCormick
  Edw 145
McPierce
  P. 173, 178, 179, 203, 218, 226
  Peter ... 10, 36, 49, 157, 160, 179, 188, 195
Meade
  Capt 153
Meade's
  D. 212, 228
  D. Jr. 212
Meades
  P. 214

237

Clarke County, Virginia Personal Property Tax Lists 1854-1870
Index

Wm 219
Mesmer
  H. J. 204
Mickey
  H. 171
Miles
  Mark 197
Miley
  Amos D. ... 204
Millwood 145, 147, 151, 152, 154, 156, 159, 161, 162, 164, 170, 173, 174, 176, 178, 181, 183, 186, 189, 191, 192, 193, 195, 196, 197, 198, 199, 201, 203, 204, 206, 209, 212, 214, 215, 217, 218, 219, 222, 226, 229
Milton
  Wm T. 155, 192
Mitchell
  J. S. 221
  J. Shep..... 196, 197
Monroe
  J. J. 206
Moore
  A. M. .. 188, 207
  Am 144, 162, 167, 177, 187
  S. J. C. 155, 178, 179, 206
Morgan
  Col. 201

  Col. B. 155, 177, 186, 194, 207
  Col. Benj ... 119
  John Jr. 194, 197, 199
  John Sr. 204
Morgan Jr.
  Jno 152, 163, 174
Morgans
  John 224
Morris
  Jno G. 155, 177, 185
Mountain 152, 174, 187, 189, 190, 191, 192, 193, 196, 199, 201, 202, 203, 204, 206, 208, 209
Murphys
  J. T. 200
Murry
  E. W. 146

N

Neadore [?] 161
Nelson
  H. M. Jr. 192
  Hugh M. Jr. ... 190, 192
  Miss A. & R. 121
  Mrs. H. 144, 149
  Mrs. H. M. 148, 164, 170

  Mrs. Hugh M. 177
  W. N. 209
Nelson's
  Capt. 212
Nelsons
  Capt. . 218, 226
Neville
  Henry 22
  No. 1 156, 157, 163
  No. 2 ...... 145, 146, 151, 155
  No. 3 ...... 146, 147, 152, 154, 158, 161, 163, 164
  No. 4 .... 149, 162
North Hill 163
Nunn
  J. R. 172

O

O'Rear's 219
O'Rears ... 214, 221
Ogden
  Thompson & 184
ORear
  Mrs. Betsy 154
  Mrs. E. 169, 177, 179
  Mrs. Susan 199

P

Page
  Dr. 150
  Dr. W. M. .. 175, 194
  Dr. Wm M. ... 167, 179

Clarke County, Virginia Personal Property Tax Lists 1854-1870
Index

Jno 157, 174, 179, 183
Jno E.145, 152, 161, 164, 179
John 189
M. R. .164, 176
Mann 199
Mann R. ... 119, 154, 157, 161, 174, 179, 185, 209
N. P. 138
Page Brook.... 151, 189, 222
Page Brooke... 201
Page's
  R. P. 227
  R. Pense ... 224
Pagebrook..... 187, 212, 217
Pagebrooke... 194, 195
Pages
  M. R. .221, 228
  R. P....223, 225
Parker
  Elliott 18
  Elliott &..4, 30, 57, 72
Pendleton
  T. P...152, 157, 158, 179
Philips
  G. C. S. 178
  G. S. 216
Philips & Wiard
  ....191, 192
Phillips
  G. E. S. 210

Pickett
  Jno 157, 180
  Rev. J.189, 204
  Rev. Jno ...174, 175, 179, 185
  Wm...152, 157
Picketts
  Wm 152
Pidgeon Hill..... 181
Pierce
  A. N..179, 191, 199
  J. N. 169
  P. M. ..173, 218
Pitzer
  Conrad R...122
Popes
  M. 226
Powers
  P. H. ..157, 179, 196, 200, 201, 203
Pulliam
  M. 145, 157, 158, 179
  Matthew..... 76
Pyle
  W. 193

R

Randoloph
  Eston 189
Randolph
  B. 145, 150, 158, 167, 172, 173, 178, 180, 181, 225

Dr. 145, 148, 151, 152, 174, 183, 207, 219
E. 204
R. C. . 158, 180, 189, 197
Randolph's 212
Maj. 225
Randolphs
Dr. 218
Maj. B. 212, 214
Reardon
  Patrick 210
Richardson
  J. D... 170, 178, 204, 211, 218
  John D. 188, 192
  Maj. 214
  Pendleton & 10, 23, 36, 63, 77
Richardsons
  J. D. 215
Richmond
  & Stoll. 129
Ridgly
  Samuel 209
Ridings
  Sanders & ... 12
Riely
  W. A. 196, 208
Riely & Adams 207
Robinson
  W. H. 148, 182, 194, 206, 210

239

Clarke County, Virginia Personal Property Tax Lists 1854-1870
Index

Wm H...... 158, 180
Romine
  A.   144
Royston
  G. R. 196
Russell
  J. E. 200
  J. W. 149
  Jas E. .158, 180
  Jesse N. 175
  John W. 193
Russells 162
  Jesse 220
Ryan
  Jas W. 158, 169, 184
  Jos F. 147, 158, 180

S

Salem 192
Saratoga. 156, 158, 159, 160, 179, 181, 189, 202, 204
Scanlands
  L.   213
Sharp
  Robt 161
Shepherd
  Champ 148, 159, 161, 174, 181, 182, 189, 197
  D. J. ...160, 165, 182, 191
  J. B. ..197, 198, 199

J. H. 198
John N. 66
Jos 145
P. D. .. 151, 157, 182, 183, 197
Shepherd Sr.
  C.   169
Shepherd's
  C.   227
  Frank 161
Shepherds
  Champ 154, 219
  J.   215
  Jas 152
  Jos 154
  P. D. 152
Shipe
  Moses 159, 182, 206
Shumate
  Mrs. 209
  Mrs. E. M. 159, 169
  Mrs. M. E. 167, 182, 185
Sibold
  D.   159, 181, 185
Smallwood
  C.   201
  Sil 165
Smith
  C.   209
  C. H. ... 185, 186
  Chas 147
  Col. 201, 222
  Dr. J. P 147, 159
  J. S. 191

Jno S. 154, 159, 182
R. R. . 159, 163, 169, 181, 185, 186, 189, 191
Roger 147
W. C. 182, 195, 197
W. D. 159, 178, 186
Warren C. 159, 172, 174
Wm D. 163, 167, 181, 182, 209
Smiths
  Wm D. 229
Snyder
  D. C.. 143, 145, 181, 189, 199
Snyders
  D.   213
Sommerville .. 150, 182, 205, 225
Sowers
  D. W. 166, 169, 178, 181, 199
  Daniel H.... 210
  Daniel W... 210
  G. H. 221
  G. K... 190, 197
  G. W. 218
  Geo K. 159, 178, 184
  Geo W. 145, 159, 178, 182

Clarke County, Virginia Personal Property Tax Lists 1854-1870
Index

J. W. . 205, 207, 210, 227
Jno W. 147, 154, 159, 176, 181, 184
W. B. 194
W. B. C. ... 160, 182, 190, 207
Sowes
  George W. 187
Spillman
  Dumphrey & 215
Springsbury 221
Sprint
  J. W. ...179, 202
Sprints
  J. W. 223
Stale
  Richmond & 78
Stephenson
  Dr. 157, 174, 218
  J. W..161, 181, 196
Stine
  F. 197, 202, 206
Stines
  F. 214
Stoll
  Richmond & 91, 117
Stolle
  Richmond & 50, 64, 138
Stone Bridge . 145, 150, 151, 169, 172, 191, 203,

209, 217, 224, 229
Stribling
  Ann 63, 76, 90, 101, 115, 137
  M 76
  Mary . 101, 115
  Miss M. 90
  Mrs. 13, 26, 39, 52, 149, 161
  Mrs. Mary ... 63
  Mrs. S. E. T. 210
  S. E. T. 163, 182
Strickler
  J. S. 206
Strider
  Mrs. 89
Strothers 213
Stryder
  Mrs. 102
Summerville ... 152, 159, 160
Swan
  P. 117

T

Tapscott
  Robert 210
Taylor
  George W. ... 65
  Mrs. 64, 78, 91, 104, 117, 191, 203
  Mrs. S. 152, 180
  S. B. Wm ... 186
  Susan 138, 158

Taylor's
  B. C. 219
Taylors
  Maj. 229
Thomas
  E. 183
  Jas 170, 184
Thomas & Adams 165, 166, 167, 173, 178, 188, 191, 192, 194, 207
Thomas'
  place 222
Thomas's 222
Thompson
  Benj .. 144, 184
  Benjamin Jr. 107
  Jno 159
  Magnus S. 183, 199
Thompson &
  Ogdan 176
Thompson &
  Ogden 167, 181, 185, 189, 193, 204, 206, 225
Thompson's
  M. 219
Thornly 32
Thos & Adams 143, 149, 151, 155, 172
Timberlake
  Mrs... 155, 161
  R. 163
Trisler
  D. 59, 74
Tristler

Clarke County, Virginia Personal Property Tax Lists 1854-1870
Index

D. 46
Trussell
   Chas .161, 176, 184
Tuleries ..147, 150, 151, 152, 157, 169, 173, 174

V

Vandevanters
   C. 224
Vandeventer. 197, 203
Vandeventers
   C. 213, 227
Vanmeter
   J. L. E. 147, 162, 184
Vorous
   Jacob 158
Vorus 162
   Jacob B. 181

W

Wadesville 160, 197, 208, 219
Wadeville 208
Walker
   Jas 130
Ware
   J. S.184, 193
   J. W. ..150, 162, 184, 196
Washington
   Furguson & 193
   M. W. 200
   Mrs. .137, 155, 177

Weir
   J. 226
   J. V. 198
   Jas V.. 157, 183
Weiss
   Jas V 215
Whaley
   Wm 119
Wharton
   Creager & 4
Wheat & Glovers 222
White Post 147, 151, 152, 154, 158, 163, 164, 172, 173, 174, 176, 181, 185, 189, 192, 194, 195, 196, 198, 201, 204, 206, 218
Whiting
   B. 160, 162, 183, 185, 191, 197
   Burwell 147, 169
   Thos 156
Whiting's
   W. H 211
Whitings
   G. 228
   Mrs. M. C.. 222
   W. H 212
Whiting's
   Mrs. M. 214
Wickliffe 178
Wiley
   G. W 199
   J. W 208

Jas W. 162, 165, 184
Wileys
   M. 212
William's
   E. P. 229
Williams
   Allen 162, 170, 184, 216
   L. E... 162, 167, 181, 184
Williams'
   P. 225
Wilson
   Jerry 127
Witherspoon . 174, 185
Wright
   Boyce & ... 166, 188
   Boyer & 144
Wyman
   S. G.. 145, 157, 162, 173, 184
Wynan
   S. G. 180
Wyndham
   S. B. . 162, 173, 186
   T. O... 154, 162
Wyndhams
   S. B. .. 159, 162

Y

Young
   W. H. 201
   Wm H. 67, 164, 223

www.ingramcontent.com/pod-product-compliance
Lightning Source LLC
Chambersburg PA
CBHW050137170426
43197CB00011B/1873